THE CAMBRIDGE COMPA
EUROPEAN MODERN

CW00554985

Modernism arose in a period of accelerating glob
century. Modernist writers and artists, while ofter
of war, aimed to rise above the national and ideological conflicts or the
twentieth century in service to a cosmopolitan ideal. This *Companion* explores
the international aspects of literary modernism by mapping the history of the
movement across Europe and within each country. The essays place the various
literary traditions within a social and historical context and set out recent critical
debates. Particular attention is given to the urban centers in which modernism
developed – from Dublin to Zürich, Barcelona to Warsaw – and to the movements of modernists across national borders. A broad, accessible account of
European modernism, this *Companion* explores what this cosmopolitan movement can teach us about life as a citizen of Europe and of the world.

A complete list of books in the series is at the back of the book.

THE CAMBRIDGE
COMPANION TO
EUROPEAN
MODERNISM

EDITED BY
PERICLES LEWIS

CAMBRIDGE UNIVERSITY PRESS
Cambridge, New York, Melbourne, Madrid, Cape Town,
Singapore, São Paulo, Delhi, Tokyo, Mexico City

Cambridge University Press
The Edinburgh Building, Cambridge CB2 8RU, UK

Published in the United States of America by Cambridge University Press, New York

www.cambridge.org
Information on this title: www.cambridge.org/9780521136075

© Cambridge University Press 2011

First published 2011

Printed in the United Kingdom at the University Press, Cambridge

A catalogue record for this publication is available from the British Library

Library of Congress Cataloguing in Publication data
The Cambridge companion to European modernism / edited by Pericles Lewis.
p.   cm.
Includes index.
ISBN 978-0-521-19941-4 (hardback)
1. Modernism (Literature) – Europe.   2. European literature – 20th century – History and
criticism.   3. European literature – 19th century – History and criticism.   I. Lewis, Pericles.
PN56.M54C355   2011
809′.9112 – dc23   2011023031

ISBN 978-0-521-19941-4 Hardback
ISBN 978-0-521-13607-5 Paperback

CONTENTS

NOTES ON CONTRIBUTORS

RODERICK BEATON is Koraes Professor of Modern Greek and Byzantine History, Language, and Literature at King's College London, a post he has held since 1988. He has published widely on Greek literature and culture from the twelfth century to the present. His books include *An Introduction to Modern Greek Literature* (1994, 2nd edn. 1999), and the award-winning biography of one of Greece's foremost modernist poets: *George Seferis: Waiting for the Angel* (2003).

TOBIAS BOES is Assistant Professor of German Language and Literature at the University of Notre Dame, where he also teaches in the Ph.D. in Literature Program. He has published articles on modernist culture and German intellectual history in journals such as *Comparative Literature Studies, PMLA,* and *ELH* and is currently completing a book on the *Bildungsroman* as a cosmopolitan genre.

NERGIS ERTÜRK, Assistant Professor of Comparative Literature at The Pennsylvania State University, University Park, is the author of *Grammatology and Literary Modernity in Turkey* (2011). Her articles have appeared in *PMLA, Modernism/Modernity, boundary 2,* and *New Literary History.*

RUDOLF KUENZLI, Professor of English at the University of Iowa, has published books on Marcel Duchamp, Dada and Surrealist Film, André Breton, Surrealism and Women, and New York Dada. He is the editor of *Dada/Surrealism* and the Director of the International Dada Archive at the University of Iowa.

PERICLES LEWIS, Professor of English and Comparative Literature at Yale University, is the author of *Modernism, Nationalism, and the Novel* (2000), *The Cambridge Introduction to Modernism* (2007), and *Religious Experience and the Modernist Novel* (2010), all published by Cambridge University Press. He is currently preparing the twentieth-century sections of new editions of the *Norton Anthology of World Literature* and *The Norton Anthology of Western Literature.* He is the founder and director of The Modernism Lab, a virtual space for collaborative research on modernism.

LEONARDO LISI, Assistant Professor of Comparative Literature at Johns Hopkins University, is the author of *Marginal Modernity: The Aesthetics of Dependency from Kierkegaard to Joyce* (forthcoming). He has published widely on Kierkegaard, Ibsen, Heiberg, and European modernism more generally, and serves as co-editor of the comparative literature issue of *MLN*.

MARINA MACKAY, Associate Professor of English and Comparative Literature at Washington University in St. Louis, is the author of *Modernism and World War II* (2007), editor of the *Cambridge Companion to the Literature of World War II* (2009), and co-editor, with Lyndsey Stonebridge, of *British Fiction After Modernism* (2007).

MEGAN QUIGLEY is Assistant Professor of English at Villanova University, where her teaching focuses on British and Irish Modernism. Her book manuscript, "Modern Novels and Vagueness," investigates the intertwined history of philosophy and literature in the modern British novel. Her work has appeared in *Modernism/Modernity*, *Philosophy and Literature*, and the *James Joyce Quarterly*.

HARSHA RAM, Associate Professor of Slavic Languages and Literatures and Comparative Literature at the University of California, Berkeley, has published extensively on eighteenth-century Russian literature, Russian romanticism, and modernism, focusing primarily on the relationship of cultural and political history to the evolution of lyric poetry. His first book, *The Imperial Sublime: A Russian Poetics of Empire* (2003), examines the sublime as a rhetorical category mediating between the imperial state and the development of lyric form and subjectivity. He is currently completing a book on the dialogue between Russian and Georgian modernism around the time of the Russian revolution.

MAURICE SAMUELS, Professor of French at Yale University, is the author of *The Spectacular Past: Popular History and the Novel in Nineteenth-Century France* (2004) and *Inventing the Israelite: Jewish Fiction in Nineteenth-Century France* (2010) as well as of many articles on nineteenth- and twentieth-century French literature and culture.

ELLEN W. SAPEGA is a Professor in the Department of Spanish and Portuguese at the University of Wisconsin-Madison. Her publications include articles and book chapters on Portuguese modernism, memory, visual culture, and commemoration since the late nineteenth century, and the contemporary Portuguese novel. Author of *Ficções Modernistas* and *Consensus and Debate in Salazar's Portugal*, she is also co-editor of the *Luso-Brazilian Review*.

MARCI SHORE, Associate Professor of History at Yale University, is the author of *Caviar and Ashes: A Warsaw Generation's Life and Death in Marxism,*

1918–1968 (2009) and the translator of Michał Głowiński's *The Black Seasons* (2005). Her new book, *The Taste of Ashes* (forthcoming), is an account of Eastern Europe's grappling with its memories of totalitarianism at the century's end. Currently she is at work on *The Self Laid Bare: Phenomenological Encounters in Central Europe*.

LUCA SOMIGLI, Associate Professor of Italian Studies at the University of Toronto, is the author of *Per una satira modernista: La narrativa di Wyndham Lewis* (1995), *Legitimizing the Artist: Manifesto Writing and European Modernism, 1885–1915* (2003), and articles on Marinetti, Bontempelli, Palazzeschi, and other figures of the Italian avant-garde. He is the co-editor of several volumes, including *Italian Modernism* (2004), and has also published extensively on Italian genre fiction, including a monograph on science-fiction writer Valerio Evangelisti.

C. CHRISTOPHER SOUFAS, JR. is Professor of Spanish at Temple University. His latest book, supported by a Guggenheim Fellowship, is *The Subject in Question: Early Contemporary Spanish Literature and Modernism* (2007), one of the first studies dedicated to mapping the scope of Spanish modernism. His current project, in preparation, is a book-length study that examines Spanish attitudes to modernity via literature and the visual arts.

SCOTT SPECTOR, Professor of History, German Studies, and Judaic Studies at the University of Michigan, Ann Arbor, is the author of the prize-winning *Prague Territories: National Conflict and Cultural Innovation in Franz Kafka's Fin de Siècle* (2002) and a host of essays on central European cultural history.

ACKNOWLEDGMENTS

The editor would like to express his gratitude to Ray Ryan, who commissioned this book, and to the rest of the staff at Cambridge University Press. At Yale University, Sam Alexander did background research for the volume as a whole; Anthony Domestico helped to put together the proposal for the press; and Elyse Graham copy-edited the contributions with her customary flair and good judgment. Their assistance was supported by the Office of the Provost.

The contributors themselves have been as gracious as they are learned. We all benefitted from a face-to-face meeting during a seminar at the 2009 conference of the American Comparative Literature Association at Harvard. For their roles in organizing that conference and for their guidance, thanks go to David Damrosch and Haun Saussy. The contributors are grateful to those members of the audience at the seminar who offered advice and criticism. We all celebrate the birth of four future readers during the year in which this volume was completed: Sophia Quigley Gill, Kalev Tristan Snyder, Matteo Eivind Somigli, and Gabriel Siro Somigli.

CHRONOLOGY

1857	Flaubert, *Madame Bovary*
	Baudelaire, *Les fleurs du mal*
1866	Dostoevskii, *Crime and Punishment*
1869	Tolstoi, *War and Peace*
1870–71	Franco-Prussian War, Paris Commune
1871	Georg Brandes initiates Modern Breakthrough in Scandinavia
1879	Ibsen, *A Doll's House* premieres at the Royal Theatre in Copenhagen
1880	Zola, "The Experimental Novel"
1889	Gerhart Hauptmann, *Before Sunrise* premieres in Berlin
1890	Knut Hamsun, *Hunger*
	Fall of Charles Stewart Parnell, leader of the Irish Parliamentary Party
1897	Founding of the Austrian Secession artistic movement
1898	Stanislavskii's production of Chekhov's *The Seagull*, Moscow Art Theatre
1899	Conrad, *Heart of Darkness*
	Freud, *The Interpretation of Dreams* (dated 1900)
1901	Death of Queen Victoria; Coronation of Edward VII
1902	Hugo von Hofmannsthal, "Lord Chandos Letter"
1904	Opening of Abbey Theatre

1905	Norway gains independence from Sweden
	Failed Revolution in Russia
1907	Strindberg founds the Intimate Theatre in Stockholm
1910	Suicide of Pericles Yannopoulos
	Death of Edward VII; Coronation of George V
	First post-impressionist exhibition in London
1912	Maiakovskii, *A Slap in the Face of Public Taste*
1913	Diaghilev's Ballets Russes stages Stravinsky's *The Rite of Spring* in Paris
1914	Unamuno, *Mist*
1914–18	First World War
1916	Easter Rising in Ireland
	First Dada performances in Zurich
	Belyi, *Petersburg*
1917	February and October Revolutions in Russia
1918	Proclamation of Weimar Republic and Czechoslovak, Yugoslav, and Polish states
1918–21	War of Irish Independence
1919	Treaty of Versailles
1919–22	Turkish War of Independence/Greco-Turkish War
1921	Arnold Schoenberg formalizes twelve-tone method of musical composition
1922	Joyce, *Ulysses*
	T. S. Eliot, *The Waste Land*
1922–23	Irish Civil War
1923	Proclamation of the Turkish Republic
1924	Breton, "Manifesto of Surrealism"
	Mann, *The Magic Mountain*

1925	Eisenstein, *Battleship Potemkin*
1926	Hugh MacDiarmid, *A Drunk Man Looks at the Thistle*
1927	Tercentenary of the death of Góngora, founding of "The Generation of 1927"
1928	Mustafa Kemal replaces Perso-Arabic script with Latin phonetic alphabet in Turkey
1929	G. Theotokas, *Free Spirit* manifesto
1930	Suicide of Maiakovskii
	Musil, *The Man without Qualities* (second volume 1932)
1932	Socialist Realism declared and mandated in the Soviet Union
1933	Nazis take power in Germany
1936–39	Spanish Civil War
1936	Assassination of Federico García Lorca
1937	David Jones, *In Parenthesis*
1939–45	Second World War
1941	Suicide of Virginia Woolf
	Brecht, *Mother Courage* premieres in Zurich
1946–49	Greek Civil War
1947	Mann, *Doctor Faustus*

I

PERICLES LEWIS

Introduction

The term 'modernism', central to English-language criticism of early twentieth-century literature at least since Laura Riding and Robert Graves published their *Survey of Modernist Poetry* in 1927, has continually widened in scope. Contemporary scholars often describe modernism, understood as a cosmopolitan movement in literature and the arts reflecting a crisis of representation, as having arisen in Europe in the middle of the nineteenth century and developing up to, and even after, the Second World War. Even so classic and wide-ranging an earlier account as the collection that Malcolm Bradbury and James McFarlane edited in 1976, *Modernism: A Guide to European Literature, 1890–1930*, today seems strangely limited in its historical timeframe. Modernism now seems to be a movement whose roots go back well over a century and whose effects are still being felt today.

This broadening of the concept's historical boundaries has not always resulted in a similarly broad geographical perspective. The reassessment of modernism in the wake of postmodernism has led to the founding of the Modernist Studies Association and many similar scholarly groups; it has led to new explorations of the historical and social context of modern literature, notably with attention to questions of empire, gender, sexuality, political commitment, the role of avant-garde journals, and the status of long-neglected authors. Yet these recent studies of modernism have tended, somewhat perversely, to take an increasingly narrow "Anglo-American" view of modernism, focusing almost exclusively on literature written in English. Even major interventions in "transnational" modernism tend to focus almost exclusively on the literature of the former British Empire.[1] A comparable reassessment of European modernism is long overdue.

Departments of foreign languages and literatures have undertaken similar investigations, but these have not resulted in a comprehensive historical reconsideration of European modernism at large, although a fine scholarly survey was recently published under the auspices of the International Comparative Literature Association.[2] The current volume brings together specialists working in a variety of national and regional literatures, many with training in Comparative Literature, to reconsider modernism as a European phenomenon. Our definition of modernism is deliberately broad and varies according to the local contexts of the literatures we study.

The reassessment of modernism in recent years has proceeded in tandem with broader critical discussions of cosmopolitanism. These discussions span the fields of literary criticism, philosophy, and anthropology, and they often echo concerns that were crucial to the modernists themselves – such as the competing claims of universal ethics and local politics, the delights and dangers of rootlessness, and the relationships between cosmopolitanism and global capitalism. Contributors to this volume have been asked to consider what this cosmopolitan movement in the arts can teach us about life as a citizen of Europe and of the world.[3] Modernism, as a field of study, has changed over the last generation. So too has Europe. The geographical center of our study here is considerably further to the south and east than those of many earlier accounts.

The crisis of representation evident in modernism has its roots in other crises: of faith, of reason, of liberalism, of empire. In an earlier volume, I explored the role of these crises in the development of English-language literature, with some reference to the European context.[4] A better understanding of how these forces shaped a broader European literature requires a collective effort. Although the essays in this volume are structured around the individual linguistic traditions in which the contributors have expert knowledge, they were written, and are meant to be read, with a comparative perspective in mind. We have tried to trace the international movement of ideas, forms, and artists themselves, from Rilke, Lorca, Joyce, Svevo, and Maiakovskii to lesser-known cosmopolitans, whether their travels were voluntary or involuntary. These contributions, and the discussion they generated at a meeting of the American Comparative Literature Association in 2009, have identified several key points for understanding the sources of European modernism: language, the unconscious, sexuality and gender, institutions, liberalism, Europe as other, empire, cosmopolitanism, and the challenges of periodization.

Language. Literary modernism has long been understood to be centrally concerned with the contingency of language and reference. This insight is often traced, fairly enough, to Ferdinand de Saussure's linguistic theories and the philosophy of Ludwig Wittgenstein, although it certainly has sources in the nineteenth century, such as Nietzsche and Flaubert. By the early twentieth century, the sense of language as contingent was widespread. The story of linguistic experimentation during a period when empires were breaking up and new nations were being formed underlines the truth of the saying that the Yiddish linguist Max Weinreich popularized, "a language is a dialect with an army and a navy." On the fringes of Europe, and even in its center, modern writers were actively involved in supporting the cause of dialects or spoken languages that were aspiring to become national literary languages – in Catalonia, Switzerland, Celtic Britain and Ireland, and throughout Central and Eastern Europe. At the same time, the invention of universal languages like Esperanto; the introduction of the Roman alphabet in Turkey as part of a political program of Westernization and modernization; and even the belated linguistic unification of Italy (which Luca Somigli discusses in his essay in this volume) contributed to the modernists' awareness of the contingency of language. In his essay on Habsburg modernism, Scott Spector traces Hoffmansthal's questioning of referentiality in his famous Lord Chandos letter partly to the multinational character of the Habsburg Empire, centered on turn-of-the-century Vienna.

The unconscious. Like the contingency of language, the unconscious might seem a discovery, or invention, of Central Europe. While Freud's explorations of the psyche were an individual achievement of world-historical significance, his debts too have been traced in part, notably by Carl Schorske, to the political situation in Freud's Vienna.[5] Other writers helped to spread awareness of the centrality of unacknowledged irrational impulses to mental life, a heritage once again going back to Nietzsche and to Dostoevskii, Dujardin, and Strindberg in the nineteenth century. In the early twentieth century, the Freudian conception of the self was diffused in very different ways by the Surrealists in France, the Bloomsbury Group in England, and the Frankfurt School in Germany. Meanwhile, Freud was parodied in the novels of Joyce, Mann, and Svevo, and challenged by the unorthodox psychoanalysts Otto Gross at Ascona and Andreas Embirikos in Athens, as Rudolf Kuenzli discusses in his essay on Switzerland and Roderick Beaton in his essay on Greece. In a modernist framework, the embrace of the unconscious was only one facet of a broader attempt to breach the traditional walls between life and art evident in Baudelaire's bohemianism, D'Annunzio's decadentism, Wilde's dandyism, the aestheticism of the George Circle, and the autobiographical poetry of Anna Akhmatova. In the manifesto of one among many ephemeral avant-gardes, the Czech poet Karel Teige captured the spirit of all such groups when he wrote that "Poetism is, above all, a way of life."

Sexuality and gender. Just as central to the radicalism of the modernists, but perhaps less often acknowledged in earlier scholarly treatments, was the exploration of new possibilities for sexual life (glimpsed but not always encouraged by orthodox psychoanalysis), or even the wholesale rethinking of the relationship between the sexes or the relationship between mind and body, as glimpsed in movements such as feminism, nudism, and vegetarianism. As well, recent criticism has addressed the homosexuality of many leading modernists with increasing candor. The current volume considers not only the famous cases of Wilde, Gide, Proust, Lorca, and Cavafy, but also the early coming-out novel, *Wings*, by Mikhail Kuzmin, which Harsha Ram analyzes in his essay on Russian modernism. Other forms of sexual experimentation are central to the expressionist theater of Frank Wedekind and the fiction of Arthur Schnitzler. English-language critics have, over the last generation, recovered the work of many important women writers, including H.D., Gertrude Stein, Dorothy Richardson, Katherine Mansfield, and Elizabeth Bowen; this collection builds on that lead with a consideration of a range of women modernists from Akhmatova to Woolf, including Rachilde, Colette, Lady Augusta Gregory, Else Lasker-Schüler, Zinaida Gippius, and Rosa Chacel.

Institutions. The rethinking of the male canon has been perhaps slower in continental traditions, where the story of modernism is often told in terms of a continual cycle of Oedipal revolt of one group of young male artists against the generation of their fathers. C. Christopher Soufas, Jr. challenges the generational model in his account of Spanish literary history. The essays collected here inquire into the formation of various modernist movements, whether tightly unified avant-gardes like the Italian futurists or the Surrealists, "schools" of like-minded individuals in Vienna or Thessaloniki, or groups sharing broader cultural affinities, like the Bloomsbury Group, which Marina MacKay analyzes in her essay on British modernism. Sometimes such groups were formed by political circumstance; Turkey, England, and Spain each had its own "generation of 1914." Whether in world capitals or provincial towns, loose affinity groups often coalesced briefly around those many little magazines that, as Gertrude Stein liked to say, "died to make verse free": these included *Blast* in London, *La Voce* in Florence, *La Ronda* in Rome, *Dada* in Zurich, *Życie* in Warsaw, *Ta Nea Grammata* in Athens, and *Dergâh* in Istanbul. Where linguistic experiment was closely tied to nationalism, such journals tended to be more explicit in their political content, as with *Irisleabhar na Gaedhilge* in Dublin, *L'Avenç* in Barcelona, *Nyugat* in Budapest, and the Yiddish *Kritik* in Vienna; more broad-based journals, such as *La Nouvelle Revue Française*, *Der Sturm*, and *The Egoist*, achieved a different level of institutional stability. In her contribution, Ellen Sapega traces the emergence of Portuguese modernism through the history of the journals *Orpheu* and *Portugal Futurista*, while Nergis Ertürk shows how the republican government in Turkey encouraged the development of a Western-style modernism as a facet of political and social modernization.

Liberalism. The case of Turkish "Occidentalism" suggests the complexity of the various relationships between modernist writers and the institutions of representative democracy, political liberalism, industrial capitalism, and modern society in its broadest sense. If Western European modernists paradigmatically sought to "*épater les bourgeois*" ("shock the middle class"), this was easier to accomplish, and a more obvious goal, where the middle class held power. Yet modernism seems to have begun very shortly after the not always successful claims of political power made on behalf of the bourgeoisie in the revolutions of 1848. France itself would not have a stable liberal democratic regime until 1871; liberalism was in continual crisis in post-Risorgimento Italy, and it did not always thrive on the rocky soil of Wilhelmine Germany and Habsburg Austria-Hungary. As Marci Shore observes in her essay on Eastern Europe, liberalism in that region came late: "it was over almost as soon as it had arrived." Even in the nation of shopkeepers, the beacon of liberal politics during the nineteenth century, George Dangerfield would analyze "the strange death of Liberal England" in the years immediately preceding the First World War. While the modernists, and especially those belonging to the more experimental avant-gardes, often found themselves attracted to utopian and sometimes totalitarian political movements of the left and the right, a few, such as Thomas Mann and E. M. Forster, did make common cause with liberalism and the middle classes from which so many writers and artists had sprung. Those who became most enamored of political revolution often turned out to be among its early victims.

Europe as other. In the context of political modernization, it is notable that for virtually every modernist, including even those in the global financial capital London, the "center" seemed to be elsewhere. Paris was perhaps the only modernist city to consider itself culturally central, the capital not only of the nineteenth century (in Walter Benjamin's phrase) but also of the early twentieth. Nonetheless, Maurice Samuels points to the limitations of Paris's centrality in his essay on French modernism. A number of the essays in this volume suggest that apparently "peripheral" regions, such as Spain or Eastern Europe, offered particularly salient contributions to the development of modernism because of their special relationship to the question of modernization. In his essay on Scandinavia, Leonardo Lisi suggests that the Scandinavians' awareness of their peripheral status with respect to Europe made them unusually open to calls for aesthetic innovation and rupture. Russian writers like Aleksandr Blok engaged in a form of "self-orientalization" when they represented themselves as Eurasian, while Turkish writers practiced a certain "Occidentalism," projecting their desires and their fears onto Europe; in both cases, debate focused on whether the

European or the Asian side of the national character should predominate, or how the appropriate fusion should be achieved.

The volume's table of contents depends on a core/periphery model based loosely on the work of sociologist Immanuel Wallerstein, which has inspired much recent scholarship on world literature. Notably, in the "core" nations, modernism was often a critique of social and technological modernity, while in the periphery nations it seemed to be a path to more complete modernization – a fuller integration into that Europe which was always conceived as elsewhere. (It is clearly somewhat arbitrary to include the Habsburg Empire, Russia, or even Italy in the core rather than the periphery, but previous literary histories tend to have seen them as part of the core of modernism, even if not the core of Europe.) Contributors also note other patterns of flow, often following migration (Russians in Germany; Americans in Paris; peripatetic Eastern Europeans), that provide alternatives to the core/periphery model. Such movements were as likely to be centrifugal (in the nationalist movements of Central and Eastern Europe) as centripetal (drawing exiles and émigrés to Paris, London, or Berlin).[6]

Empire. Even more than the crisis of liberalism, the crucial historical context for these political considerations is the decline of empire. If, during the high tide of literary modernism, Britain reached the apogee and started to envisage the decline of its imperial power, leaving its mark on the works of Joseph Conrad, W. B. Yeats, James Joyce, E. M. Forster, and others, the decline of empire in continental Europe was much more pronounced and sudden. In the course of 1917–18, four great transnational empires – the Wilhelmine, Habsburg, Romanov, and Ottoman – quite suddenly dissolved. Much recent criticism of English-language modernism has been concerned with the British Empire and its break-up.[7] Studies of European modernism seem to have paid less attention to the aftermath of empire. This volume calls attention to the broader post-imperial character of modernism, not by drawing on a one-size-fits-all post-colonial theory, but through historical analysis of the unique situations in various regions of Europe. The essays take up some of the issues created by this sudden redrawing of the map of Europe, including the rebirth of Poland, the growth of irredentism in Italy, the emergence of smaller nation-states throughout the former territories of the Romanovs and Habsburgs, and the emergence of the modern Turkish Republic. In Western Europe, France (like Britain) began to foresee the possibility of losing its overseas empire, while Portugal and Spain looked back nostalgically to their former imperial power. Italy unwisely, and fatefully, undertook its own imperial adventures in Libya and Ethiopia.

Cosmopolitanism. The inhabitants of the erstwhile Habsburg and Ottoman lands, born into multinational empires and often transformed willy-nilly into citizens of tiny nation-states, were cosmopolitans perforce. So too were the three generations of Irish writers who revolutionized literature in English ("a language not their own," Joyce called it). As Megan Quigley shows in her essay on Irish modernism, these writers often had to leave Ireland in order to have their plays produced or their novels printed, although some, like Joyce and Beckett, left their homeland behind quite willingly. Certainly the cosmopolitanism of a German-speaking Jew in Prague differed in character from that of a Cambridge-educated intellectual in Bloomsbury; and certainly there were modernists who clung with ferocity to their local attachments; but for the most part, the writers this volume considers saw themselves as engaged alike in a universalistic enterprise. As recent debates about cosmopolitanism have reminded us, it is possible to perceive the international aspirations of global elites as part of a quest for global democracy, or as facilitating the exportation of Western capitalist values to the rest of the world.[8] Modernism arose in a period of accelerating globalization in the late nineteenth century. From its origins, it faced criticism from those who deemed it too cosmopolitan – lacking local or national ties, politically uncommitted, and open to dangerous foreign influences. Sometimes "cosmopolitan" was a code word for Jewish; and several contributors underline the centrality to modernism of Jewish writers, such as Kafka, Joseph Roth, Georg Lukács, Svevo, and Lasker-Schüler, as well as the appeal of Judaism as a theme even for gentiles, like Joyce, or those of mixed parentage, like Proust. Modernism was a fundamentally cosmopolitan movement, in the root sense of that word, a movement of citizens of the world and of world-cities, from Woolf's London to Belyi's Petersburg to Cavafy's Alexandria.[9] The prevalence of pseudonyms among the famous names of modernism – Joseph Conrad, Guillaume Apollinaire, Blaise Cendrars, Tristan Tzara, Man Ray, Italo Svevo, Flann O'Brien, Witkacy – points in part to the role of migration in the formation of modern literature, but equally perhaps to the writers' desire to invent new, cosmopolitan identities for themselves. A surprising number of modernists could claim that their national origin made them uniquely cosmopolitan; thus Fernando Pessoa wrote that "The Portuguese are original and interesting because, being strictly Portuguese, they are cosmopolitan and universal." More than a few would have celebrated Leopold Bloom's vision, in Joyce's *Ulysses*, of the "new Bloomusalem": "New worlds for old. Union of all, jew, moslem, and gentile... General amnesty, weekly carnival with masked license, bonuses for all, Esperanto the universal language with universal brotherhood... Mixed races and mixed marriage." In the event, these utopian visions were not to be realized.

Periodization. The trials of Flaubert's *Madame Bovary* and Baudelaire's *Les fleurs du mal* in 1857 serve as a convenient starting-point for modernism, marking as they do the growing antagonism between advanced literature and state censorship, as well as the growing disillusionment with the legacy of 1848. The following decade saw the publication (but not yet production) of Ibsen's great modern play *Peer Gynt* (1867, performed 1876). Yet if these works seem obvious precursors of modernism, should not Dickens's *Bleak House* (1853), with its playful use of first- and third-person narration and its unforgettable portrayal of the modern city, also belong to the genealogy traced in this volume? In the final two decades of the nineteenth century, that characteristic modernist form, the manifesto, became widespread, representing such arguably proto-modernist movements as naturalism and symbolism. It was in the decade leading up to the First World War that the manifesto as art-form achieved its finest efflorescence in such movements as futurism, acmeism, vorticism, sensationism, and (during the war) Dada; after the war, surrealism, formism, and zenithism followed. Virginia Woolf claimed famously that "On or about December 1910, human character changed." There can be little dispute that the experimental literature produced between 1910 and 1930 deserves the label modernist (although the applicability of that term to less obviously experimental literature is indeed debatable). So when did modernism end? Clearly the coming to power of the Nazis in 1933 put an end to the movement in Germany, as did the start of the Civil War in Spain in 1936; more broadly, the politically committed anti-fascist literature of the 1930s tends to shy away from the overt experimentalism of the earlier avant-gardes or "high modernists." Yet many contributors to this volume make a case for the continuity of modern literature in various traditions even after the Second World War. Tobias Boes argues in his essay on German modernism that the identification of the term with the Weimar Republic (1918–33) is misleadingly narrow. The modernist legacy can clearly be discerned in the later work of Brecht and Mann, as well as in such diverse writers from across Europe as Paul Celan, Samuel Beckett, Nathalie Sarraute, Flann O'Brien, Carlo Emilio Gadda, Vladimir Nabokov, Friedrich Dürrenmatt, Jean Rhys, Milan Kundera, Nikos Kazantzakis, and Orhan Pamuk. If the borders of Europe remain subject to change, so too do the boundaries of the multifarious expression of literary and cultural crisis that we have come to call modernism.

NOTES

1. See Laura Doyle and Laura Winkiel, eds., *Geo-Modernisms: Race, Modernism, Modernity* (Bloomington: Indiana University Press, 2005) and "Modernism and Transnationalism," special issue, *Modernism/Modernity* 13.3 (September 2006).
2. Astradur Eysteinsson and Vivian Liska, eds., *Modernism*, Comparative History of Literatures in European Languages, vol. XXI (Amsterdam: John Benjamins,

2007), 2 vols. Two contributors to the current volume, Luca Somigli and C. Christopher Soufas, Jr., also contributed to the earlier collection.

3. Most of us are based in North America but are frequent visitors to Europe; we would not want to claim to advise Europeans on their current political arrangements.

4. Pericles Lewis, *The Cambridge Introduction to Modernism* (Cambridge University Press, 2007). Considerations of space and of linguistic competence meant that the earlier volume was essentially an introduction to English modernism. It is my hope that the current volume makes up for the deficiency of the earlier one in this regard.

5. Carl E. Schorske, *Fin-de-Siècle Vienna: Politics and Culture* (New York: Vintage, 1970).

6. The matters discussed briefly in this paragraph are explored at much greater length in Pascale Casanova, *The World Republic of Letters*, trans. M. B. DeBevoise (Cambridge, Mass.: Harvard University Press, 2004); Franco Moretti, "Conjectures on World Literature," *New Left Review* 1 (2000): 54–66; David Damrosch, *What is World Literature?* (Princeton University Press, 2003). See also Immanuel Wallerstein, *The Modern World-System*, 3 vols. (New York: Academic Press, 1974–89) and Fredric Jameson, *A Singular Modernity: Essay on the Ontology of the Present* (London: Verso, 2002).

7. See for example the excellent collection *Modernism and Colonialism: British and Irish Literature, 1899–1939*, ed. Richard Begam and Michael Valdez Moses (Durham, N.C.: Duke University Press, 2007).

8. For broad philosophical defenses of cosmopolitanism, see Martha Nussbaum *et al.*, *For Love of Country: Debating the Limits of Patriotism*, ed. Joshua Cohen (Boston: Beacon Press, 1996); Amanda Anderson, *The Powers of Distance: Cosmopolitanism and the Cultivation of Detachment* (Princeton University Press, 2001); Kwame Anthony Appiah, *Cosmopolitanism: Ethics in a World of Strangers* (New York: Norton, 2006). For a more critical assessment, see Pheng Cheah and Bruce Robbins, eds., *Cosmopolitics: Thinking and Feeling Beyond the Nation* (Minneapolis: University of Minnesota Press, 1998). For the modernist context, see Jessica Berman, *Modernist Fiction, Cosmopolitanism, and the Politics of Community* (Cambridge University Press, 2001) and Rebecca L. Walkowitz, *Cosmopolitan Style: Modernism Beyond the Nation* (New York: Columbia University Press, 2006).

9. Lewis, *Cambridge Introduction to Modernism*, p. 97.

PART I

"Core" modernisms

2

MAURICE SAMUELS

France

Paris might rightfully claim to be the capital of modernism. It was there that the first experiments in both poetry and the novel – as well as in painting, sculpture, architecture, and music – led to a rupture with the classical tradition. It was there that the avant-garde first launched its attacks on an ossified bourgeois culture. In the century spanning 1850 to 1950, Paris attracted writers and artists not only from all corners of France, or even Europe, but from around the world, who saw in the City of Light a beacon of artistic freedom, as well as a particularly fertile climate for artistic experimentation. The fact that so many of the terms and slogans we associate with modernism originated in French – *la modernité*, *l'avant-garde*, *l'art pour l'art* ("art for art's sake"), *il faut être de son temps* ("you must be up to date"), *épater les bourgeois* ("shock the middle class") – signals the extent to which modernism, despite its cosmopolitan ethos, bears a Gallic imprint.

And yet modernism as a critical category has never played a particularly enabling role in French cultural history. Unlike in other national literatures, such as the Anglo-American tradition, modernism in France does not designate a school or a movement. Few French writers or artists labeled themselves modernists. Instead, the characteristics we associate with modernism elsewhere took on, in France, more specific or local designations: naturalism, impressionism, post-impressionism, symbolism, decadence, Dada, surrealism, the New Novel, etc. This chapter will explore all of these movements, but will do so against the grain of traditional French cultural history by linking them together under the common heading of modernism. This strategy has the advantage of illuminating shared features among them, as well as of signaling similarities with forms and practices in those national traditions that more self-consciously adopted the label modernism.

But what does modernism mean in France? Antoine Compagnon has usefully distinguished between the German sense of modernity, which often implies a faith in the Enlightenment, and the much darker sensibility of modernist French authors, who were often in revolt against the power of reason. Although in France the drive toward innovation was one of the main features of modernist artistic and literary practice, according to Compagnon, French modernism was less future oriented, and more pessimistic, than its counterparts in other European countries or in the Anglo-American tradition.[1]

In the pages that follow, I will not argue that modernism was ever a single form or style in France. Nevertheless, most of the writers and artists who claimed affiliation with the various "isms" mentioned above shared a common set of concerns or postures: a privileging of formal experimentation; an attempt to discover new subject matter for art, often in "modern life" or, as I will emphasize, in taboo forms of behavior, especially alternative sexualities; a self-consciousness about artistic production and a foregrounding of their own methods; and a self-conception as a renegade in relation to middle-class society or the social changes known as "modernization." These features have become so ingrained in French artistic and literary life, they so define what it means to be an artist or writer in France even today, that it might come as a surprise that such was not always the case – that they, too, have a history. Indeed, it seems likely that the reluctance of French critics to acknowledge modernism as a historical category stems from their refusal to see it as a movement with a beginning and an end, rather than as an eternal aspect of artistic and literary production.

Second-empire origins

Virginia Woolf famously located the origin of British modernism "on or about December 1910," when everything, including human character, seemed suddenly to change.[2] In France, a similar watershed occurred in 1857, with the publication of both Charles Baudelaire's book of poems, *Les fleurs du mal* [The Flowers of Evil] and Gustave Flaubert's novel, *Madame Bovary*. These two works revolutionized poetry and prose respectively, and any account of modernist literature in France must begin with them. The publication of these two works is significant, however, not only for their introduction of new forms and figures into the literary imagination, but also for the way in which they called down the wrath of the government's censors. Both authors were put on trial because of their works, for outrages to religion and to public morals. These trials testify to the consecration of the modern writer as *provocateur*, and helped forge an image of the oppositional status of literary modernism.[3]

Like many periods of political repression, the Second Empire (1852–70) gave rise to a great deal of artistic experimentation. Ross Chambers has argued that writers such as Baudelaire sought creative ways to register their dislike for a regime they could not openly criticize. Their attempts at coded protest resulted in a new self-consciousness in art and a unique attentiveness to language's multiple layers of meaning.[4] To be sure, Baudelaire was reacting to more than just the petty tyranny of Napoleon III. As Walter Benjamin describes him, Baudelaire was the writer of the period who most clearly registered the shocks to subjectivity caused by the industrialization and urbanization that had begun to take root in France by the middle of the nineteenth century.[5] In Baudelaire, a modernist style emerges in response to the new political, social, and economic structures of what he would be among the first to label "modernity." Baudelaire drew inspiration for his dark vision above all from the poetry and fiction of the American Edgar Allan Poe, another writer in revolt against the progress of his century, whose work Baudelaire translated into French.

Most of the poems in *Les fleurs du mal* make use of traditional forms, such as the sonnet, and feature conventional rhyme schemes with a standard number of syllables per line. (Syllables determine meter in French poetry.) Baudelaire's radical achievement was to make classical forms fit new subjects. Baudelaire explores the dark side of the human psyche, the moods of melancholy and despair, as well as unconventional forms of behavior, such as lesbianism and drug use. He is a poet of lust rather than love, devoting poems to the smell of his lover's hair, or to descriptions of the body of a prostitute, which he likens to a cadaver. The "Parisian Scenes" section of *Les fleurs du mal* takes Paris as its subject, but this is a city haunted by terrifying old men who remind the poet of demons and hideous crones, who mirror the inner torment of the poet's soul. Baudelaire also lamented the changes that Napoleon III and his prefect Baron Haussmann had wrought upon Paris in their effort to "modernize" the city, and bemoaned his sense of displacement and exile in his own home.

Like most modernist authors and artists in France, Baudelaire came from a prosperous bourgeois background. His identification with the capital's low-life was both a political stance and an artistic gesture. Baudelaire formed part of the artistic "bohemia" that his contemporary Henry Murger would chronicle in a series of stories – *Scènes de la vie de bohème* [Bohemians of the Latin Quarter] (1851) – that later formed the basis for Giacomo Puccini's opera, *La Bohème* (1896), and that helped forge the myth of the modern artist as a merry garret-dweller, suffering poverty for the sake of his art. That this image was very much a myth even Murger realized: the story that ends his collection shows his bohemians selling out to the bourgeoisie, compromising their artistic principles for a more comfortable life. Baudelaire, on the other hand, remained true to the bohemian myth to the end. Dying poor at forty-six, he became a hero to his modernist followers who nevertheless took advantage of the increasing autonomy of the artistic field (which no longer conceived of artists as servants to wealthy patrons) to consolidate their positions within the bourgeois society they purported to scorn.[6]

Baudelaire was important not only as a modern poet and myth-maker, but also as one of the first theorists of artistic modernism. In his essay *Le peintre de la vie moderne* [The Painter of Modern Life] (1864), Baudelaire elevates the minor illustrator Constantin Guys to the status of modernist hero, an artist-dandy who celebrates the bustling urban spectacle in rapid sketches free of the strictures of classical artistic training. In this essay, Baudelaire distinguishes between two types of beauty: one kind classical or eternal, and the other fleeting or ephemeral, linked to the current moment. The painter of modern life can achieve the former only by focusing on the latter: rejecting the traditionally noble subjects drawn from history and religion, he focuses instead on "la modernité," which Baudelaire defines as "the transitory, the fugitive, the contingent." Guys's more illustrious contemporary, Edouard Manet, might be seen as the truly great painter of modern life: Manet's canvases revolutionized art through their use of subjects drawn from contemporary life, as well as through their bold, sketchy brushstrokes, which observers at the time considered hasty and unfinished – like the very modernity they were meant to represent. Impressionist painters such as Claude Monet, Auguste Renoir, and Camille Pissarro were his disciples.

Brought to trial on the same charges as Baudelaire, Flaubert was accused of producing a series of "lascivious pictures" in *Madame Bovary,* his novel about a provincial doctor's wife who embraces adultery and reckless spending to relieve her boredom. Many of the themes that Flaubert explored in the 1850s had already been sounded by Honoré de Balzac in the 1830s and 1840s.

Flaubert would become a modernist hero by transforming writing into a heroic labor. Whereas Balzac wrote in a hasty fury, producing as many as thirty manuscript leaves a day, Flaubert's *Correspondence* reveals an artist agonizing to find "le mot juste" ("the right word"). Flaubert helped to invent a new social role for the novelist as well. Although he was the son of a prominent doctor and lived off his family's money, in his novels Flaubert heaped scorn on the bourgeoisie, wielding irony as a weapon to denounce the hypocrisy and banality of modern middle-class life. As for many of his generation, the Revolution of 1848 represented a turning point for Flaubert. The spectacle of the forces of order crushing the urban proletariat on the barricades, which Flaubert would describe in his later novel *Sentimental*

Education (1869), led to the writer's realization that the bourgeoisie no longer could claim to speak for the people as they had during the first French Revolution. Roland Barthes dates the beginning of modernism in France to the disillusion of this historical moment, when writers such as Flaubert realized that the meaning of words was no longer transparent and began to subject language to a lacerating scrutiny.[7]

Flaubert also pioneered new narrative techniques. Balzac had not hesitated to use his novels as platforms for his political and social opinions, most of them conservative, which he put into the mouths of his narrators. In *Madame Bovary*, on the other hand, the narrator never tells the reader what to think. This reticence would land Flaubert in trouble with the authorities; it was because the narrator never intervenes to censure Emma Bovary's actions that the government prosecutor blamed the author for glorifying adultery. Indeed, Flaubert's elaborate use of free indirect discourse – a kind of precursor to the stream-of-consciousness monologue, in which reported speech represents the thoughts or words of a character, but is not put in quotation marks – could easily lead to a confusion over whether opinions are those of the character or author. The reader sees Emma Bovary's adultery from her point of view alone – which is to say, through the eyes of a spoiled provincial woman who has read too many romance novels. Only the purity of Flaubert's language offers a counterweight to the stupidity and banality of the world he represents – and only to those readers attentive and sophisticated enough to appreciate it. Although the judges denounced his "realism" as "a negation of the beautiful and the good," Flaubert was exonerated by the court – thanks, in part, to his important connections. He would remain, however, no less a hero to modernist writers than Baudelaire, who was forced to pay a fine and to suppress some of his most scandalous poems.

The fin-de-siècle

The fin-de-siècle period (1880–1900) was in France a time of social crisis and artistic ferment. The nation had suffered a humiliating defeat in the Franco-Prussian War of 1870, and had been forced to surrender its eastern provinces of Alsace and Lorraine to a newly unified Germany. For the rest of the century, the French would attempt to understand the reasons for this debacle. Politicians, sociologists, psychologists, and medical doctors, as well as artists and writers, probed the wounded nation for the causes of its weakness, which many diagnosed as a form of "degeneration" with both social and biological symptoms. Some would lament this state of affairs and seek to reverse the decline by exposing the nation's ills, while others would exult in the decay, turning it into the basis of a rarefied form of aesthetic pleasure. Both tendencies helped to fuel modernist literature and art.

Émile Zola and his "naturalist" followers saw the novel as a tool for social criticism. Like Balzac and Flaubert, Zola set out to analyze the dangers of capitalist modernity, only he did so in a more systematic manner, by devoting entire novels to specific modern economic and social institutions – the railroad, the department store, the stock exchange, the mine, etc. – which he portrayed with lavish and highly metaphoric visual descriptions. He also endeavored to test recent scientific (or pseudo-scientific) theories about the effects of heredity and environment on character in the novels that he described as laboratories in his influential essay, "The Experimental Novel" (1880). His twenty-volume Rougon-Macquart cycle of novels relates what becomes of an extended family tainted by alcoholism. Zola's naturalist associates, such as the brothers Edmond and Jules de Goncourt and Guy de Maupassant, engaged in more subtle novelistic explorations of similarly scabrous themes.

By 1900, naturalism had become a model for an emerging modernist literature in other parts of Europe, North and South America, and Asia. In France, however, self-consciously decadent writers began to reject Zola's positivistic method as early as the 1880s. In 1884, Joris-Karl Huysmans, who began as a member of the naturalist school by writing documentary novels about prostitution and other social ills, published *A Rebours* [Against the Grain], which portrays an effeminate and neurasthenic aristocrat who retreats from the world to cultivate recondite aesthetic pleasures. Whereas Zola would have treated Des Esseintes as a "case" of morbid degeneration to be diagnosed for the sake of the moral health of the nation, Huysmans revels in his protagonist's odd tastes, which include raising rare blossoms, encrusting a tortoise with precious gems, and corrupting lower-class boys he picks up on the street. It is not hard to see why *A Rebours* came to be considered a "breviary of decadence" for young rebels (or why it was one of the favorite books of Oscar Wilde, the creator of Dorian Gray). A rejection of the materialism of modern industrial society, the novel is imbued with mystical overtones that intersect with the symbolist movement's emphasis on hidden spiritual meanings lurking within objects in the material world – a preoccupation that presaged Huysmans's later conversion to Catholicism.

As Huysmans saw it, Zola and his followers had reached an impasse by focusing exclusively on the vulgar masses, on typical human psychologies. He turned instead to unique specimens, whose rarefied inclinations he catalogued in excruciating detail, thereby emptying his novel of anything resembling a plot. In their investigations into the dark recesses of the human psyche, Huysmans and his fellow decadents pioneered other new narrative techniques as well. James Joyce would credit his discovery in the 1920s of stream-of-consciousness – a defining feature of much modernist fiction in English – to Édouard Dujardin's neglected novel, *Les lauriers sont coupés* [The Laurels are Cut Down], published in the symbolist journal *La revue indépendante* in 1887. An attempt to render the thought processes of its protagonist with a new kind of mimetic fidelity, Dujardin's novel consists of an extended interior monologue.

The reaction against naturalism was codified in *The Symbolist Manifesto*, published in *Le Figaro* in 1886, which declared its hostility to "plain meanings, declamations, false sentimentality, and matter-of-fact descriptions."[8] Symbolists and decadents rejected the crass scientism of Zola and the naturalists, attempting instead to give form to the ideal and the mystical. Many of these mystical ruminations involve fantasies of female dismemberment. One of the most famous symbolist novels, *L'Ève future* [The Future Eve] (1886) by the impoverished count Auguste Villiers de l'Isle-Adam, describes the efforts by a fictionalized Thomas Edison to construct an android endowed with the highest form of female beauty but lacking what he sees as the mundane and annoying aspects of the female personality. Decadent women writers contested this misogyny by producing novels that reversed traditional gender stereotypes while celebrating perversity from a female perspective.[9] In Rachilde's *Monsieur Vénus* [Mister Venus] (1884), for example, a cross-dressing female aristocrat transforms her lower-class male lover into a canvas on which she inscribes her sadistic fantasies.

Just as symbolist and decadent authors rejected what they considered the shallow observations of the naturalists, so too did symbolist painters turn away from the optical experiments of the impressionists and post-impressionists. Whereas Georges Seurat had pioneered a pointillist style in the 1880s that broke down vision into tiny spots of color, even while continuing to paint subjects drawn from "modern life," symbolists painted bizarre, unrealistic images taken from mythology and dreams. Gustave Moreau's paintings of Salomé ordering the head of John the Baptist on a platter are crowded with jewel-like colors and convey a feeling of otherworldly ecstasy. Odilon Redon displays a similar fascination with severed heads, but his no less strange charcoal drawings and pastels attain an ethereal simplicity. Huysmans's Des Esseintes would praise both artists in *A Rebours*.

It was really in poetry, however, that symbolism achieved its fullest expression. Poets such as Gustave Kahn, Paul Verlaine, and Arthur Rimbaud crafted images to convey spiritual longings and mystical ideals. But it was another of Des Esseintes's favored artists, Stéphane Mallarmé, who most decisively broke with prior poetic conventions. (Mallarmé returned Huysmans's tribute with his "Prose pour Des Esseintes" [Prose for Des Esseintes] (1885). Mallarmé's early poems resemble those of Baudelaire in their use of traditional forms, such as the sonnet, and traditional syllabic verse structures such as the *alexandrine* (twelve syllables per line). His *Hérodiade*, an unfinished poetic drama that he worked on for decades beginning in the 1860s, took up the story of Salomé that the symbolists so fetishized. In Mallarmé's version, however, the dance itself remains invisible. "I want to reproduce not the thing itself but the effect it produces," Mallarmé wrote of his inverted poetic program.[10] *Hérodiade* ends with a lyric fragment entitled "The Canticle of Saint John," told from the perspective of the Baptist's head at the very moment it is severed from the body. Critics have read the poem as a manifesto for a kind of abstract or pure poetry that would detach itself – like John's head – from the mundane task of representing objects in the material world. And indeed, the dense syntax and abstruse imagery of much of Mallarmé's poetry frustrates any form of mimetic reading.[11]

Nearly all of Mallarmé's poems lend themselves to such allegorical readings: poetry itself becomes his primary subject even when the surface of the poems contain references to nature or history. This turning inward, wherein art concerns itself with the conditions of its own production, is a typical modernist gesture. Mallarmé would also speculate on the possibilities of modernist poetry in his theoretical prose writings. In "Crise de vers" [Crisis of Verse] (1886), written after the death of Victor Hugo, Mallarmé speculates that the passing of the master will liberate French poetry by sundering it from conventions of rhyme and meter. "On a touché au vers" ("Verse has been tampered with"), Mallarmé declared in a lecture in 1894, referring to the advent of "free verse" that would be unrhymed and contain an irregular number of syllables in a line.[12] While for the most part, Mallarmé would continue to use conventional forms for his poetry, his one monumental experiment in free-verse, "Un coup de dés n'abolira jamais le hasard" [A Dice-Throw Will Never Erase Chance] (1897), carries the idea of a pure, non-representational poetry to its logical extreme: nominally about a shipwreck, the almost abstract poem conceives of the blank page as a canvas on which words appear in what Barbara Johnson calls "a typographical symphony" of different sizes and shapes.[13]

Mallarmé also played a crucial social role in the development of French modernism. His Tuesday salon gatherings – *les mardis* – grouped together leading writers and artists of the younger generation, many of them from abroad, over whom Mallarmé exerted an enormous influence. Regular visitors included Paul Valéry and Paul Verlaine, but also Rainer Maria

Rilke and William Butler Yeats. This group became a center for modernist innovation across the arts. Many of Mallarmé's associates were devotees of the music of Richard Wagner; Mallarmé wrote one of the most significant essays on Wagner in French ("Richard Wagner, rêverie d'un poète français" [Richard Wagner: A French Poet's Reverie]). Claude Debussy set Mallarmé's *L'Après-midi d'un faune* to music, and Mallarmé himself served as a subject for leading modernist visual artists, including Manet.

The First World War

The period leading up to the First World War, often called the *belle époque*, saw French political, financial, and artistic power reach its zenith. It was in this period that the American writer Gertrude Stein and her brother Leo opened their salon on the rue de Fleurus to luminaries including the painters Pablo Picasso, Henri Matisse, and Georges Braque, and the poet Guillaume Apollinaire (pseudonym of Wilhelm Albert Włodzimierz Apolinary Kostrowicki). Picasso's famous cubist portrait of Stein stands as a symbol of the artistic experimentation of the era.

The leading French novelists of the period, such as Anatole France, Roger Martin du Gard, and Romain Rolland, all three of whom won the Nobel Prize for Literature, largely confined themselves to refining realist and naturalist techniques. Rolland's ten-volume novel, *Jean-Christophe* (1904–12), which tells the story of a fictional German composer who settles in France, describes the political and social transformations of the French Third Republic (1870–1940) in great detail. Martin du Gard's *Les Thibault* (1922–40), similarly examines the members of a family against the background of historical events. An exception to the starchy conservatism of the literary establishment, Colette (pseudonym of Sidonie-Gabrielle Colette) published racy and linguistically inventive novels, such as the pre-First World War *Claudine* series, that reversed gender stereotypes by depicting sexually empowered female heroines. Known for her scandalous cross-dressing music-hall performances, Colette also collaborated on a modernist opera with the composer Maurice Ravel, entitled *L'Enfant et les sortilèges* [*The Child and the Spells*] (performed 1925).

However, the two novelists of the period who most clearly exemplify modernist tendencies are André Gide and Marcel Proust. Though less radical in their ruptures of novelistic form than Virginia Woolf or James Joyce, both Gide and Proust experimented with new narrative techniques in their effort to attain a heightened form of psychological realism. It is not a coincidence that this formal innovation accompanied a revolution in novelistic content: Gide and Proust both made homosexuality a major theme in their work, and it was the effort to speak new truths about desire that led both authors into some of their most revolutionary achievements.

If the theme of homosexuality remains a subtext in *L'Immoraliste* [The Immoralist] (1902), Gide would bring it to the surface in his later works, especially *Amyntas* (1904) and *Corydon* (1911), as well as in his autobiography, *Si le grain ne meurt* [If the seed dies] (1921). Although homosexuality was not criminalized in France as it was in England, Gide's open discussion of same-sex sexual relations – especially in *Corydon* – still aroused controversy. In his memoirs, Gide describes a discussion he had with Proust on the topic of writing about homosexuality in which Proust advised him, "'You can tell everything... but on the condition you never say: I.'"[14] As we will see below, this was odd advice coming from an author whose own first-person novel dwells at length on homosexuality in all its forms. As Michael Lucey and others have argued, it was this struggle to develop a way of speaking of same-sex sexual relations in the first-person that led both authors, as well as Colette, to revolutionize prose forms in French.[15]

Gide would theorize these issues in fictional form in *Les Faux-monnayeurs* [The Counterfeiters] (1925), a novel about novel-writing. The plot centers on two adolescents from good bourgeois families, Olivier and Bernard, who long to be writers. After discovering that his father is not really his father, Bernard runs away, eventually becoming the secretary to Édouard, Olivier's uncle, who happens to be writing a novel entitled "The Counterfeiters." Olivier falls in with a trendy but cynical novelist named Robert de Passavant (a caricature of Jean Cocteau) and attempts suicide after what the reader presumes is a night of love. Bernard, meanwhile, stumbles upon a ring of counterfeiters who are attempting to use local boys to pass false money. The fathers of Bernard and Olivier, both magistrates, manage to stop the counterfeit ring, and the novel ends with Bernard returning home. In *Les faux-monnayeurs*, the novel takes itself as subject, and leaves us wondering whether the novel we have just read is the novel that Édouard has struggled to write.

Gide occupied a strategic place in the Parisian literary world. The *Nouvelle Revue Française* [New French Review], a literary journal that he cofounded in 1909, published much of the most advanced modernist writers in French, including Paul Valéry. Under the direction of Gaston Gallimard, the *NRF* became a publishing house that brought leading modernist novels into print – although it famously refused Proust at first. It was through Gide, moreover, that the influence of various foreign novelists made itself felt in French literature. His reading of Dostoevskii can be seen in the novel *Les Caves du Vatican* (The Vatican's Cellars, also translated as *Lafcadio's Adventures*, 1914), which features an apparently unmotivated crime and challenges expectations about the novel's ability to account for its characters' psychology. The influence of Henry James (perhaps even more than Freud) makes itself felt in Gide's drive to scrutinize conflicting emotions and to make these the very subject of his fiction: "[...] who's to say how many passions and how many warring thoughts can cohabit in a man?" Gide wrote at the end of *L'Immoraliste*, his tale of a man who brings about his wife's death even while proclaiming his love for her.[16] Like James and Gide, Proust would make the complexity of human psychology, the multiple selves making up the individual, the guiding principle of his art.

And yet, despite comparisons, Proust's multi-volume modernist masterpiece *A la recherche du temps perdu* (In Search of Lost Time, also translated as *Remembrance of Things Past*, 1913–27) is like nothing else in the history of literature. At once the story of the developing consciousness of a single individual – the narrator, Marcel – and a panoramic history of French society of the Third Republic, particularly as it passes through the difficult periods of the Dreyfus Affair and the First World War, the novel (which I will refer to as the *Recherche*) is at once psychological, sociological, and philosophical. No aspect of human perception or reflection is either too small or too large for its examination. Proust devotes entire pages to the sight of a church steeple, the smell of hawthorns in bloom, the taste of a cookie dunked in tea, or the feel of uneven paving stones beneath the feet. Each of these sense impressions, moreover, unlocks intensely personal memories and associations in the narrator, who in turn provides generalizable meditations on their significance that rival the theories of Proust's contemporaries Bergson, Durkheim, and Freud concerning time, social formations, and the self. In the *Recherche*, the novel of bourgeois consciousness reaches its apogee, but it also dissolves into something resembling a collective account of human experience.

Proust's style is also completely unique. The *Recherche* begins with a deceptively simple utterance – "For a long time, I used to go to bed early" – but it contains many extremely long sentences, with multiple subordinate clauses enclosing elaborate metaphors that draw unexpected connections between apparently divergent realms of experience. Like Gide, Proust occupied a position within French society that was at once central and marginal. He, too, came from a wealthy background: his father was a prominent doctor and his mother's relations were successful Parisian financiers. But the Jewishness of his mother's family, as well as his homosexuality, provided him with a unique perspective from which to observe the social and sexual mores of his world. As we have seen, Proust advised Gide never to say "I" when discussing thorny topics such as same-sex sexual relations – advice that Gide rejected. Proust likewise did not follow his own dictum.

Or rather, he followed it even while circumventing it. The first-person narrator of the *Recherche* shares a first name with the author, but he does not share the author's Jewish background or his homosexuality. Instead, these traits are projected onto secondary characters whom the narrator observes with a kind of good-natured fascination. The knowledge the novel produces about Jewishness and same-sex sexual relations is both specific and general. It constitutes a profound reflection on what it means to live as a minority group in modern society, while at the same time drawing universal conclusions about the laws of desire and of social adhesion from these seemingly marginal cases.[17]

Proust also evinces the typical modernist self-reflexivity. As much as the *Recherche* is a novel about human perception or society, it is also about the process of artistic creation. The novel contains numerous creative characters in all fields of artistic endeavor – painting, music composition, acting, writing. But it is the narrator's struggle to become a writer that represents the single unifying thread of the narrative. This struggle is linked for Marcel with the drive to recover his past in all its complexity. He has inklings of the wealth of insight and emotion lurking in the deep recesses of his memory from the very start of the novel, when he first dunks his madeleine into a cup of tea and is transported to the small town of Combray, where he spent much of his youth. He eventually stumbles upon – quite literally – the key to his involuntary memory at the end of the novel, when crossing an unevenly paved courtyard on the way to a party, and this in turn enables him to begin, finally, to write. The novel the reader has finally finished, one assumes, is the novel the protagonist has struggled for a thousand pages to begin.

The party that finally turns the narrator into a writer in the final volume occurs after the rupture of the First World War, which took place while Proust was composing his novel in his cork-lined bedroom on the Boulevard Haussmann. Proust doesn't depict battlefields or trenches, but he does show the effects of the War on the individuals who survived it, as well as the structural changes it produced in French high society. For those authors who were also soldiers – such as Apollinaire – the War would have an even more immediate impact on their writing.

Before the War, Apollinaire had written extensively on the cubist painters Braque and Picasso, and published a volume of poetry entitled *Alcools* [Alcohol] in 1913. According to Tom Conley, while most of the poems in *Alcools* reflect a more traditional conception of poetry as music, the final poem in the volume, "Zone," written just as the volume was going to press, displays a more modern kind of visual imaginary.[18] Although it moves out toward exotic geographic locations, the poem is set in the area surrounding a modern industrial city, the type of landscape that is neither urban nor rural, and that traditional lyric poets and painters eschew. Baudelaire had shared an affinity for this kind of liminal space, as had Vincent Van Gogh in certain of his drawings and paintings of the outskirts of Paris. Like them, Apollinaire sees this no-man's-land as an emblem of modernity: "A la fin tu es las de ce monde ancien" ["In the end you are tired of this old world"], the poet declares, in free verse, in terms that announce a desire for both geographic and poetic liberation.

The First World War (1914–18) would bring an end to this old world sooner than the poet could have imagined. War on this scale had never before been seen: over the course of the four years of conflict, over 70 million military personnel were mobilized and over 15 million people were killed. The War damaged not only populations, but entire landscapes. The trenches turned large swaths of Northern France into "zones" of destruction, and new technologies such as the airplane, the machine gun, and poisonous gas generated death on an industrial scale. Soldiers returned profoundly traumatized – shell-shocked, in the terminology of the day – to a society they found transformed by the conflict and an economy in ruins.

Although the son of a Polish noblewoman, born in Rome, Apollinaire fought for France during the War. He received a serious shrapnel wound in the head in 1916, and he died in 1918 during the Spanish Flu epidemic that followed the War. Shortly after his death, his radically innovative volume of poems entitled *Calligrammes: Poèmes de la paix et de la guerre* [Calligrams: Poems of Peace and War] (1918) appeared. In "Fusée" [Rocket], the poet tells his mistress, "Tes seins sont les seuls obus que j'aime" ["Your breasts are the only artillery shells that I love"]. The poem ends with a wish that the shells will "Carillonnez pieusement" ["sound piously"], like bells announcing the end of the "vieux monde du XIXe siècle" ["old world of the nineteenth century"]. Other poems in the collection are titled "Guerre" [War] and "Les feux du bivouac" [The Fires of the Bivouac], and all bear the trace of the conflict in their form as well as in their content.

Between the Wars

The destruction of the First World War produced a violent reaction in the worlds of literature and art. Formed in Cabaret Voltaire in Zurich, Switzerland in 1916, the Dada movement rejected not only the political institutions and technologies that had sown destruction on such a vast scale, but also the social institutions that defined the bourgeois world and that had led to war. Art itself was their primary target. Led by the Franco-Romanian poet Tristan Tzara (pseudonym of Samuel Rosenstock), the Dadaists issued manifestos that in their absurdity punctured the aura of seriousness that surrounded art production – even in its innovative modernist guise. Marcel Duchamp's "ready-mades" represent perhaps the quintessential Dadaist art objects: Duchamp displayed an everyday shovel with the title, "In Advance of a Broken Arm," and a urinal entitled "Fountain" that he signed R. Mutt. He painted a moustache on a reproduction of the Mona Lisa and labeled it "L.H.O.O.Q," a pseudo-acronym with lewd connotations in French. Dadaist poetry, in randomly assembling words and phrases, rejected not only emotion, but the very idea of meaning. Although it had branches in other major European capitals, the Dadaist center was Paris, where Tzara and his colleagues, many of whom, such as André Breton and Max Jacob, later became Surrealists, staged anti-art shows, readings, and even ballets.

The Surrealist movement, which took up where Dada left off in the 1920s, sought a different kind of liberation. While still rejecting bourgeois proprieties and artistic conventions, the Surrealists also aimed at attaining a psychological – and for some, a political – freedom through the exploration of the unconscious. Breton's 1924 *Manifesto of Surrealism* linked its practice with "automatism," the attempt to express pure thought ungoverned by reason. Surrealist writing experiments such as the "cadavre exquis" [exquisite corpse], in which different writers each add a word or phrase to a poem, sought to break beyond the bounds of the repressed. Surrealist poets such as Louis Aragon, Philippe Soupault, Paul Eluard, and Robert Desnos also attempted more individual forms of poetic expression by giving voice to supposedly unconscious fears and desires. Breton's surrealist novel, *Nadja* (1928), describes the narrator's fascination with a woman he meets through a chance encounter and follows through the streets of Paris. Surrendering to the logic of chance, the narrator experiences odd longings and mystical communions brought about by the random juxtapositions of the urban spectacle.

The Surrealist movement lasted for several decades and included adherents throughout the world, although the center of the movement would remain Paris. Surrealist artists, photographers, and filmmakers – such as André Masson, the American Man Ray (pseudonym of Emmanuel Radnitzky), and the Spaniards Salvador Dalí and Luis Buñuel – attempted to give visual form to their unconscious drives through visual experiments modeled on automatic writing. Antonin Artaud, the author of *Le théâtre et son double* [The Theater and its Double] (1938), which advocated a destabilizing "Theater of Cruelty" in opposition to the staid conventions of the bourgeois stage, was for a time a Surrealist, but he broke with the group over questions of political engagement. Certain Surrealists – including Breton – believed that the liberation of the individual psyche could lead to larger societal liberation, and attempted to link their aesthetics to the political program of revolutionary Marxism. Titles of major Surrealist publications signal this affiliation: *La Révolution Surréaliste* [The Surrealist Revolution] and *Le Surréalisme au service de la Révolution* [Surrealism in Service of the Revolution]. The occultism and individualism of the Surrealists rendered the match with Marxism problematic, however, and Breton would be expelled from the Communist Party in 1935.

Historians of culture have tended to characterize Dada and Surrealism as "avant-garde" movements, rather than as part of modernism proper. According to Andreas Huyssen, the main difference between modernism and what he terms the "historical avant-garde" lies in their opposite relationships with mass culture.[19] Modernists have tended to eschew mass culture by reducing art to its purest form, eliminating all elements considered extrinsic to the nature of the medium. The difficulty of modernist aesthetics often winds up eschewing the masses along with their culture; modernist writers and artists speak only to the elect few. Mallarmé's opaque verses stand as the epitome of this striving toward radical aesthetic autonomy. Dada and Surrealism, on the other hand, sought to lower bridges from the ivory tower by embracing the forms of mass culture. Duchamp's "Fountain" stands as the epitome of this opposite strategy. The distinction between the historical avant-garde and modernism is a fine one, however, and may obscure the manifold similarities between the two kinds of movements. Both modernism and the avant-garde shared the primary goal of using formal experimentation to access new realms of human experience. Both adopted an outsider posture in relation to bourgeois society, and both sought a rupture with prior forms of art and literature.

A writer like Céline (pseudonym of Louis-Ferdinand Destouches) reveals how tenuous this distinction can be. On one level a classic modernist – the oxymoronic conjunction of "classic" and "modernist" here reflecting the increasing acceptance of the modernist challenge to the artistic establishment by the 1930s – Céline invented a distinctive new prose style in novels like *Voyage au bout de la nuit* [Journey to the End of the Night] (1932) that by later novels such as *D'un chateau l'autre* [*Castle to Castle*] (1957) became increasingly difficult if not totally impenetrable. Céline's radical populism eventually veered toward anti-Semitism, and one finds the same modernist prose innovations that made his *Voyage* a revelation used in hate-filled pamphlets such as *Bagatelles pour un massacre* [Trifles for a Massacre] (1937) denouncing the Jews. Debates still rage over whether to consider his artistic innovation tainted by his politics.[20]

While modernist painters such as Picasso had looked to the so-called primitive art of France's African colonies for inspiration, the post WWI period saw the first colonial writers rise to prominence in France. Aimé

Césaire was born in Martinique and came to Paris to study at the École normale supérieure in the 1930s. His book-length poem, *Cahier d'un retour au pays natal* [Notebook of a Return to My Native Land], written in the late 1930s, was eventually published in 1947 with a preface by André Breton. It describes the social as well as psychological conflicts faced by colonial subjects in a poetic form as radically innovative as its content. Along with Léopold Sédar Senghor, Césaire helped found the *négritude* movement in the 1930s, a political and artistic group with links to the Harlem Renaissance that celebrated the cultural distinction of the African diaspora. The fight against racism and colonialism, maintained throughout Césaire's writings, would contribute to France's retreat from empire by the 1960s.

After the Second World War

The postwar French literary scene was dominated by the existentialists – Albert Camus, Jean-Paul Sartre, Simone de Beauvoir – who wrote philosophical and politically engaged novels that privileged an ethics of commitment over formal innovation. In the 1950s and 1960s, the practitioners of the so-called *nouveau roman*, or New Novel, took up the torch of modernism by subjecting both the language and philosophical assumptions of prose fiction to radical critique. Closely associated with the Éditions de Minuit publishing house, the new novelists – who included Alain Robbe-Grillet, Michel Butor, Claude Simon, Nathalie Sarraute, and Marguerite Duras – continued the modernist tradition of self-reflexivity by calling into question the ways in which novels organize perception and thereby shape reality. Guided by polemical treatises such as Sarraute's *L'Ère du soupçon* [The Age of Suspicion] (1956) and Robbe-Grillet's *Pour un nouveau roman* [For a New Novel] (1963), these writers based their aesthetic on a systematic undoing of what they took to be the conventions of nineteenth-century realism. Omniscient narrators, linear plot development, and psychological motivation all gave way to novels that challenge notions of space and time, and even what constitutes human subjectivity.

As Gerald Prince points out, such questioning of novelistic convention was not really all that new in French literature. Writers like Valéry and Gide had already subjected the novel to critical scrutiny, calling into question its attempt to present objective experience.[21] In the New Novelists, however, the experiment yields narratives with no beginning, middle, or end; and "characters" lacking not only coherent psychologies but anything resembling identifiable traits. In Sarraute's *Portrait d'un inconnu* [Portrait of an Unknown Man] (1947, published 1956), finely calibrated psychological states are analyzed without attributing them to flesh and blood beings, to characters with a physical presence or history. Claude Simon – who won the Nobel Prize – decomposes the historical novel: in *La Route des Flandres* [The Flanders Road] (1960), he views an episode from the Second World War from multiple angles in a chronology without sequence. Objective reality, in these works, does not precede its discursive instantiation. The New Novelists carried these experiments with storytelling into cinema as well. The screenplay by Duras for Alain Resnais' *Hiroshima mon amour* [Hiroshima My Love] (1959) reconceives plot through an innovative use of flashbacks, but Robbe-Grillet's screenplay for Resnais' *L'Année dernière à Marienbad* [Last Year at Marienbad] (1961) evacuates plot almost entirely: the two main characters spend the film debating whether they have met before.

Perhaps the most formally innovative and philosophically challenging modernist writer in French of the postwar period was not even French. Born in Ireland, Samuel Beckett, another Nobel Prize winner, produced novels and plays that expressed a sense of humanity reduced to its barest essence, confronting an absurd universe. Between 1946 and 1956, he worked mainly in French in order to write, as he put it, "without style." Although he produced a critical study of Proust, Beckett strove for a nearly opposite effect. His minimalist syntax belies a complex inquiry into the possibilities for communication in a world devoid of transcendent meaning. The characters in his play *En attendant Godot* [Waiting for Godot] (1952) repeat the same questions and the same gestures as they await the arrival of a mysterious visitor, so that the play is constructed around an absence. His trilogy of novels *Molloy* (1951), *Malone meurt* [Malone Dies] (1951) and *L'Innommable* [The Unnamable] (1953) ends with the paradoxical proclamation, "I can't go on, I'll go on," which can be read as a heroic affirmation of writing itself in the face of cosmic emptiness, or as a final farewell to literary modernism.

Most critics would acknowledge that Paris ceased to be the center of cutting-edge art and literature after 1960. This mantle passed to New York with the rise of abstract expressionism, pop art, and postmodernism, and to hundreds of smaller capitals of the newly consecrated "world literature." Indeed, one could argue that the idea of a single capital or center lost its importance after the decline of modernism; once radical innovation and the quest to produce absolute novelty ceased to be the point, and writers and artists no longer needed immediate access to the latest trends.

The French themselves have been slow to recognize this change. The sociologist of literature Pascale Casanova celebrates Paris as the once and future capital of a "world republic of letters" and only provisionally acknowledges its recent eclipse.[22] But it comes as no surprise that all her examples of Parisian domination come from the modernist century that I have outlined in this essay, and particularly the period of high modernism from 1920 to

1950, when writers such as Joyce and Beckett left behind their outdated homeland for the up-to-date "central time" of the Latin Quarter and Montparnasse. What Casanova fails to recognize is that the centrality of Paris is less a permanent or eternal feature of the literary field than a byproduct of modernism.

French writers and critics have remained so invested in certain modernist assumptions about art, especially the belief in art's oppositional role, that they have been slow to acknowledge not only the eclipse of Paris, but that of modernism as well. Or perhaps modernism never really faded in France. The radical French rethinking of culture that took place after 1968, which helped to define postmodernism for Anglo-American critics, was in France anything but a radical break with the past. Roland Barthes, Jacques Derrida and their fellow post-structuralists celebrated modernist strategies and drew largely on modernist artists and writers for their case studies.[23] Their critique of reason and decentering of the self had much in common with the revolts of Baudelaire and Flaubert against the smug positivism of the nineteenth century. Seen from this angle, postmodernism in France came not to bury modernism, but to praise it.

NOTES

1. Antoine Compagnon, *The Five Paradoxes of Modernity*, trans. Franklin Philip (New York: Columbia University Press, 1994), p. x.
2. Virginia Woolf, "Mr. Bennett and Mrs. Brown" (1924), in Vassiliki Kolocotroni, *et al.*, eds., *Modernism: An Anthology of Sources and Documents* (Edinburgh University Press, 1998), p. 296.
3. On Flaubert's trial, see Dominick LaCapra, *Madame Bovary on Trial* (Ithaca, N.Y.: Cornell University Press, 1982). Elisabeth Ladenson discusses both trials, along with other attempts to censor modernist literature, in *Dirt for Art's Sake: Books on Trial from Madame Bovary to Lolita* (Ithaca, N.Y.: Cornell University Press, 2007).
4. Ross Chambers, *The Writing of Melancholy: Modes of Opposition in Early French Modernism* (University of Chicago Press, 1993).
5. Walter Benjamin, *Charles Baudelaire: A Lyric Poet in the Era of High Capitalism* (London: Verso, 1997).
6. On bohemianism, see Jerrold Seigel, *Bohemian Paris: Culture, Politics, and the Boundaries of Bourgeois Life, 1830–1930* (New York: Viking 1986); Mary Gluck, *Popular Bohemia: Modernism and Urban Culture in Nineteenth-Century Paris* (Cambridge, Mass.: Harvard University Press, 2005).
7. Roland Barthes, *Writing Degree Zero*, trans. Annette Lavers and Colin Smith (New York: Hill and Wang, 1977).
8. Jean Moréas, "Le symbolisme," *Le Figaro* (September 18, 1886), Supplément littéraire, pp. 1–2.
9. Rachel Mesch, *The Hysteric's Revenge: French Women Writers at the Fin-de-Siècle* (Nashville, Tenn.: Vanderbilt University Press, 2006).

10. Mallarmé, Letter to Henri Cazalis (October 30, 1864), cited in Rosemary Lloyd, *Mallarmé: The Poet and His Circle* (Ithaca, N.Y.: Cornell University Press, 2005), p. 48.

11. Charles Bernheimer, *Decadent Subjects: The Idea of Decadence in Art, Literature, Philosophy, and Culture in Fin-de-siècle Europe* (Baltimore, Md.: Johns Hopkins University Press, 2002), p. 109.

12. Cited in Barbara Johnson, "The Liberation of Verse," *A New History of French Literature*, ed. Denis Hollier (Cambridge, Mass.: Harvard University Press, 1989), p. 799.

13. Johnson, "The Liberation of Verse," p. 800.

14. Cited in Michael Lucey, *Never Say I: Sexuality and the First Person in Colette, Gide, and Proust* (Durham, N.C.: Duke University Press, 2006), p. 4.

15. Along with Lucey, other recent treatments of homosexuality in French modernism include Elisabeth Ladenson, *Proust's Lesbianism* (Ithaca, N.Y.: Cornell University Press, 1999) and Lawrence Schehr, *French Gay Modernism* (Urbana: University of Illinois Press, 2004).

16. André Gide, *The Immoralist*, trans. Richard Howard (New York: Vintage, 1996), p. 151.

17. Pericles Lewis discusses the question of "race" in Proust in *Modernism, Nationalism, and the Novel* (Cambridge University Press, 2000), pp. 153–66. Also see the conclusion to Maurice Samuels, *Inventing the Israelite: Jewish Fiction in Nineteenth-Century France* (Stanford University Press, 2009).

18. Tom Conley, "Lyrical Ideograms," in Hollier, ed., *A New History*, p. 843.

19. Andreas Huyssen, *After the Great Divide: Modernism, Mass Culture, Postmodernism* (Bloomington: Indiana University Press, 1986), p. vii.

20. See Alice Yaeger Kaplan, *Reproductions of Banality: Fascism, Literature, and French Intellectual Life* (Minneapolis: University of Minnesota Press, 1986), pp. 110–24.

21. Gerald Prince, "The Nouveau Roman," in Hollier, ed., *A New History*, p. 990.

22. Pascale Casanova, *The World Republic of Letters*, trans. M. B. DeBevoise (Cambridge, Mass.: Harvard University Press, 2004), p. 165.

23. See Barthes, *Writing Degree Zero* and Jacques Derrida, *Writing and Difference*, trans. Alan Bass (University of Chicago Press, 1978).

FURTHER READING

Bourdieu, Pierre. *The Rules of Art: Genesis and Structure of the Literary Field.* Trans. Susan Emanuel. Stanford University Press, 1992.

Chambers, Ross. *The Writing of Melancholy: Modes of Opposition in Early French Modernism.* Trans. Mary Seidman Trouille. University of Chicago Press, 1993.

Clark, T. J. *Farewell to an Idea: Episodes from a History of Modernism.* New Haven, Conn.: Yale University Press, 1999.

The Painting of Modern Life: Paris in the Art of Manet and His Followers. Princeton University Press, 1983.

Compagnon, Antoine. *The Five Paradoxes of Modernity.* Trans. Franklin Philip. New York: Columbia University Press, 1994.

Culler, Jonathan. *Flaubert: The Uses of Uncertainty.* Ithaca, N.Y.: Cornell University Press, 1974.

Gay, Peter. *Modernism: The Lure of Heresy.* New York: Norton, 2008.

Huyssen, Andreas. *After the Great Divide: Modernism, Mass Culture, Postmodernism.* Bloomington: Indiana University Press, 1986.

Kritzman, Lawrence, ed. *The Columbia History of Twentieth-Century French Thought.* New York: Columbia University Press, 2006.

Ladenson, Elisabeth. *Dirt for Art's Sake: Books on Trial from Madame Bovary to Lolita.* Ithaca, N.Y.: Cornell University Press, 2007.

Lemke, Sieglinde. *Primitivist Modernism: Black Culture and the Origins of Transatlantic Modernism.* Oxford University Press, 1998.

Lucey, Michael. *Never Say I: Sexuality and the First Person in Colette, Gide, and Proust.* Durham, N.C.: Duke University Press, 2006.

Peyre, Henri. *The Contemporary French Novel.* Oxford University Press, 1955.

Terdiman, Richard. *Present Past: Modernity and the Memory Crisis.* Ithaca, N.Y.: Cornell University Press, 1993.

3

TOBIAS BOES

Germany

The popular perception of German modernism in the English-speaking world is defined by an almost exclusive preoccupation with the Weimar period, those fertile fifteen years stretching from the end of the First World War in 1918 to the Nazi seizure of power in 1933. That such a thing as a popular perception of German modernism exists at all has largely to do with the allegorical subtext that we now invariably read into the period: the frenzied dance around the volcano by brilliant yet morally louche artists, and the eventual eruption of that volcano in the greatest political catastrophe of the twentieth century.[1] Yet such a reading is deeply flawed, and not just because German modernism, like all of its European counterparts, had roots that reached back into earlier decades and an afterlife that continued long after Weimar had perished. More importantly still, it suggests that German modernism was a self-contained phenomenon, an exceptional case that went exceptionally wrong. The political development of the Weimar Republic was indeed without parallels, but the culture that accompanied it was enmeshed in transnational networks that stretched from Paris to St. Petersburg, from Oslo to Milan. The fabulous diversity of German modernism, along with all the characteristics that make it so distinctive, would not have come into being without these multifold exchanges.

Ibsenism and Nietzscheanism at the turn of the century

The origins of the modernist movement in Germany are impossible to understand without reference to the country's violent and belated unification during the 1860s and the eventual proclamation of King William I as German emperor in 1871, following the Franco-Prussian War. Germany's new imperial fortune created an urgent need for a corresponding imperial culture that might bestow the semblance of dignity and legitimacy upon the rather ham-fisted Hohenzollern dynasty. This resulted in an ambitious public building program, the erection of much statuary, and a vogue for historical novels and plays. A younger generation of German writers, many of whom first announced themselves to the public via the anthology *Moderne Dichter-Charaktere* [Modern Poet Characters] (1885) found an easy target for satire in these official, as well as officious, manifestations of imperial culture. The theoretical foundation for the new movement came in 1886, via a lecture that the historian Eugen Wolff gave to the Berlin literary association *Durch!* [Through!]. Wolff declared that "our highest ideal is no longer antiquity, but rather the modern period," and "the task of the present-day writer is to give a poetic shape to all the meaningful forces of contemporary life [...] as well as to blaze a prophetic path for the future."[2] Within the span of a few hundred words, he thus not only proclaimed the dawn of a new artistic era, but also provided it with an energetic program.

To "give a poetic shape to all the meaningful forces of contemporary life" meant, first of all, to find an artistic response to the Second Industrial Revolution. The natural resources of the Rhineland as well as savvy investments in chemical and electrical technology allowed the Wilhelmine Empire to quickly overtake Britain as the leading industrial power in Europe, a development that gave rise to astonishing changes in the urban landscape. The population of Berlin, for instance, nearly trebled during the period from 1870 to 1905, as the formerly quaint garrison town, which had been the ridicule of cosmopolitan travelers earlier in the century, spawned ever more factories, train yards and tenement slums. A group of writers that included Gerhart Hauptmann, Arno Holz, and Otto Brahm set out to chronicle these social transformations along with their attendant ills of disease, prostitution, and alcoholism.

Although they opposed Wilhelmine pieties, many of these proto-modernists nevertheless participated in the proud nationalism that characterized their era. Hermann Conradi, for instance, wrote in his preface to *Moderne Dichter-Charaktere* that, "the spirit which moves us [...] is the spirit of a reawakened nationality. It is a Germanic creature, which can make do without foreign tinsel and trumpery."[3] This curious mixture of revolutionary sensibility and conservative nationalism produced tensions from the very outset. For German modernism was, like the national unification that gave rise to it, a belated phenomenon. French naturalist writers, foremost among them Émile Zola, had begun exploring the darker side of industrialization at least a decade before their German colleagues, yet in the heady nationalist context of the Reich, founded in the Mirror Hall of Versailles, French achievements, though universally read, were sometimes difficult to publicly acknowledge. As late as 1915, Heinrich Mann still provoked the ire of his more nationalistic brother, Thomas, when he proclaimed Zola a model poet and intellectual.

This internal asynchrony between a rapidly developing industrial economy and a cultural sphere that was, in many regards, still playing catch-up helps to explain the rise of Ibsenism on the Berlin stage during the 1870s and 1880s. Ibsen was Norwegian, and thus easy to accommodate to the chauvinistic theories of a pan-Germanic cultural heritage that were gaining currency at the time. And he added to Zola's anti-bourgeois outlook a determined focus on the cataclysmic inner life of the modern individual. The German poets, who came from a national tradition in which inwardness and spirituality had long been valorized over social realism (and in which the novel had also never displaced the play as the dominant form of high artistic expression) could intuitively relate to this. The first Ibsen play to premiere in Berlin was *The Pretenders* in 1876, followed in quick succession by *Pillars of Society* in 1878 and *A Doll's House* in 1880. *Ghosts* and *An Enemy of the People* were put on in 1887, and they opened the floodgates to a whole series of productions that helped to establish Ibsen as a household name not only in Germany, but throughout the rest of Europe as well.

Many of these early performances were hamstrung by incompetent directors or overly zealous censors. But even if they did not immediately resonate with a large public, they nevertheless provided inspiration for such German works as Gerhart Hauptmann's *Before Sunrise* (1889) and *The Weavers* (1893). In another important development for the history of modernist literature, the controversy over Ibsen's plays also accelerated the creation of a counter-public that intentionally segregated itself from the public at large. In order to evade the compulsory state review of all public theater performances, Otto Brahm in 1889 founded a private theater association, *Freie Bühne* [The Free Stage], which immediately went on to premiere *Before Sunrise*. The paying members of *Freie Bühne* still possessed, for the most part, strictly conventional tastes, and *Before Sunrise* caused a riot not at all unlike the one in Dublin that James Joyce so memorably depicted in his "The Day of the Rabblement" (1901). Over the following decade, however, Berlin's theater life became increasingly liberal, and the nascent avant-garde found artistic outlets in an ever-increasing array of little magazines, literary associations, clubs, cabarets, and galleries.

The cultural transfer between Scandinavia and Germany did not just consist of texts, however. It had a human face as well. Ibsen himself lived in Dresden and Munich from 1868 to 1879. The Danish critic Georg Brandes, considered the father of the "modern break-through" in Scandinavian letters, settled in Berlin from 1877 to 1883. By the time of the first full flowering of German modernism in the 1890s, the Prussian capital, despite the ongoing conservatism of official Wilhelmine culture, had turned into an asylum for a variety of other Nordic artists who sought to escape an even more chilling cultural climate back home. The tavern *The Black Piglet* became a meeting place for such poets and painters as Edvard Munch, August Strindberg, and Holger Drachmann. Here they mingled with German modernists like Richard Dehmel and Max Klinger, as well as the Polish poet Stanislaw Przybyszewski, to create a kind of "literary Hansa," an artistic community founded on a shared cultural patrimony centered on the Baltic Sea.

The importance of Ibsenism for the development of a naturalist tradition in Germany already demonstrates that the cultural transfer within this transnational network was far from one-way. Modernist techniques didn't merely move from what might be called the "Prussian semi-periphery" on the edges of industrialized Western Europe into the genuine "periphery" in Northern and Eastern Europe; the inverse was true as well. Yet another example of this dynamic appears in the rise of Nietzscheanism in Germany, which came roughly a decade after the discovery of Ibsen and at last provided German modernists with a genuinely indigenous aesthetic program. Nietzsche had published *The Birth of Tragedy*, his first major work, in 1872, but for almost two full decades he remained virtually unread in Germany. In 1888, however, Brandes, who had by then returned to Copenhagen, delivered an important lecture series on Nietzsche's "aristocratic radicalism," which was published in the *Deutsche Rundschau* in 1890, and which set off a veritable tidal wave of interest in the philosopher. Nietzsche's theories thus traveled from German-speaking Switzerland to Denmark and back to Germany, from whence they were disseminated throughout the world, via the universities, the publishing industry, and through multi-national artist circles such as the one centered on *The Black Piglet*.

The influence of Nietzsche on German modernism was profound and multi-faceted. Three elements of his thought, however, were especially pertinent. The first was his rejection of academic historicism. In one of his *Untimely Meditations* of 1874, entitled "On the Uses and Disadvantages of History for Life," Nietzsche averred that "[a] man who wanted to feel historically through and through would be like one forcibly deprived of sleep."[4] For such an enforced insomnia, he prescribed the "unhistorical" ability to forget the past, as well as the "suprahistorical" capacities of art and religion to refocus attention from the "process of becoming" towards the eternal.[5] The notion of art as an agent through which we might effect an irreconcilable break with the past resonated with many modernist manifestos of the period; it plays a central role, for instance, in the important essay "Die Moderne," which the Austrian critic Hermann Bahr published in 1891.

The second important aspect of Nietzsche's thought, closely related to the first, was the philosopher's scathing attack on positivism, a term used here to refer to the tendency to describe human behavior using vocabulary drawn from the natural sciences. As Nietzsche asked rhetorically, "Is life to dominate knowledge and science, or is knowledge to dominate life? Which of these two forces is the higher and more decisive? There can be no doubt: life is the higher, the dominating force."[6] Nietzsche's spirited argument for the supremacy of life had tremendous influence not only on the so-called *Lebensphilosophie*, or "vitalist" school of philosophy, but also on the artistic movement that would eventually come to be known as expressionism.

A third important element of Nietzsche's thought is to be found in his critique of language. A pivotal text in this regard is the short essay, "On Truth and Lie in an Extra-Moral Sense" (1873), which contains one of the most frequently quoted sentences by this eminently quotable philosopher. Truth, Nietzsche there proclaims, is nothing more than a "mobile army of metaphors, metonyms and anthropomorphisms – in short, a sum of human relations [...] which after long use seem firm, canonical, and obligatory to a people."[7] "On Truth and Lie in an Extra-Moral Sense" was not published until 1896 and received scant attention even then, but it collects ideas that can be found throughout Nietzsche's writings, and that contributed greatly to the so-called modernist "crisis of language" (*Sprachkrise*). This term signifies a general mistrust in the ability of language to represent external reality, as well as its ability to serve as a neutral medium in which competing claims about facts and values might be adjudicated. If words are, as Nietzsche claimed, really just worn-out metaphors, how can words ever keep up with what is new in the world or, even more importantly, be used to formulate new truths? This question is the driving force behind Fritz Mauthner's voluminous *Contributions to a Critique of Language* (1901/02); but the most important response to the *Sprachkrise* came in poetic form. In October of 1902, the Berlin literary periodical *Der Tag* [The Day] published a short piece, by the Austrian poet Hugo von Hofmannsthal, entitled simply, "A Letter," in which the fictitious sixteenth-century poet Lord Chandos complains to his friend and mentor, Sir Francis Bacon, that "the abstract terms of which the tongue must avail itself as a matter of course in order to voice a judgment [crumble] in my mouth like moldy mushrooms."[8] The sentiment underlying this statement would be shared by many other German poets over the following decades.

The Nietzsche euphoria of the 1890s spawned an army of second-rate disciples, prophets, and exegetes, but it also produced writers of undeniable genius. Among the first of these was the playwright Frank Wedekind. Only two years younger than Hauptmann, Wedekind wrote plays whose themes – sexual repression and the abasement of women in a hypocritical society – are basically naturalist; but his treatment of these themes is not.

In pioneering works such as *Spring Awakening* (1891, though not performed until 1906), *Earth Spirit* (1895), and *Pandora's Box* (1902), Wedekind abandons the naturalist preoccupation with verisimilitude and introduces fantastic, grotesque, and even explicitly anti-theatrical elements. *Spring Awakening*, for instance, concludes with the appearance of a *deus ex machina*, identified only as the "masked gentleman." Wedekind also transcends the naturalists' sometimes facile sexual politics. For instance, Lulu, the protagonist of *Earth Spirit* and *Pandora's Box*, although she is a prostitute, is hardly a victim in the traditional sense. Her irrepressible lust for life is instead presented as a threat to her suitors, who regard her only as a plaything for their carnal desires. Her eventual death, at the hands of Jack the Ripper, can thus be read as a grotesque personification of social prejudice.

The Nietzsche cult was strongest, however, where it mixed with the influence of French symbolism, another artistic current imported from abroad, and one eagerly received by a new generation of artists who had no personal memories of 1871. The poet Stefan George, for example, served a kind of personal apprenticeship to Stéphane Mallarmé during a trip to Paris in 1889, taking from him the idea of literature as the expression of an aristocracy of the spirit. This notion was thoroughly Nietzschean at the core, but George took it to even further extremes than Nietzsche. He was obsessed with the notion that society needed to be revitalized by the powers of creative genius; only poetry, he believed, was capable of this task, in which philosophy had failed. For the final two lines of his poem, "Nietzsche" (1907), George quoted the philosopher's self-critical lament, in *The Birth of Tragedy*, that "it should have sung, this 'new soul,' and not spoken," leaving little doubt that he, George, believed himself to be this "new soul" capable of song where others had been confined to mere speech. [9] He lent concrete form to his vision of a spiritual aristocracy by forming the so-called "George Circle," an especially interesting example of the cliquish nature of so many literary and intellectual movements during the modernist period.

Another poet deeply influenced by both Nietzsche and French symbolism was Rainer Maria Rilke, who lived in Paris during the early years of the new century, and whose famous description of an "Archaic Torso of Apollo" (1907) owes much to Nietzsche's description of the "Apollonian element" in *The Birth of Tragedy*: "We cannot know his legendary head / with eyes like ripening fruit. And yet his torso / is still suffused with brilliance from inside, / like a lamp, in which his gaze, now turned to low, / gleams in all its power." [10] Through his poetry and his pioneering novel, *The Notebooks of Malte Laurids Brigge* (1910), in which he worked to counter the crisis of language by giving symbolic forms to the interior experiences that exterior objects occasioned, Rilke established himself as one of the most important, as well as one of the most influential, practitioners of German modernism.

Futurism, expressionism and the search for a modern voice

In the first two decades of the twentieth century, Rilke's achievement and influence were rivaled only by those of Thomas Mann, whose early short stories sold poorly, but who leaped into prominence with the success of his first novel, *Buddenbrooks* (1901, although sales did not take off until the second edition of 1903). *Buddenbrooks* is symptomatic of a new stage in the reception history of German modernism, which by the turn of the century had made far greater inroads into official Wilhelmine culture. Whereas the plays of Hauptmann and Wedekind had been *succès de scandale*, *Buddenbrooks* was simply a success.[11] Perhaps partly due to this popular success, *Buddenbrooks* has sometimes been classified as a "late realist" novel, but in truth, it reflects the most advanced artistic currents of its day: the influence of Scandinavian literature (especially the genealogical novels of Alexander Kielland and Jonas Lie), the flirtation with naturalist elements (Mann's original title had, in fact, been *Downwards*), Nietzscheanism, symbolism, irony, and decadence.

One of the factors that helped bridge the gap between modernist and official culture was the rise of the feuilleton. The new century brought with it the birth of the modern German newspaper industry, exemplified by the *Berliner Illustrirte Zeitung* (founded 1892), the *Berliner Morgenpost* (1898), and the *BZ am Mittag* (1904). Many of these new papers were tabloids, but their success changed the form of bourgeois periodicals as well, creating, among other things, a steady demand for punchy pieces of cultural criticism. This need was filled with gusto and genius by such writers as Alfred Kerr and Siegfried Jacobsohn. It wasn't just that these journalists were willing to defend and explain modernist authors; they also created an entirely new *style* of writing that was very much of its own time. The critical miniature has a long tradition in German letters, reaching at least as far back as Friedrich Schlegel's philosophical fragments, but Kerr and his colleagues gave it a new edge. The literary culture of the Weimar Republic would owe much to their achievements.

Another important new arrival on the German literary scene in the first decade of the twentieth century was the poet Else Lasker-Schüler. Lasker-Schüler, whose short lyrics rival those of Rilke in their linguistic inventiveness and symbolic compression, and whom Gottfried Benn would later call "the greatest female poet that Germany has ever had,"[12] suffered decades of neglect because she was a woman and a Jew. Her husband, Herwarth

Walden, on the other hand, quickly became a figurehead of the modernist movement and vociferously defended the avant-garde just when some of its more moderate elements were being absorbed by the mainstream culture. One of the most telling of these defenses came in an article entitled "The Jungles of Berlin," which he published in 1911 in *Der Sturm* [The Storm], a journal that he himself had founded a year earlier and which he continued to edit until his emigration to the Soviet Union in 1932. In this article, Walden depicts his circle of friends as a cosmopolitan clique plugged into the latest artistic developments throughout Europe:

> With a resounding thud, the daily papers are being tossed into a corner, the Brockhaus encyclopedia has been burnt along with Goethe and Schiller, but the works of [minor modernist poet] Alfred Mombert make the rounds. [Peter] Altenberg unfortunately can't stand to travel, but Hermann Bahr comes twice a week, while Alfred Kerr calls on the telephone and Karl Kraus sends dispatches from the [Viennese journal] *Die Fackel* by telegraph. The wires are full of news about Ibsen and Hauptmann, Strindberg and Wedekind, Hofmannsthal and Maeterlinck, Shaw and d'Annunzio.[13]

The description is pure satire: the Berlin avant-garde was at that time neither as prolific nor as international as Walden suggests. It is a deeply telling satire, however, appropriating the breathless style of the newspaper extra edition to enumerate the qualities he thought the mainstream press considered suspicious about the modernists: their mistrust of the bourgeois canon, their scorn for public opinion makers, their enthusiasm for modern technology, and, finally, their organization into transnational networks that defied the national distribution channels (and frequently nationalist rhetoric) of the daily papers.

During his years at the helm of his journal, Walden turned *Der Sturm* into a veritable media empire, through which he tirelessly promoted the kind of artistic internationalism that he could still only dream of when he wrote "The Jungles of Berlin." At various times, this empire included a publishing house, a book store, a theater, an arts academy, and a gallery. It was through the last of these that German modernism received its next great fertilizing inspiration from abroad. The larger-than-life avatar of this inspiration was Filippo Tommaso Marinetti, who arrived in Berlin in April of 1912 to publicize an exhibition of futurist manifestos and paintings at the Sturm-Galerie. Marinetti and Walden drove through Berlin in an open car, distributing leaflets, waving placards and yelling *evviva futurista*! It was a giant advertizing stunt that once again used the methods of a modern media society to disseminate a subversive message. When the Prussian authorities reacted with predictable force against this "disturbance of the peace," the avant-garde had successfully completed its guerrilla raid into the public sphere: up to 1,000 visitors a day now streamed into the Sturm-Galerie to view the scandalous new paintings.[14] Among them were many of the most radical poets and painters of the time, who reacted to futurism with a mixture of fascination and anxiety comparable to that which had greeted naturalism forty years earlier.

Just a month prior to the futurist exhibition, the Sturm-Galerie had hosted a number of works by the *Blaue Reiter* group, a painters' circle held together by the brilliant and temperamental Russian émigré Wassily Kandinsky. The term "expressionism" was then still new and not yet in universal use. It had been coined by Lovis Corinth in 1911 to refer to the art of Vlaminck and Matisse. Deeply inspired by these two provocative exhibitions shown in quick succession in the same gallery, the German modernists began the difficult task of explicating what they had seen. One critic, for instance, sought a common ground for futurism and expressionism in the legacy of cubism, which he defined as a "feeling for the profound relationship of things, a cosmic world feeling," and which he claimed futurists and expressionists alike harnessed to rebel against the cold, analytical stance of impressionism.[15] Gottfried Benn, who first burst upon the literary scene with his poetry collection, *Morgue*, in 1912, soon applied a similar analysis to futurist and expressionist verse. He defined both of them through their "inner disposition to smash up reality, their tendency to dig down to roots, to a point where individualism and sensualism can no longer taint, falsify and soften things in order to appropriate them for the psychological process."[16] Alfred Döblin also expressed admiration for the "energy, hardness and masculinity" of futurism, for its rhetorical power and its effort to become an "art without wrapping paper." His "Open Letter to F. T. Marinetti" nevertheless concludes with a defiant vow to depart in a different direction: "Go on and cultivate your futurism. I will cultivate my Döblinism."[17]

Tellingly, this "Döblinism," which bore first fruit in *The Three Leaps of Wang-Lun: A Chinese Novel* (1915), involved a return to the living totality of the epic, as opposed to the joyous fragmentation of experience that the futurists advocated. For futurism and expressionism were never in reality as closely related as some critics made them out to be. Futurism was the brain-child of a small group of radical intellectuals aiming to create a modern Italian culture through a categorical break with the past. German modernism, on the other hand, as we have already seen in the earlier tempering of French naturalism with Ibsenism, was essentially a compromise formation, seeking to build bridges between a deeply entrenched cultural tradition and more recent industrial advances. Expressionist poets such as Georg

Heym, Ernst Stadler, Gottfried Benn, and Jakob van Hoddis wrote about modern life, but they always attempted to synthesize and impose meaning – frequently of a religious kind – onto what they observed. Ernst Stadler's sonnet "Ride Across the Cologne Rhine Bridge at Night" (1913), for instance, begins with a celebration of the vertiginous speed of the machine age: "The express train feels and jerks its way through the darkness / No star dares appear. The entire world is but a narrow mine-gallery railed round by night, / Into which now and then haulage stations of blue light tear abrupt horizons." But the poem ends with an invocation of "Reflection. Contemplation. Communion. And ardor and the urge / To the ultimate, to what blesses. To the feast of procreation. To ecstasy. To prayer. To the sea. To extinction."[18] As much as they rearranged their syntax and abandoned conventional meter, the expressionists never succeeded in treating words as pure materials, in the way that the futurists did with their *parole in libertà*. In short, expressionism remained wedded to a poetics of depth, whereas the great conceptual breakthroughs of cubism and futurism arguably lay in their discovery of a poetics of surface.

Expressionism remained the dominant literary paradigm in Germany throughout the rest of the decade, but as political events hurtled forward, it soon outlived itself. The outbreak of the First World War, that ultimate conflict between the souls of men and the horrors of modern mechanized warfare, confronted the expressionists with a challenge they could not handle. Carried through to its logical conclusion, the search for depth in the trench experiences could only lead to the kind of psychotic self-reification celebrated by Ernst Jünger in works such as *In Storms of Steel* (1920) and *Battle as an Inner Experience* (1922). Kurt Pinthus published his great expressionist anthology, *The Dawn of Humanity*, in 1919. The German word for "dawn" (*Dämmerung*), however, notoriously can also mean "dusk"; and many of the voices commemorated in this work had already been silenced with bayonets and mustard gas.

Exiles and émigrés in Weimar and beyond

The armistice of 1918 marked a monumental turning point not only in the political history of Germany, but also in its cultural history, and it is worth pausing to consider some of its most significant ramifications for the development of modernist literature. The defeat in the war turned the country from an autocratic empire into a representative democracy practically overnight, a transformation that brought almost as many problems as it did blessings. The conditions for peace that had been dictated at Versailles were oppressively harsh, while the actions undertaken by the founding fathers of the new republic waffled between the farcical and the tragic. From the beginning, Weimar Germany thus had to confront a serious legitimation crisis. Among intellectuals, this manifested most clearly in the phenomenon of the so-called "republicans of reason," who supported the new state with their minds, but not with their hearts. Thomas Mann's *The Magic Mountain* (1924) has been read persuasively as the supreme product of this mindset, even as Mann himself became over the course of the 1920s a staunch supporter of liberal democracy.

Contributing to this problem was the fact that the Wilhelmine Empire's rigid social hierarchy and ideological narrow-mindedness had prevented a younger generation from acquiring the skills and experience necessary to run a state. The same was true in the cultural arena as well, where state censorship was abolished (at least in its most overt forms) and the conservative gatekeepers of culture departed along with the regime that they had propped up for so long. The modernists suddenly found themselves no longer confined to the periphery of cultural life, but rather at its very center. The result was a flurry of activity, in which new theaters, cabarets, galleries, or literary magazines seemed to open up almost every week – and often closed just as quickly. The Weimar Republic undoubtedly represented a golden age for the performing arts. But it is equally important to remember that for many dramaturges, musicians, and bit players, this artistic frenzy represented above all a source of uncertainty. There was always the chance to make it big, but a more likely fate would be to find oneself on the street once again, in a society that was infamous for its lack of a social net to protect the poor.

Modernist artists are not expected to hold sinecures, of course. Still, the economic uncertainty of the Weimar years had lasting effects on both their outlook and output. The hyperinflation of 1922 and 1923, in particular, hit the intellectuals harder than most other strata of society. Unlike farmers, intellectuals produced no consumable commodities; unlike workers, they did not receive weekly salaries and could not fall back on union protection. Their income was instead tied to royalties, contractual advances, and the interest earned on prior investments. During the peak of inflation, sums that might have seemed princely when they were originally written into a contract would often no longer cover even the cost of a single breakfast. As a result, many artists and intellectuals turned cynical, frequently withdrawing their support from the new democracy that had failed to protect them. The rise of so-called "reactionary modernism," which embraced the technological aspects of modernity while rejecting the emancipatory legacy of the Enlightenment, is at least partially tied to these economic conditions. Ernst Jünger and the later Gottfried Benn are prime examples of this tendency, as, for that matter, is Joseph Goebbels, who held a doctoral degree in literature and published the expressionist novel *Michael* in 1924.

Cynicism and the need to earn a steady income in rough times marked other directions of cultural production as well. The years following the inflation saw the rise of a new aesthetic ideology that valued practicality and adaptability above all else, and that demanded that all art possess a *Gebrauchswert*, or "value for everyday life." The precise ramifications of this are perhaps best expressed by a famous anecdote about the composer Paul Hindemith, who, during a performance tour of England in January of 1936, was told that the British premiere of his viola concerto, *Der Schwanendreher*, would have to be cancelled due to the recent death of King George V. With less than twenty-four hours before the performance, Hindemith gutted his composition, rearranged several of its themes, and thereby produced a new piece, the *Funeral Music*.[19]

The very best *Gebrauchsliteratur* was ironically conscious of its ambivalent status between art and mere functionalism. This is especially true of the works of Bertolt Brecht. Brecht first made a name for himself immediately after the First World War, when he wrote a series of plays that deconstructed the expressionist pathos to which many of the older poets still clung. In the early 1920s, both in poetry and in such plays as *Man is Man* (1926), he developed a sophisticated aesthetic that tasked itself with leading the reader or spectator toward critical reflection, rather than mere artistic appreciation. His *Manual of Piety* (1926) groups poems into functional rubrics, such as "supplications," "spiritual exercises," or "chronicles," and suggests different occasions on which individual works might be used, even as it wryly subverts the standard expectations that one might bring to a manual of piety. Thus the final stanza of his "Great Hymn of Thanksgiving" runs: "Praise ye the coldness, the darkness, the decomposition! / Look at the sky / And without qualms you can die / Knowing that you count for nothing."[20] Around the same time, Brecht also advised theater directors to make their houses more like sports arenas ("More Good Sport," 1926), and he caused a major uproar when he refused to award a prize to any of the 400 entries to a poetry competition for which he was the judge, suggesting that the laurel instead be awarded to a piece of doggerel he had found in a cycling journal ("A Short Report Concerning 400 (Four Hundred) Young Poets," 1927).

Gebrauchsliteratur was itself part of a larger trend that has come to be known as "the New Objectivity," or *Neue Sachlichkeit*, and which was crucially influenced by the reception of American culture in Germany during the 1920s. The works of Sinclair Lewis and especially Upton Sinclair left a lasting impression upon the literature of the Weimar Republic and led to the development of the so-called "journalistic style" (*Reportagestil*), in which writers commented on contemporary events of popular significance. Other hallmarks of the New Objectivity included factual observation, anti-psychologism, neutrality of view, and emotional distance between narrator and subject. Needless to say, this kind of writing was especially suited for publication in the newspapers that provided many of the most innovative Weimar authors – among them Joseph Roth, Lion Feuchtwanger, and Erich Kästner – with their principal source of income. Women writers, such as Irmgard Keun, Marieluise Fleißer, Gabriele Tergit, or Mascha Kaléko, profited from the commercial appeal of the new aesthetics as well. For perhaps the first time in literary history, they could live off the fruits of their labors (although the case of Fleißer, who attempted suicide after her publisher did not renew her contract, shows that this foothold was often tenuous). The women modernists also tackled subjects – such as gender relations in the new democratic state – that their male colleagues had sorely neglected. The Marxist Left was nevertheless quick to attack the New Objectivity as an intellectual surrender to the alienating effects of industrial capitalism (see Walter Benjamin's "Left-Wing Melancholia," 1931), although this did not prevent the movement from remaining artistically dominant throughout the life of the Weimar Republic.

The journalistic style was far from the only cultural influence that America exerted upon Germany during this period. Without America, the development of Brecht's epic theater would have been impossible, for it was Sinclair's *The Jungle* (1906) that first inspired the young playwright to search for an aesthetic method capable of representing the workings of global capitalism. Brecht abandoned an early project about the international grain trade, but he returned to Sinclair with his play *St. Joan of the Stockyards* (1930); a little earlier he had also relied on Charles Lindbergh's memoir, *We* (1927), as the principal inspiration for his innovative learning play, *Lindbergh's Flight* (1929). Looking beyond high culture, *Amerikanismus* was a great influence (as well as a major source of anxiety) on almost every facet of life during this period. Factories were Taylorized, modern offices were constructed on the American model, and at night, the weary masses danced their troubles away in the countless night clubs that pretended to be straight out of Chicago. Theodor Adorno's cantankerous grumblings notwithstanding, most strains of Weimar musical modernism would have been impossible without the influence of jazz – or at least what the Germans took to be jazz. One of the composers who learnt the most from this musical style was Kurt Weill, who collaborated with Brecht on several projects (including *The Threepenny Opera*, 1928); Weill repaid his international debt during his later American exile, when he revolutionized the Broadway musical.

Another cultural influence on the Weimar Republic that was very differ-ent from what America provided came from the large number of Russian émigrés who arrived in Germany in the wake of the Soviet Revolution. The young republic was a logical destination for such émigrés; most of the Russian intelligentsia spoke at least a little German, and many of the aristo-crats had family connections there. More importantly, however, Germany during the time of hyperinflation was incredibly cheap for anyone who pos-sessed gold or foreign currency. In the years 1922–23, roughly 300,000 Russians migrated to Berlin, then a city of just over four million inhabitants (the unflappable Berliners rechristened the ritzy district of Charlottenburg "Charlottengrad"). These numbers dwindled rapidly after the end of the inflation, but it is estimated that more than 100,000 émigrés were still living in Berlin when the Nazis seized power in 1933.

The Russian diaspora included many first-rate writers and literary critics, among them Vladislav Kodasevich, Viktor Shklovsky, and, most famously, Vladimir Nabokov. Between 1918 and 1924, Berlin's eighty-six Russian publishing houses printed over 2,100 different titles, more than Moscow or Petrograd.[21] For all this, however, cultural relations between Germans and the Russian émigrés remained underdeveloped. Many of the intellectual leaders of the diaspora were aristocrats who looked down on plebeian Berlin, with its tenement slums and petty bureaucrats. The émigrés were also acutely aware of the political instability of the Weimar Republic and the strong influence of the Communist Party: what had happened in Russia might also happen in Germany. A much more substantial impact was made by the new Soviet avant-garde during its brief efflorescence. German–Soviet relations did have an institutional dimension (for instance, in the form of exchanges between the Bauhaus and the Russian state design academy in Moscow, the VChUTEMAS), but in the face of pervasive mistrust between the two young states, individual encounters played an even larger role. German intellectuals like Walter Benjamin, George Grosz, and Egon Erwin Kisch traveled to the Soviet Union to examine the new workers' state, while a number of Russian artists found inspiration in the turbulent life of the Weimar Republic. Among the many figures who exerted a profound impact on the German avant-garde were the graphic artists El Lissitzky and Alexander Rodtschenko, the playwright and poet Sergei Tretyakov, as well as the director Vsevolod Meyerhold. As so often, Bertolt Brecht stood at the center of things. He derived numerous inspirations from Meyerhold for his own epic theater, and he adapted Tretyakov's play, *I Want a Child!* (1926).

Of course, not everyone who chose to relocate to Germany during the 1920s came as an exile or an émigré. Artists and writers from all over the world flocked to the Weimar Republic, attracted by the low cost of living, the intellectual vibrancy, and the legendary night life. Unlike their Russian counterparts, these modernists were free to leave whenever they chose, as most of them did when Hitler came to power in 1933. W. H. Auden, Christopher Isherwood, and Thomas Wolfe are just the best-known English voices to report on these tumultuous times. In masterpieces such as *Good-bye to Berlin* (1939) and *You Can't Go Home Again* (1940), they carried back to their own countries a disciplined and socially engaged approach to literature thereby preserving the cultural legacy of the Weimar Republic even as Nazi stormtroopers were burning books within Germany.

The most important international art form of the Weimar Republic was film, however. The famous Universum Film AG (UFA) was founded in 1917 and quickly reached a golden age as the home of expressionist directors like Robert Wiene, Fritz Lang, and F. W. Murnau. The economics of inflation meant that movies could be shot cheaply and earn great profits in foreign markets; for a brief while, German cinema enjoyed world-wide success. Audiences in the 1920s, however, quickly developed a preference for melodramas and physical comedies – genres in which German films found stiff competition from Hollywood productions anchored by Charlie Chaplin, Mary Pickford, Buster Keaton, and similar stars. As a result, UFA went bankrupt in 1925 and was purchased by the American studios MGM and Paramount, who in turn sold it back to the right-wing industrialist Alfred Hugenberg in 1927. Ironically, some of the most successful American movies were made by the German-born director Ernst Lubitsch, who came to Hollywood of his own accord in 1922 but was followed, a decade later, by a number of his former colleagues upon whom this decision was thrust by the Nazi seizure of power.

After 1933, the landscape of modernism shifted once again, as most of its German practitioners were forced into exile. The diaspora was international in scope, taking prominent modernists as far from home as Mexico (Anna Seghers), Brazil (Stefan Zweig), or Moscow (Herwarth Walden and others). Most of the émigré writers – Bertolt Brecht, Heinrich and Thomas Mann, Alfred Döblin, Carl Zuckmeyer, to name but a few – ended up in the United States, however, where ironically they found themselves in a situation not unlike the one that Russians in Berlin had experienced fifteen years earlier: they spoke at least the rudiments of their new country's language, but nobody understood their own; they established tight social networks among themselves, but encountered utter indifference among their hosts. Just like the Russians, they were also shocked by the hyper-modernism and what they regarded as the inherent barbarism of their new surroundings.

Most accounts of the German diaspora in America have emphasized the tragic dimensions of emigration, telling stories of once powerful artists who, having made the tragic realization that cultural capital is rarely portable, had to contend daily with poverty and ignominy. The suffering was certainly real and should not be underestimated. It is given memorable form in some famous lines by Bertolt Brecht: "Every morning, to earn my daily bread / I go to the market where lies are bought. / Hopefully / I take my place among the sellers."[22] But despite what Brecht claims, there were among the émigrés some who managed to sell their books without succumbing to lies: Lion Feuchtwanger, Anna Seghers, and Franz Werfel all produced bestsellers; Thomas Mann even enjoyed celebrity status. Cultural exchange, furthermore, frequently takes unpredictable forms. Brecht himself, for instance, was slighted and mistreated during his stay in the United States, but his plays were rediscovered in the 1960s by such institutions as the Living Theater, and helped launched a new stage in the development of the theatrical avant-garde in America. Many other artists underwent career changes that previous generations of scholars have lamented as compromises, but which are slowly being reevaluated now that the old barriers between "high" and "low" art are breaking down in the academy.

Erwin Piscator, for instance, failed in his attempts to inject American theater with the experimental spirit over which he had presided at the Volksbühne in Berlin. His Dramatic Workshop at the New School in New York, however, almost single-handedly produced an entire generation of Hollywood stars, including Marlon Brando, Tony Curtis, and Shelley Winters. Along the same vein, none of Kurt Weill's American compositions may have risen to the same level of genius as his score for *The Threepenny Opera*, but they nevertheless shaped musical theater on Broadway, helping to usher in a golden age for what has become one of America's most distinctive art forms. Arnold Schoenberg, who taught John Cage at the University of Southern California, Josef Albers, who mentored Robert Rauschenberg, Donald Judd, and Eva Hesse, and Ludwig Mies van der Rohe, whose students at the Illinois Institute of Technology included Gene Summers and Helmut Jahn, formed vital institutional links between modernism and postmodernism in the United States.

There is an inherent irony here, in that the restrictive understanding of the modernist legacy that prevailed for many decades is, in part, the product of a certain kind of exile experience. With works like *The Dialectic of Enlightenment* (1947) and *The Philosophy of Modern Music* (1949), the Frankfurt School theorists Max Horkheimer and Theodor Adorno laid the foundation for later accounts of an unbridgeable rift between modernist art and the popular "culture industry." Their pessimistic outlook was undoubtedly reinforced by their distance from American society: their failure to understand how cultural formations that to them seemed crudely reductive actually possessed deep roots in collective experience. In a kind of vicious circle, this understanding of modernism then led to cultural histories that inevitably cast the American years as a time of crisis and compromise. The almost inevitable association of German modernism with political catastrophe has come about in a similarly circular fashion, in that it was largely created by German émigré historians during the 1960s, at a time when there was much fearful talk in intellectual circles about possible parallels between Weimar and Vietnam-era America. Fifty years later, in an era when globalization has emerged as the leading socio-political challenge of the day, the time is ripe for a new understanding of German modernism as an internationally connected phenomenon of astonishing inclusiveness and diversity.

NOTES

1. The canonical shape of this narrative largely derives from Peter Gay's *Weimar Culture: The Outsider as Insider* (New York: Norton, 1968).
2. I quote from the condensed version of the lecture that Wolff published anonymously in the *Allgemeine deutsche Universitätszeitung* the following year. See *Die literarische Moderne: Dokumente zum Selbstverständnis der Literatur um die Jahrhundertwende*, ed. Gotthard Wunberg (Frankfurt am Main: Athenäum Verlag, 1971), pp. 1–2. Unless otherwise indicated, all translations are my own.
3. Hermann Conradi, "Unser Credo," in *Die Berliner Moderne, 1885–1914*, eds. Jürgen Schutte and Peter Sprengel (Stuttgart: Reclam, 1987), p. 184.
4. Friedrich Nietzsche, "On the Uses and Disadvantages of History for Life," in *Untimely Meditations*, trans. R. J. Hollingdale (Cambridge University Press, 1983), p. 62.
5. *Ibid.*, p. 120.
6. *Ibid.*, p. 121.
7. Friedrich Nietzsche, "On Truth and Lie in an Extra-moral Sense," in *The Portable Nietzsche*, trans. Walter Kaufmann (New York: Viking, 1954), p. 46.
8. Hugo von Hofmannsthal, "The Letter of Lord Chandos," in *Selected Prose*, trans. Mary Hottinger (New York: Pantheon Books, 1952), pp. 133–34. Translation modified.
9. Friedrich Nietzsche, *The Birth of Tragedy and the Case of Wagner*, trans. Walter Kaufmann (New York: Vintage, 1967), p. 20. George's poem was later reprinted in *The Seventh Ring* (1907).
10. Rainer Maria Rilke, *The Selected Poetry of Rainer Maria Rilke*, ed. and trans. Stephen Mitchell (New York: Vintage, 1980), p. 61.
11. At least this was true for most of Germany. In Mann's provincial hometown of Lübeck, *Buddenbrooks* was rightly recognized as a *roman-à-clef*, and did cause a good deal of outrage.
12. Gottfried Benn, "Erinnerungen an Else Lasker-Schüler," in *Essays und Reden in der Fassung der Erstdrucke* (Frankfurt am Main: Fischer, 1989), p. 542.
13. "Der Sumpf von Berlin: Spezialbericht 'Café Größenwahn'" ("The Jungles of Berlin: Special Report on the Café Megalomania") in *Der Sturm*, no. 2 (October 1911): 651–52. Reprinted in Schutte and Sprengel, eds., *Die Berliner Moderne,*

pp. 662–70. "Café Größenwahn" was a popular nickname for the bohemian Café des Westens on the Kurfürstendamm in Berlin.

14. On this episode, see Nell Walden, *Herwarth Walden: Ein Lebensbild* (Mainz: Kupferberg, 1963), p. 127.

15. Adolf Behne, "German Expressionists, Lecture for the Opening of the New Sturm Exhibition," in *German Expressionism: Documents from the End of the Wilhelmine Empire to the Rise of National Socialism*, ed. Rose-Carol Washton Long (Berkeley: University of California Press, 1993), p. 60. The original appeared in *Der Sturm*, nos. 17–18 (December 1914): 114–15.

16. From Gottfried Benn's introductory remarks to *Die Lyrik des expressionistischen Jahrzehnts* (Wiesbaden: Limes Verlag, 1955), p. 11.

17. Alfred Döblin, "Futuristische Worttechnik: Offener Brief an F. T. Marinetti," in *Schriften zu Ästhetik, Poetik und Literatur*, ed. Erich Kleinschmidt (Olten: Walter-Verlag, 1989), pp. 113–19.

18. Kurt Pinthus, ed., *The Dawn of Humanity – A Document of Expressionism*, trans. Joanna M. Ratych, Ralph Ley, and Robert C. Conard (Columbia, S.C.: Camden House, 1994), p. 221.

19. Hindemith related the details of this episode in a letter he sent to his publisher, Willy Strecker, the following day. The letter is signed, "Paul Hindemith, Bespoke Tailor." See Geoffrey Skelton, ed. and trans., *Selected Letters of Paul Hindemith* (New Haven, Conn.: Yale University Press, 1995), p. 91.

20. Bertolt Brecht, *Manual of Piety*, trans. Eric Bentley (New York: Grove Press, 1966), p. 123.

21. I derive these figures, as well as the ones pertaining to the Russian diaspora more generally, from Karl Schlögel, *Das russische Berlin: Ostbahnhof Europas* (Munich: Pantheon, 2007).

22. John Willett, Ralph Manheim, and Erich Fried, eds., *Bertolt Brecht: Poems 1913–1956* (New York: Methuen, 1976), p. 382.

FURTHER READING

Aschheim, Steven. *The Nietzsche Legacy in Germany: 1890–1990*. Berkeley: University of California Press, 1992.

Bahr, Ehrhard. *Weimar on the Pacific: German Exile Culture in Los Angeles and the Crisis of Modernism*. Berkeley: University of California Press, 2007.

Berman, Russell. *The Rise of the Modern German Novel: Crisis and Charisma*. Cambridge, Mass.: Harvard University Press, 1986.

Herf, Jeffrey. *Reactionary Modernism: Technology, Culture, and Politics in Weimar and the Third Reich*. Cambridge University Press, 1984.

Horowitz, Joseph. *Artists in Exile: How Refugees from Twentieth-Century War and Revolution Transformed the American Performing Arts*. New York: Harper, 2008.

Jefferies, Matthew. *Imperial Culture in Germany, 1871–1918*. New York: Palgrave Macmillan, 2003.

Lethen, Helmut. *Cool Conduct: The Culture of Distance in Weimar Germany*. Trans. Don Reneau. Berkeley: University of California Press, 2001.

Midgley, David. *Writing Weimar: Critical Realism in German Literature, 1918–1933*. Oxford University Press, 2000.

Schönfeld, Christiane, and Carmel Finnan, eds. *Practicing Modernity: Female Creativity in the Weimar Republic*. Würzburg: Königshausen & Neumann, 2006.

Sokel, Walter H. *The Writer in Extremis: Expressionism in Twentieth-Century German Literature*. Stanford University Press, 1959.

4

SCOTT SPECTOR

The Habsburg Empire

The historiography of central European modernism has been characterized by a set of oppositions that have sometimes appeared to be paradoxical. These contradictions relate to the context of the late Habsburg Empire and (after its dissolution following the First World War) its successor states, which include Austria, Hungary, Czechoslovakia, and the formerly Habsburg regions absorbed by Poland, Italy, Romania, and the new state of Yugoslavia. On the one hand, scholars have identified Habsburg Europe as the laboratory of many creations and movements that have been considered seminal to modernism in its myriad forms: in literature, in the visual arts, in architecture and design, in music, and in other intellectual spheres from the philosophy of language to psychoanalysis. Modernist literary giants from the Empire include Rainer Maria Rilke, Franz Kafka, Robert Musil, Paul Celan, and many others. These contributions, moreover, have been seen not simply as prime exemplars of modernism but as innovations of a radical type, producing lasting legacies for the twentieth century and beyond. In fact, some critics have claimed the term "modernism" itself, as applied to literature in particular, as an innovation of the Viennese critic Hermann Bahr, although that genesis is a matter of debate.[1] Yet in terms of *modernity*, the Habsburg monarchy has often seemed – to later historians, to contemporary onlookers, and even to Habsburg subjects themselves – to be less characteristically "modern" than its Western European neighbors, as well as its rival German Empire to the north. In one of European modernism's masterworks, *The Man without Qualities*, Robert Musil would in 1930 describe the old monarchy in this way:

> There, in Kakania, that misunderstood State that has since vanished, which was in so many things a model, though all unacknowledged, there was speed too, of course; but not too much speed. [...] Of course cars also drove along those roads – but not too many cars! The conquest of the air had begun here too; but not too intensively. Now and then a ship was sent off to South

America or the Far East; but not too often. There was no ambition to have world markets and world power. Here one was in the center of Europe, at the focal point of world's old axes; the words "colony" and "overseas" had the ring of something as yet utterly untried and remote. There was some display of luxury; but it was not, of course, as over-sophisticated as that of the French. One went in for sport; but not in madly Anglo-Saxon fashion. One spent tremendous sums on the army; but only just enough to assure one of remaining the second weakest among the great powers. The capital, too, was somewhat smaller than all the rest of the world's largest cities, but nevertheless quite considerably larger than a mere ordinary large city.

Contemporary skeptics regarded the Habsburg state itself as out of step with modernity in political, economic, and cultural terms: supranational in the age of nation-states, authoritarian in an age of liberalism, clerical and aristocratic in an age of bourgeois secularism. There is much to dispute in these condemnations, but the fact is that they belonged to the time and place we are discussing.

The indigenous character of this standoff between pastness and futurity cohabiting in the space of the empire's present has a special importance for Habsburg modernism in all its varied forms. This incongruous self-image of the central European empire is a central part of what we must interrogate in order to find a way to speak of the varied manifestations of modernism from Vienna to Czernowitz, and from Secession to Holocaust.

Habsburg myths

The themes outlined thus far converge on literature poignantly in Joseph Roth's *Radetzky March* (1932). This work is another ironic reflection on the Habsburg Empire by one of its former subjects. Written after the dismemberment of the Empire, by a Jew from Galicia who learned German as a foreign language, it is a self-conscious revision of the poem "Feldmarschall Radetzky," written by the very differently Austrian Franz Grillparzer in the revolutionary year 1848; furthermore, it does not on its surface represent the radical formal experimentation often associated with the modernist novel. Roth's example is hence a peculiar choice to begin an inquiry into central European modernism, and he cannot be called representative; his position is in fact too complex to actually represent anything fixed. Yet the modernist contribution of the otherwise ostensible bourgeois family historical epic lies precisely in this motility. While the work is immensely lucid and readable, the narration shifts constantly – yet sometimes almost imperceptibly – from the perspective of the narrator to that of various characters, and it is often colored by a subtle yet sharp irony, rendering the whole easier to read than to interpret, as one critic has aptly put it.[2] To ignore this modernist inscrutability is to accept the text as an homage to the Slovene field marshal and Habsburg patriot Radetzky, and hence to claim the novel, as has often been done, as a nostalgic valorization of a past supra-national Habsburg identity. One could argue, however, that the novel articulates nothing more than the *dis*placement represented by Roth himself – the Galician Jew writing in the German language from the tiny rump remaining of the Habsburg Empire after its dissolution. Whether we try to think of this literary moment in terms of time or space, language or history or politics, Roth seems to be free-floating, unanchored, always "elsewhere." This eternal elsewhere is intimately connected to a Habsburg mystique at the heart of the historiographical problem of central European culture, a mystique that is present both in the historiographical clichés about Habsburg central Europe and in the articulations of some of its famous subjects. Roth's Radetzky occupies this function differently from the Radetzky of Grillparzer's patriotic poem of 1848, from that of Johann Strauss the elder, whose "Radetzky March" (op. 228) was composed in the same year, and from the Bohemian-born noble who was to become the historical field marshal; and yet they share a place within its frame.

Writing from post-Habsburg Trieste, Claudio Magris was to read Roth as a paradigmatic voice, but he would not take that voice at its word. Instead he identified it as an embodiment of what he named, consequentially, the "Habsburg Myth." According to his interpretation, Roth's forever-tenuous position was an exemplar of the overall displacement of central European identity, the view from the periphery. "His empire is the empire of the *crown lands*, of the distant provinces on the Russian border and on the Slavic-Jewish world of Galicia and the Bukovina." Roth's fantasy production of a grounded central European identity and patriotism was a kind of defense mechanism (in psychoanalytic terms, a "reaction-formation"), an inversion of both this peripheral condition within central Europe and also, more pointedly, the "confusion, insecurity of sentiment, and nihilistic despair" of the years after the collapse of the monarchy.[3] Further – and here Magris' interpretation is particularly compelling – the nostalgia within this Austrian interwar literature for a place that had never existed harkened back to a powerful nineteenth-century myth of Habsburg dynastic history, a myth that arose in order to resist the centrifugal force of national movements after 1848. This is why Roth's *Radetzky March* embodies the myth so well, so literally. Magris' contribution allows us to think about German-language central European literature in terms other than, but comparable to, discussions of "national" cultures proper. The "Habsburg Myth" thesis allows us to see a unity in central European literature from 1806 on – not through the ascription of a thesis of national essence, but rather through ideological necessity.

The idiosyncrasy of the cultural regime in central Europe in the late nineteenth and early twentieth centuries may thus cast light on aspects of European modernism that have remained obscured by its ordering within various national cultures. The survey here of the Habsburg modernist landscape may only begin to cast such a light. Most of the families of Habsburg modernists hailed from crown lands or from Habsburg possessions beyond what is today's Austria; but there is no doubt that it was in Vienna at the turn of the century that the movement's most prized innovations were forged.

The Vienna crucible

In his classic study, *Fin-de-Siècle Vienna: Politics and Culture*, the historian Carl E. Schorske posited a peculiar answer to what is posed above as the Habsburg problem, or discrepancy, of modernism and modernity. The anachronism of Habsburg politics, Schorske reasons, must have been expressly – if inversely – linked to the innovations of central European culture.[4] The politically "peripheral" becomes "central" to the modernist project. Some of the power of this overly simple thesis comes from the appealing correspondence between, on the one hand, the displacement of the Habsburg cultural producer, and on the other hand, the "fugitive" or "marginal" status of the modernist subject. Modernism is itself a notoriously slippery category, but regardless of whether we decide to define it by its pervasive sense of self-reflection and self-consciousness, its self-irony and ironic stance toward the outside world, its moods of alienation, neurosis, or paranoia, or its play with the category of language, we could fruitfully see the anachronism of central Europe as "central." That is, the creative minds of the Habsburg Empire arguably had privileged access to the hallmarks of modernism by virtue of the story they told themselves about the place of central Europe in the modern world.[5]

Vying with Schorske's account of the fin-de-siècle for explanatory power in approaches to Habsburg modernism was the roughly contemporary volume by one philosopher and one intellectual historian, Janik and Toulmin's *Wittgenstein's Vienna*.[6] Their distinctive account is less well-known than Schorske's, and hence arguably has been less influential, but one of their principal theses has proven irresistible to many observers. In concert with a distinctive philosophical tradition, the historical context of a polyglot empire – rife with nationality conflict taking form in public discourse about language – placed Habsburg subjects in a privileged place vis-à-vis a central insight of modernism: the radical contingency of language.

Much points to the possible relevance of this context to Austrian modernism. First, two of the most important early philosophical projects pointing to the contingency of language sprang from this ground: the Bohemian Fritz Mauthner's three-volume *Contributions to a Critique of Language* (1901–03), and the Viennese Ludwig Wittgenstein's sustained and shifting reflections on language. These projects do not in some senses share a common philosophical genealogy, and yet both saw in the critique of language a radical challenge to standing assumptions about epistemology and metaphysics. While the work of the mature Wittgenstein of the *Tractatus Logico-Philosophicus* (1922–23), with its crystalline proofs of the parameters of language, is easily appropriated by analytic philosophers, the work's final pages describe language as ultimately extremely limited, and logic itself as a "ladder" to be kicked away once the goal of understanding has been reached.

In modernist literature, such skepticism of language had its paradigmatic expression in the significant publication in the German literary journal *Der Tag* [The Day] of October 18, 1902, of a fictive letter of 1603 from Lord Chandos to his mentor, Francis Bacon. The piece – called "Ein Brief" [A Letter], but widely known as the Chandos Letter – confesses a personal crisis on behalf of the young author, which he describes as a failure of language:

> My case, in short, is this: I have completely lost the ability to think or to say anything coherent. [. . .] I experienced an inexplicable unease upon even pronouncing the words "mind," "soul" or "body" . . . the abstract words to which the tongue must naturally avail itself in order to make the simplest judgment on the day collapsed in my mouth as moldy mushrooms.

The potent epistolary essay electrified young modernist audiences of the day, particularly in German-speaking Europe, but its very eloquence raises the problem of accepting as a "fact" such self-declared crises among this generation of modernists as the crisis of language, of subjectivity, or of masculinity. While scholars like Jacques Le Rider (in *Modernity and Crises of Identity*) argue that central Europe experienced such crises and responded to them with modernism, Suzanne Stewart-Steinberg's *Sublime Surrender*, focusing on the presumed fragility of masculine subjectivity in this period, suggests persuasively that such claims were self-empowering, and (as this key passage from a key text suggests) an occasion for writerly innovation.[7] Similarly, the self-declared outsider status of so many young writers and artists in turn-of-the-century Vienna can be seen as a context for artistic innovation that they created, in no small degree, for themselves.

In the period bridging the nineteenth century and the twentieth, a quasi-institutional setting for Hofmannsthal and a small but influential group of young literati was the Café Griensteidl. The circle of young writers, calling themselves "Jung-Wien" [Young Vienna], included such aesthetically oriented poets as Arthur Schnitzler, Felix Salten, Peter Altenberg, and Richard von Beer-Hofmann; and central to the circle was the aforementioned literary critic and publicist Hermann Bahr.[8] The brilliant writer and critic Karl Kraus was an early adherent, and later adversary, of the group. The qualifier of "young" was a characteristic marker of this literary generation's self-identity; and such circles arose throughout central European cities with similar designations. The setting of the coffee house had a special significance in Vienna in particular, highlighting the ways in which the space of aesthetic modernism overlapped with a self-conscious intervention in the public sphere. Viennese and other Habsburg coffee-house intellectuals conceived of themselves not as iconoclasts, but clearly as outsiders of a particular kind: mildly unconventional in the "bohemian" style; bourgeois and educated, but outside of the center of cultural as well as political power. Many were of Jewish origin, for instance – which is not to endorse the thesis that Viennese modernism was in some way a "Jewish phenomenon." Rather, Jewishness was simply one of an array of markers that allowed for a claim of displacement of the sort explored in this chapter.[9]

Among the young writers of the Griensteidl group, Arthur Schnitzler was to become particularly prominent and contentious, and at the same time to make a distinctive mark on European modernist literature. In short fiction such as *Fräulein Else* (1924) and the *Dream Story* (*Traumnovelle*) (1925), but also already in much earlier work such as *Lieutenant Gustl* (1901) and *Anatol* (1893), he ventured into the psychic lives of his characters in complex ways, including the stream-of-consciousness narrative technique, which he developed before it appeared in English in the works of James Joyce and Virginia Woolf. His frank depiction of sexuality (perhaps no less than his focus on social hypocrisy) placed him beyond the circle of most highly respected writers in the high culture of Vienna; he was even branded a pornographer in light of the now famous piece *Reigen* (best known in English as *La Ronde*, the title of Max Orphül's celebrated 1950 film version). Yet Schnitzler was prolific and popular, and particularly successful with his dramas, the field in which he remains best known. His dramatic modernism was also resisted, however, by the official high culture of Vienna (represented by the *Burgtheater*), and was instead performed chiefly at the more popular *Volkstheater*.

The brilliant poet Georg Trakl – born in Salzburg to Protestant parents of Czech and Hungarian origin – was one of the great modernist masters of the German lyric. Tapping into a German Romantic tradition, his lyric style bridges fin-de-siècle decadence and twentieth-century expressionism of the "contemplative" mode. Bestowing a worldly beauty upon the darkest themes, his poems exercise a purity of language of an extraordinary intensity. Although he was supported (largely anonymously) by the patronage of Ludwig Wittgenstein, both Trakl's work and his life were marked by morbidity and pain. His early death by suicide during service as a medic in the First World War is one reason for his relatively muted recognition in the canon of European modernism; another is his personal isolation (in spite of inclusion in expressionist anthologies); ultimately, the opacity of his poetry, and the difficulties in translating it, interfere with its accessibility.

Karl Kraus is himself an important if complicated case, and his importance to Habsburg modernism cannot be overestimated. This writer and critic never completed his academic degree, and after early adherence to the Jung-Wien circle, he dissociated himself even from the company of these self-proclaimed outsiders with a satirical attack on them called "die demolirte Literatur" [Demolished Literature] – published on the occasion of the demolition of the Griensteidl coffee house. While central European journalists and men of letters were typically outsiders to the still relatively closed academic world (and often Jewish), Kraus came to embody a form of public discourse that was as oppositional to journalism as it was to formal academic or official discourse. His journal, *Die Fackel* [The Torch], railed endlessly and in pointed, pun-filled prose against the contemporary political, social, and cultural worlds, and hence came to embody the modernist enterprise in form, intent, and aesthetic content. The journal was further a source of powerful influence for the central European literary avant-garde – Kraus was an avid supporter of the German and Austrian journals *Der Sturm* [The Storm] and *Der Brenner* [The Burner] – and he also became an influence as a personality, through lectures that acquired a mass following.

Kraus's ceaseless critique of virtually all areas of contemporary culture included modernist literary movements as well: not only the Young Vienna movement, but also other forms of symbolism, and expressionism later on. Withal, he cannot be considered a conservative per se, or even an anti-modernist. He extolled many modernists, including Austrians ranging from Trakl (he was responsible for calling the attention of Trakl's future patron, Wittgenstein, to his work) to Kokoschka, Loos, and Schoenberg; but he was suspicious of literary movements as such, and ruthless toward adherents whom he deemed mediocre. The ultimate direction to which his writing pointed was the abolition of boundaries between public engagement, journalism, and literature; his primary literary aim was to liberate language from the confines of fictively transparent referentiality. Walter Benjamin would much later note "the strange interplay between reactionary theory and revolutionary practice that is met everywhere in Kraus."[10] In the last analysis, Kraus has been an underappreciated contributor to international, and especially central European, modernism.

Vienna 1900: beyond literature

Vienna was as much a crucible of modernism in the visual arts as it was in literature; and there is evidence that the impulse of the visual in Viennese modernism is more than casual.[11] Central to artistic innovation in all media was an institution that sprang in 1897 from a group that broke away from Vienna's official academy: the Union of Visual Artists Austrian Secession (or simply, the Secession). The nineteen artists in the original group included Gustav Klimt (who was its leader), along with painters, craftsmen, and architects including Carl Moll, Koloman Moser, Josef Hoffmann, and J. M. Olbrich, who designed the famous Secession building in the shadow of the Academy's official House of Art (Kunsthaus). In contrast to the House of Art's heavy historicist style – it was built between 1865 and 1868 and resembles an inflated Italian Renaissance villa – the Secession building was designed to be unmistakably modern: white, small, and ornamented with a prominent sphere of gilded laurel, and the motto, "To each time its art, to art its freedom." In all these ways, the Secession announced itself as a rupture from official academic art, from historicism and derivative styles.

The story of the Vienna Secession is a familiar one, in that such splits within the artistic establishment took place in other cities and nations, and in fact the Vienna example followed similar secessions that had already taken place in such cities as Munich and Berlin. These secessions were closely associated with other terms relating to modernist aesthetic style, such as symbolism, *Jugendstil*, and art nouveau. Critics typically see these styles, with their stress on aesthetic ornamentation and the reproduction of organic forms, as pre-modernist. Yet they are clearly important precursors of the emancipation of art from its conventional representational moorings in movements like cubism, fauvism, expressionism, and finally formal abstraction. Furthermore, as the example of the Secession shows, these movements self-consciously imagined themselves to be breaking away from historical forces in order to embrace the forces of aesthetics itself: to embrace art on its own terms (as in the slogans "l'art pour l'art," or "to art its freedom"). Like the contemporary group of café literati who bore the banner of Jung-Wien, the Secession deliberately used a vocabulary of modernity and youth. Another parallel to the "young" literary circles of central Europe lies in the claim of outsider status: as the word "secession" was designed to imply, these artists were self-declared exiles from the largest and oldest organ for artistic education and association. Yet they were not expelled from any academy; they were its competitors in an evolving culture market. The Secession itself was built with private funds, including the participants', but the City of Vienna donated the land for the building. The members and students of the Secession vied for public commissions as well as, significantly, the burgeoning market of private bourgeois enthralled by the new forms.

From the start the exhibitions of the Secession included design and craft elements, moving not only toward a greater inclusiveness of various media, but also toward the fusion of different artistic elements within a unified vision. By 1902, when the Secession opened its fourteenth exhibition, on the theme of Beethoven, this tendency had evolved into a manifestation of the conception of a total work of art (*Gesamtkunstwerk*).

These themes of the total work of art and unity of art and life were manifest in another of Vienna's lasting contributions to the Modern: the applied arts and design of the Wiener Werkstätte, or Vienna Workshop community. This group evolved directly out of the Secession when some of its members were motivated, after the 1900 Secession exhibition of British and European workshop communities, to found a group which, as in other "arts and crafts" movements, unified contemporary high aesthetic principles with practical artisanry and design. The Werkstätte included architects, furniture designers, textile creators, and innovators of industrial design. While, like the Secession, it was neither unique in Europe nor the first organization of its kind, it was particularly influential. Uniting all these efforts were a commitment to high-quality craftsmanship and its status as an art; the rejection of conventionality and the search for new, aesthetically pleasing forms to correspond to modern life; the communal value of individual artistic achievement; and the project to unite daily life and art both by making the everyday more aesthetic and by bringing the artist's concerns to bear on quotidian human needs. The linkage of all of these tendencies to Arts and Crafts movements in Northern Europe and North America is clear, as is the stylistic continuity from French art nouveau and symbolism to the Vienna Secession. In short, the remarkable confluence of different forms of modernist innovation associated with Vienna 1900 was from the start, and self-consciously, a cosmopolitan manifestation.

The Habsburg architects Otto Wagner and Adolf Loos were key figures in the modernization of the built environment, and they were centrally active in the modernist circles of Vienna. Wagner designed the magnificent church at Steinhof, a mental institution on the outskirts of Vienna, where the beauty of the building theoretically corresponded in large part with its functionalist innovation. (The building was also designed as a collective arts project, with mosaics, stained glass, sculptures, and other decorative elements designed by Koloman Moser and other artists of the Wiener Werkstätte and Secession movements.) The supposed turn to function was a central hallmark of architectural modernism, and was wittily and programmatically outlined by Adolf Loos in several essays, most notably the influential "Ornament and Crime," which rejected the decorative flourishes of the Secession and *Jugendstil* movements. "The evolution of culture is synonymous with the removal of ornament from objects of everyday use," Loos declared, suggesting that while ornament was the origin of fine art and connected to primitive eroticism, in modern life it was associated with degeneracy and criminality.[12]

The Austrian high cultural tradition was deeply invested in music, and not only because of the towering legacies of Haydn, Mozart, Schubert, and Beethoven. The operatic tradition, the operetta, and the waltz were at the heart of the myth of Habsburg high culture. The Viennese musical establishment was in many ways resistant to modernization, and yet it was the reluctant host to the earliest and most important moves toward truly modernist musical innovation. Springing from the neo-Romantic strains of chromaticism of Gustav Mahler and Richard Strauss, the next generation of Viennese musical innovators would be the first set of composers to aim to liberate Western music from the classical rules of harmony (or, as they were to put it, "tonality"). Arnold Schoenberg is the chief figure of what came to be called the Second Vienna School of composition. With his students Anton Webern and Alban Berg, Schoenberg mounted an atonal revolution that aimed to completely rethink the fundamentals of composition. This rethinking motivated an evolution from chromaticism (or the use of a broader scale of tones within each octave than major and minor keys traditionally allowed, producing more pronounced dissonances) to disharmony, and then later yielded to new rules of composition which, though it was inconsistently adopted by all these composers, was as regimented as the old system. The "dodecaphonic" or twelve-tone system of composition regulated composition to a series of manipulations of an initial row of twelve notes.

As a term that classically refers to the arts, modernism has only exceptionally been applied to branches of early twentieth-century scholarship and science. Yet if any of the European modernisms reach into the academic sphere, it is the Viennese variant. In the philosophical realm, we have already discussed Ludwig Wittgenstein, whose work on language transformed epistemology into a modernist metaphysics. The critic Terry Eagleton (who also wrote the screenplay for Derek Jarman's avant-garde film *Wittgenstein*) calls the Viennese Wittgenstein the "first philosophic modernist," a philosopher whose project owed more to the Viennese scene of Schoenberg, writers like

Joyce, and painters like Picasso, than to the logicians to whom he formally responded.

This birth of philosophic modernism in Vienna is odd, in a certain way. Vienna's recent philosophical tradition was above all empiricist, rationalist, and positivist, as the prominence of the physicist and empirico-positivist philosopher Ernst Mach and his followers testifies.[13] For cultural–historical reasons, the human sciences in Austria were not saturated with Romanticism in the early nineteenth century, as was the case in Germany and elsewhere in northern Europe, and Austrian philosophy steered strongly away from the metaphysical. Part of the power of the *Tractatus* is the way in which it feels its way through this steely positivism to lyrical metaphysical and, indeed, mystical insights.

The modernist scientific specialty par excellence, however, is psychoanalysis. Like the philosophical modernism of his fellow Viennese, Ludwig Wittgenstein, Sigmund Freud's disciplinary innovation emerged out of a powerful scientistic context: neurological medicine in the most advanced medical school in the world at the time, the University of Vienna. Freud's struggle throughout the foundation of psychoanalysis was for a professional recognition of its scientific character, and yet, as he noted, its findings were remarkably similar to those of another thinker earlier in the nineteenth century who had no access to medical knowledge at all: Friedrich Nietzsche. While Carl Schorske identified the major parallel of Freudian thought and painterly aestheticism in that both were a "retreat from the world" – one into the work of art, one into the psyche – in practice psychoanalysis aimed at anything but a retreat. Nonetheless, in its revolutionary abandonment of old ways of representing the world and the place of humans in it, in its turn to the sometimes apparently senseless and random meanderings of the individual consciousness, and in its amalgamation of the nineteenth-century scientistic confidence with a fin-de-siècle skepsis, psychoanalysis is easily associated with other modernist movements. As modernism continued to develop through the twentieth century, the insights of psychoanalysis, and indeed an arguably psychoanalytic model of artistic subjectivity, fed into various modernist styles, from stream-of-consciousness narrative to Surrealist imagery. This was perhaps less the case in Vienna itself than in centers of modernism all over the continent and in Britain, as well as the United States and further abroad.

Beyond Vienna

To the north of Vienna and its surrounding provinces lay the Habsburg crown lands of Bohemia and Moravia. These provinces, with borders closely mapping on to those of today's Czech Republic, were host to a majority of Czech speakers, plus a large minority of German speakers who were concentrated in the north, west, and south as well as in mixed-population areas, especially cities and towns of the interior. The German-speaking Jews of Bohemia and Moravia, and especially the population of Prague, made an important contribution to German literature, and indeed to modernism more generally. For the most part, these figures were writing in their native language, in a context in which German was an indigenous tongue, even if it was not the language of the majority of the population. While the temptation today is to think of this as a "marginal" space of the Empire, in terms of contemporary perception, these crown lands, which were direct possessions of the Emperor, belonged to the cultural, economic, and geographical core of the Habsburg lands. Prague itself lay geographically about halfway between Vienna and Berlin. Yet the context of the large surrounding Slavic-speaking population is a fact that must be considered inseparable from any understanding of this region's contribution to German literature in general and modernism in particular.

Some of the Jews residing in the German-language "islands" within the majority-Czech interior identified particularly strongly as cultural Germans. Among these was the journalist, novelist, and philosopher Fritz Mauthner. Mauthner resided in Berlin for much of his career, but his staunch German-nationalist sympathies emerged out of the Czech–German conflict in Bohemia that started to emerge in the last third of the nineteenth century. Although his novels, including many that were desperately defensive of German life in the borderlands, do not bear the marks of modernist innovation, this same context has been thought to inform his prescient two-volume philosophical critique of language – not least by the author himself in a much-cited memoir.[14]

Probably the greatest poet to emerge from Bohemia was Rainer Maria Rilke, born René Karl Wilhelm Johann Josef Maria Rilke in Prague in late 1875. Rilke is clearly a writer of great importance to literary modernism, although his literary contribution, like his life, was a product of experience far afield of the Habsburg Empire, taking place first in Germany, then Russia, and finally in France and Switzerland. His lyric style is similarly peripatetic, temporally as well as geographically: it interfolds a classicism and a Romanticism that are both informed by a profound immersion in the history of lyric, just as it hails the literary abstraction of the word and even seems to anticipate movements, like existentialism, that he would not live to see. In spite of the poet's self-mythology of creative isolation, his works display a rich convergence of contemporary cultural currents, from aestheticism to the modernist formal innovation that he did much to further through his own poetry, and including visual culture and other arts as well.[15] As difficult as modernism is to define through a set of features, Rilke's embrace of fragmentariness, his experimentation with the representation of subjectivity, his self-referentiality, and the metapoetic operation of many of his pieces, all contribute to his reception as one of the greatest modernist poets. Central European themes are rare and scattered in his works (with the exception perhaps of the crucial and markedly modernist work the Duino Elegies, written in that Adriatic corner of the Empire under the patronage of a Habsburg aristocrat). It is internationalism, rather than any grounding in central Europe, that characterizes his work; and hence the name of Rilke must be pronounced in several chapters of this volume.

In the elite Prague German literary association known as "Concordia," the dominant figures around 1900 were well connected to European literary circles. They were also adherents of the then-fashionable literary trends of neo-Romanticism and neo-Classicism. Hence their work was rich in historical and classical references, but eschewed any mark of local peculiarity. The same would not be the case of the generation which would follow. It is interesting that the truly great Prague German writers of Jewish origin would come from this latter generation.

The best known of these authors was Franz Kafka, who is considered a towering figure of European modernism. Kafka was part of a generation of German-speaking Jews from Prague that included such others as the prolific and important writers Max Brod and Franz Werfel, the blind expressionist prose writer Oskar Baum, the expressionist poets and translators Otto Pick and Rudolf Fuchs, and the socialist journalist Egon Erwin Kisch, among others. These writers, all born in the decade between 1880 and 1890, came of age in a period when the German cultural domination of this region had been forcefully challenged by the political ascendancy of the Czech national movement. At the same time, due to the rise of the more racialist or ethnicist strand of German nationalism that developed in the late nineteenth and early twentieth century, even within the boundaries of Prague the status of Jews as members of the German minority was increasingly challenged. It was in this volatile cultural–political context that a Prague German literature dominated by Jews, far out of proportion to the relatively small absolute numbers of Prague German-speaking Jews, flourished and gained extraordinary attention abroad. In the German literary world, publishers like Axel Juncker and Kurt Wolff actively marketed Prague German authors as inhabitants of a modernist island-world in the heart of Bohemia.

Among these writers, known retrospectively as the "Prague Circle" (although they did not share an aesthetic program), Franz Werfel and the dramatist Paul Korngold were significant contributors to modernism, particularly in their participation in the expressionist movement between 1910 and the 1920s. Werfel wrote dramas and novels, yet his most modernist work was arguably his poetry; the recitation of one of his poems from the collection *Der Weltfreund* [Friend of the World] by Max Brod in Berlin is even credited as the founding moment of the German literary movement. Korngold has not remained canonical in the way Werfel and especially Kafka have, but his dramaturgic theory, which stressed that the actor's art is not to represent reality naturalistically, but to express spiritual essences outward, was key to modernist stage practice. Another Prague German writer of this generation was Egon Erwin Kisch, who used the reportage form in innovative ways, although this work does not belong to modernism in the sense of formal innovation in high culture. Of this generation Max Brod was by far the most prolific and also, with Werfel perhaps, the most famous, although his venerated place in the history of modernism was not earned through his own writing so much as from his determined and successful efforts to save his best friend's unpublished work from destruction (twice: first from destruction by his own hand, as his friend's will had specified, and then from eternal loss with the Nazi occupation of Prague). The name of that friend, which remains known as a result of these and other efforts of Max Brod, was Franz Kafka.

Kafka's place in literary modernism can hardly be questioned, yet the precise nature of his linkage to modernist movements as such is complicated. Part of the difficulty arises from the problem of the interpretation of Kafka's notoriously ambiguous texts – a quality that itself is perceived as linked to modernism. While the terms "modern" and "die Moderne" (referring both to "modernity" and to modernism), as they relate to literature, were already current in the period in which Kafka lived and wrote, he did not explicitly identify with the terms nor express concern about what literary modernism should entail. He did not rush to join any of the programmatically avantgarde artistic circles current in his day, and his letters and diaries do not betray a preoccupation with the specific concern of how to modernize literature. Nonetheless, the texts he produced have earned him an undisputed place in the modernist canon.

The writers and artists of the secessionist Young Vienna, as well as the parallel "young Prague" movements, were by and large a half-generation older than Kafka and his fellow students. At first the college-aged Kafka and others of his generation of German-speaking Jewish Praguers demonstrated a strong identification with the aestheticist tendencies of these self-identified "moderns," but their work soon departed from these styles. Several members of this cohort were part of a reading group at the German university in Prague (called the Reading and Discussion Group of German Students in Prague), whose program at the time was markedly modernist and aestheticist, while also respectful of the older generation of neo-Classicist poets in Prague that included Hugo Salus and Friedrich Adler. The literary and artistic section of this group, where Kafka befriended Brod and others of the Prague Circle, at the time admired the work of German aestheticist poets; and Brod for a while after his university period imagined himself to be working along the lines of the French symbolist writers such as Jules Laforgue. Kafka scholars have long noted the uncharacteristically florid style of Kafka's early work, particularly *Betrachtung* [Contemplation]. In contrast to those who would see this work as immature and underdeveloped, discontinuous with the crystalline, stripped-down style of work after the 1912 "breakthrough," some scholars have appreciated the continuities of these equally modernist contributions.[16]

Kafka is generally not identified under the labels of aestheticism, decadence, art for art's sake, etc., yet one could argue that his attitude toward writing was an extension and intensification of aestheticist positions. Certainly, life and art may seem for Kafka to have been at times opposing realms, as Max Brod asserted early in Kafka scholarship, or as readers of his letters to Felice Bauer have had reason to assume.[17] On the other hand, Kafka's more consistently held position was not the segregation of art and life, but rather a view of art that was deeply connected to living, or that promised or threatened to consume it; his remark that "writing is a form of prayer" is one oft-cited example of such an expression. Indeed, it is in one of the letters to Felice that he makes the well-known claim that "I have no literary interests, but rather I consist of literature, I am nothing else and can be nothing else." As extravagant as these claims may seem to be, they belong to Kafka's time and place. Rather than representing a retreat into literature (as Schorske understood the Viennese modernist turn of a disenfranchised bourgeoisie), Kafka's claim represents merging of artistic language, self-conception, and context in ways expressly linked to his place within central European cultural politics. At the same time, his singular contribution to modernism may lie precisely in what appears as a resistance to specific reference to any historical context, his determined referential ambiguity. Language itself would seem to be the self-referent of this work.

Many Bohemian and Moravian German writers beyond the so-called Prague Circle contributed more peripherally to modernism. A significant, if also idiosyncratic, exemplar is Alexander Friedrich Roda Roda, whose early work would come to characterize the "Habsburg spirit," according to Gregor von Rezzori. He was born in Drnowitz, Moravia in 1872, but his family soon moved to Zdenci in Slavonia, the furthest eastern province of today's Croatia. Roda Roda's central Europe ranged into German Austria and Germany itself, where he became famous as a satirist and cabarettist, rubbing elbows with leading literati and political writers of the age and active notably in the *Simplicissimus* circle. In his peripatetic engagements bridging high and popular culture, his focus on language play and irony, and his insertion of himself as a figure in his work, he embodied a strand of modernism of the particularly central European variety.

Beyond German: other central European languages

While the main focus of this chapter is German-language central European modernism, it is important to note the distinct, and in fact unique, modernist formations taking place in other languages. A brief mention of some of these will help put the general discussion in perspective. In the case of Bohemia and Moravia, the relevant language competing with the powerful German tradition was Czech. As a literary language, Czech had needed to be revived earlier in the nineteenth century, due to the long Habsburg domination of all Czech speakers. From the start, modern Czech writers distanced themselves from German-language central European modernism by identifying their cultural production as forward-looking, youthful, healthy, and connected, in contrast to an alienated Prague German literature. At the same time, in looking abroad for models, the writers of the 1890s became attached to French symbolism and other trends of fin-de-siècle decadence in art as well as literature. The strong influences of Young Vienna (especially the influence of Bahr) and also the Berlin scene on the first modernist movements in Czech Prague were crucial, if often understated.[18] By 1895, a set of Czech artists and critics organized under the rubric of the Czech *Moderna* produced a manifesto designed to distance itself at once from a detached aestheticism and an overly journalistic Czech artistic mainstream; modernist journals began to appear at the same time. In the 1920s, avant-garde poets and artists joined in a formal association known as Devětsil; the group was not consistently associated with a single style or tendency, although its most active critic, Karel Teige, produced varied manifestos and programmatic writings. The "poetist" movement came out of this movement and is considered a Czech form of Surrealism. While many other Czech literary figures may be considered modernist in some way – including more well-known writers, like Jaroslav Hašek, Karel Čapek, and Karel's brother Josef – none have the stature within the modernist canon that some of the German Habsburg writers do. Still, even if Czech national culture played a lesser role within broader modernist movements, these movements were extremely important in the self-determination of Czech national culture.

While Slovak speakers would later be joined with the Czechs in interwar and postwar successor states, in the Habsburg period Slovakia belonged to the Hungarian half of the Austro-Hungarian monarchy. Unlike the situation in Bohemia and Moravia, this region was subjected to an intensive Magyarization policy. The resurgence there of a distinctively national literature was a form of resistance to what was definitely perceived as cultural imperialism. While most of this literature was not modernist as such, the work of the poet Ivan Krasko and the fiction writers Gejza Vámos (who hailed from a Hungarian-speaking Jewish family) and Ivan Horváth was its most cosmopolitan strain.

In the Hungarian language, the pattern of modernist innovation is thought to have been different from that of German-language central Europe as well. As in Czech modernism, Hungarian poets and painters were attracted to European currents of decadence and symbolism; yet the metaphors of displacement that motivated so much of German-language Habsburg modernism held less resonance for Hungarian poets, who stood grounded in ascendant national movements. The late Hungarian historian Péter Hanák has offered an apt comparison of Budapest and Vienna at the end of the nineteenth century. Where Carl Schorske saw Vienna moderns' retreat into the aesthetic "garden," Hanák offered the metaphor of the "workshop" to characterize a project that was for Hungarian creative forces both self-consciously modernist and central to a nation-building project.[19] The poet most often credited with creating modernist poetry in Hungary was Endre Ady, whose contemporary poetic style aimed to advance Hungarian literary culture at the same time as it (and Ady's journalistic work as well) offered an implicit critique of a political and cultural scene that was not progressive enough. The journal Nyugat [West], founded in 1908 by a young generation of enthusiastic modernists proclaiming Ady as their exemplary poet, was attacked by conservative critics offended at "the treason and slander" represented by the journal's malicious aims "under the pretext of civilizing the barbarian Magyars."[20] As elsewhere, Hungary never possessed a consistent aesthetic program of the modernist movement, even within the Nyugat circle; but the tension between innovation in Hungarian culture as nation-building and the suspicion of modernism as a hostile foreign import would survive the fall of the Empire.

One of the modernist epoch's more powerful critics was Georg/Györgi Lukács, an intellectual of Jewish origins from Budapest. Lukács, like many Hungarian Jews of his generation, studied in Germany, and was fluent in German as well as Hungarian; his early essays, published first in German in 1910–11 as Die Seele und die Formen [Soul and Forms], were composed in Hungarian and translated by himself. These elegant and subtly complex essays, informed by a Hegelian dialecticism and covering a range of literary and philosophical production, are driven by a modernist imaginary concerned with the fusion of artistic form, world, and subject. Turning to Marxism in the wake of the Russian Revolution, Lukács's criticism and philosophy from the 1920s must be considered foundational for what would become known as Western Marxist thought, a decidedly and important modernist intellectual movement that was much more powerful in Germany than in the Habsburg realm, including its successor states. Lukács was a central figure in the rethinking of Marxist aesthetics, the concept of reification, and the relationship of consciousness to political processes. His sophisticated understanding of realism yielded, however, to a critical rejection of literary modernism in many of its forms; his debates with German defenders of modernist formal innovation (notably expressionism), especially Bertolt Brecht and Ernst Bloch, have become required reading for students of the potential intersections and conflicts of modernism and Marxism.[21]

Innovative writing in other languages also flourished in the Empire, including in those languages where a majority of speakers and writers were subjects of other nations and empires. These languages included Polish, for the writers of Galicia and especially Cracow, which became a center for Polish modernism. Cracow's first literary review, *Zycie* [Life], founded in 1897 by poet Ludwik Szczepanski and then directed by the leading figure of aestheticist Young Poland, Stanisław Przybyszewski, followed Viennese and Parisian models. In the case of Polish modernist literature, Habsburg and Habsburg-influenced areas of both Galicia and the nominally free city of Cracow suffered less national oppression than did their counterparts under Russian and even German rule. Moreover, Young Poland and other Habsburg movements were more markedly decadent or aestheticist, less overtly politicized, and more tied to Viennese and West European trends. Romanian-speaking areas of the Empire were divided: the polyglot Bukovina, in the eastern part of the monarchy's Austrian half, was under German cultural and linguistic dominance, whereas Transylvania was part of the Hungarian half, and hence subject to Magyarization policies and the repression of Romanian cultural activity. Romanian modernism was hence most active outside the Empire, in Bucharest. In many of these examples – the Polish, Romanian, and also Hungarian cases – modernist tendencies vied with avowedly non-modernist, traditional, or "indigenist" forms, with proponents accusing modernists of non-nativist cosmopolitanism.[22]

An interesting case of the central European context informing the modernism of one of these language groups is that of Italo Svevo, the Italian modernist of Jewish origin born Aron Ettore Schmitz in Habsburg Trieste. Championed by James Joyce, Svevo is certainly accommodated by our thesis of Habsburg displacement; even his pen name refers to him as a Germano-Italian hybrid of sorts (Svevo referring to "Swabian"), and his work displays a swaying play of language, even as it is anchored in the local atmosphere of Trieste. All of this, as well as a connection to the Freudian landscape of the unconscious, mark his modernist contribution as distinctly central European.[23] An extended discussion of his work, however, is best left for discussion in our chapter on Italy.

Habsburg Jews and modernism

Yiddish may also be seen as one of these languages with one foot in the Empire, largely in the eastern province of Galicia. In fact there were several movements within Yiddish literature that were self-consciously modernist, "young-Yiddish," expressionist, or avant-garde; yet these were really strongest in the Russian Empire and especially the Soviet Union (Kiev was an important center), and to some degree in the United States. During and after the First World War a group of innovative writers arose in Galician Lemberg, today L'viv; the most remembered of this group was Uri-Tzvi Grinberg, an expressionist Yiddish poet influenced by Rilke, whose work bears a Habsburg mark. After the First World War, with the dissolution of the Empire and an influx of refugees from Galicia, Vienna became something of a center for the mediation of Yiddish, and a modern Yiddish literary journal (*Kritik*) was established there. The Habsburg Empire was also an important continental source of modern literature in the revived or reinvented language of Hebrew, and this literature, too, participated in modernist movements. The Galician poets Avraham ben Yitzhak Sonne and Dvoyre Fogel are two examples of genuine and successful aesthetic experimentation in Hebrew, though the latter was born in 1902 and wrote in the 1920s and 1930s, after the fall of the Habsburg Empire. Jewish Habsburg subjects, as we have seen, were most active in modernist innovation within the German language (if also, in examples above, in Hungarian, Slovak, and Italian, among others).

A final region of the Austrian half of the Habsburg Empire where German-speaking Jewish inhabitants made a substantial contribution to modern literature is the Bukovina. Bukovina was the northeastern corner of what was considered Romania, and was the part of Romania under Austrian control; this imperial context and the history of the multi-cultural region led the Habsburgs to encourage Germanization there, especially among the region's Jewish subjects. In the early twentieth century, German-speaking Jews made up nearly half of the population of the regional capital Czernowitz (Romanian Cernăuți, today Chernivtsi in western Ukraine). Much of the most important modernist poetry of Bukovina was created after the

First World War and the secession of the region to Romania. Another important intellectual influence is said to have been that of the so-called "Ethical Seminar" at the University of Czernowitz, where some future poets, notably Rose Ausländer, were steeped in a German neo-idealist philosophical tradition. A further influence was the German classical tradition, which, in part due to the relative isolation of the province, was highly cherished there; as a result, most of the numerous excellent poets to emerge from this small population were not modernist as such. The case of the region's most extraordinary poet, Paul Celan, was somewhat different. Born in Czernowitz shortly after the First World War and the dissolution of the Empire, he experienced and survived the Holocaust, then becoming active as a poet and translator in Romania, the Soviet Union, Vienna, and finally and for the longest period in Paris. His poetry, the most powerful and canonical sections of which reflected obliquely on the Holocaust, has all of the marks of high modernist poetry – especially, as the classical definition of modernist poetry has it, an obscurity rendering it often difficult to decipher, where the effects of language seem at times to be liberated from a strict connection to worldly referents.[24] It is notable that Celan was himself aware of this classical definition, and rebutted it in a lecture and then an essay entitled "Meridian." There, he argued that modern poetry might seem obscure, but that its obscurity is not a turn from referentiality, but rather the only access to an obscure contemporary world. The obscurity of such poetry in German is due to the "thousand darknesses of death-bringing speech" in recent central European history.[25]

Certainly many other central European writers and artistic movements could be named as contributing to European modernism. These contributions could be said to have continued even through the postwar period, where innovative and controversial playwrights such as Thomas Bernhard and George Tabori, for example, seem to follow very clearly in the traditions set by the likes of Karl Kraus, Arthur Schnitzler, and Robert Musil. Traces of this tradition continue in contemporary Czech literature, among others, whereas in many corners of the former Empire the remains of the polyglot empire, with its unlikely fusion of abrasively modernist and staunchly traditionalist impulses, are only faintly present, or where self-styled marginality and displacement has been overrun by more centered national cultural consciousness. It may be true, as some have claimed, that the fragile status of language, the contingency of subjective experience, the lack of foundations for making empirical claims, and so on – in other words, features that we identify with modernism, whatever it was – were elements of modern life that Habsburg subjects experienced more directly than did other Europeans at the century's turn. Or perhaps this was just a story some modern central

Europeans liked to tell about themselves, hoping that it would be repeated by their audiences, their critics, and their historians.

NOTES

1. Fritz Martini, "Modern, Die Moderne," in Werner Kohlschmidt and Wolfgang Mohr (eds.), *Reallexikon der Deutschen Literaturgeschichte*, vol. II (Berlin: Walter de Gruyter & Co., 1965), p. 409.

2. See the excellent reading of Philip Manger, "The 'Radetzky March': Joseph Roth and the Habsburg Myth," in Mark Francis, ed., *The Viennese Enlightenment* (London and Sydney: Croom Helm, 1985), pp. 40–62; on earlier work, see Jon Hughes, *Facing Modernity: Fragmentation, Culture and Identity in Joseph Roth's Writing in the 1920s* (London: Modern Humanities Research Association, 2006).

3. Claudio Magris, *Il mito absburgico nella letteratura austriaca moderna* (Turin: Einaudi, 1963), based on his doctoral dissertation, and later *Lontano da dove: Joseph Roth e la tradizione ebraico-orientale* (Turin: Einaudi, 1989). William M. Johnston critiques the view of the former work in his classic intellectual history *The Austrian Mind: An Intellectual and Social History, 1848–1938* (Berkeley: University of California Press, 1972), pp. 32–33.

4. Carl E. Schorske, *Fin-de-Siècle Vienna: Politics and Culture* (New York: Vintage, 1970). Critiques of this arguably reductive thesis have ranged widely, and in some cases gone some way toward explaining how the power of the work so vastly exceeded the limits of the paradigm. See Dominick LaCapra, *History and Criticism* (Ithaca, N.Y.: Cornell University Press, 1983), pp. 83–86; Michael Roth, "Performing History: Modernist Contextualism in Carl E. Schorske's *Fin-de-Siècle Vienna*," *American Historical Review* 99 (1994): 729–45; Scott Spector, "Beyond the Aesthetic Garden: Politics and Culture on the Margins of *Fin-de-Siècle Vienna*," *Journal of the History of Ideas* 59 (1998): 691–710.

5. Nor is this historiographical circle broken by the much-heralded passage from the modern to the so-called postmodern. Witness Stefan Jonnson's insightful book, in which the conventional historiography on the Habsburg nationality conflict merges seamlessly with anti-foundationalist philosophy's critique of the existence of a modern self: Stefan Jonnson, *Subject Without Nation: Robert Musil and the History of Modern Identity* (Durham, N.C.: Duke University Press, 2000).

6. Allan Janik and Stephen Edelston Toulmin, *Wittgenstein's Vienna* (New York: Simon and Schuster, 1973).

7. See Jacques Le Rider, *Modernity and Crises of Identity: Culture and Society in Fin-de-siècle Vienna* (New York: Vienna Continuum, 1993); Suzanne R. Stewart, *Sublime Surrender: Male Masochism at the Fin-de-Siècle* (Ithaca, N.Y.: Cornell University Press, 1998).

8. Paul Reitter, *The Anti-Journalist: Karl Kraus and Jewish Self-Fashioning in Fin-de-Siècle Europe* (University of Chicago Press, 2008). See also Peter Sprengel and Gregor Streim, *Berliner und Wiener Moderne: Vermittlungen und Abgrenzungen in Literatur, Theater, Publizistik* (Vienna: Böhlau, 1998); Edward Timms, *Karl Kraus, Apocalyptic Satirist: Culture and Catastrophe in Habsburg Vienna* (New Haven, Conn.: Yale University Press, 1986).

9. The thesis that Viennese modernism was specifically linked to Jewishness in that city is posited by Steven Beller, *Vienna and the Jews, 1867–1938: A Cultural History* (Cambridge University Press, 1989). For a critique of that position, see Ernst H. Gombrich, *Kokoschka and His Time* (London: Tate Gallery, 1986), and Gombrich, "The Visual Arts in Vienna c. 1900: Reflections on the Jewish Catastrophe" (London: The Austrian Cultural Institute, 1997); see also Scott Spector, "Modernism without Jews: A Counter-Historical Argument," *Modernism/modernity* 13 (2006): 615–33.

10. Walter Benjamin, *Reflections: Essays, Aphorisms, Autobiographical Writings*, ed. Peter Demetz, trans. Edmund Jephcott (New York: Harcourt Brace Jovanovich, 1978), p. 247. See also António Ribeiro, "Karl Kraus and Modernism: A Reassessment," in *The Turn of the Century / La tournant du siècle: Modernism and Modernity in Literature and the Arts / Le modernisme et la modernité dans la littérature et les arts*, eds. Christian Berg, Frank Durieux, and Geert Lernout (Berlin and New York: De Gruyter, 1995), pp. 143–54.

11. Andreas Huyssen, "The Disturbance of Vision in Vienna Modernism," *Modernism/Modernity* 5.3 (1998) 33–47.

12. Adolf Loos, *Ornament and Crime: Selected Essays*, ed. Adolf Opel, trans. Michael Mitchell (Riverside, Calif.: Ariadne, 1988).

13. William M. Johnston, *The Austrian Mind: An Intellectual and Social History, 1848–1938* (Berkeley: University of California Press, 1972).

14. Fritz Mauthner, *Erinnerungen*, vol. I, *Prager Jugendjahre* (repr. Frankfurt am Main: Fischer, 1969).

15. See Judith Ryan, *Rilke, Modernism, and the Poetic Tradition* (Cambridge University Press, 1999).

16. Cf. G. Kurz, ed., *Der junge Kafka* (Frankfurt am Main, 1984). Particularly relevant is Mark Anderson's argument in *Kafka's Clothes: Ornament and Aestheticism in the Habsburg Fin de Siècle* (Oxford University Press, 1992), where the high modernist and alienated, stripped-down style of the later Kafka is described as an unmistakably aestheticist self-fashioning of a different kind.

17. Cf. Max Brod, *Franz Kafka: Eine Biographie* (1937); Elias Canetti, *Der andere Prozeß. Kafkas Briefe an Felice* (Munich, 1969).

18. See Katherine David-Fox, "Prague–Vienna, Prague–Berlin: The Hidden Geography of Czech Modernism," *Slavic Review* 59 (2000): 735–60.

19. Péter Hanák, *The Garden and the Workshop: Essays on the Cultural History of Vienna and Budapest* (Princeton University Press, 1998).

20. See Mary Gluck, *Georg Lukács and his Generation, 1900–1918* (Cambridge, Mass.: Harvard University Press, 1991), pp. 111–14.

21. See Theodor Adorno *et al.*, *Aesthetics and Politics* (London: Verso, 2007).

22. See the forum "The Other Modernisms: Culture and Politics in East Central Europe," *Austrian History Yearbook* 33 (2002): 141–238.

23. The connection to psychoanalysis is most prominent in the novel *La Coscienza di Zeno* [Zeno's Conscience]. The author's own psychoanalyst, Ottocaro Weiss, also a friend of Joyce's, had been trained by Freud in Vienna.

24. Cf. Paul de Man, "Lyric and Modernity," in *Blindness and Insight: Essays in the Rhetoric of Contemporary Criticism* (Minneapolis: University of Minnesota Press, 1983), pp. 166–228. De Man makes use of the classic definition found in Hugo Friedrich, *The Structure of Modern Poetry: From the Mid-nineteenth to*

the Mid-twentieth Century, trans. J. Neugroschel (Evanston, Ill.: Northwestern University Press, 1974).

25. Paul Celan, *Der Meridian: Rede anläßlich der Verleihung des Georg-Büchner Preises*, in *Selected Poems and Prose of Paul Celan*, trans. John Felstiner (New York: Norton, 2001), pp. 401–13. Quoted in Ulrich Baer, "Modernism and Trauma," in A. Eysteinsson and V. Liska, eds., *Modernism* (Amsterdam and Philadelphia: John Benjamins, 2007), vol. I, p. 312.

FURTHER READING

Janik, Allan, and Stephen Edelston Toulmin. *Wittgenstein's Vienna*. New York: Simon and Schuster, 1973.

Le Rider, Jacques. *Modernity and Crises of Identity: Culture and Society in Fin-de-siècle Vienna*. New York, Continuum, 1993.

Loos, Adolf. *Ornament and Crime: Selected Essays*. Ed. Adolf Opel, trans. Michael Mitchell. Riverside, Calif.: Ariadne, 1988.

Magris, Claudio. *Danube*. Trans. Patrick Creagh. New York: Farrar, Straus, Giroux, 1989.

Reitter, Paul. *The Anti-Journalist: Karl Kraus and Jewish Self-Fashioning in Fin-de-Siècle Europe*. University of Chicago Press, 2008.

Ryan, Judith. *Rilke, Modernism, and the Poetic Tradition*. Cambridge University Press, 1999.

Schorske, Carl E. *Fin-de-Siècle Vienna: Politics and Culture*. New York: Vintage Books, 1981.

   Thinking with History: Explorations in the Passage to Modernism. Princeton University Press, 1998.

Spector, Scott. *Prague Territories: National Conflict and Cultural Innovation in Franz Kafka's Fin de Siècle*. Berkeley: University of California Press, 2000.

5

LUCA SOMIGLI

Italy

In order to outline a history of Italian modernism, we must begin with a reflection on the category of modernism itself, which in recent years has substantially broadened its scope. From a term indicating a particular moment in Anglo-American literature (what we might now call "high modernism"), modernism has grown into a period label encompassing much of Western literature from the middle of the nineteenth century to the Second World War. This re-interpretation has tended to privilege the northern Paris–London–Berlin–Moscow axis, as in the case, for instance, of the critical anthology edited by Malcolm Bradbury and James McFarlane, arguably the key text in redefining the boundaries of modernism.[1] At the same time, as a historiographic category, modernism has played a very minor role in the Italian critical debate. The question with which we might begin, then, is to ask precisely what is at stake for Italian literature in the appropriation of modernism. I should point out that this is not a peculiarly Italian problem. Indeed, as Edward Możejko has argued in a recent essay, the "internationalization" of modernism as a term – its increased adoption on the part of critical traditions to which it was, until recently, foreign – entails a continuous process of redefinition of its meaning and implications.[2]

Until the 1970s, "*decadentismo*" might have seemed to cover much the same ground as modernism in Italian literary history.[3] However, *decadentismo* was always a problematic term, one that, even when used in the most neutral sense, could not be easily disjoined from the implicit moral judgment that its relation with "decadence" entails. Indeed, its fortune has had much to do with its negative implications, and was the result of the unlikely convergence of two otherwise rather distant currents of thought: Benedetto Croce's idealism, which censured modernist art in its defense of classical aesthetic values, and postwar Marxist criticism, which, following Georg Lukács, regarded modernism as a kind of irrationalist response to the crisis of the bourgeois social order. Since the 1980s, though, *decadentismo* has practically disappeared from the critical discourse as a general category, and now "seems more like a relic of past polemics."[4] Other, less ideologically charged terms, like "modernità" or even "modernità letteraria," have been used to define the period with which we are concerned – but there is a certain vagueness about them, their boundaries often stretching to include late twentieth-century phenomena that might be more often associated with postmodernity.

So, what is to be gained by introducing "modernism" into the debate?[5] As it has escaped the narrow boundaries of Anglo-American literature, modernism has become a productively "soft" literary category, an "-ism" which denotes not a set of specific stylistic–rhetorical options or a particular articulation of the relationship between aesthetics and politics, but rather a series of strategies to engage and come to terms with the challenges of modernity. For this reason, it might be useful to take as our point of departure a very minimal characterization of modernism, such as Matei Calinescu's account of a "culture of crisis," which also has parallels in Italian historiography. This "crisis" can be inflected in several ways, but it seems to me that, at its core, it entails a constant process of questioning and re-negotiation of the function of art and the artist within the political, social, economic, and, of course, artistic institutions of dominant bourgeois society. Our initial task will be to see what the articulations of that "crisis" might be in turn-of-the-century Italian culture, and where some of the fault lines delineating a properly modernist culture might lie.

Realists and aesthetes

To fulfill this task, it is also necessary to consider some of the peculiarities that distinguished late nineteenth-century Italy from the other major European powers, in particular its very late formation as a nation-state. While at the cultural level, the peninsula had been de facto united by the language of literary Italian since the fourteenth century, political unification was achieved only partially in 1861, with the foundation of the Kingdom of Italy, and completed over the following decade, culminating with the conquest of Rome in 1870 (the period of political activism and insurrections leading to unification is known as *Risorgimento*). However, unification in many ways only brought into relief the divisions – both social and cultural – of the peninsula: for instance, the uneven development between a moderately industrialized north and a fundamentally agrarian south; or the low level of literacy and the fact that Italian was spoken by a small minority of the population, with local dialects being used virtually everywhere for everyday interaction. As was said at the time, once Italy was made, the problem became how to make Italians. Indeed, well into the Fascist regime, the cultural and political debate would be oriented by two questions: how to forge a shared Italian identity, and how to improve the nation's status on the world stage.

Unification also affected the status of intellectuals. Like their colleagues in other European nations, they faced the "loss of aura," of moral and even political authority, incisively represented by Charles Baudelaire's *poème en prose* "Perte d'auréole" (1865), and the consequent integration of their works into the marketplace. The loss was felt more acutely in this context because during the Risorgimento, in the absence of Italy as a political entity, it had been precisely writers and artists who had been vested with the task of representing the nation and its aspirations, as in the paradigmatic case of composer Giuseppe Verdi, whose operas were often interpreted as national allegories. After unification, on the contrary, the work of intellectuals became subaltern to that of politicians, who were now the legitimate representatives of the unified nation. Writers benefitted from the expansion of publishing venues made possible by the new technologies for the production and distribution of printed matter, but at the same time literature became "subjected to the laws of other industries, and, like other industries, it [was] exploited by capitalists," as writer and librettist Arturo Colautti put it in an interview in 1895.[6] Furthermore, the cultural life of the nation remained relatively scattered, as no individual city – neither those that in quick succession had the role of political capital, namely Turin (1861–65), Florence (1865–71), and Rome (1871–), nor the industrial capital Milan – emerged as a cultural center comparable for its influence to the great cultural capitals of Europe.

Of course, for Italian writers, as for many of their European colleagues, the true center of intellectual life was Paris. In Italy, as in France, the turn of the century was characterized by the conflict between two opposing, but also complementary tendencies: realism and aestheticism. Italian culture metabolized quickly the lesson of Émile Zola, especially through the mediation of the great literary historian Francesco De Sanctis and novelists Luigi Capuana and Giovanni Verga, who with their works and theoretical writings laid the ground for *verismo*. Informed, like naturalism, by the scientific paradigm of positivism, *verismo* entrusted narrative with the task of producing objective and "true" ("*vero*") knowledge of its object of study, to be achieved through the practice of strict impersonality. Behind this veneer of objectivity, however, lies a profound skepticism regarding modernity and its promise of progress, especially in Verga's two masterpieces, *I Malavoglia* (1881), about a poor family of fishermen, and *Mastro Don Gesualdo* (1889), about a laborer who ascends the social ladder to marry into an aristocratic family. In both novels, the characters' struggle to improve their material conditions culminates in defeat, as suggested by the very title of the projected and incomplete narrative cycle of which they were part: the "cycle of the vanquished." Thus in Verga the *tranche de vie*, the objective representation of a particular social milieu, acquires an ethical dimension, and the task of the artist becomes that of giving voice to the weak who are overwhelmed by what Verga calls the "fiumana," the deluge of life. If the urban proletarian of Zola's fiction is a victim of the new economic and political institutions of capitalist modernity, the characters of Verga's rural and semi-feudal Sicily appear rather the victims of historical cycles that have the inevitability of natural phenomena, and in which today's conquerors are tomorrow's victims. A similar pessimism underlies *I Viceré* [The Viceroys] (1894), the last great novel of *verismo*, in which, through the vicissitudes of the corrupt noble Sicilian family of the Uzedas, Federico De Roberto expresses the failure of the ideals of the Risorgimento.

At the other end of the spectrum, we have a literary production characterized by the rejection of the materialism of *verismo* in favor of a form of writing that plumbs the depths of the human psyche or elevates the subject from the mundane to the ideal. At the core of this poetics, we find a vindication of the peculiar function of art: art does not simply provide an account of what exists, but rather makes it possible to give shape to experiences that, because they have no material substance, cannot otherwise be articulated. Once again, France led by example, as the younger generation of Italian writers turned to the writers grouped under the labels of "decadents" and "symbolists" – Huysmans, Verlaine, Rimbaud, Mallarmé – who became synonymous with literary modernity *tout court*. In this respect, the critic Vittorio Pica, in his essays on contemporary French literature collected in *All'avanguardia* (*Avant-Garde*, 1890) and *Letteratura d'eccezione* (*The Literature of Exception*, 1898), played a crucial role in defending the conception of art as an aristocratic activity.

Yet critical opinion on the Italian fin-de-siècle was shaped quite early on by Croce's condemnation. In the essay "Di un carattere della più recente letteratura italiana" [On a Characteristic of the Most Recent Italian Literature], published in his journal *La critica* in 1907, Croce linked this literary production with the decay in the moral and political conditions of the country. For him, "modern Italian spiritual and literary life" divided into two periods, with the dividing line placed somewhere between 1885 and 1890.[7] The literary culture of the first phase was dominated by the figure of Giosué Carducci, the national poet of the new state; the second, by a triad composed of Gabriele D'Annunzio, Giovanni Pascoli and Antonio Fogazzaro. Whereas Carducci and his contemporaries represented the healthy ideals of the Risorgimento (patriotism in politics, realism in literature, positivism and historicism in the natural and social sciences), the "triad," which Croce famously dubbed the laborers "in the great industry of emptiness," represent the degeneration of those ideals: imperialism (and authoritarianism), mysticism, aestheticism. Making recourse to what Barbara Spackman has called "the rhetoric of sickness,"[8] Croce describes D'Annunzio *et al.* as "malati di nervi" [neurotics]; and although he did not actually use here the term "decadence," this essay would become one of the foundational texts in the historiographic tradition that described Italian modernism as "*decadentismo.*"

In fact, the "triad" and the other authors influenced by decadent and symbolist poetics constitute a far less unified group than Croce's account suggests. The Catholic novelist Fogazzaro is very much a transitional figure, and his novels of characters caught in the struggle between religious faith and the demands of the modern world – *Piccolo mondo antico* [Little World of the Past] (1895), *Il santo* [The Saint] (1905) – are indebted less to the contemporary avant-garde than to Catholic modernism, the current of thought that sought in the early twentieth century to reconcile Church doctrine and scientific thought.[9] Pascoli, in such works as *Myricae* [Tamarisks] (1891) and *Canti di Castelvecchio* [Songs of Castelvecchio] (1903), reframed the symbolist idea that poetry probes the mysteries of life and of the soul in terms of a series of personal, homely myths, which he expressed in a subtle and modulated language that accommodates vocabulary ranging from regional and foreign languages to the canon of modern and classical poetry (he was also a fine poet in Latin). For Pascoli, the model for the poet is not the visionary prophet, but rather the little child (*Il fanciullino* is the title of his statement of poetics published in 1897), who can look at the world with wonder and astonishment, and who remains uncorrupted by modernity.

Among the minor figures of Italian aestheticism, the symbolist poet Gian Pietro Lucini played an especially important role in renewing Italian versification. While most of his contemporaries still clung to traditional forms, he championed free verse, used for instance in his *I drami delle maschere* [Tragedies of Masks], only partially published before his death and collected in 1973, and theorized in his massive *Il verso libero* (1908). In prose fiction, Grazia Deledda, winner of the Nobel Prize for literature in 1926, achieved a unique synthesis of *verismo* and decadentism with her narrative rooted in the culture of her native Sardinia.

The figure who dominated the landscape of turn-of-the-century Italian literature, however, was without a doubt D'Annunzio, who enjoyed literary success quite precociously with the poems of *Primo vere* [First Spring] (1879), published when he was just sixteen. His initial influences were Carducci in poetry and *verismo* in fiction, but his voracious interests quickly spanned the whole of turn-of-the-century European culture, from the then-fashionable Russian novelists to French symbolism, from Wagner to Nietzsche, and he demonstrated an uncanny ability to absorb and use for his own purposes the most diverse contemporary currents of thought.

The central problem of D'Annunzio's major works is the conflict between the protagonist, who is invariably male and often an artist, and a modern society governed by material rather than spiritual values. The motto that governs the life of Andrea Sperelli, the protagonist of his first and still most widely read novel, *Il piacere* [Pleasure] (1889) – "one must *fashion* one's own life, as one fashions a work of art" – might well summarize D'Annunzio's approach to the modernist question of how to renegotiate the relationship between art and life. In his novels in particular, D'Annunzio attempted (through the figure of the aristocrat) to weld together art and politics; these he presents as activities in which an exceptional man can heal the community's divisions and return order to a social body torn apart by the rise of new forces: the materialistic bourgeoisie of the founding fathers of the nation, and later the proletariat, eventually represented by the Socialist Party (founded in 1892). In *Il piacere*, set in the fashionable sites of the Roman *beau monde* with which D'Annunzio had become familiar as a journalist in the 1880s, Sperelli's struggle to assert his authority remains mostly confined to the domain of sexual politics. However, in later works, such as *Le vergini delle rocce* [The Virgins of the Rocks] (1895), which was influenced by the Nietzschean theory of the *Übermensch*, the broader socio-political implications of his project, as well as its chimerical aspects, come into focus. Claudio Cantelmo, another variation on the aristocratic aesthete, goes into self-imposed exile to his ancestral country estate, abandoning Rome to the hands of the rapacious middle class. Faced with the stark choice of either accepting the values of the new dominant class and becoming a cultural laborer, or recognizing his superfluity and marginality, the Dannunzian artist–aristocrat seeks a third alternative: the reassertion of his cultural–political authority by collapsing essence and performance, by closing the circle between nobility of birth and nobility of deed. Cantelmo dreams of generating a child, a new "King of Rome" who will redeem the nation from the vulgarity of its new masters; to this end, he intends to take as his bride one of the three daughters of the ancient and noble Capece-Montaga family, proudly loyal to the deposed King of the Two Sicilies. Yet the Capece-Montagas, plagued by neuroses and madness, appear rather to epitomize the decadence of their class. It is significant that D'Annunzio was unable to imagine their redemption through Cantelmo and his scion: the second and third volumes of the trilogy begun with *Le vergini delle rocce* were never written. In the end, it is not the ivory tower, but rather direct

contact with the masses, that can endow the artist with a new guiding role –
as in *Il fuoco* [The Flame] (1900), where rhetoric is the instrument that
allows the protagonist, Stelio Èffrena, to translate words into action.

As Sperelli's maxim suggests, the circuit between aesthetics and politics
could flow not only from art to life, but also inversely, turning life into a
work of art. This offers a key for understanding D'Annunzio's own political
activity, both inside and outside established practice. His most important
intervention in the political domain occurred in 1919, when, at the head of
an army of volunteers, he marched on the Istrian city of Fiume (now Rijeka),
over which Italy had failed to obtain control at the Paris Peace Conference of
1919. Dubbing the territory "Reggenza del Carnaro," D'Annunzio turned
it into a semi-independent, libertarian state, to which streamed artists and
adventurers from Italy and the rest of Europe until the state's suppression
by the Italian army on December 21, 1920 (the territory having been ceded
to Italy by the allies the previous November). As Claudia Salaris has written,
Fiume was "a sort of small experimental 'counter-society,' with ideas and
values not exactly in line with current morals, open to the transgression of
rules, to the mass practice of rebelliousness."[10] After the bloody conclusion of the "adventure of Fiume," D'Annunzio retired to "Il Vittoriale," his
estate in Gardone, in a sort of self-imposed exile, honored but not particularly loved by the Fascist regime. He devoted the later years of his life to
memorialistic labors, of which the best result is *Notturno* (*Nocturne*, 1921),
a series of short pieces mostly written during the war while recovering, in
total darkness, from an eye injury.

The integration of art and life: the avant-garde

D'Annunzio's aristocratic aestheticism – *dannunzianesimo*, as it was called –
cast its shadow over much of early twentieth-century literature, and for
younger writers, an engagement with this poetics, if only by negation, was
an inevitable starting point. For instance, the *crepuscolari* [twilight poets],
an informal grouping of poets thus described by the critic Giuseppe Antonio
Borgese, rejected the heroic version of the artist that D'Annunzio proposed.
Instead, they used as a subject of their poetry the diminished status of the
poet – sometimes considered ironically, as in the case of Guido Gozzano,
sometimes dolefully, as in the case of Sergio Corazzini – and focused on
the banal aspects of their own emotional experiences and their daily lives.
The most pressing problem for many young intellectuals at the turn of
the century, however, was that of finding new means to reconcile culture
and politics, especially in light of a political establishment that was seen as
hopelessly corrupt.

The major center of this debate in the first decade of the twentieth century was Florence, where militant journals and little magazines proliferated, starting with the foundation in 1903 of *Leonardo*, edited by Giuseppe Prezzolini and Giovanni Papini. Steeped in the rhetoric of fin-de-siècle aestheticism, *Leonardo* articulated in more openly political terms a number of decadent themes, such as the decline of the bourgeoisie, the call for national regeneration, and scorn for the political liberalism embodied by Prime Minister Giovanni Giolitti. In its short life (it closed in 1907), *Leonardo* also played an important role in introducing to Italy a number of currents and figures of European thought (in particular pragmatism), that its editors championed. In 1908, Prezzolini launched *La Voce* [The Voice], a more ambitious project that shed the Dannunzian frills of its predecessor for a more active engagement with Italian political and cultural life. Its goal, as its director put it with an intentionally plain-spoken expression, was "star sempre al sodo" ("to stand on firm ground"), and the journal went on to provide a space of confrontation for many of the most important intellectuals of the period, from Croce and his fellow philosopher, Giovanni Gentile, to political leaders such as the Socialist Gaetano Salvemini. In this context, literature, too, was called to rediscover its moral mission, and artists to come out of the ivory tower. Rejecting the rhetorical excesses of decadent literature, the writers of *La Voce* and the publishing house that it established – Piero Jahier, Clemente Rebora, Giovanni Boine – turned to writing as a means of investigating their own consciences and their relationships with the world, in an exercise of autobiographical investigation that eschewed the order and coherence of traditional genres in favor of brief moments of illumination narrated through short prose fragments (as a result this poetics is often called *frammentismo*). An example is *Il mio Carso* [My Carso] (1912), in which the Triestine writer Scipio Slataper explores his complex relationship with his homeland and with Gioietta, the woman he loved and whose suicide prompted the writing of the book, which is built through the juxtaposition of narrative blocks characterized by sudden shifts in tense, narrative point of view, and linguistic register.

The most ambitious and influential project of cultural renewal, however, was that proposed with characteristic iconoclasm by the futurist movement, which the poet Filippo Tommaso Marinetti founded on February 20, 1909 with a manifesto on the front page of the Parisian paper *Le Figaro*. Born in Egypt of Italian parents, Marinetti began his career as a symbolist poet, writing most of his works in French, the language in which he was educated. Initially an advocate for a revolution in Italian poetic language through the adoption of French innovations like *vers libre*, in 1909 he proposed a much more radical program. Arguing that the progress of Italian culture had been hindered by its obsessive worship of the past, he called for the suppression of academies and museums, and for an art that would represent the energy and dynamism of modernity, exemplified by the machine. (As he famously put it, "a roaring automobile [. . .] is more beautiful than the *Victory of Samothrace*".) At the core of the futurist program lay the faith in the regenerative power of rebellion and struggle, as opposed to the stagnation resulting from traditional artistic and social values. Futurism quickly expanded into other domains: music, theatre, architecture, and even fashion and cookery. It had a particularly profound impact on the figurative arts. In 1910, the painters Umberto Boccioni, Giacomo Balla, Carlo Carrà, Gino Severini and Luigi Russolo urged modern artists to rethink the relationship between the work of art and its audience. Whereas traditional art, they argued, had sought simply to fix a moment in time to be contemplated at a distance, futurist painting would render the continuous flow of existence in all its dynamism, placing "the spectator in the center of the picture." Meanwhile, in the literary domain, Marinetti experimented with a form of writing that freed language not only from traditional prosody, but from syntax itself, in a practice that he called "words in freedom," and of which he gave the best known example with *Zang Tumb Tumb* (1914), based on his experience as a war correspondent during the First Balkan War. Although they are less radically experimental, the futurist works of Aldo Palazzeschi (pseudonym of Aldo Giurlani), especially the poems in *L'Incendiario* [The Arsonist] (1910) and the allegorical fable, *Il codice di Perelà* [Perelà's Code] (1911), undermine through laughter the institutions of middle-class social life.

Like the *vociani*, although with very different means, the futurists saw themselves involved in far more than an artistic project: Marinetti issued a political manifesto as early as 1909. The movement is an example of what historian Emilio Gentile has called "modernist nationalism" – that is, a project of cultural revolution, aimed at "the regeneration of the Italians and the creation of a 'New state' and a 'New Man'."[11] Indeed, the rubric of nationalism allowed Marinetti to bring together, in a union that was sometimes unstable, different strands of turn-of-the-century political and cultural thought, from anarchism to Sorelian syndicalism to republicanism. After the war, nationalism became the means to reconcile the initially rather libertarian politics of the movement with those of Mussolini's Fascism. At the same time, however, Marinetti's cosmopolitan background naturally led him to conceive futurism as a means for Italian culture to expand beyond the narrow confines of the nation. Through his international contacts, his considerable managerial skills, and his personal fortune, Marinetti embarked on a continental campaign of cultural promotion that earned him the nickname of "the caffeine of Europe." There is no doubt that on the eve of the Great War, futurism played a crucial role in the formation of an avant-garde culture throughout the continent, even when Marinetti's heavy-handed self-promotion led him to clash with his erstwhile supporters, as in the case of English vorticism or Russian futurism. Furthermore, futurism's attack on traditional sites of artistic legitimation and its ridicule of the sacralization of the work of art paved the way for other forms of anti-institutional avant-garde, such as Dada.

Pirandello and Svevo

The two Italian writers whose contribution to European modernism was most significant and long-lasting, the Sicilian Luigi Pirandello and the Triestine Italo Svevo, stand rather apart from these collective projects and avant-garde movements. In order to understand Pirandello's poetics, it may be useful to consider the notion of humor articulated in his 1908 essay *L'umorismo*. Half historical survey, half theoretical statement, the study distinguishes "humor" from other forms of comic writing by emphasizing the centrality of reflection. While the moment of reflection, in the organic work of art, becomes invisible in the harmonious coming together of form and content, in the humorous work it is foregrounded, thus precluding such reconciliation. The bitter laughter of the humorist reveals the simultaneously comic and tragic dimension of human illusions, the unredeemable contradiction between the real and the ideal.

Indeed, a surfeit of reflection is what distinguishes and alienates Pirandello's protagonists from their social environment. An early example is *Il fu Mattia Pascal* [The Late Mattia Pascal] (1904), the story of a man who attempts to escape his stifling existence in a provincial town and build a new life for himself in Rome after he is believed dead. Inspired by the advertisement for a puppet show based on a Sophoclean play, the protagonist's landlord, the arm-chair philosopher Anselmo Paleari, explains to him the difference between classical and modern tragedy:

> If at the climactic moment, just as the puppet representing Orestes is about to take revenge on Aegisthus and his mother for his father's death, the paper sky of the theatre were to be torn up, what would happen then?
>
> [...]
>
> Orestes would still feel his thirst for revenge, he would still want to pursue it with feverish passion, but his eyes would look up there, at the tear from which all sorts of ill influences would come in, and his arms would drop. Orestes would then become Hamlet.[12]

The tragic–comic – that is, humorous – condition of the modern subject lies precisely in his inability to live fully his passions and desires, as he is haunted by the awareness that there are no outside agents to endow his actions with meaning: neither the gods of classical or Christian mythology, nor the gods of the bourgeois fathers, science and material success. The torn paper sky is Pirandello's homespun version of the Nietzschean death of god.

The opposition between Orestes and Hamlet is one of a series of dichotomies that underlie Pirandello's narrative and theatrical production. Another fundamental opposition is what critic Adriano Tilgher described as the "Dualism of Life and Form": "In Pirandello's vision," he wrote, "it is essential for Life to take on a Form and yet not exhaust itself in it."[13] In this sense, identity is nothing more than the construction and fixation of an image of the self by isolating certain elements from the flow of existence: hence the Pirandellian theme of the impossibility of human relations, as they are predicated on the fundamental misunderstanding that each individual construction of the other (including one's self-image) is the truth. As the title of Pirandello's last novel, *Uno, nessuno e centomila* [One, No One and One Hundred Thousand] (1926), makes clear, under our layers of constructed selves there lies no core, no ultimate truth, only the mutable stream of becoming.

Pirandello turned to the theater in earnest relatively late, in 1910, but it quickly became his favorite medium, and the one which ensured his international reputation. Like the works of the group of dramatists who created what became known as "grotesque theater" – Luigi Chiarelli, Pier Maria Rosso di San Secondo, Enrico Cavacchioli – Pirandello's early plays subverted from the inside out the bourgeois theatrical tradition, founded on the themes of adultery and betrayal, that dominated the Italian stage. The critical function of exposing, through the paradoxes of *umorismo*, the pettiness of the conventions of middle-class life was entrusted to the figure of the *raisonneur*, who, like the protagonists of Pirandello's novels, is plagued by the demon of self-reflection. In his later works, self-reflection even becomes a formal principle through the device of the theater-within-the-theater. This device is employed most famously in his best-known work, *Sei personaggi in cerca d'autore* [Six Characters in Search of an Author] (1921), in which the titular six characters irrupt into a theatre during rehearsals (of a Pirandello play, of course!) and demand that the company take on the task of staging their own stories. A veritable *summa* of Pirandellian themes, *Sei personaggi* is also a play about the failure of art: as they repeat obsessively the actions that led them to disaster and death, the characters are unable to give an organic shape – and therefore a meaning, a moral – to their stories.

If Pirandello was one of the most public and influential artists of the period between the wars, especially after the Nobel Prize consolidated his status in 1934, Italo Svevo was perhaps the least visible of the major Italian modernists. Born Aron Hector Schmitz, Svevo carefully chose his pen-name, which can be loosely rendered as "Italian Swabian," to reflect the multi-cultural dimensions of his city, Trieste, a crossroad of Italian, German, and Slavic cultures and until 1919 the major port of Austria–Hungary, as well as his own experiences as an Italophone partly educated in Germany. After his first two novels, *Una vita* [A Life] (1892) and *Senilità* [As a Man Grows Older] (1898), failed to attract critical attention, he withdrew from writing almost completely, devoting himself to his work in his father-in-law's business, and returned to fiction only in 1919 – in part thanks to the encouragement of his English teacher and close friend, James Joyce (according to Richard Ellmann, Svevo, who came from a Jewish family, was a model for Leopold Bloom).[14] In 1923, Svevo published his masterpiece, *La coscienza di Zeno*, which Joyce recommended to the French critics Valéry Larbaud and Benjamin Crémieux. They edited a special issue of *Le navire d'argent* on Svevo in 1926, while in Italy Eugenio Montale devoted a long essay to him in 1925. Thus, after over thirty years of neglect, he was almost simultaneously "discovered" in Italy and France just before his death in 1928.

Unlike many of his contemporaries, Svevo was influenced above all by Central European culture, in particular Schopenhauer and, in his final novel, Freud. Indeed, *La coscienza di Zeno* (the title can be translated as *Zeno's Conscience* or *Zeno's Consciousness*) is the first work in Italian literature to use psychoanalysis as its frame of reference (albeit with serious reservations about its therapeutic effectiveness), as it is purported to be an exercise in self-examination written by the protagonist as part of his psychoanalytic treatment for nicotine addiction. This addiction is, of course, only a symptom of a more profound neurosis, a kind of existential alienation that characterizes the individual who is unable to live life unreflexively. Zeno is the greatest incarnation of the central figure of Svevo's narrative, the "inept," the character who is too estranged from others and himself to be able to act (the original title for *Una vita* was *Un inetto*). Like the Pirandellian *raisonneur*, the inept is obsessed to the point of paralysis with self-reflection and self-analysis, as exemplified by one of the funniest scenes in the novel, where Zeno develops a limp when his thoughts become fixated on the complicated muscle movements involved in taking a step. In this view, life itself is an illness, and social relations and institutions – marriage, business, friendships – are mere palliatives that do not cure the subject of his existential dis-ease. We stand once again in a universe empty of meaning, as is suggested by the series of missed opportunities, misunderstandings, coincidences, and misinterpretations that shape the life of Zeno and the other characters. What sets this novel apart from Svevo's previous fiction is the vein of humor that runs through it, as the protagonist's retrospective gaze brings out the disconnection between the characters' plans and their fates.

Modernism under Fascism

Although it divided the general population, Italy's entry into the Great War enjoyed widespread support among artists and intellectuals, especially those of the younger generation. Once again, what appeared to be at stake were the two complementary projects of defining Italy's role on the international scene and forming a national identity. Coming on the heels of an aggressive colonial policy that had yielded decidedly mixed results – Italy wrested Libya from the Ottoman Empire in 1912, but was thwarted in its attempt to conquer Ethiopia by the disastrous defeat at Adowa in 1896 – the European war seemed to provide a new opportunity for national redemption. Furthermore, many saw the prospect of shared sacrifice against a common enemy as a means of forging a strong sense of national unity that would cut across all classes – especially when that enemy was Italy's "natural" adversary, the Habsburg Empire, which held the so-called "unredeemed territories" of Trent and Trieste claimed by the Italian state. Indeed, for many interventionists, the European war was nothing less than the final phase of the Risorgimento.

Perhaps because of this initial enthusiasm, the literature produced during the war and in its aftermath does not reflect the same sense of disillusionment and disgust that characterizes that of other European countries. The most profound expression of the dehumanizing effects of the war is found in Giuseppe Ungaretti's *Il porto sepolto* [The Buried Harbour] (1916) and *Allegria di naufragi* [The Happiness of Shipwrecks] (1919), which includes the previous collection. A son, like Marinetti, of fin-de-siècle cosmopolitanism (he also grew up in Egypt and spent part of his formative years in Paris), Ungaretti had already begun to dismantle the highly stylized conventions of Italian poetry by fragmenting traditional verse and using direct and evocative language. Though not always free of nationalist rhetoric, his highly compressed war poems often achieve a remarkable balance in expressing the horrors of trench warfare, the existential loneliness of human beings confronted by their own mortality, and the human solidarity that is fostered by shared danger.

In many ways, the aftermath of the war played a more important role in shaping Italian modernism than did the war itself, as it precipitated the liberal state into a period of instability that eventually shattered its institutions. The economic crisis following the war radicalized social conflict between urban and rural proletariat and property owners, and land and factory occupations characterized the so-called "red biennium" of 1919–20. Among the nationalists, the failure to obtain territorial control over parts of Dalmatia fostered the myth of the "mutilated victory" – the term was coined by D'Annunzio – according to which the victory obtained with the sacrifice of thousands of Italian soldiers had been rendered vain by the ineptitude of Italian politicians and by the machinations of international diplomacy. In founding the Fascist party in 1919, Benito Mussolini, the former socialist leader and erstwhile author of the anti-clerical historical potboiler *L'amante del cardinale* [*The Cardinal's Mistress*] (1910), drew heavily upon disappointed interventionists, officers, and elite soldiers, but he also found support among property owners who relied on Fascist squads against socialist insurrectionists. The "March on Rome" of October 28, 1922 dealt the final blow to the liberal state. King Victor Emmanuel III refused to let the army intervene to stop the rebellious Fascists, and he appointed Mussolini prime minister: thus, with apparent respect for the form of parliamentary monarchy, began the *ventennio*, the twenty-year Fascist regime.

In this context, the most remarkable aspect of cultural life immediately after the war is the gradual withdrawal of art from direct engagement with social reality and the re-articulation of that autonomy that so many artists had challenged a decade earlier. Two journals, one in the figurative arts, the other in literature, best represent this general "return to order": *Valori plastici* [Plastic Values] (1918–22) and *La Ronda* [The Patrol] (1919–23). *Valori plastici*, founded in Rome by the critic and painter Mario Broglio and published simultaneously in Italian and French, aimed at defining aesthetic modernity not in terms of an antagonistic relationship with the past, but rather as the recovery of a series of classical formal values through which the experience of modernity can be articulated. The paradigmatic expression of this form of artistic research was the "metaphysical painting" of Giorgio De Chirico, another cosmopolitan Italian – born in Greece, educated in Germany and France – who had returned to serve in the army during the war. In De Chirico's works, it is precisely the manipulation of traditional tropes and techniques, such as perspective, classical figures, and statuary, that generates a sense of mystery and unease lurking behind the composure of the surface of the canvas. Many artists of *Valori plastici* also contributed to *La Ronda*, which was founded by a group of intellectuals that included poet Vincenzo Cardarelli, critic Emilio Cecchi, and novelist Riccardo Bacchelli. This journal proposed a similar program for literature, which they understood as a polished and controlled exercise of stylistic research, the highest example of which was the works of the nineteenth-century poet, Giacomo Leopardi. Like the *vociani*, the *rondisti* identified in short prose the most effective means of literary expression, but whereas the fragment of the *vociani* was the instrument for investigating the torments and anguishes of the modern subject, the "prosa d'arte" of the *rondisti* appeared rather as a means of sublimating the shock of modernity through the superior harmony of art.

The policy of the Fascist regime regarding cultural production developed gradually. After the outcry in 1924 over the kidnapping and murder, by Fascist thugs, of the socialist Member of Parliament Giacomo Matteotti threatened to topple Mussolini's government, the Duce enacted a series of laws that, among other things, outlawed other political parties and curtailed freedom of the press. The regime did not, however, use censorship alone to assert its control over artists and intellectuals. To be sure, a number of them were silenced by force, and even paid with their life for their anti-fascism, as in the case of the Liberal Piero Gobetti and the Communist Antonio Gramsci. Nevertheless, a perhaps more effective strategy was the establishment of a complex system of patronage, "designed to contain dissent and draw creative individuals into a collaborative relationship with the state."[15] Literary and artistic prizes, public commissions, new institutions such as the Accademia d'Italia (Pirandello and Marinetti were among its members), all ensured the apparently non-coercive integration of intellectuals into the Fascist system. This was only one component in the broader totalitarian project of Fascism, which aimed to identify the nation with the regime. Other cultural strategies were quickly developed for that purpose, including the expansion of and control over mass media (cinema and, above all, radio), and the sponsorship of youth organizations, leisure activities, mass spectacles and rallies, and other events that aimed to link individuals into a collective social body. As Emilio Gentile puts it, "mass politics in Fascist Italy took the form of permanent totalitarian education."[16]

Nevertheless, the Fascist regime did not impose a coherent cultural program beyond a generic defence of "Italianness." Modernism was never the object of Fascist opprobrium that it was for Nazism, and under Fascism the arts maintained a degree of autonomy. A paradigmatic example is that of architecture: the functionalist and anti-decorative rationalist style, in dialogue with the experiences of the "international style" of Le Corbusier or Gropius, flourished during the *ventennio*, along with a more rhetorical neo-Classicism meant to evoke the continuity between Fascism and imperial Rome. Literature, too, remained relatively open to an engagement with foreign models, if only as a means of defining the peculiarities of Italy's own approach to modernity: indeed, one of the salient characteristics of the period was the "discovery" of American modernism. (Hemingway and Dos Passos were particular favorites.) Yet anxiety over foreign influences could also result in very public polemics, like the one that opposed Massimo Bontempelli to *Strapaese* [Supercountry], an anti-bourgeois, anti-intellectual artistic and literary movement that took the view that true Fascist culture was to be rooted in the rural traditions of provincial Italy. (Its organ was Mino Maccari's periodical *Il Selvaggio* [The Savage] (1927–43).) Bontempelli's journal *900* (1926–29), initially published in French and with an editorial board that included Joyce, Georg Kaiser, and Ilya Ehrenburg, was attacked for its cosmopolitanism, and it did not survive long after its conversion to Italian in 1928.

In general, the atmosphere of "return to order" continued in the inter-war years, and even the futurists renounced their old political ambitions, retreating into the secure ambit of art. Whereas in other countries new movements, such as Surrealism, continued the anti-institutional project of the avant-garde, in Italy the most innovative program of the 1920s was Bontempelli's *novecentismo*, which proclaimed as its aim the reconstruction of the ordered and structured universe that futurism had sought to demol-ish. In Bontempelli's "moderate avant-garde,"[17] the mission of the artist becomes the creation of "new myths," narratives characterized by "realist precision and a magical atmosphere" (hence the description of this style as "magical realism"), in which archetypal characters and situations could structure and order lived experience. In his own literary practice, Bontem-pelli moved from the ironic social commentary of the highly compressed and meta-literary micro-novels of *La vita intensa* [Intense Life] (1920) to the rar-efied atmospheres and the carefully crafted language of his late, fable-like narratives, such as *Il figlio di due madri* [The Son of Two Mothers] (1929). In this period, fantastic literature also flourished. Its more famous practition-ers included De Chirico's brother Andrea, better known by the pseudonym Alberto Savinio, and Dino Buzzati, whose allegorical novel, *Il deserto dei Tartari* [The Tartar Steppe] (1940), has been compared to Kafka's fiction for its disturbing atmosphere.

In poetry, Umberto Saba (pseudonym of the Triestine Umberto Poli) sought to find a new authenticity for art through the exploration of per-sonal experience, while Eugenio Montale, whose *Ossi di seppia* [Cuttlefish Bones] (1925) was one of the seminal works of the period, derived from the arid landscape of his native Liguria symbols through which to express the bleakness and desolation of a world empty of meaning although occasionally lit by elusive moments of epiphany (for instance, in "Limoni" [Lemons]). Ungaretti and Montale have traditionally been regarded as the "first gener-ation" of *ermetismo* (hermeticism). The second generation, which includes

Vittorio Sereni, Mario Luzi, and the 1959 Nobel Prize winner Salvatore Quasimodo, was a more self-conscious movement. Its poetics harked back to the symbolist notion of poetry as an absolute language, removed from, and even antagonistic to, material experience – a detachment from the world that has been read politically as an attempt to preserve individual freedom in the midst of Fascist repression.

In 1929, Alberto Moravia (pseudonym of Alberto Pincherle) gained immediate notoriety with *Gli indifferenti* [The Indifferent Ones], a withering portrayal of the hypocrisy and moral squalor of the Italian bourgeoisie, written in a direct and detached style that reflected, in its distance from its subject, the disturbed human relations represented in the novel. Moravia was not alone in wishing for literature to play a more critical role. For many novelists of the new generation, too young to have been "Fascists of the first hour," the time had come to return Fascism to its supposed original revolutionary purity, which they saw as threatened by the progressive bureaucratization and bourgeoisification of the regime. Indeed, they considered their attacks on middle-class complacency and mediocrity not as subversive gestures, but rather as the recovery of the idealism of "original" Fascism. Such works as Carlo Bernari's *Tre operai* [Three Workers] (1934), the story of three poor laborers before and after the First World War, Alba De Cespedes's *Nessuno torna indietro* [No Turning Back] (1938), which follows the life of eight young women in a religious boarding house, Elio Vittorini's *Il garofano rosso* [The Red Carnation], serialized in the magazine *Solaria* (1933–34), the story of a personal and political coming of age, Paola Masino's *Nascita e morte della massaia* [Birth and Death of the Housewife], published in its final form in 1945, a surreal tale of female oppression, are all examples of novels that sought to explore the social contradictions of Fascist Italy. This new engagement with social reality did not come at the expense of formal experimentalism. Ranging from Masino's grotesque take on magic realism to Bernari's expressionistic mixture of direct and indirect discourse to Vittorini's stylized and hieratic language, evident in particular in *Conversazione in Sicilia* [Conversations in Sicily] (1941), stylistic experimentation remained a central feature of the fiction of the 1930s and 1940s. The most experimental writer of the period is Carlo Emilio Gadda, whose work is often described as "plurilinguistic," not only for its characteristic impasto of standard Italian and regional languages, but also for its mixture of registers and genres. Although Gadda's major works appeared – often unfinished – after the war, the first version of *La cognizione del dolore* [Acquainted with Grief], his complex meditation on familial and social alienation, was serialized in *Letteratura* in 1938–41.

When the sanctions that the League of Nations imposed after Italy's invasion of Ethiopia in 1935–36 isolated the regime on the international scene, Mussolini responded with his official policy of autarchy. Censorship then became more heavy-handed, though it could not completely stifle literary debate. Fascism attempted to co-opt the new generation of intellectuals with the journal *Il Primato* (*Supremacy*), founded in 1940 by Giuseppe Bottai, who, as Minister of National Education, had presided over the purge of Jews from Italian schools, universities, and cultural institutions after the promulgation of the anti-semitic Racial Laws in 1938. This attempt to provide an official venue for dissenting voices came, of course, too late: Italy was about to enter another world conflict that would bring about the collapse of the regime in 1943, followed by two years of de facto civil war. Pinpointing an end of modernism is no easier than determining its precise beginning. Certainly, the postwar reconstruction and the need to come to terms with the legacy of Fascism, a task that culture accomplished much more effectively than other sectors of Italian society, meant that the questions that oriented the intellectual debate were quite different from those that governed the first half of the century. In this sense, it can be argued that the war put an end not only to Fascism and the monarchy, but also to modernism.

NOTES

1. Malcolm Bradbury and James McFarlane, eds., *Modernism* (Harmondsworth: Penguin, 1976).
2. Edward Możejko, "Tracing the Modernist Paradigm: Terminologies of Modernism," in Astradur Eysteinsson and Vivian Liska, eds., *Modernism* (Amsterdam: John Benjamins, 2007), vol. I, pp. 11–33.
3. Cf. Matei Calinescu, *Five Faces of Modernity*, 2nd edn. (Durham, N.C.: Duke University Press, 1987), pp. 211–21.
4. Paolo Giovannetti, *Decadentismo* (Milan: Editrice Bibliografica, 1994), p. 24. Other major studies of the period include: Carlo Salinari, *Miti e coscienza del decadentismo italiano* (Milano: Feltrinelli, 1960), Leone de Castris, *Il decadentismo italiano* (Bari: De Donato, 1974), and Elio Gioanola, *Il decadentismo*, 2nd edn. (Roma: Studium, 1977), this last notable because it spans the whole of European modernism.
5. Of course, this is not to say that the term is completely new to Italian Studies, especially in the English-speaking world, e.g. Cinzia Sartini Blum, *The Other Modernism: F. T. Marinetti's Futurist Fiction of Power* (Berkeley: University of California Press, 1996).
6. In Ugo Ojetti, *Alla scoperta dei letterati* (1895; Florence: Le Monnier, 1946), p. 288.
7. Benedetto Croce, *La letteratura della nuova Italia* (Bari: Laterza, 1915), p. 187.
8. Barbara Spackman, *Decadent Genealogies: The Rhetoric of Sickness from Baudelaire to D'Annunzio* (Ithaca, N.Y.: Cornell University Press, 1989).

9. On Catholic modernism, see Daniela Sarasella, *Modernismo* (Milan: Editrice Bibliografica, 1995).

10. Claudia Salaris, *Alla festa della rivoluzione: Artisti e libertari con D'Annunzio a Fiume* (Bologna: Il Mulino, 2002), p. 12.

11. Emilio Gentile, *The Struggle for Modernity: Nationalism, Futurism, and Fascism* (Westport, Conn.: Praeger, 2003), p. 5.

12. Luigi Pirandello, *Tutti i romanzi*, ed. Giovanni Macchia (Milan: Mondadori, 1973), vol. I, pp. 467–68.

13. Adriano Tilgher, *Saggi sul teatro contemporaneo*, 2nd rev. edn. (Rome: Libreria di Scienze e Lettere, 1923), p. 203.

14. Richard Ellmann, *James Joyce*, rev. edn. (Oxford University Press, 1982), p. 374.

15. Ruth Ben-Ghiat, *Fascist Modernities: Italy, 1922–1945* (Berkeley: University of California Press, 2001), p. 9.

16. Emilio Gentile, "The Totalitarian Experiment," in Adrian Lyttleton, ed., *Liberal and Fascist Italy* (Oxford University Press, 2002), p. 162.

17. Luigi Baldacci, *Massimo Bontempelli* (Turin: Borla, 1967), p. 65.

FURTHER READING

Adamson, Walter. *Avant-Garde Florence. From Modernism to Fascism.* Cambridge, Mass.: Harvard University Press, 1993.

Biasin, Gian Paolo, and Manuela Gieri, eds. *Luigi Pirandello: Contemporary Perspectives.* University of Toronto Press, 1999.

Curi, Fausto. *La poesia italiana d'avanguardia: Modi e tecniche.* Naples: Liguori, 2001.

Dombroski, Robert S. *Properties of Writing: Ideological Discourse in Modern Italian Fiction.* Baltimore, Md.: Johns Hopkins University Press, 1994.

Minghelli, Giuliana. *In the Shadow of the Mammoth: Italo Svevo and the Emergence of Modernism.* University of Toronto Press, 2002.

Poggi, Christine. *Inventing Futurism: The Art and Politics of Artificial Optimism.* Princeton University Press, 2009.

Raimondi, Ezio. *Le poetiche della modernità.* Milan: Garzanti, 1990.

Somigli, Luca, and Mario Moroni, eds. *Italian Modernism: Italian Culture between Decadentism and Avant-Garde.* University of Toronto Press, 2004.

Storchi, Simona. *Valori Plastici 1918–1922.* Supplement to *The Italianist* 26 (2006).

Valesio, Paolo. *Gabriele D'Annunzio: The Dark Flame.* New Haven, Conn.: Yale University Press, 1992.

6

MARINA MACKAY

Great Britain

Modernism has traditionally been considered a denationalized enterprise – axiomatically the work of "exiles and émigrés," "an art without frontiers," "the product of an era of artistic migration and internationalism."[1] In the context of British modernism this conventional story of deracinated internationalism contains an essential truth, but it narrows and simplifies the area of inquiry unnecessarily. It is a curiosity of the field of Anglo-American modernism that London is among the most studied of modernist locations, yet *British* modernism is thought to be virtually non-existent, on the grounds that most of the major London-based modernists were expatriates rather than British-born writers. I hope to demonstrate, however, that if "British modernism" sounds like a contradiction in terms, this is not merely because so many of its important participants were British only by adoption if at all (and this is the enduringly useful insight at the heart of the exiles-and-émigrés narrative), but also because a number of the British-born writers of the period identified most strongly not with the *political* nation-state of the United Kingdom of Great Britain and Northern Ireland, but with one of its constituent *cultural* nations and regions.

London, England

Before turning later in this chapter to the issue of how "native" British modernists reconciled their political and artistic cosmopolitanism with (often powerfully felt) local allegiances, it is important to acknowledge the significance of the British metropolis in the wider contexts of transatlantic and transnational modernism. It is certainly striking that many centrally canonical works take London as their setting. Following Franco Moretti's argument that location is not extraneous to literature, but rather exerts a force that shapes it from within ("*what* happens depends a lot on *where* it happens"[2]), I propose that pausing briefly on some of these highly canonical

94

representations of the metropolis can help to clarify what we mean by *modernism* in the first place, in terms of its origins, interests, and characteristic styles.

Consider, for example, the case of Joseph Conrad's *The Secret Agent* (1907), a novel about a counterrevolutionary attempt to blow up the Royal Greenwich Observatory, and about the tragic domestic aftermath of the plot's failure. Unlike their colleagues in some other national literatures (most notably French), scholars of British literature seldom speak of modernism prior to the turn of the century, and *The Secret Agent* is a suggestively transitional novel. On the one hand, its London of obscuring fog and crepuscular state bureaucracies recalls Charles Dickens's classic *Bleak House* (1853), a novel about national and imperial systems already grown so inhumanly vast as to render oversight and intervention impossible; and one sees in Conrad's debt to Dickens how British modernists may have inherited from earlier writers their deployment of the modern city as a site of epistemological doubt and anxiety. (Modern urbanization, bureaucratization, and industrialization had happened earlier, of course, for this imperial superpower than for most European countries.) On the other hand, Conrad refuses the nineteenth-century novel's habit of mastering its deeply unsettling cities by bringing about revelation and closure. Defying traditional ideas of novelistic containment, *The Secret Agent* ends with a terrorist walking through London with a bomb in his pocket, wholly invisible to his fellow citizens. Explaining his choice of setting, Conrad described London as "a monstrous town more populous than some continents," with "darkness enough to bury five millions of lives."[3] Metropolitan modernity means not knowing who or what walks among us; and the radical sense of insecurity and contingency this generates becomes at once a thematic interest of modernism – *The Secret Agent* is a novel about the harrowing impossibility of knowing even those with whom one shares a home, let alone a city – and one of its most instantly recognizable formal principles (evidenced here in Conrad's refusal to close the narrative in a reassuringly complete way).

A more affirmative version of the interplay of (modern) metropolitan theme and (modernist) experimental form appears in Virginia Woolf's *Mrs. Dalloway* (1925), when the heroine steps out onto a London street and is bombarded exhilaratingly by sensory impressions: "the bellow and the uproar, the carriages, motor cars, omnibuses, vans, sandwich men shuffling and swinging; brass bands; barrel organs; in the triumph and the jingle and the strange high singing of some aeroplane overhead was what she loved; life; London; this moment of June." The link between "life" and "London" is more than alliterative; it is as if encountering London's constantly shifting urban spectacle is equivalent to consciousness itself. "Examine for a moment an ordinary mind on an ordinary day," Woolf urged in what would become one of the most famous statements on modernist fiction: "The mind receives a myriad impressions – trivial, fantastic, evanescent, or engraved with the sharpness of steel. From all sides they come, an incessant shower of innumerable atoms."[4] The impressionistic style of modernist narrative and the apprehension of a fragile, permeable boundary around the city self become mutually reinforcing. Merely living in London becomes an act of improvisatory artistic composition: "making it up, building it round one, tumbling it, creating it every moment afresh," as she writes in *Mrs. Dalloway*.

Although modernist novels like *The Secret Agent* and *Mrs. Dalloway* reveal very different attitudes toward the contingency and haphazardness of modern metropolitan existence, what they share is a sense of living at the very center of the world. This is the illusion fostered by London's status as one of the major imperial capitals, and both novels allude to that status by including characters newly returned from outposts of empire: Conrad's Assistant Commissioner, who has been reluctantly fetched back from the tropics, and Woolf's Peter Walsh, who is home briefly from India. The imperial context is more forebodingly articulated in T. S. Eliot's modernist masterpiece *The Waste Land* (1922), in which London is but one "unreal city" among many, taking its place alongside other ancient and modern imperial capitals, some obsolete and others – ominously – obsolescent: "Falling towers / Jerusalem Athens Alexandria / Vienna London / Unreal." This capaciously transnational and transhistorical poem places London at the end of a long line of doomed metropolises and collapsing civilizations. This most canonically modernist of poems thus makes the very idea of modernity a central theme: another epoch has come to an end – what now?

In these high modernist years, late imperial London was for artists a powerfully attractive city – drawing most of the luminaries of the Anglophone canon. Along with Conrad, Woolf, and Eliot, there were Henry James, Ezra Pound, Wyndham Lewis, Ford Madox Ford, and W. B. Yeats, as well as Nancy Cunard, H. D., Mina Loy, Katherine Mansfield, Dorothy Richardson, and Jean Rhys, important women modernists whom the canon-extending scholarship of recent decades has restored to critical view. Some were simply passing through, and a few became British by choice; fewer still were British by birth. For instance, Conrad (born a Pole in what is now the Ukrainian town of Berdychiv) and Eliot (born in St. Louis, Missouri) anticipated or followed James (born in New York City) in becoming naturalized British subjects. Others had differently complicated relationships to nationality. Yeats was "British" in the sense that he was born in Ireland before independence, while Mansfield and Rhys were born in colonial New Zealand and

Dominica, respectively; Lewis was born in Canada to an English mother and an American father; Cunard's mother was American and her father British; Ford was born Ford Hermann Hueffer, the son of a German father and an English mother; and the English-born Loy, part-English and part-Hungarian, would travel continental Europe before settling in the United States. Pound retained his American citizenship from his birth in Idaho to his death in the Italian city of Venice; his sojourn in London was just one stage of an eventful career. Of all these modernists who resided, for a spell or a lifetime, in London, only Woolf and Richardson were uncomplicatedly British, biographically speaking; and yet their feminist politics gave them good reason to stand somewhat apart from Britain's resiliently patriarchal national culture.

Like many major European cities, London had the networks of artistic production and exchange that have come to be considered central to the modernist endeavor: the salons, the little magazines, the collaborations they made possible. Ford Madox Ford, for example, was not only an accomplished modernist novelist in his own right – (the four novels of his "Parade's End" sequence [1924–28], along with his most widely read novel, *The Good Soldier* [1915], are masterworks of his signature "impressionist" style) – but was also vital to a nascent London modernism in his role as founder of *The English Review* in 1908 and *The Transatlantic Review* in 1924. Ford would publish many of the most influential modernist writers: James, Conrad, and Yeats, as well as Pound, Joyce, Lawrence, Rhys, Stein, Hemingway, and Lewis.

Soon to become leader of another London modernist movement, Lewis was an early contributor to *The English Review*. He later repaid the favor (or had it repaid) by publishing the first part of the novel that would become *The Good Soldier* in his short-lived avant-garde magazine, *Blast*. Bearing an ominous title for a periodical that came on the scene in the summer of 1914, *Blast* would be hastened to an end by the First World War ("a bigger *Blast* than mine," Lewis commented dryly). Lewis's work as a painter had already attracted the tag "vorticist," a designation also attached to, among others, the English painters Edward Wadsworth and David Bomberg and the expatriate sculptors Henri Gaudier-Brzeska and Jacob Epstein. Owing much to cubism in its heightened attention to the dimensionality of the medium, and even more to the industrial-geometrical abstraction of Italian futurism (from which, admittedly, Lewis tried furiously to distance himself), vorticism proved less important, perhaps, for what it accomplished than for what it appeared to be in the context of the domestic art scene: a rare example of an avant-garde "-ism" grown on Britain's philistine soil.

Nonetheless, it is telling not only that many of vorticism's major names were foreign by birth (Gaudier-Brzeska was born in France, Epstein in the United States), but also that it took the American impresario Pound, with his talents for organization and publicity, to give the movement a name. Meanwhile, Pound was also exercising these gifts on the politically radical London magazine *The New Freewoman*, formerly *The Freewoman* and soon to become the modernist mouthpiece *The Egoist*. Although London could not credibly claim to have an avant-garde art scene along the energetic lines of, say, Berlin and Vienna, it certainly had a vital culture of socialist and suffragette protest upon which artistic radicalism could be grafted. Indeed, Pound became the literary editor of *The New Freewoman* on the recommendation of Rebecca West, who was one of the most celebrated political polemicists of the modernist era.

Looking back on this moment of political and artistic upheaval, Lewis announced that "the day was lost, for art, at Sarajevo." As he tells the story in his memoir *Blasting and Bombardiering* (1937), the First World War brought to an untimely end the pan-European ferment of 1914, rendering "the Men of 1914" – as he termed himself, Pound, Eliot, Joyce, and the critic and poet T. E. Hulme – "the first men of a Future that has not materialized":

> We belong to a "great age" that has not "come off." We moved too quickly for the world. We set too sharp a pace. And, more and more exhausted by War, Slump, and Revolution, the world has *fallen back*. Its ambition has withered: it has declined into a listless compromise – half "modern," half Cavalcade.

That last sentence refers to Noel Coward's populist *Cavalcade* (1931) and the Oscar-winning film it became, which tell the story of the quintessentially English Marryot family as their lives are caught up in the major public events of the early twentieth century: the death of Queen Victoria, the sinking of the *Titanic*, the Great War. Lewis's charge was that the gloriously futuristic promise of prewar modernism had ultimately been sold out to postwar pathos and nostalgia, the groundbreaking achievements of the generation of 1914 giving way, in the 1920s, to a mediocre compromise between modernism and the middlebrow.

Although Lewis's taste for provocation makes him a less than disinterested judge of his peers' accomplishments, here he put his finger on something important: the difference between the self-consciously path-breaking, future-oriented modernism of 1914 and the melancholy, even elegiac retrospection of the writing that replaced it (understandably enough, as this shift accompanied a devastating war). Even if Lewis pretended not to know her well enough to spell her name ("Woolfe," he calls her), Virginia Woolf rather supports his diagnosis of a postwar modernism that combined technical innovation with elegiac sensibility. *Cavalcade* it emphatically is not, but Woolf's *To the Lighthouse* (1927) directs its extraordinary formal experiments toward telling the story of one English family, which becomes a national story of loss and mourning when the First World War comes and splits the novel down the middle. "The War is such a tremendous landmark that locally it imposes itself upon our computations of time like the birth of Christ," Lewis wrote: "We say 'pre-war' and 'post-war', rather as we say B.C. or A.D." Although Woolf had famously dated the seismic rupture to "on or about December 1910" – 1910 was the year in which the Edwardian era ended, and also of Roger Fry's highly publicized exhibition of post-impressionist painting – her major novels rather confirm Lewis's sense of the war as modernity's sharpest dividing line.[5]

Predictably, in view of the close ties obtaining among modernism's metropolitan coteries, Lewis and Woolf had links to one another through common friends and collaborators. Lewis's connection to the "Bloomsbury Group" with which Woolf is customarily associated dated back to 1913, when Woolf's friend the artist and critic Roger Fry opened his design collective, Omega Workshops. Woolf's sister, Vanessa Bell, and Bell's lover, the painter Duncan Grant, were among the artists who contributed – as was Lewis himself, until a rift with Fry led him to form the aptly named Rebel Art Centre.

When critics speak of "Bloomsbury," they typically include the writers Woolf, Forster, and Lytton Strachey; the painters Bell, Fry, and Grant; the psychoanalysts Adrian Stephen and James Strachey; the critic Desmond MacCarthy and his memoirist wife Mary ("Molly"); the aesthetician Clive Bell; and the economist John Maynard Keynes. While it is tempting to characterize this group as analogous to the metropolitan salons of continental modernism, this was a more domestic affair in every sense, as the personal ties among all these notably and diversely gifted individuals long predated their individual accomplishments. Bound by family, friendship, and romantic interest, the members of the Bloomsbury Group constituted more a distinct social "set" than a modernist movement as such. To the extent that it had a common program, this was more a shared moral philosophy than a prescription for art: personal relationships always take priority over public causes, candor over convention, private integrity over social respectability.

Writing of her move from the repressive Victorian family home in Kensington to her own airy Bloomsbury house ("the most beautiful, the most exciting, the most romantic place in the world"), Woolf wrote that "46 Gordon Square could never have meant what it did had not 22 Hyde Park Gate preceded it."[6] These lines appear in an ephemeral paper written for a circle of intimates, but there is a lasting truth in Woolf's claim that one can understand the significance of Bloomsbury only by recognizing the stuffy, late Victorian world into which its members had been born, and from which they had aimed collectively to escape. To put it another way, Bloomsbury makes most sense when we take into account that its members were all essentially insiders to the national culture.

For even if their personal and familial closeness makes them anomalous when seen in relation to the international avant-garde, it makes them entirely predictable in relation to the longer history of Britain's cultural elite, which has traditionally been drawn from a socially narrow, upper-middle-class metropolitan base. Writing as another insider, Noel Annan (Baron Annan), summarized the early twentieth-century British "intellectual aristocracy" in an instructive way:

> There was the Macaulay–Cripps–Hobhouse–Babington–Booth–Beatrice Webb clan. There was the Arnold–Trevelyan–Huxley–Darwin–Wedgwood clan, which contained members of the Keynes, Vaughan-Williams, Sidgwick, Cornford and Barlow families. Or the Fry–Hodgkin–Haldane–Mitchison–Butler–Faber–Adam Smith connection. Or the Stephen–Venn–Elliot–Strachey–Barnes–Shuckburgh strain, and so on.[7]

Woolf and her sister belonged to the last of these "clans" (as Virginia and Vanessa Stephen prior to their marriages), but other Bloomsbury names such as Fry, Strachey, and Keynes also appear in that catalogue of distinguished English families with pedigrees reaching back to the intelligentsias of earlier centuries. As Perry Anderson pithily wrote of the national culture, British intellectuals have traditionally been "related by family to their class, not by profession to their estate."[8] Polyglot, pacifist, and socially liberal, the Bloomsbury Group was certainly internationalist in its politics but it was deeply English in its constitution.

England and Englishness

In view of her status as the preeminent British-born modernist, Woolf's conflicted feelings about national affiliation are telling. Her anti-war treatise *Three Guineas* (1938), written with the Spanish Civil War ongoing and the Second World War soon to break out, remains the classic statement of feminist anti-nationalism:

> "Our country" . . . throughout the greatest part of its history has treated me as a slave; it has denied me education or any share in its possessions . . . Therefore if you insist upon fighting to protect me, or "our" country, let it be understood, soberly and rationally between us, that you are fighting to gratify a sex instinct which I cannot share; to procure benefits which I have not shared and probably

will not share; but not to gratify my instincts, or to protect myself or my country. For . . . as a woman, I have no country. As a woman I want no country. As a woman my country is the whole world.

Sub-citizens of their own country, excluded from their share of its vast economic and cultural resources, women are perforce cosmopolitans. Even this "native" British modernist seems unable to resist the familiar modernist vocabulary of expatriation and exile, even if in her case the voluntary de-racination is spiritual rather than actual. "I hate the idea of causes," her friend Forster would similarly and very publicly declare in wartime: "and if I had to choose between betraying my country and betraying my friend, I hope I should have the guts to betray my country."[9]

Yet this is only half the story. When, in *Howards End* (1910), Forster asks whether the nation belongs to its businessmen and imperialists or its cultured liberal elite, it is difficult to ignore Forster's sense of a decent, tolerant, humane, and unchauvinistic England available to those who are willing to jettison the baggage of imperialistic and materialistic exploitation. Likewise, Woolf's position is more complicated than self-exile. In the same passage of *Three Guineas* where she liberates women from the claims made by the state, Woolf goes on to acknowledge the resilience of national feeling:

And if, when reason has had its say, still some obstinate emotion remains, some love of England dropped into a child's ears by the cawing of rooks in an elm tree, by the splash of waves on a beach, or by English voices murmuring nursery rhymes, this drop of pure, if irrational, emotion she will make serve her to give to England first what she desires of peace and freedom for the whole world.

How close these waves and rooks bring us to the pastoral lyricism of Woolf's major modernist novels, to *Mrs. Dalloway, To the Lighthouse,* and *The Waves.* But with what ironic closeness, too, this passage recalls the patriotic soldier of her dead friend Rupert Brooke's famous poem "The Soldier," "whom England bore, shaped, made aware, / Gave, once, her flowers to love, her ways to roam / . . . Washed by the rivers, blest by suns of home," and who in death "Gives somewhere back the thoughts by England given." This is not to imply that Woolf's cosmopolitanism was only half-hearted, much less that it was insincere, but rather to suggest, first, that Bloomsbury's modernism is probably better read as an engagement with the prewar national mythos (Brooke's "forever England") rather than as a negation of it; and, second, that Britain's major modernists understood cosmopolitanism not as the opposite of national feeling, but as the best of its possible outcomes – the worst being, à la Brooke's "The Soldier," militaristic imperial jingoism.

The seemingly contradictory possibility of an outward-looking, anti-imperialist cosmopolitanism that is yet rooted in local affiliation is at the heart of many modernists' treatment of national and regional sympathies. It is what Woolf means when she proposes that the "pure, if irrational, emotion" of patriotism can fuel the desire for a counter-empire of English-style pastoral serenity. In the most internationalist and formally modernist of Forster's novels, *A Passage to India* (1924), the love of country is an exasperated affair, but the final impression the novel leaves is that imperialism has been as corrupting a force on the English colonizers as it is destructive to the Indian colonized.

A writer of the same generation as Forster, Ford Madox Ford shared many of his auto-ethnographic impulses. Some of his most interesting non-fiction was explicitly about the national culture, as in his "England and the English" trilogy: *The Soul of London* (1905), *The Heart of the Country* (1906), and *The Spirit of the People* (1907). The meaning of Englishness is also extensively explored in his novels; the central concern of *The Good Soldier* is, as Malcolm Bradbury put it, "sounding the false beat of the pre-war English heart," while the "Parade's End" series traces the transformation of the national consciousness from the complacency of a prewar *belle époque* to the disorder of the postwar present via the martyrdom of Christopher Tietjens of Groby.[10] Tietjens is "the last surviving Tory," "the most brilliant man in England of that day," someone "who never told a lie or did a dishonourable thing in his life"; and he is victimized not only by the war he barely survives, but also by the self-interest, greed, and opportunism that have come, in Ford's narrative, to define postwar England.[11]

This worried attention to the state of the national culture also finds expression in the novels of the restlessly migrant Lawrence, who was born in Eastwood, Nottinghamshire, and buried near Taos, New Mexico. Modernist myth-making and the material realities of modern England come together in the apocalyptic ending of his family saga, *The Rainbow* (1915), with the cosmopolitan heroine, Ursula Brangwen, seeing in a rainbow "the earth's new architecture, the old, brittle corruption of house and factories swept away." (The reference to jerrybuilt housing and factories reminding us that this is not so much a new world as a new England, with the traces of an industrialism that Lawrence abhorred now obliterated.) However far Lawrence traveled, his best novels invariably returned him to the Midlands of his birth, and he had lived away a long time when he produced his final (and some think finest) major work, *Lady Chatterley's Lover* (1928). This novel tells a love story of a notoriously frank kind, but it is no less passionately outspoken in its treatment of the wider cultural questions – of war, class, industrialism – represented by the relationship between the novel's lovers and dissidents, the Scottish aristocrat Constance Chatterley and the working-class war veteran Oliver Mellors. Quite literally at the center of *Lady Chatterley's Lover* is a lengthy denunciation of a national culture in ruins, when the heroine, driving through the ugly new villages sprung up around the coalmines, is forced to confront for the first time "this terrifyingly new and gruesome England." Here the narration takes a discursive turn, as Lawrence intervenes with a sardonic replay of the Victorian patriot's address: "England, my England! But which is *my* England?" Industrialism – and mechanized war, its most brutal expression – has annihilated the traditional ways of life without replacing them with anything worth having. This sense of a vulnerable and self-endangered national culture is a staple of the late imperial novel.

Nor was this attention to English places, and to the place of England in the world, exclusive to fiction. One of the most impressive of English-born modernist poets, Basil Bunting was both expansively Europeanist in his outlook and acutely local in his concern with his native Northumbria. This is perhaps most visible in his late modernist poem *Briggflatts: An Autobiography* (1966), which returns repeatedly to the question of what connects region to nation, nation to continent. Here, for example, Bunting pauses on a carved epitaph to a tenth-century Viking, the Norwegian king Eric Bloodaxe:

> Bloodaxe, king of York,
> king of Dublin, king of Orkney.
> Take no notice of tears;
> letter the stone to stand
> over love laid aside lest
> insufferable happiness impede
> flight to Stainmore,
> to trace
> lark, mallet,
> becks, flocks
> and axe knocks.

This is a characteristic example of this poet's celebrated musicality: "lark" to "becks" to "flocks" to – superlatively – the onomatopoetic "axe knocks," which annihilate time by linking Bloodaxe's weapon to the memorializing mallet, the mason's mallet to the poet's pen. Adamant that poetry addresses itself more productively to the ear than to the reasoning mind, Bunting typically underplayed questions of "meaning." Yet the topographical content of his musical forms is hard to ignore, as when Bloodaxe's name aurally unifies his heterogeneous kingdom: "Bloodaxe" and "Dublin"; "Bloodaxe" and "Orkney"; "Orkney" and "York." Historical regression makes it possible to redraw the national and continental maps, Bunting shows here, as again when he cites the sixth-century Welsh poet Aneirin – Welsh not in the geographical sense, but in terms of the language, Old Welsh, in which he wrote about the Britons of the land now divided between southeastern Scotland and northeastern England. *Briggflatts* is Bunting's story, its subtitle tells us; and it is equally a story of the north of England. More importantly, though, this regional story is also necessarily a Scandinavian story – and a Scottish, Irish, and Welsh one, too.

"Marginal" modernisms

Just as Bunting's poetry shows there need be no contradiction between local allegiances and transnational awareness, the ambition to unite the regional and the continental was also characteristic of the writers of the Scottish Literary Renaissance – a movement coterminous with high modernism, but not often read alongside it. Like more widely known political modernisms such as the Irish Literary Revival and, across the Atlantic, the Harlem Renaissance, the Scottish Renaissance took as its premise that cultural regeneration is the necessary precursor to political regeneration.

Prior to the 1707 creation of the Kingdom of Great Britain (the forerunner to the modern-day United Kingdom of Great Britain and Northern Ireland), Scotland was a sovereign state. The early twentieth century saw the first sustained attempts to restore Scottish independence. National self-determination was in the air in the years immediately following the First World War: central and eastern European territories formerly under Habsburg rule were being reconstituted as sovereign nations while, closer to home, the Irish Free State would emerge in 1922. No doubt inspired by the Irish example, the Welsh nationalist party Plaid Cymru was founded in 1925; and in Scotland, the pro-independence National Party of Scotland came together in 1928, with the leading light of the Literary Renaissance, the poet Hugh MacDiarmid (Christopher Murray Grieve), among its founding members.

Other major Scottish Renaissance figures included the poet Edwin Muir and the novelists Lewis Grassic Gibbon, Catherine Carswell, Neil M. Gunn, and Willa Muir. (Instructively, the Muirs are now recognized in the context of literary modernism only as early translators of Kafka.) Many of these writers, and most famously MacDiarmid, were committed to the regeneration and transformation of the Scots language as a literary medium. Of course, the politics of language were generally important to Anglophone modernism more broadly: in his satirical "The Oxford Voice" (1929), for example, the Midlands-born Lawrence had mocked the "languishing / and hooing and cooing" of educated southern speech (and "worse still / the would-be oxford [sic] voice"). Yet the modernist concern with the materiality and agency of speech would lend itself even more powerfully to the political interests of the non-English but "British" writer. "Modernism was an essentially provincial phenomenon," Robert Crawford contends: "the roots of [modernists'] creativity came from Hailey, Idaho, from Poland, from Dublin, St Louis, Langholm, or the Nottinghamshire pits. Their language is not the language of English gentlemen, nor is it meant to be."[12] Perhaps the most famous instance of a politically denaturalized English comes in the passage in Joyce's *A Portrait of the Artist as a Young Man* (1916) when Stephen Dedalus's use of the word "tundish" (in modern English, the ironically French-derived "funnel") is remarked by his English dean of studies, who assumes that this Middle English word is a quaint Irishism. (Although here the joke is also on the young artist for taking at face value the dean's mistake: "The language in which we are speaking is his before it is mine," Stephen infers; "His language, so familiar and so foreign, will always be for me an acquired speech.")

Widespread though such attention to the politics of language surely was, Ian Duncan had good reason to single out MacDiarmid's modernist long poem *A Drunk Man Looks at the Thistle* (1926) as "unique among the major modernist works for forcing its topical preoccupation with national identity upon the reader as a linguistic problem."[13] Probably the best known of Scottish modernist texts, *A Drunk Man* is written in Scots dialect – but one drawn less from ordinary Lowland vernacular than from raids on the preexisting body of Scots poetry. As Duncan rightly says, the "linguistic problem" is such that the poem's difficulty is apprehended even by Scottish readers, forced thus to confront their severance from their national heritage. As its title makes plain – (the thistle is a familiar national symbol) – this is a poem that apostrophizes Scotland and the Scots:

> And let the lesson be – to be yersel's,
> Ye needna fash gin it's to be ocht else.
> To be yersel's – and to mak' that worth bein',
> Nae harder job to mortals has been ge'in.[14]

The pawky sentiment and the use of the ballad-like end-rhyming quatrain may evidence a self-consciously folksy rootedness, but the stanza immediately prior to this one cites Spengler, Dostoevskii, and Nietzsche, "To show what Scotland micht ha'e hed instead / O' this preposterous Presbyterian breed." That Scotland must learn to understand itself as a European country is among the main claims of a poem that extensively cites continental contemporaries such as the Russian Aleksandr Blok and the German-Jewish

Else Lasker-Schüler, long passages of whose work MacDiarmid freely adapts here.

Such linguistic estrangement is also central to the most original of Scottish modernist novels, *Sunset Song* (1932), the first novel in Lewis Grassic Gibbon's trilogy *A Scots Quair*. Set in a farming community in the northeast of Scotland during the years leading up to the First World War, the novel is told in the second person ("you") of ordinary speech. This device allows Gibbon to turn the novel into something authored not by a privileged individual looking in on a dying world, but by the community itself:

> Maybe there were some twenty to thirty holdings in all, the crofters dour folk of the old Pict stock, they had no history, common folk, and ill-reared their biggings [buildings] clustered and chaved [labored] amid the long, sloping fields. The leases were one-year, two-year, you worked from the blink of the day you were breeked to the flicker of the night they shrouded you, and the dirt of gentry sat and ate up your rents but you were just as good as they were.[15]

This is rural Scotland seen from the perspective of those who work it from dawn to death. Breaking with the realist hierarchy that separates narrative voice from the speech of characters, "standard" English from dialect, the narrator speaks the same language as the people about whom he writes.

In a magical realist gesture *avant la lettre*, *Sunset Song* includes ghosts: the ghost of an ancient Caledonian soldier from the time of the Roman occupation, and also the ghost of the heroine's soldier husband, shot as a deserter by his own side during the First World War. On the one hand, the yoking of antiquity (a first-century soldier) and the modern present (unnecessary victim of a war newly ended) recalls Eliot's treatment of the Great War in the first part of *The Waste Land* (the speaker of which famously addresses the American "Stetson" as a fellow veteran of the ancient wars between Carthage and Rome), as well as his famous praise for Joyce's "mythical method": "a way of controlling, of ordering, of giving a shape and a significance to the immense panorama of futility and anarchy which is contemporary history."[16] On the other hand, it is noteworthy that strategies that use temporal conflation to bypass modernity's political borders should have appealed so widely to writers with nonmetropolitan affiliations: not only to Joyce himself, but also to Bunting, MacDiarmid, and Gibbon, as well as to the sometime self-identified Scot Rebecca West, who adopted this strategy for her epic *Black Lamb and Grey Falcon* (1941), when she used the two Serbian myths to which the title refers to explain, in mythic terms, the capitulation of contemporary Europe to totalitarianism.

Such transhistorical tactics also appealed to the major Welsh modernists. The London-born and Welsh-identified David Jones was very literally one of the "Men of 1914": his greatest work, the book-length prose-poem, *In Parenthesis* (1937), is based on his experiences serving in the Royal Welsh Fusiliers in the First World War. Here and in *The Anathemata* (1952), the modern and the ancient coexist, as do the insistently localized and the pan-European. There is no single mythology expounded in Jones's writing, but mythology is everywhere in his characteristic juxtapositions of the fragments ("deposits" he typically calls them) that constitute a culture, the stratified remains of multiple civilizations and their heterogeneous temporalities. "[T]here are the basic things . . . the *materia* we all draw upon, whether we know it or not," he wrote in his preface to *The Anathemata*: "the early mixed racial deposits, the myth (mythus) of this Island, and the Christian Liturgy, and the Canon of Scripture, and the Classical deposits . . . a great complex of influences and interactions which have conditioned us all."[17]

A generation younger than Jones, the Welsh writer Dylan Thomas – a man of 1939 rather than of 1914 – was producing his most important work during the same years. Many of his best-known poems locate the Second World War's home front within a timeless setting of violence. Just as "A Refusal to Mourn the Death, by Fire, of a Child in London" (1945), for example, both is and is not an elegy, it both is and is not a poem about the bombing of London. Deep time supplies consolations that a poet cannot, but those consolations have an obscurely macabre tenor, the consolations of communion with the already dead: "Deep with the first dead lies London's daughter, / Robed in the long friends, / The grains beyond age, the dark veins of her mother / Secret by the unmourning water." Another important poetic recorder of the Second World War, the Northern Irish Louis MacNeice writes in a different but no less death-haunted idiom when, in his Blitz poem "Brother Fire," he designates the fire that despoils London both "enemy and image of ourselves": "Did we not . . . / Echo your thoughts in ours? 'Destroy! Destroy!'" Like Thomas's, too, MacNeice's poems of place are sharply attentive to the ways in which the past persists in the present. Dublin, in MacNeice's poem of that title, is "not an Irish town / . . . not English" but made up of all the peoples, histories, and styles the city has absorbed: "Fort of the Dane, / Garrison of the Saxon, / Augustan capital / Of a Gaelic nation." His poem "Iceland" sees in this spare and remote landscape how "Corrugated iron / Farms inherit / The spirit and phrase / Of ancient sagas."

Dylan Thomas's style has been aptly characterized as "a Gothicised, even grotesque modernism,"[18] and the epithet holds good for a number of his mid-century Celtic contemporaries, with their attention to the presence of the past in the very ground beneath our feet. Among them is the Scottish Gaelic poet (because it bears mentioning that Britain has indigenous languages other than English) Somhairle MacGill-Eain/Sorley MacLean whose incantatory "Hallaig" restores to life those lost communities forced from their ancestral settlements by the ignorance and greed of metropolitan masters: "They are still in Hallaig / MacLeans and MacLeods /... The dead have been seen alive" ["Tha iad fhathast ann a Hallaig / Clann Ghill-Eain's Clann MhicLeòid, /... Chunnacas na mairbh beò"].[19] As the "regional" American modernist William Faulkner so famously put it, "The past is never dead. It's not even past."[20]

Late modernism

Until recently, however, the mid-century era of these major writers and major works would have been excluded from consideration under the conventional understanding of modernism, with its emphasis on the 1910s and early 1920s, and its reluctance to look beyond the metropolitan centers. This narrower understanding of British modernism is starting to change, thanks to arguments such as those of Jed Esty, who has described how English modernism was transformed through the 1930s and 1940s. Turning to well-known late modernist works that make a key theme of the concept of Englishness – works such as Eliot's *Four Quartets* (1943) and Woolf's *Between the Acts* (1941) – Esty takes this new and almost communitarian attention to the particularities of the national culture as indicative of an imperial nation renouncing its sense of itself as the universal culture and coming to recognize itself as merely one culture among many.

To say that these late modernist texts are preoccupied by questions of national identity is not, however, to say that they are somehow parochial or introverted. On the contrary, *Between the Acts* is a more *continentally* aware book than any of Woolf's others, as may be inevitable in view of its wartime context. Notice, for example, how often the main characters refer to the news from Europe ("Had he not read in the morning paper... that sixteen men had been shot, others prisoned, just over there, across the gulf, in the flat land which divided them from the continent?"). Another character reads not of her own catastrophic present, but of a differently barbarous time, "when the entire continent, not then, she understood, divided by a channel, was all one." (Yet of course this return to the prehistoric past is no flight from the chilling present, for "what's the channel, come to think of it, if they mean to invade us?") Meanwhile, the contemporary poem *The Dry Salvages*, the third of Eliot's *Four Quartets*, looks across another war-endangered stretch of water, west toward the United States rather than east toward occupied Europe. Here the newly explicit concern with his adopted nation that characterizes Eliot's poems of the war years ("History is now and England") is accompanied by a return to the sensitively particularized locations of his altogether un-British origins: *The Dry Salvages* opens with the Mississippi River of his St. Louis childhood ("His rhythm was present in the nursery bedroom, / In the rank ailanthus of the April dooryard . . . / The river is within us").

Although Esty focuses on the canonical figures of Eliot, Forster, and Woolf, the reappraisal of the mid-century period of which his study is an important part has expanded the British modernist canon in exciting ways. For a start, thinking again about this period allows us to revisit those British modernists whose writing was preoccupied all along by the communal, the local, the non-metropolitan, and the auto-ethnographic. "A Scottish poet maun assume / The burden o' his people's doom," learns MacDiarmid's drunk man, and many other minority modernists shared that sense of not-voluntary but not-rejected collectivity. Long neglected mid-century novelists who have now returned to view include the Anglo-Irish Elizabeth Bowen and the white West Indian Jean Rhys, whose sharp attention to group feeling is brilliantly evidenced in their stories of women displaced by the demise of their once privileged settler caste (the "white cockroaches" of Rhys's novel of dispossession, *Wide Sargasso Sea* [1966]). It is tempting to attribute their sharp attention to the complexities of social affiliation to their late-colonial or "peripheral" origins: certainly Bowen's *The Last September* (1929), a novel about the end of British power in Ireland, shares Rhys's interest in the tangled allegiances of those who, though not "native," cannot see themselves or be seen as English either. Even so, reading these novelists alongside their English-born contemporaries suggests that there is a period component as well as a geographical one.

For example, other second-generation modernists like Evelyn Waugh and Henry Green are, in their way, as group-conscious as Bowen and Rhys, although the groups with which they concern themselves are invariably English: interwar socialites, metropolitan pseudo-intellectuals, wartime fire-fighters and bureaucrats, Birmingham factory workers, servants in an Anglo-Irish mansion. (Waugh's commitments are generally to the various sub-categories of posh, but it is hard to think of another English modernist with Green's unforced social range.) On the level of style, this group consciousness is most obvious in the sensitivity to sociolect that makes for their novels' celebrated dialogue – and novels like Waugh's satirical *Vile Bodies* (1930) and Green's offbeat *Loving* (1945), *Nothing* (1950), and *Doting* (1952) consist of little *but* dialogue. It was with these writers in mind that David Lodge summarized late modernism as the substitution of "stream of consciousness" with "stream of talk" – a suggestive way of thinking about modernism and its longer history beyond the dominant perception of 1920s modernism as the writing of lonely interiority, of the solitary and alienated perceiving subject (which is not a useless model, but useful only up to a certain historical point).[21] Late modernist fiction in England tends to be socially inquisitive to a high degree even when, as in the cases of, say, Henry Green, Ivy Compton-Burnett, and Patrick Hamilton (to name just a few of the period's neglected talents), that sociability is put into the service of the most rewardingly idiosyncratic narrative effects.

In his essay "When was Modernism?" Raymond Williams argued decades ago for the need to rethink the periodization of the twentieth century into, on the one hand, a hegemonic modernism – (the modernism of the canon, its radical potential neutralized by the very fact of its institutionalization) – and, on the other hand, the depthless "postmodernism" to which later decades found themselves condemned by the artificial "ending" imposed upon modernism for institutional purposes. To think beyond the established modernism of metropolitan alienation and isolation would mean recovering all "the neglected works left in the wide margin of the century," Williams argued, and it was high time to look outside the paradigms offered by modernism's most vocal spokesmen:

> The life of the émigré was dominant among the key groups, and they could and did deal with each other. Their self-referentiality, their propinquity and mutual isolation all served to represent the artist as necessarily estranged, and to ratify as canonical the works of radical estrangement. So, to *want* to leave your settlement and settle nowhere... becomes presented, in another ideological move, as a normal condition.[22]

In searching for a modernism that was still capable of imagining affiliation and community, Williams was speaking not only as a Marxist critic, but also as a Welsh one. London in the 1910s and 1920s has long been at the core of the modernist canon, but, as Williams suspected, there were other British modernisms – of later times and non-metropolitan places, with altogether different values and concerns.

NOTES

1. Terry Eagleton's *Exiles and Émigrés: Studies in Modern Literature* (New York: Schocken, 1970); Raymond Williams, "When was Modernism?" *The Politics of Modernism: Against the New Conformists*, ed. Tony Pinkney (London: Verso, 1988), p. 34; Malcolm Bradbury and James McFarlane, *Modernism: A Guide to European Literature 1890–1930*, rev. edn. (Harmondsworth: Penguin, 1991), p. 13.
2. Franco Moretti, *Atlas of the European Novel, 1800–1900* (London: Verso, 1998), p. 70.

3. Joseph Conrad, "Author's Note," *The Secret Agent* (London: Penguin, 2007), p. 250.

4. Virginia Woolf, "Modern Fiction," *The Virginia Woolf Reader*, ed. Mitchell A. Leaska (San Diego: Harcourt, 1984), p. 287.

5. Virginia Woolf, "Mr. Bennett and Mrs. Brown," *The Virginia Woolf Reader*, p. 194.

6. Virginia Woolf, "Old Bloomsbury," *Moments of Being: A Collection of Autobiographical Writing*, 2nd edn., ed. Jeanne Schulkind (San Diego: Harcourt, 1985), pp. 184, 182.

7. Noel Annan, *Our Age: English Intellectuals Between the World Wars – A Group Portrait* (New York: Random House, 1990), p. 7.

8. Perry Anderson, *English Questions* (London: Verso, 1992), pp. 59–60.

9. E. M. Forster, "What I Believe," *Two Cheers for Democracy* (San Diego: Harcourt, 1968), p. 68.

10. Malcolm Bradbury, *The Modern British Novel* (Harmondsworth: Penguin, 1994), p. 89.

11. Ford Madox Ford, *Parade's End* (New York: Vintage, 1979), pp. 598, 48, 226.

12. Robert Crawford, *Devolving English Literature*, rev. edn. (Edinburgh University Press, 2000), p. 270.

13. Ian Duncan, "'Upon the thistle they're impaled': Hugh MacDiarmid's Modernist Nationalism," *Modernism and Colonialism: British and Irish Literature, 1899–1939*, ed. Richard Begam and Michael Valdez Moses (Durham, N.C.: Duke University Press, 2007), p. 246.

14. Hugh MacDiarmid, *A Drunk Man Looks at the Thistle*, *Selected Poetry*, ed. Alan Riach and Michael Grieve (Manchester: Carcanet, 2004), p. 51.

15. Lewis Grassic Gibbon, *Sunset Song* (London: Penguin, 2007), p. 12.

16. T. S. Eliot, "Ulysses, Order, and Myth," *Selected Prose of T. S. Eliot*, ed. Frank Kermode (Orlando, Fla.: Harcourt, 1975), pp. 178, 177.

17. David Jones, *The Anathemata: Fragments of an Attempted Writing* (1952; New York: Chilmark Press, 1962), p. 40.

18. John Goodby and Christopher Wigginton, "'Shut, too, in a tower of words': Dylan Thomas' Modernism," *Locations of Literary Modernism: Region and Nation in British and American Modernist Poetry*, ed. Alex Davis and Lee M. Jenkins (Cambridge University Press, 2000), p. 90.

19. Somhairle MacGill-Eain, *Reothairt is Contraigh: Tagadh de Dhàin, 1932–1972/ Spring Tide and Neap Tide: Selected Poems, 1932–72* (Edinburgh: Canongate, 1977), p. 143.

20. William Faulkner, *Requiem For a Nun*, *William Faulkner: Novels 1942–54* (New York: Library of America, 1994), p. 535.

21. David Lodge, "Dialogue in the Modern Novel," *After Bakhtin: Essays on Fiction and Criticism* (London: Routledge, 1990), p. 81.

22. Raymond Williams, "When was Modernism?" p. 35.

FURTHER READING

Begam, Richard, and Michael Valdez Moses. *Modernism and Colonialism: British and Irish Literature, 1899–1939*. Durham, N.C.: Duke University Press, 2007.

Cunningham, Valentine. *British Writers of the Thirties*. Oxford University Press, 1988.

Davis, Alex, and Lee M. Jenkins. *Locations of Literary Modernism: Region and Nation in British and American Modernist Poetry*. Cambridge University Press, 2000.

Esty, Jed. *A Shrinking Island: Modernism and National Culture in England*. Princeton University Press, 2004.

Goldman, Jane. *Modernism, 1910–1945: Image to Apocalypse*. Basingstoke: Palgrave Macmillan, 2004.

Levenson, Michael. *A Genealogy of Modernism*. Cambridge University Press, 1984.

Marcus, Laura, and Peter Nicholls, eds. *The Cambridge History of Twentieth-Century English Literature*. Cambridge University Press, 2004.

Nicholls, Peter. *Modernisms: A Literary Guide*. Berkeley: University of California Press, 1995.

Stansky, Peter. *On or About December 1910: Early Bloomsbury and Its Intimate World*. Cambridge, Mass.: Harvard University Press, 1996.

Walkowitz, Rebecca L. *Cosmopolitan Style: Modernism Beyond the Nation*. New York: Columbia University Press, 2006.

7

HARSHA RAM

Russia

The achievements of Russian modernism appear all the more extraordinary given how recent, if rapid, have been many of the major developments of Russian literature. Medieval Russia possessed little in the way of secular *belles lettres*; and when modern Russian literature arose in the eighteenth century, it was as the tentative by-product of a state-sponsored program of political modernization and cultural enlightenment. Acquiring new confidence, verbal suppleness, and cultural breadth with Aleksandr Pushkin and his romantic contemporaries, Russian literature finally came of age with realism and the nineteenth-century novel. In their epic reach, their social engagement, and their insistence on linking the nuances of psychology and character development to the larger metaphysical dimensions of human experience, the works of Tolstoi and Dostoevskii seemed to bend or extend novelistic form in ways unimaginable to the western European author. The Russian nineteenth-century novel vividly expresses the characteristic tendency of Russian literature to question the autonomy of the aesthetic sphere and the discursive mediation of institutional forms, in favor of a direct appeal to the antinomies of the spirit and the hope of renewed human solidarity. This impatience with conventions and distinctions, preceding but also fueling Russian modernist experimentation, can be attributed to many local factors. European norms of discourse and behavior were perceived by many Russians as a foreign imposition, emulated unevenly and frequently questioned. The severe restrictions placed upon civil society paradoxically gave Russian literature a greater charismatic charge. The Orthodox religious tradition stressed the integration and transfiguration of life over dualism and differentiation. And while the recently emancipated peasantry was still largely separated from the practices of high literacy, the gap between intellectuals and the Russian people weighed heavily on the conscience of the writing class.

It was through the translation and diffusion of this recent, but already impressive, past that Russian literature acquired its international reputation in the early twentieth century. To the English reader, Russian literature revealed, in the words of Virginia Woolf, a "new panorama of the human mind," in which "the old divisions" of bourgeois decorum and conventionally paced narrative "melt into each other."[1] In the closing pages of *The Theory of the Novel*, Georg Lukács would hail Russian literature's "greater closeness to certain organic natural conditions," intimating the possibility of a "new form of artistic creation," the "renewed epic."[2] To many critics the Russian writer seemed to be rooted in a still-vivid agrarian world, able prophetically to glimpse an alternative cultural synthesis that would dissolve or bypass the limits of bourgeois modernity. The international renown of Russian literature coincided, in Russia itself, with the advent of modernism, which in Russia as elsewhere called into question the assumptions of realism and the shape of the novel as a genre. Thus the very works by which Russia was appearing urgently new to the rest of the world – above all the works of Dostoevskii, Tolstoi, and Chekhov – were subject at home to reappraisal in the light of still newer trends.

Modernism in Russia served first and foremost as a means of synchronizing native culture with recent developments in the West, resulting in the accelerated absorption of a literary history that had been more prolonged and internally differentiated in Europe. Yet unlike Russian classicism or romanticism, which never achieved the nuanced richness of the models from which they derived, Russian modernism would equal, if not outstrip, the modernisms of Europe in quality, radicalism, and breadth. Stimulated but also repelled by the belated growth of a dynamic local bourgeoisie, and witness to the looming confrontation between the tsarist state and the forces of social revolt, the Russian modernists would fuse the aesthetic sensibility, self-reflexivity, and formal preoccupations of their European counterparts with the messianic role that the nineteenth-century intelligentsia had bequeathed to Russian literature. Rarely was modernism's much-trumpeted freedom from the constraints of the church, the state, and the academy put to such probing use as in Russia, where utopian artistic experimentation and metaphysical speculation coincided with the proximity, and then the reality, of political revolution.

The question of Russian modernism's temporal and aesthetic boundaries remains widely debated to this day. Its beginnings – described in the pages to come – are relatively clear, but not its end. The October revolution of 1917 was doubtless a watershed in the history of Russian modernism, but it was by no means its endpoint. The revolution galvanized as well as polarized Russia's writers, fragmenting an already factionalized literary community without eliminating – at least initially – the factions themselves. The deepest fissure was geographical, separating those who left as émigrés in the revolution's wake from those who remained behind. The émigrés, though motivated to leave by their deep distaste for Bolshevism, were by no means all political or aesthetic conservatives. Linguistic barriers and cultural orientation confined major poets such as Marina Tsvetaeva and Vladislav Khodasevich to the lively but isolated Russian communities of Europe, while those more attuned to the cosmopolitan experimentalism of the international avant-garde, such as Il'ia Zdanevich (Iliazd), strove to dialogue with their European counterparts. Vladimir Nabokov was the rare figure capable of reconciling his nostalgic outsider status with an exceptional linguistic dexterity and cultural mobility.

The cultural politics of those who remained in Russia varied greatly. The Bolsheviks were anxious to draw sympathetic intellectuals to their cause: their initial goal was simply political hegemony, rather than cultural uniformity. The absence of a coherent cultural policy allowed numerous literary factions, modernist or otherwise, to coexist and compete for the largesse of the new regime. For artists, the collapse of the material conditions of everyday life, along with the nationalization of cultural enterprises, made state patronage all the more desirable. The futurist avant-garde in particular embraced the new Soviet reality with enthusiasm, viewing political revolution as complementary to the aesthetic revolution they had already been advocating. Outside of the avant-garde, modernist writers such as Boris Pasternak typically regarded the revolution more philosophically, as an elemental force that was abhorrent in its excesses, but nonetheless an organic expression of the Russian historical process. These multiple redactions of modernism had a profound impact on a new generation of "fellow-travellers": younger writers of the 1920s who strove to fuse revolutionary themes with modernist form. All of those who remained in Soviet Russia – symbolists, acmeists, futurists, as well as their younger successors – would struggle to find a place in the new order. Their success or failure depended as much on the contigencies of party policy as on their actual literary practice.

The harassment, imprisonment, and execution of so many major modernist artists during the Stalin era have frequently led critics to view Russian modernism as antithetical to a Soviet literary establishment that eventually destroyed it. In Russia and abroad, the term "Silver Age" has become entrenched as a means to identify this period – the cultural ferment of the first two decades of the twentieth century, second only in its brilliance to the "Golden Age" of Pushkin. The term has little intrinsic merit, except in revealing a profound nostalgia for a period whose spiritual values and material basis were destroyed or profoundly transformed by communism. More controversially, Boris Groys has advanced the opposite argument: that the Soviet literary dogma of socialist realism was in fact a complex extension of the utopian, totalizing vision of the symbolists and the avant-garde.[3] Yet given the historical absence in Russia of a differentiated and autonomous aesthetic sphere, homologies between politics and aesthetics have been the norm more than the exception, and cannot be adduced to establish precise genealogies such as that which would obtain between the avant-garde and socialist realism, without careful investigation. The historical record, as always, is messier: Russian modernism's post-revolutionary existence grew out of a compound of unique historical conditions including the adaptive capacities of Soviet writers, the emergence of a Russian modernist culture in emigration, and the vicissitudes of Soviet cultural policy, which led in the 1930s to the creation of a multi-ethnic socialist literature sustained by state sponsorship.

The pages to come provide a very partial account of this overall story. They focus on two major literary currents – symbolism and acmeism – and on two important writers – Innokentii Annenskii and Mikhail Kuzmin – whose work serves as a bridge between the two movements. They also illuminate many of the debates on aesthetics and poetics, on spirituality, sexuality, and class, on national identity and the crisis of empire, that informed the cultural production of the time. My preference has been to flesh out one dominant tendency in Russian modernism, which might be termed neo-traditionalist, instead of surveying the myriad names and groupings associated with Russian modernism as a whole.

Polemics and patronage in Russia's *belle époque*

Beginning in the 1890s, Russia's literary elite saw a trickle of new converts to the doctrines of European symbolism and decadence, which proclaimed the purity of art and the primacy of lyric poetry, and which explored the burden of belonging to a cycle of cultural history that had reached its zenith and was experiencing a sumptuous decline. To an even greater extent than in Europe, however, Russian modernism did not seek the absolutization of art, but rather what Nietzsche had called the "transvaluation of all values." The first generation of Russian symbolists, such as Valerii Briusov, Dmitrii Merezhkovskii, Zinaida Gippius, and Fedor Sologub liked to invoke as their credo the lines of the decadent writer Nikolai Minskii, a minor poet remembered mainly for dramatizing the shift away from the populist and utilitarian values which had dominated Russian culture during the latter half of the nineteenth century: "A hostility to whatever is, the dim light of premonitions, / And a searing thirst for sacred things that never are." The decadents shared with the progressive intelligentsia from which they emerged a critical negation of the present, but they replaced the radicals' didacticism, epistemological positivism, and moral rigidity with a new poetics of indeterminacy and inbetweenness. This implied the refusal of programmatic content, epistemological certainty, and immediate social utility, the transgression of cognitive and discursive boundaries, and the preponderance of suggestive nuance and epiphanic insight over objective reality and delineated contours; but none of this necessitated for Russian artists the fetishizing of aesthetic experience as something separate from religious experience or social engagement. The latter was hardly possible, given the political turbulence and spiritual restlessness of turn-of-the century Russia.

Russia's *belle époque* was indeed far from tranquil: economic modernization, rapid urbanization, and political repression were punctured by moments of geopolitical crisis and domestic dissent – the latter escalating, in 1905, into broadly based popular revolt. Increasingly conscious of the lability of the existing order, and gripped by intuitions of apocalyptic change, the Russian modernists refocused their attention on the great and unresolved questions of national identity, historical destiny, geographical location, and spiritual fulfillment that the nineteenth-century tradition had posed. This did not necessarily imply a return to tendentiousness or the social content of art. Rather, modernist writers and artists explored multiple ways of conceiving change, creating spiritual community and physical intimacy, and evaluating the relationship between language and the world. The erosion of the distinction between art and non-art, which Western critics often attribute to Dada and Surrealism, began earlier in Russia, where the symbolists saw art as a vehicle for the transformation, rather than the evasion, of everyday life. In the extraordinary efflorescence of heterodox theology and in the new cultural visibility of Russia's long-persecuted schismatic sects, there was a palpable if diffuse desire for spiritual communion outside the purview of church and state.

The influence of literary modernism in prerevolutionary Russia should not be underestimated, although it arose in a diverse and contested literary field. Inexpensive editions of the Russian classics, adventure novels, regional prose, popular women's fiction, and the work of the younger neorealists such as Maksim Gor'kii all vastly outsold their modernist rivals. Widely derided by opponents for repudiating the literary intellectual's traditional civic consciousness, the modernists nevertheless succeeded, over two decades, in fostering a reading public within the ascendant bourgeoisie. These newer consumption patterns fostered distinctions of taste based on social alignments that were not entirely stable. On the one hand, Russia's modernist bohemia retained and even intensified the intelligentsia's traditional disdain for the *meshchane* (the urban lower middle classes) and more broadly for *meshchanstvo*, the cultural philistinism of those who placed social consensus and personal comforts above the unfettered growth of human potential. On the other hand, the modernists welcomed the patronage of the wealthy merchant class and the more enlightened members of the gentry. The emergence of modernism as a privileged cultural commodity was financed by such wealthy art patrons as the cloth merchant Sergei Shchukin and the textile manufacturer Ivan Morozov, who were among the earliest private collectors of European impressionist and post-impressionist painting, not to mention the mercurial dilettante Nikolai Riabushinskii, whose willingness to use his vast family fortune to bankroll new art reflected the maturation of Moscow's merchant community into a culturally engaged and politically liberal entrepreneurial class during the final decades of the tsarist era. No less important for the propagation of the new sensibility were the coordinated efforts of luxury literary periodicals and art exhibitions, such as *The World of Art* (1898–1904), *Libra* (1904–09), and *The Golden Fleece* (1906–09).

Senses and spirit

The period from 1890 to 1914 saw the rapid circulation and critical assimilation in Russia of modernist literary currents ranging from European decadence and French symbolism to the Italian futurist avant-garde, as well as the rediscovery of past Russian writers whom the radical populists had dismissed or misconstrued. Thus the larger historical trajectory of European literature acquired in Russia an accelerated development, with truncated cycles of innovation and intellectual crisis occurring nearly simultaneously or in rapid succession. Until the revolutions of 1917, these cycles were dominated by lyric poetry, involving various redactions of symbolist and post-symbolist poetics, and encompassing major offshoots such as acmeism and futurism. In its richness, diversity, and sophistication, Russian modernist poetry ranks among the greatest achievements of the lyric genre in any language.

The opening volley of Russian modernism was fired by Dmitrii Merezhkovskii, an author who once enjoyed Europe-wide celebrity on the basis of his philosophically charged historical novels on such figures as Leonardo da Vinci and Peter the Great. In his article, "On the Causes of the Decline and on the New Currents in Contemporary Russian Literature" (1892), Merezhkovskii spoke of modern art as distinguished by three elements, "mystical content, symbols, and the broadening of artistic receptivity." In his formulation, the symbol functions as a tenuous bridge between mystical idealism and aesthetic impressionism. The symbol permits either a radical and fragmentary perspectivism, or the integration of these perceptions into a higher unity. This thesis unleashed a diverse range of poetic responses. Zinaida Gippius, arguably Russia's first major woman writer, exercised considerable influence in the literary and religiously inflected philosophical circles of the time. She urged the abandonment of orthodox faith for the sake of a new spirituality, which would arise both from personal inquiry and from the construction of interpersonal relations beyond the confines of conventional marriage and family life. Her lyric persona, often masculine in gender, is typically spiritually sluggish but struggling to awaken. Her poem, "The Seamstress" (1901), depicts a solitary heroine bent from overwork and cut off from religious communion. For a brief instant, the silk cloth she is embroidering transforms into a streak of fiery blood, which she interprets as a "sign of that which we call Love." The revelation is instantaneous but transitory: the poem's originality lies in its marriage of symbolist intuition to the humdrum routine of women's labor and a subjectivity that is lucid but bereft of conventional feminine charm.

Valerii Briusov, the leading symbolist of the first generation, emphasized the technical mastery of poetic form. Today his original verse, flawless but frigid, has been eclipsed by his vast output of poetic translations, primarily from the French, and by his novel *The Fiery Angel* (1908). Set in sixteenth-century Germany, the novel meticulously reconstructs an early modern Europe of exalted passions and occult practices. Even as it adheres to the genre of historical fiction, *The Fiery Angel* is an intensely modern *roman à clef*, addressing the vexed relationship between sexuality and spirituality that was an ongoing preoccupation of the Russian modernists.

With the second generation of Russian symbolists, Merezhkovskii's premise of contradictory inclusiveness would give way to more sharply edged distinctions. In his 1908 article, "The Two Elements in Contemporary Symbolism," Viacheslav Ivanov sought retroactively to separate what Merezhkovskii had once conflated. For Ivanov, aesthetic experience in the form of sensory and psychological enrichment was the legacy of decadence. This was a subjective idealism, to be distinguished from symbolism proper, which subordinated art to the higher "realism" of mystical cognition. The sensory *and* the mystical could not be indiscriminately embraced, since they served different goals. For Ivanov, Russian symbolism acquired its positive content from religious experience, allowing it to overcome the temptations of decadence and acquire an epistemologically more solid footing. Art thus became a hieratic activity, but one for which Ivanov sought to cultivate a popular base. Although the Russian symbolists remained a coterie phenomenon and differed considerably in their understanding of society from the left, they were, like the Marxists, deeply drawn to totalizing and collectivist categories of thought.

The greatest poet of Russian symbolism was Aleksandr Blok. Revered in his own lifetime and still widely read today, he enjoys a status akin to that of Yeats in the English-speaking world. His prolific output of poetry and drama is unified by an exquisite musicality and an intuitive capacity that is allusive and associative rather than didactic, anchored in a lyric persona at once vulnerable and ironically self-reflexive, introspective yet deeply engaged in the drama of Russian history. Blok's early lyrics celebrate the poet's future wife as a hypostasis of spiritual wisdom, a role, it seems, that hardly corresponded to the conventional expectations of the hapless bride: Russia possessed a rich theological and liturgical corpus but little in the way of an indigenous poetic tradition of courtly or mystical love. Blok's originality lay in grafting a foreign mode onto a recognizably Russian landscape of twilight, flickering icon-lamps and snow-swept plains. Blok's lyric hero is similarly a hybrid blend of the masculine abjection of the courtly lyric, the psychosexual neuroses of the fin-de-siècle, and the spiritual meekness that Russian Orthodoxy stressed. The archaic modalities of chivalrous love could not survive unaltered in Blok's work. Menacing motifs of urban squalor and civil unrest, juxtaposed alongside a bourgeois world of theatrical artifice, coarse pleasure, and frivolous excess, would soon blur – without dissolving – the polarities of spirit and flesh, eternity and history.

The pressures of Russian history would impel Blok to reconsider the typically decadent dialectic of aristocratic ennui and spiritual exaltation. In the major lyric cycle "The Native Land" (1907–16), the poet views the political tensions of his time through the prism of the fourteenth-century battle of Kulikovo Field, a watershed event that signaled the end of Tatar–Mongol suzerainty over Russian lands and the eventual rise of the unified Muscovite state: "Oh, my Russia! My wife! Painfully clear / To us is the long path! / Our path has pierced our breast / with the arrow of the ancient Tatar will." The allegory here is complex: Blok sympathizes with the goal of liberating Russia's divided lands from Tatar domination, but he also acknowledges the transformative impact of Russia's prolonged contact with the Turkic peoples of the East. "Our path is through the steppe," he exclaims, envisioning Russia as an unbridled mare galloping through the Eurasian hinterland. Russia's future liberation, Blok suggests, will have to fuse the Christian patriotism of the medieval past with the drive and mobility of the Turkic nomads, Russia's erstwhile adversaries.

The Eurasian dilemma

Blok's vision had its roots in a larger exploration of the Eurasian dimension of Russian identity that would prove central to Russian modernism.

Although Eurasianism was given a name and a codified doctrine only in the 1920s, the term subsumed what was by then a long-standing (and still current) debate on Russia's geographical identity, caught as the nation was between the western tilt of the Petrine reforms and the centuries-long eastward expansion of the Russian state. The Eurasian dilemma was formulated for the Russian modernists by Vladimir Solov'ëv's influential poem, "Pan-mongolism" (written in 1894 and published in 1905). The nine-stanza poem read the ongoing crises of empire and revolution as part of a civilizational clash between East and West, whose meaning lay within a larger providential scheme of history. In Solov'ëv's formulation, the memory of past defeats inflicted on Christendom by the Turkic peoples became the pattern of Russia's immediate future:

> From the Malay waters to the Altai,
> Leaders from the Eastern islands
> At the walls of flagging China
> Have amassed their vast troops . . .
> O Russia! Forget your former glory:
> The two-headed eagle is smashed,
> And the shreds of your banners have been given
> To yellow children for their amusement.

Solov'ëv's vision was easily simplified into a Russian variant of the Yellow Peril myth, projecting a generic but racially colored Orient (whose threat appeared very real in the wake of the devastating Russo-Japanese War of 1905) onto an eschatological scheme that collapsed the political present of Russian imperial policy into a remote past (the Tatar yoke or the defeat of Byzantium) and an impending future (the Apocalypse). A cluster of racial pathologies, class anxieties, and archaic historical traumas were thereby interpreted as signs of the impending end of history and the possible renewal of humanity.

If what we might call "horizontal" Eurasianism – focusing on the burden of Russia's geographical liminality, the sense of being sandwiched between East and West, Asia and Europe – was a search for commonalities or analogies, the synthesis of civilizational polarities, then "vertical" Eurasianism stressed the notion of social hierarchy as racial or cultural difference. At stake was the contrast between Russia's Europeanized elite and its backward, "Asiatic," peasant masses. This conflation of race and class reflected the profound gap between the rulers and the ruled, a legacy of Peter the Great's westernizing reforms, and the lingering consequences of serfdom, no less than of Russia's eastward expansion into Central Asia and the Far East. "Asia" served as a loose, mobile and polemical toponym that could embrace anyone from the rapidly modernizing Japanese to the Central Asian subjects of the Russian empire to the restive masses of Slavic peasants and workers. With the tide of revolution rising, many Russian artists reversed the terms of vertical Eurasianism by identifying with the "Asiatic" masses. In his later celebrated poem, "The Scythians," (1918) Blok was moved to exclaim: "Yes, we are Scythians! Yes, we are Asians, / With slanted and avaricious eyes!" In the wake of the October revolution, Russians could pose as a new barbarian horde destined to shatter and revivify a bourgeois Europe in decline. Although they were by and large poorly versed in Marxism, many Russian modernists were willing to embrace the socialist internationalism of Lenin and the Bolsheviks as a revolutionary extension of the Eurasian impulse. The futurist poet Velimir Khlebnikov offered the most positive literary solution to the "horizontal" dilemma of Russia's geographical liminality and the "vertical" dimension of imperial or class oppression: Khlebnikov proposed nothing less than a new theory of time that determined the historical regularity by which empires rose and fell. Khlebnikov believed that his revolutionary epistemology, which for him reconciled poetry and science, could free the Eurasian landmass from the vicious cycles of violence that had long pitted East against West. While he was universalist in his utopian ambitions, Khlebnikov connected his project to the cause of pan-Asian liberation, which it was Russia's destiny to champion.

One could in fact trace much of the trajectory of Russian modernism, from Diaghilev's Ballets Russes to the Asiatic primitivism of the Russian avant-garde, to the program of self-orientalization alone. Andrei Belyi's masterpiece *Petersburg*, first published in book form in 1916 and easily the most significant work of prerevolutionary modernist prose, linked the Eurasian question aesthetically to symbolism and historically to the literary mythology surrounding the city of St. Petersburg. St. Petersburg had been the primary source of a fantasizing or de-realizing impulse at the heart of nineteenth-century Russian realism, dissolving the solidity of reality and questioning the very ability of language to represent and narrate the world. Belyi's novel further radicalized this impulse by marrying the incipient modernism of this Petersburg tradition to the newer poetics of symbolism. "Outside of speech," Belyi asserted in "The Magic of Words" (1909), "there is neither nature, world, nor cognizing subject. The original act of creation is given in the word." The demiurgic power to reshape Russia, once the privilege of monarchs, was now accorded to the artist.

Set during the revolutionary upsurge of 1905, *Petersburg* is a meditation on the crisis of empire viewed simultaneously from the apex of political power and from the related, but competing, perspective of the Russian literary tradition. The novel's external plot focuses on the Ableukhov household, a dysfunctional family from the tsarist elite: its Oedipal drama becomes a political thriller when the son Nikolai Apollonovich, a cerebral and amateurish radical, is instructed by an amorphous group of provocateurs to blow up his father, a senator and high-ranking bureaucrat. The confrontation between father and son, reaction and revolution, is re-enforced by the related opposition of East and West. Borrowing from Solov'ëv's eschatological schema, the narrator repeatedly predicts a new Mongol invasion, of which the assassination conspiracy would appear to be a symptom. Nikolai Apollonovich even imagines himself as "a mandarin from the Middle Empire dressed up in a frock-coat for passage to the West," his mission being to "destroy all foundations." Yet the novel is ultimately dominated by a dynamic of cultural hybridization rather than by the conflict of racial or metaphysical polarities. (As *Petersburg*'s English translators Robert Maguire and John Malmstad note, "the most useful rhetorical model for this novel is not either/or, but both/and.")[4] The Ableukhovs, we quickly learn, are all descendants of a Mongol clan that was baptised and assimilated into the Russian nobility: their mixed Eurasian heritage, like that of Russia as a whole, precludes a real clash of civilizations. This inclusive logic, however, also fails to produce a genuine reconciliation: East and West, fantasy and reason, terrorist subversion and the status quo reinforce each other in cycles of mutual contamination and inconclusive action.

Earthly aesthetes and spiritual sodomites

The successors of the symbolists both adapted and productively resisted their dogmas. The poet Innokentii Annenskii is a striking example: the most self-reflexive Russian embodiment of French decadence and the *poètes maudits*, Annenskii was little known in his lifetime but hailed posthumously by the cognoscenti as a crucial figure of transition. Annenskii acknowledged the "power of things" as a means of circumventing both the solipsism of decadence and the metaphysical certainties of high symbolism: his best poems are essentially *paysages d'âmes*, finely balanced calibrations between the pathologies of a neurasthenic heart and a world both nightmarish and shabby, humdrum yet capable even in its mundaneness of yielding enigma. A classically trained philologist, Annenskii was at the same time acutely attuned to the resonances of modernity. At its most extreme, Annenskii's verse assimilates the repetitive mechanical noises – the tick-tock and the ding-dong – that punctuate our daily routine, foregrounding the psychopathologies of everyday life. His "Sleigh Bells" (1906) blurs the distinction between human language and the jingling of bells, anticipating the futurists' "beyonsense" experiments with sound. At the same time, Annenskii remained anchored in the traditional moral and historical consciousness of the Russian intellectual. In the poem "Petersburg" (1909), he contemplates the Bronze Horseman, Falconet's celebrated equestrian statue of Peter the Great located in St. Petersburg's Senate Square and the symbol, since Pushkin, of Russia's state-sponsored modernization. "The dark-wreathed giant on the rock," the poet says of Peter's statue, "will tomorrow become the plaything of children." In predicting the end of the Romanov dynasty eight years before the tsar's abdication, the poem turns Falconet's Baroque allegory on its head. While the original statue shows Peter's horse trouncing a serpent – said to represent the tsar's external foes and internal adversaries – for Annenskii it is the snake, which the tsar "was unable to crush," that has since "become our idol." This line reflects a major intellectual event of 1909: the publication of *Landmarks*, a collection of essays by liberal political theorists and religious philosophers who rejected the populism and materialism of the left as a form of secular idolatry. Annenskii's poem, and with it much of prerevolutionary modernism, here reveals its ideological contours. By reinterpreting the snake as a figure for the oppressed masses, Annenskii acknowledges the ineluctability of revolution as well as the role of the radical intelligentsia in fomenting it. Yet the poet's own role in this history remains ambiguous, hovering between an avowed complicity in the revolutionary tradition and the acute if impotent "consciousness of an accursed mistake." What might this mistake be? Nothing less, perhaps, than the fate of St. Petersburg itself, encompassing two centuries of repressive modernization, cultural ferment, and political dissent that would end in 1918 when the Bolsheviks took Russia's capital back to Moscow.

A more visible contemporary presence than Annenskii is the poet, novelist, dramatist, diarist, and composer Mikhail Kuzmin. In linking a recognizably modernist aestheticism to the articulation of homosexuality in its erotic, affective, and spiritual dimensions, Kuzmin belongs in the company of Oscar Wilde, André Gide, and the Greek poet Constantine Cavafy. "Kuzmin came to us from the shores of the Volga," declared Osip Mandel'shtam in 1922, highlighting Kuzmin's ability to bring the traditions of the Russian hinterland into contact with Europe, "bringing with him the songs of the Russian schismatics, the Italian comedy of a homely native Rome, and the entire culture of old Europe to the extent that it had been transformed into music." Unlike his symbolist counterparts, Kuzmin wore his erudition lightly, cultivating only the aesthetic modes and symbolic forms needed for his own self-realization as an artist and seeker. From the mannered playfulness of eighteenth-century rococo, recently revived in Russia by the painter Konstantin Somov, to the syncretism of the Hellenistic and early Christian eras, Kuzmin's work reflects diverse but carefully selected models, stylized in a way that seemingly evokes cultural specificity, yet anachronistic enough to serve as a marker of artistic virtuosity rather than historical accuracy.

Kuzmin debuted almost simultaneously as a poet and a novelist. His "Alexandrian Songs," published in 1906, was popularly hailed for its freshness of theme and liberty of form. The first substantial Russian experiment in free verse, the cycle of thirty-two poems reads as if composed in ancient Alexandria, reanimating the lives and textures of the city's distant past. The "Alexandrian Songs" strike a wistfully voluptuous tone reminiscent of the Greek Anthology, markedly prosaic in their orientation toward conversational speech and everyday objects while gently probing the ultimate questions of love, time, and mortality:

> So what
> . . . If I should cease to see
> your face,
> to hear your voice?
> If all the wine is drained,
> if all the fragrances dissolve into thin air
> and the costliest fabrics
> decay
> over the centuries?
> Would I love
> these dear, fragile things any less
> for being perishable?

Delight, if properly understood, could be a path to self-knowledge. The city of Alexandria, then, represented not just a fantasy of sensuous release, but a spiritual signpost and cultural palimpsest: a repository of the classical world where philosophers had sought to reconcile various esoteric and mystical traditions before the codification of orthodox Christian doctrine.

The appearance of *Wings* (1906), surely the world's first gay coming-out novel, in the symbolist journal *Libra*, won Kuzmin even greater attention and notoriety. Neither Wilde's *The Picture of Dorian Gray* (1890) nor Gide's *L'Immoraliste* (1902) had allowed the heavily veiled sexual orientation of its protagonists to succeed in their transgressions of convention: the inscription of homosexuality into the cult of artistic beauty or sensuous immediacy propels the heroes into the blind alley of decadent subjectivity, with its furtive hedonism and transient epiphanies. The programmatically positive tone of *Wings* appears all the more remarkable by contrast. How then did Kuzmin succeed where Paris and London had failed? The publication of *Wings* was doubtless made possible by the active support of symbolist impresario Valerii Briusov, as well as by the radical loosening of ideological constraints, including censorship, in the wake of the 1905 Revolution. Male sexual activity, particularly within elite circles, was in any case not regulated with any consistency in late imperial Russia, allowing for the emergence of an urban gay subculture that mirrored the wider class inequalities of the time, extending upwards to the court intrigues of the ruling aristocracy and downwards to the paid services of bathhouse attendants. Kuzmin's novel refracted elements of this late imperial world while drawing its idealism from debates within the Russian modernist intelligentsia about the possibilities of erotic love as a vehicle for spiritual transfiguration.

In "The Meaning of Love," (1892–93) Vladimir Solov'ëv had denounced both the subordination of sexual desire to reproduction and its sublimation into a "dreamy, sterile sentimentality." The "negation of the flesh," he declared, is "false spirituality," while "true spirituality" involves "its rebirth, salvation and resurrection." In *Tolstoi and Dostoevskii* (1901) Dmitrii Merezhkovskii, too, had argued for a "holiness of the flesh" that complemented the "holiness of spirit," a "pagan or at least Old Testament holiness, not abolished but only transformed by the Son [of God]." Properly understood, Christ's act of kenosis, his voluntary acceptance of bodily suffering as the extreme consequence of incarnate life, deepened and clarified the earthly ecstasies of pagan religion, offering a new synthesis of spirit and flesh. In his important work, *The Meaning of Creativity* (1916), the philosopher Nikolai Berdiaev declared the "universal differentiation into male and female principles" to be a consequence of Adam's fall from the state of grace: "in truth not man or woman is the image and likeness of God, but the androgyne, the maiden-youth, the bisexual human in its wholeness." The era's most sustained investigation of sexuality belongs to Vasilii Rozanov, a thinker still little known outside Russia, whose ideas are inseparable from an idiosyncratic style based on aphoristic provocation and meandering digression. "Gender," Rozanov asserted in *People of the Moonlight* (1913), "trembles, oscillates, vibrates, illuminates" within a fluid spectrum of orientations that vary between and even within individuals. Assuming the procreative urge to be necessary, if not normative, Rozanov regarded homosexuality negatively, believing it to be a visceral horror of heterosexual coitus. Aligning homosexuality with monastic celibacy, Rozanov claimed to find a pervasive "spiritual sodomy" at the heart of the Christian tradition. As much an androgyne as Adam before Eve, the sodomite had a remote past but no future: he did not work for the "progress" of the human species, but heralded a "new type of history," based on "spiritual union" rather than biological continuity. While uncomfortable with same-sex desire, Rozanov acknowledged homosocial intimacy as the very basis of a "selfless" spiritual life.

Strikingly metaphysical and at a notable remove from the psychologizing vocabulary of Western sexology, Russian modernist debates on sexuality sought the transcendent truths required for the ultimate divinization of humanity, rather than the stability of existing social norms. This frequently permitted artistic creativity and interpersonal relations to be conceived in contradistinction to procreative sex and gender conventions. Although popularly misread as "pornographic," despite the absence of erotic detail, Kuzmin's *Wings* is, in this sense, quite characteristic of its time and place: a gay *Bildungsroman* that translates the young hero's nascent homosexuality into a paradigm for aesthetic and spiritual growth. A loosely autobiographical "story in three parts," the novel relates the evolution of Vania, a poor orphan from the provinces who must choose between the limited horizons of his family and the mentorship of cultivated foreigners. Structurally, the novel is little more than a series of loosely related dialogues that vacillate between banal banter and fervent affirmations of the cult of beauty. Refracted through the mind of the adolescent hero, reported speech highlights the spiritual gap between bourgeois family life and the lofty aestheticism of a mobile and cosmopolitan gay elite, even as the novel's intersecting fictional worlds confirm their shared roots in a larger context of social privilege. Aware of his modest background and stirred by still inchoate desires, Vania is ushered into an alternative world of "men, wine and light conversations," of "raptures" provoked by the "sharply etched beauty of every nation and epoch." To become a truly "modern man," the hero must learn to sprout wings and fly to the "originary homeland" first glimpsed by the Greeks, who rejected both the "vulgar lust" of heterosexual intimacy and the "intolerant monotheism" of the Jews in favor of the "true idea of beauty." Implicitly equating the patterns of aesthetic and erotic consumption available to the upper classes of Europe's *belle époque*, *Wings* interprets both according to the classical Greek model of *paideia*, which it views as superseding Judaeo-Christian morality. Not fully convincing as a *roman à thèse*, *Wings* deserves wider recognition as the first novelistic affirmation of homosexuality as a process of socialization and acculturation of which sex is a natural but not even primary component.

Mourning and memory

The search for a post-symbolist idiom that would adequately convey embodied experience took on an even more organized form with the emergence of the "acmeist" group of poets in 1912. Acmeism was a poetic revolt of aesthetic moderates, one that acknowledged symbolism to be, in the words of its key founding figure Nikolai Gumilëv, a "worthy father." The acmeists rejected the Baudelairean premise of symbolic correspondences, which they believed undermined the weight and heft of each constitutive element of the knowable world. Poetry for them was not a mystical conduit but a craft, one that coincided with the material resources of language and with the poet's conscious creative impulse.

Acmeism also signaled a shift away from the androgynous ideal of the symbolists towards a primal masculinity, an "Adamism" that celebrated a "virilely firm and clear view of things." Nikolai Gumilëv was inspired by the French Parnassian school of Théophile Gautier and José-María de Heredia to apply the ideals of chiseled craftsmanship and sculptural plasticity to a Kiplingesque representation of heroic voyages, exotic beasts, and remote landscapes. For his colleague Osip Mandel'shtam, the revolutionary epoch demanded the participation of the "man" (the Roman *vir*) no less than of the citizen: this heroic masculinity was to be complemented by the feminized realm of lamentation, prophecy and remembrance, both equally necessary for cultural continuity.

The very literary group to insist so pointedly on the masculine principle also gave Russia her most celebrated woman poet, Anna Akhmatova. Beginning with her earliest volumes, *Evening* (1912) and *Rosary Beads* (1914), Akhmatova won rapid recognition for a voice that was at once distinctively modern and distinctly feminine. Vulnerable yet unsentimental, her early lyrics convey the experience of a young woman for whom love is already loosened from the stable routine of marriage and family life. Akhmatova cannot escape the transience of intimacy, the cycle of passion and abandonment, but she transcends her subordinate role in the game of courtship by distilling and objectifying her experiences: her acquisition of a voice, her arduous dialogue with her "sister muse," ultimately lifts her above the pain of love ("To the Muse," 1911). Many of Akhmatova's poems read like abbreviated narratives, snippets of a nineteenth-century novel – replete with dialogue – transposed into verse:

> Music rang out in the garden
> With such indescribable sorrow.
> The fresh and sharp smell of the sea
> wafted from the dish of oysters on ice.
>
> He said to me: "I am a faithful friend!"
> And touched my dress.
> How unlike an embrace
> Is the feel of these hands.

> That is how cats or birds are petted,
> That is how people eye slender women on horseback . . .
> There is only laughter in his calm eyes
> Beneath the light gold of his lashes.
>
> ("Restaurant," 1913)

The sonic ambience of the restaurant, with its tipsy smalltalk and musical accompaniment, had already been popularized by Aleksandr Blok; yet for Blok the restaurant's bourgeois setting functioned only as a profane contrast to the archetypal woman, at once alluring and unreachable:

> You darted forth with the movement of a frightened bird,
> You passed by, light as my dream . . .
> And the perfume sighed, the lashes drowsed
> The silks whispered with unease.
>
> (From Blok's "In a Restaurant," 1910)

Akhmatova offers a female acmeist's revision of her male symbolist precursor. She dismisses Blok's fragmentation of the female body as dehumanizing, and restores the equilibrium between psychological projection and the external world which symbolism had distorted. The authority and dignity of her voice derive, then, not merely from her articulation of an embodied female subjectivity; her best poems anchor the poet's inner life in a concrete world of carefully observed detail:

> You cannot mistake real tenderness
> For anything else, and it is quiet.
> In vain do you carefully swathe
> My shoulders and breast in furs.
>
> ("You Cannot Mistake Real
> Tenderness," 1913)

Here a meditation on love is couched in a tactile realm of gestures, actions, and objects. The world at large is present, capable of obliquely mirroring emotional states without dissolving entirely into symbols.

Akhmatova's vision broadened with the outbreak of the First World War. Her hollowed memory, she claimed, would no longer be the receptacle of "songs and passions" but the bearer of "thunderous tidings" ("In Memory of June 19, 1914," 1916). Assuming the mantle of public mourner and doomed prophetess bestowed on her – and indeed on all women – by Mandel'shtam, the later Akhmatova would elevate feminine experience to the level of moral witness to an epoch. Arising from Akhmatova's experience as a mother driven to despair by the arrest of her son, the poem-cycle *Requiem* (composed chiefly between 1935 and 1940) identifies the poet's anguish with the fate of a nation crushed by the arbitrary terror of Stalin's regime. The poem invokes the iconic figure of the grieving Virgin Mary to sanctify the collective sorrow of Russia's wives and mothers. Still more complex is Akhmatova's crowning achievement, the triptych *Poem Without a Hero* (1940–65), a dense and ambitious settling of accounts with life, the poet's contemporaries, and the passage of time. Arguably the last great work of Russian modernism, *Poem Without a Hero* abandons Akhmatova's customary clarity for a poetic mode that partly resembles Dantesque allegory. Not only do the poem's tripartite structure and sequence of rhyming tercets loosely recall those of the *Divine Comedy*; the setting effectively plunges the reader into a modern inferno in which the life of the poet, her city, and her creative milieu become indices of the moral compass of her generation and of the fate of Russia itself. Unlike Dante's work, though, the poem deliberately obscures the details of its biographical frame of reference, upholding the modernist principle of poetic ambiguity even as it condemns the ethical failures of modernism as a lifestyle. Akhmatova evokes Petersburg's modernist bohemia on the eve of the First World War, in all its playful theatricality and libertinism, as a "hellish harlequinade" whose masked participants become emblems of the sins of Russia's *belle époque*. The central episode of the poem revolves around the suicide in 1913 of a young, handsome, and largely forgotten bisexual poet whose romantic life implicated a range of Petersburg artists and writers in a tangled web of competing intimacies. The efforts of critics to decode these historical references has led to a treatment of the poem as a kind of cryptic palimpsest: *Poem Without a Hero* has become a poem with multiple heroes – and heroines – whose prototypes critics feel called upon to decode and amass. Yet whatever the merits of this or that interpretation, the work of these critics might be seen as a predictably positivistic response to the poem's central philosophical dilemma: the ambiguous relationship between the personal, the collective, and the seemingly impersonal force of time. Unifying these dimensions is the moral drama of conscience: the poet willingly assumes the cross of her generation, making the text a personal confession that is deflected onto the poet's unidentified peers, projected outwards as a sweeping judgment upon her epoch.

Osip Mandel'shtam was the other great poet to arise from within acmeism. A telling example of acmeist poetics is his youthful lyric of 1909: "On the window pane of eternity have come to settle / my breath, my warmth. // A pattern is imprinted on it, / Unrecognizable of late. // Let the surface dregs of the moment drip away – / The beloved pattern cannot be erased." In these closing lines, which recall Shelley's *Adonais*, the distinction between eternity and the limits of mortal existence is essentially collapsed: eternity is only as durable as the poet's imprint, whose material effect is uniquely his and yet, in repeating the divine act of creation, also universal.

Mandel'shtam's first volume, *Stone* (1913), brings an organicist model of creativity into contact with the realm of architecture. In "Notre Dame" (1912), Paris's great cathedral acquires a human anatomy, "nerves," and "monstrous ribs" that are likened to Adam's. Each act of artistic creation, the poet concludes, relives the miracle of embodied form as it was first molded lovingly from inert matter. In a later poem of 1914, the poet goes so far as to declare that "Nature is just like Rome": we glimpse "images" of Rome's "civic power" in the "forum of the fields" and in the air which stretches over us like a "sky-blue circus." Here culture absorbs nature entirely, wresting its organic properties for its own monumental creations. "The word . . . is stone," Mandel'shtam had declared in his 1912 manifesto "The Morning of Acmeism": architecture was to displace the symbolist principle of musicality as the primary model for poetry. Indeed, the great edifice of culture – humanistic, classicizing, accretive, Eurocentric – sustains all of Mandel'shtam's work through a vast scaffolding of intertextual references. For example, when in "Notre Dame" he compares the cathedral to an "elemental labyrinth" and an "unfathomable forest," he is invoking a passage from Chateaubriand's *Le Génie du Christianisme* that describes the "labyrinthine forests" of Gaul as the original inspiration for Gothic architecture. Baudelaire himself had reworked and questioned this passage in his closely related sonnets, "Correspondances" (1857) and "Obsession" (1861). Thus Mandel'shtam quotes Chateaubriand in order to marshal his organicist defence of Christian faith against Baudelaire (as he had been commonly understood in Russia). If in symbolism the word had pointed beyond itself to an allegorical plane, for Mandel'shtam the word was immanently divine, generating a field of verbal reverberations that spread, like expanding ripples, into the vaster realm of world culture. Mandel'shtam saw the salvific function of Christ as inherent in the poetic word: literature, in its potentially infinite intertextual dialogue with itself and with time, is always already a spiritual activity, and the poet its supreme adept and willing martyr.

Mandel'shtam's confidence as an artist quickly outgrew the humble submission to three-dimensional reality which had been acmeism's initial premise. In his poem "The Admiralty" (1913), dedicated to the headquarters of the Russian Imperial Navy whose gilded spire and ship-like weathervane have made it a distinct Petersburg landmark, Mandel'shtam muses that "free man" had created the conditions to "deny the supremacy of space." Once the "bonds of the three dimensions have been sundered / the seas of all the world open up." Fueled by the Russian mystic Peter Ouspensky's recent discovery of the invisible "fourth dimension" of time, this ringing endorsement of Petrine-era optimism about Russia's expanding place in the world also had its darker side. For Mandel'shtam, as for much of the Russian tradition, St. Petersburg was a Janus-faced symbol: at once the glorious creation of *homo faber* and prey to the forces of dematerialization and destruction that human intervention had unleashed in a vengeful nature. After the revolution, witnessing the appalling carnage and the material collapse of everyday life unleashed by the civil war, Mandel'shtam came to see the inadequacy of the incremental model of cultural history implied by the word-as-stone. Mandel'shtam's second major manifesto "The Word and Culture" (1921) formulates a significant shift in the poet's orientation:

> A heroic era has arrived in the life of the word. The word is flesh and bread. It shares the fate of bread and flesh: suffering [. . .] Do not demand from poetry an excessive thingliness, concreteness, materiality [. . .] Above all, why identify the word with the thing, with the object it designates? Is the thing truly the master of the word? The word is Psyche. The living word does not designate the object, but freely chooses, as if for its dwelling place, this or that objective meaning, thingliness, dear body. And the word wanders freely around the thing, like the soul around its body, abandoned but not forgotten.

Mandel'shtam here blends three distinct elements – the embodied Christ, Psyche the bride of Cupid, and the semiotic distinction between the linguistic sign and the object to which it refers – into a new model of poetic creativity. Common to all three elements is a fundamental disjuncture in human experience, be it of flesh and spirit, or of word and thing. These fissures, perhaps constitutively human but understood differently at different moments in history, were related by Mandel'shtam to the Russian revolution as an unprecedented rupture in time. "Who will pick up the word and show it to time?" he asked. Mandel'shtam's brilliance as a poet lay in marshaling the resources of pagan mystery, the Christian Eucharist, as well as the linguistic volatility of modernism itself to forge a poetic response to the great upheavals of his day. This was in part a return to symbolist mythopoesis, but with a new sense of civic urgency and without the totalizing utopian vision that symbolism shared with the revolutionary avant-garde. Mandel'shtam's mature poems read like extraordinary shamanic incantations, obscurely powerful exorcisms of loss and forgetting that rank among the greatest achievements of twentieth-century poetry. Their spiritual independence from the new Soviet reality is counterbalanced by a deeper engagement with the transfiguring potency of time, the hidden correlations between past and future.

The acmeist treatment of language as memory was by no means the only response of Russian modernism to the world's first socialist revolution, in its transformative potential or in its coercive bureaucratic realization. Aleksandr Blok's long poem, *The Twelve* (1918), one of the earliest and most celebrated literary responses to the events of 1917, unequivocally rejected the old order while – somewhat ambivalently – embracing the new. A polyphonic tour de force that blends folk ditties, political slogans, and snatches of dialogue overheard on the snow-swept streets of revolutionary Petrograd, the poem depicts a group of Red Guards on patrol as an unruly force whose sense of historical purpose is difficult to distinguish from wanton lust and violence. Their destructive passion seems to be redeemed at the poem's end by the startling appearance of Jesus Christ at their helm, part victim and part leader. Soviet critics canonized *The Twelve*, along with Blok himself, as an essential bridge between two epochs. After him, the role of preserving and extending symbolist poetics into the Soviet era fell to Andrei Belyi, who published actively into the 1930s; his rhythmic prose, and his historiosophical meditations on national destiny, exerted a profound influence on early Soviet literature.

The Russian futurists, meanwhile, embraced the revolution with great enthusiasm. Their early insistence on the autonomy of language, on the "word as such," should not be misread as a desire to shield literature from politics: they merely sought to purge from language its quotidian references and established conventions. After 1917, they came to view the renewal of language as one with the goal of radical social change. For the futurist Velimir Khlebnikov, language contained the keys to time and space: its workings revealed the copresence of the remote past and the utopian future in ways that defied notions of sequential progress. In this sense, Khlebnikov is the twentieth century's great bard of what Leon Trotsky called "uneven and combined development," a condition that Trotsky believed to characterize the peripheries of global capitalism. An even better known poet, the immensely influential Vladimir Maiakovskii, ranges in his work from lamentations over urban alienation and unrequited love to agitational verse on behalf of the new Soviet state. Unquestionably sincere, he predicated his political commitment on a kind of cosmic narcissism, absorbing the collective concerns of society into the projections of an unmistakably individuated lyric voice. Maiakovskii's ability to fuse revolutionary idealism with a neo-Romantic lyric persona made him an essential point of reference for those who believed in the possibility of socialism with a human face.

Like modernisms elsewhere in Europe, Russian modernism embraced a range of stylistic and ideological possibilities, stretching from the stoic neo-traditionalism of the acmeists to the formal and political radicalism of the avant-garde. What united these competing modernist tendencies was a desire to contemplate one of the greatest ruptures in modern history through the inherent polyvalency and charismatic authority of the Russian language. The suppression and selective appropriation of the modernist legacy by the Soviet state, and its selective appropriation by Russia's postwar liberal intelligentsia, constitute one of the most poignant chapters in Russia's literary history. As more of this legacy becomes available in translation, its impact outside Russia's borders continues to grow.

NOTES

1. Virginia Woolf, "The Russian Point of View" (1925), *The Common Reader* (New York: Harcourt, 1984), p. 179.
2. Georg Lukács, *The Theory of the Novel*, trans. Anna Bostock (Cambridge, Mass.: The MIT Press, 1971), pp. 145, 152.
3. See Boris Groys, *The Total Art of Stalinism: Avant-garde, Aesthetic Dictatorship, and Beyond*, trans. Charles Rougle (Princeton University Press, 1992), pp. 18, 34, 36.
4. Robert A. Maguire and John E. Malmstad, Translators' Introduction, *Petersburg* by Andrei Belyi (Bloomington: Indiana University Press, 1978), p. xix.

FURTHER READING

Cavanagh, Clare. *Osip Mandelstam and the Creation of the Modernist Tradition.* Princeton University Press, 1995.

Clark, Katerina. *Petersburg: Crucible of Cultural Revolution.* Cambridge, Mass.: Harvard University Press, 1995.

Engelstein, Laura. *The Keys to Happiness: Sex and the Search for Modernity in Fin-de-Siècle Russia.* Ithaca, N.Y.: Cornell University Press, 1992.

Gasparov, Boris, Robert P. Hughes, and Irina Paperno, eds. *Cultural Mythologies of Russian Modernism.* Berkeley: University of California Press, 1992.

Gibian, George, and H.W. Tjalsma, eds. *Russian Modernism: Culture and the Avant-garde, 1900–1930.* Ithaca, N.Y.: Cornell University Press, 1976.

Hutchings, Stephen C. *Russian Modernism: The Transfiguration of the Everyday.* Cambridge University Press, 1997.

Kelly, Catriona, and David Shepherd, eds. *Constructing Russian Culture in the Age of Revolution: 1881–1940.* Oxford University Press, 1998.

Keys, Roger. *The Reluctant Modernist: Andrei Belyi and the Development of Russian Fiction, 1902–1914.* Oxford University Press, 1996.

Malmstad, John E., and Nikolay Bogomolov. *Mikhail Kuzmin: a Life in Art.* Cambridge Mass.: Harvard University Press, 1999.

Matich, Olga. *Erotic Utopia: The Decadent Imagination in Russia's Fin de Siècle.* Madison: University of Wisconsin Press, 2005.

Paperno, Irina, and Joan Delaney Grossman. *Creating Life: The Aesthetic Utopia of Russian Modernism.* Stanford University Press, 1994.

Pyman, Avril. *A History of Russian Symbolism.* Cambridge University Press, 1994.

Rosenthal, Bernice Glatzer, and Martha Bohachevsky-Chomiak, eds. *A Revolution of the Spirit: Crisis of Value in Russia, 1890–1924*. New York: Fordham University Press, 1990.

Rylkova, Galina. *The Archeology of Anxiety: The Russian Silver Age and Its Legacy*. Pittsburgh: University of Pittsburgh Press, 2007.

Seifrid, Thomas. *The Word Made Self: Russian Writings on Language, 1860–1930*. Ithaca, N.Y.: Cornell University Press, 2005.

PART II

"Peripheral" modernisms

8

ELLEN W. SAPEGA

Portugal

In the history of Portuguese literature and art, the term "modernism" generally refers to the production of two generations of writers and artists spanning the period 1914–40. The first generation of Portuguese modernist poets (Fernando Pessoa, Mário de Sá Carneiro, and José de Almada Negreiros) is closely tied to the short-lived literary review *Orpheu* (1915); their work evolved out of a late-symbolist aesthetic that explored intensely subjective themes in traditionally metered verse. Members of the group soon succeeded in breaking with these practices, however, and their most celebrated texts often engage with such European avant-garde movements as futurism, simultaneism, and cubism.

The second modernist generation in Portugal is associated with the magazine *Presença* (1927–40). Members of the *Presença* group (José Régio, João Gaspar Simões, Adolfo Casais Monteiro, and Miguel Torga until 1930) were the first to call attention publicly to the value and importance of the *Orpheu* generation's literary experiments; they were also the first to refer consistently to the *Orpheu* poets as "modernists," implicitly positioning themselves as that generation's literary disciples. However, while the two groups shared many formal strategies (free verse, abstract language and imagery, stream of consciousness, etc.), the work of the *presencistas* is far less experimental than that of the earlier generation, and less committed to pushing the boundaries of mimetic representation. Still, as active practitioners of literary criticism, many of the *presencistas* were responsible for bringing modernist forms and themes into the mainstream in Portugal, and for disseminating and promoting works by other European modernists.

Orpheu began and ended publication in 1915. Its two issues, appearing in March and June, launched a generation of young poets and painters that had begun to form several years earlier. A third issue, planned for September 1916, never saw the light of day, although the page proofs have been discovered, archived, and reprinted. In 1917, a single edition of a magazine, entitled *Portugal Futurista*, was published, which included the collaboration of the principal members of the *Orpheu* group; soon thereafter, several key members had died and the first, experimental, phase of the modernist project in Portugal came to a close. During the short period 1913–17, the poet Fernando Pessoa briefly theorized a series of self-styled literary currents that quickly evolved from a post-symbolist aesthetic, which he termed *paulismo* ("swampism," from the title of a poem he published in 1913), to a more openly avant-garde technique, which he gave the name "sensationism." Pessoa's enthusiasm quickly spread to other members of the group, such as Sá-Carneiro and Almada Negreiros, both of whom produced works identified as inspired by these movements. Moreover, Pessoa's experiments with sensationism were contemporaneous to the emergence in 1914 of his major heteronyms (literary alter egos with distinct writing styles and personalities).

Fernando Pessoa's literary sensationism

In an unpublished preface to an anthology of the Portuguese sensationists that he drafted in English, probably around 1916, Fernando Pessoa explained that "The Portuguese are original and interesting because, being strictly Portuguese, they are cosmopolitan and universal." Here, the poet articulates an apparent paradox that governed his creative impulses, and which would reappear under different guises in subsequent decades: by staging a national literary revival, the Portuguese modernists would fuel a spiritual revival of the cosmopolitan ethics and practices that governed the nation during the Age of Discovery. As Pessoa observed in the same preface: "An original, typically Portuguese literature cannot be Portuguese, because the typical Portuguese are never Portuguese . . . No people depersonalizes so magnificently. That weakness is its great strength . . . That indefiniteness of soul is what makes them definite."

This preface is one of many texts that Pessoa wrote around this time with a view of promoting *Orpheu* and its contributors in Portugal and abroad. In it, he begins to sketch out the historical and theoretical foundations of sensationist practice. Sensationism and its precursor, intersectionism, were Pessoa's attempts to relate Portuguese modernism to contemporary avant-garde techniques, and so to create a uniquely Portuguese avant-garde aesthetic. As Pessoa would observe in another unpublished text, this movement enjoyed certain affiliations with futurism and cubism, yet it added a novel intellectual dimension to their experimental practices:

> As to our influences from the modern movement which embraces cubism and futurism, it is rather owing to the suggestions we received from them, than to the substance of their works properly speaking.

We have intellectualized their processes. The decomposition of the model they realize (because we have been influenced, not by their literature, if they have anything resembling literature, but by their pictures), we have carried into what we believe to be the proper sphere of that decomposition – *not things, but our sensation of things.*[1]

Pessoa and his critics alike cite as the best examples of sensationist theory put into practice Álvaro de Campos's *Odes* and other long poems written in the period 1914–16. In these, the poetic voice strives to effect a decomposition of experience and being that is both spatial and temporal; his desire is, in effect, to "To feel everything in all ways."

Sensationism, as expressed by Campos and elsewhere in Pessoa's work, enabled the poet to be all things, to bring together a series of different avant-garde composition techniques, and to make sense of the heteronyms' differences and similarities. Sensationism led Pessoa to introduce a new objectivity into his poetry, albeit a fictionalized one, and to embrace a view of the present that was not predicated on a post-symbolist dream-like state. It also allowed him to give a dramatic quality to an existential topic, to realize a decomposition of the self as well as of the exterior world.

From *Orpheu* to *Portugal Futurista*

The formative years of members of the *Orpheu* generation closely correspond to the period leading up to the proclamation of the Portuguese Republic in 1910. Republican politicians championed the ideals of a secular state that was firmly grounded in nationalist symbols and sentiments. In the literary field, these ideals found a voice in the Portuguese Renaissance movement, which comprised poets and philosophers who supported the republic's political goals, and who searched in their art to express a uniquely Portuguese sentiment embodied in the term *saudade* (a sort of nostalgia comprised equally of memory and desire). Pessoa, in particular, was inspired by the tension within the *saudosistas'* works between nationalist sentiments and cosmopolitan practices, which he praised in 1912 for conveying a "transcendental pantheism." While he would soon move on to investigate new forms and subject matter, the tension to which his interpretation of *saudosismo* alluded would continue to hold as a productive contradiction, fueling much of his generation's subsequent productivity.

Events surrounding the First World War were significant in bringing the *Orpheu* group together in Lisbon in early 1915, since several key participants in the launching of *Orpheu* and *Portugal Futurista* came together in Portugal after the outbreak of the War in 1914. Pessoa and Sá-Carneiro had met several years earlier, probably in 1911 or 1912; in April 1913, Pessoa had also met the painter and poet José de Almada Negreiros, when he published a review of Almada's first solo exhibit of caricatures. Sá-Carneiro had moved to Paris in October of 1912, where he matriculated as a law student at the Sorbonne; in truth, though, he only attended classes briefly, and he spent most of his time frequenting cafés and theatres, where futurism, cubism, and other avant-garde aesthetic movements ruled the day. Sá-Carneiro's letters to Pessoa are filled with accounts of these activities, as well as descriptions and analyses of his own prose and poetry, in addition to in-depth commentaries on the articles and poems that Pessoa would send from Lisbon. Sá-Carneiro was not the only collaborator in *Orpheu* to be found in Paris at this time, moreover: the painters Amadeo de Souza Cardoso and Guilherme de Santa Rita (most often referred to as Santa Rita Pintor) were also residing in the French capital. Although Sá-Carneiro's letters record only passing references to the former, who is now considered the finest Portuguese modernist painter of the time, many comments in his letters to Pessoa mention the work of Santa Rita Pintor, as well as that of other poets, sculptors, and painters with whom Sá-Carneiro had contact.

With the outbreak of war, Sá-Carneiro was forced to leave Paris, traveling first to Barcelona, and arriving in Lisbon in early September 1914. That same year, the poet Luís de Montalvor returned from Brazil, where he had worked as a secretary in the Portuguese embassy in Rio de Janeiro. While in Rio, Montalvor, together with the Brazilian poet Ronald de Carvalho, had conceived a new literary review that would bring together poets from both sides of the Atlantic; he gave this review the name *Orpheu*. Thus, the inaugural number of *Orpheu* identified Carvalho and Montalvor as the editorial directors, and the title page of that issue promoted *Orpheu* as a trans-Atlantic enterprise. There is no indication, however, that *Orpheu* was ever distributed in Rio de Janeiro, and the three numbers of the review (two published, one projected) included works by only two Brazilian poets (Carvalho and Eduardo Guimaraens). With the publication of the second number, in June 1915, the designation "Portugal – Brazil" had disappeared from the magazine's opening page, as had the names of Montalvor and Carvalho. The directors of *Orpheu* 2 were now identified as Fernando Pessoa and Mário de Sá-Carneiro, both of whom had (to be sure) undoubtedly constituted a driving force behind the content of the previous issue as well.

With the exception of the magazine's closing text – "Triumphal Ode," signed by Pessoa's heteronym, Álvaro de Campos – most of the contributions to the inaugural issue of *Orpheu* exhibited a late symbolist aesthetic that favored highly interiorized evocations of experience, constructed with elaborate correspondences and synesthesias. Such was the case with the series of twelve poems by Sá-Carneiro dated 1913–15, and with Pessoa's "own" contribution to the issue: a "static drama" titled "The Mariner," dated October 1913. In the drama's single scene, three women, identified only as "veladoras" ("keepers of vigil"), converse during the late hours of the night. Their discourse puts a paradoxical relation of dream to reality into play: by the drama's close, the women discover themselves to be no more real than their own dream of the mariner. The compositions of both Pessoa and Sá-Carneiro, (as well as those of the other contributors) were clearly intended to emphasize the arrival of the characters or narrator at *o além* [the beyond], as well as in communicating a sense of *o vago* [the vague] and *o subtil* [the subtle], which Pessoa had grouped in 1912 alongside *o complexo* [the complex] as the "new Portuguese" poetry's defining elements. That long closing poem bearing the signature of Álvaro de Campos goes a step further still, however, for it abandons a post-symbolist fascination with the subjective world of dream imagery and exhibits a new complex objectivity that "The Mariner" had lacked. Although "Triumphal Ode" is not identified as belonging to any specific literary current, its style and content were clearly inspired by the futurist example.

The influence of avant-garde techniques would be much more in evidence in the second number of *Orpheu*, published in June 1915. There, following the collaboration of a poet (Ângelo de Lima) who had been long confined to a state mental institution, Sá-Carneiro published two poems dedicated to Santa Rita Pintor. The second of these poems, "Manicure," marks his belated attempt to effect a rupture in form, syntax, and subject matter, as the incorporation of varied typefaces, verbal montages, and onomatopoeias announce. These techniques appear somewhat forced, however. By contrast, Álvaro de Campos's magisterial "Maritime Ode," which occupies thirty-six pages of *Orpheu* 2 and which is also dedicated to Santa Rita Pintor, employs a similar method of montage to surprising effect. Aside from the work of Campos, Pessoa's "own" contribution to this issue was a series of six "intersectionist" poems titled "Slanting Rain." While significantly less daring than Campos's ode, the poems that comprise this series are noteworthy for their use of free verse and for their attempt to introduce and theorize a new equilibrium between poetic objectivity and subjectivity. Aside from all this, the second issue of the journal, unlike the inaugural number, which had no illustrations or other visual content, included reproductions of four paintings by Santa Rita Pintor.

Portugal Futurista, the final publication of the experimental phase of Portuguese modernism, appeared in November 1917, more than two years after *Orpheu* 2. *Portugal Futurista* was markedly different from *Orpheu*, both in its oversize format and in its display of manifestos and criticism along-side the poetry and prose. (In this review greater emphasis was placed on the visual, and it also contained a great many references to, and texts by, non-Portuguese writers and artists.) Clearly the organizers of *Portugal Futurista* were invested in realizing concrete social and political interventions, in addition to presenting original literary creations. After the appearance of *Orpheu*, several events staged in the public sphere generated interest and debate about their projects. In 1916, Amadeo de Souza Cardoso organized public exhibitions of his paintings in Lisbon and Oporto, introducing his cubist-inspired works to sectors of the Portuguese public that were already familiar with *Orpheu*'s literary provocations. Like Sá-Carneiro, Souza Cardoso had returned to Portugal in 1914, but rather than set up a studio in Lisbon, he had moved to his family's home in northern Portugal. Robert and Sonia Delaunay lived in nearby Vila do Conde, where they would spend two years waiting out the war. Souza Cardoso's entry into the newly formed circle of modernists, as well as his friendship with the Delaunays, afforded several young Portuguese painters, among them José de Almada Negreiros, the opportunity to exchange new ideas and to develop plans with the Delaunays for future *simultanéiste* collaborations.

Although works by Robert and Sonia Delaunay are not found in the pages of *Portugal Futurista*, the presence there of previously unpublished poems by Apollinaire and Blaise Cendrars must be ascribed to their influence. Other works the review published in the original French include Saint-Point's "Futurist Manifesto of Lust" and the "Manifesto of Futurist Painters." Additionally, a version of Marinetti's "Music Hall" appeared in Portuguese. The original programmatic texts signed by Portuguese modernists that the review printed include a manifesto in support of the *Ballets Russes*, by Almada Negreiros, Ruy Coelho, and José Pacheko, and a copy of a "Futurist Ultimatum to the Portuguese of the Twentieth Century," which Almada had presented in Lisbon in April of that year. Both Santa Rita and Amadeo included reproductions of several of their paintings, and an "Ultimatum" by Álvaro de Campos appeared in its pages. In the event, the police immediately seized the magazine upon publication, most likely in response to alleged obscenities in Almada's novella, *Saltimbancos*, or to the virulent language of Campos's "Ultimatum" (which opens with multiple insults directed at European statesmen and artists, followed by the observation, "SHIT!!").

Not every text in *Portugal Futurista* exhibits the avant-garde's anarchic qualities, however. Poems that both Pessoa and Sá-Carneiro had contributed continued to evidence the hermetic subjectivism typical of post-symbolism. Sadly, the review had to publish posthumously its selection of Sá-Carneiro's poems, dated "Paris – November 1915," for their author had committed suicide in Paris the previous year. In this respect and others, *Portugal Futurista* signals the end of the short-lived enthusiasm of the *Orpheu* group for avant-garde experimentation, and of its publicly proclaimed desire to shake up a nation that Almada had described in his "Ultimatum" as "sleeping since the time of Camões." Both Souza Cardoso and Santa Rita Pintor would die the following year. By 1918, the original group of Portuguese modernists was reduced to just a handful of members; of these, Fernando Pessoa and José de Almada Negreiros stand out for their continued efforts to build upon *Orpheu*'s promise of literary and artistic renewal. During the 1920s, the two would collaborate in a series of publications dedicated to promoting modernist arts and letters.

Fernando Pessoa's heteronyms

In 1928, in a Bibliographical Chart that he sent to the editors of *Presença*, Fernando Pessoa coined a phrase that has since become a much-quoted description of the heteronymic process: "It is a drama divided into people instead of acts." As part of this explanation, Pessoa called attention to the existence of his literary alter egos as distinct entities or personalities, which made them, he took care to note, quite unlike pseudonyms. In several posthumously published fragments, he likened his relationship with the heteronyms, and their relationships with one another, to that of characters in a drama; in other pieces, he stressed that their ideas, feelings, and writing styles were very different from his own: "Each of these authors is not just conceived differently but created as a wholly different entity. That's why poetry predominates here. In prose it is harder to other oneself." The act of the poet working to "other himself" is a key concept in understanding the tension between absence and presence that constitutes the structuring paradox of Pessoa's aesthetics of depersonalization: "The human author of these books has no personality of his own. Whenever he feels a personality well up inside, he quickly realizes that this new being, though similar, is distinct from him." Besides publishing the work of his three principal heteronyms (and one "semi-heteronym") in a variety of literary journals between 1913 and 1935, Pessoa also published a good deal of poetry signed with his own name. The author referred to the work that bears the signature "Fernando Pessoa, himself" as belonging to the "orthonym." Yet since it presents a distinct poetic voice, or rather a variety of voices writing in both Portuguese and English, critics agree that the orthonym's writing is no more subjectively "sincere" than that of the other heteronyms.

Fernando Pessoa constructed fairly elaborate biographies for his best-known and most fully developed heteronyms, Alberto Caeiro, Ricardo Reis, and Álvaro de Campos. These biographies were most likely constructed after the early poems of each imaginary author had been written. In both his published and his unpublished descriptions of their work and their lives, Pessoa unfailingly refers to Caeiro as the "Master," whose poetry of the senses influenced his disciples to cultivate their own sensationist aesthetic. According to Pessoa's many notes on him, Caeiro was a simple, uneducated man who spent most of his life in the country. In his poetry, Caeiro eschews rhyme, meter, and figurative language in an effort to capture the "real" without the intrusion of consciousness or thought. His emphasis on experiencing the world through his senses (particularly through sight) allegedly taught the other heteronyms, and even Pessoa himself, to break free of symbolist excesses and explore the possibilities that their master's pagan materialism presented.

In an oft-cited letter that Pessoa wrote in January 1935, some ten months before his death, he described the first appearance of Caeiro, on March 8, 1914, as the "triumphal day" of his life. First he recalls that, having already in 1912 experimented with and abandoned the idea of writing poetry from a pagan perspective, he decided in 1914 to "invent" a bucolic poet as part of joke on Sá-Carneiro. Pessoa then explains that, several days after having given up on attempts to envision this poet, he "walked over to a chest of drawers, took a sheet of paper and began to write standing up . . . " He then notes that "I wrote thirty-some poems at once, in a kind of ecstasy I'm unable to describe . . . I began with a title, *The Keeper of Sheep*. This was followed by the appearance in me of someone whom I instantly named Alberto Caeiro. Excuse the absurdity of this statement: my master had appeared in me."[2] Upon completing this sequence of poems, Pessoa writes that he immediately grabbed a sheet of paper and wrote "Slanting Rain," in what to him seemed to constitute "the reaction of Fernando Pessoa against his nonexistence as Alberto Caeiro."[3] Recent studies of the manuscript of *The Keeper of Sheep* have cast doubt on Pessoa's account of this day, and another manuscript provides a slightly different date for Caeiro's arrival; nonetheless, it seems fair to assume that Caeiro's appearance did occur in early 1914, since evidence shows that some twenty-five of his poems were written in March of that year.

Any appraisal of Pessoa's commentaries on the heteronyms must take into account their author's often playful tendency to construct elaborate fictions; as he said, "The poet is a faker." Yet while Pessoa may have fabricated several of the details of the letter on Caeiro and other documents describing the appearance of the heteronyms in order better to serve the rules of his "fiction," there is no doubt that the poetry of Caeiro preceded the poetry of Reis and Campos. By the summer of 1914, Pessoa was feverishly at work writing in the name of all three. The following year, in the pages of *Orpheu*, Pessoa would begin publication of such mature works signed under his own name as "Slanting Rain" and "The Mariner." There, he also introduced the reading public to the first ambitious compositions of his most modern and experimental heteronym, Álvaro de Campos, a naval engineer who had studied in Scotland and traveled to the Far East.

According to the aforementioned letter, Pessoa's other principal heteronym, Ricardo Reis, was the first of Caeiro's disciples, having appeared to the poet shortly before Campos: "From Caeiro's false paganism I extracted the latent Ricardo Reis, at last discovering his name and adjusting him to his true self, for now I actually *saw* him. And then a new individual, quite the opposite of Reis suddenly and impetuously came to me." Pessoa did not begin to publish Reis's poetry until several years later; Reis's first public appearance was in the pages of the review *Athena*, which Pessoa co-edited in 1924–25. Given the strictly metered neo-Classical style that characterizes Reis's *Odes*, it is not surprising that Pessoa chose not to include Reis's work in *Orpheu* or *Portugal Futurista*. Reis was a self-styled (so to speak) neo-pagan whose poems lay claim to life's transitory character and to the fleeting passage of time; there was little room for his perspective in such unabashedly avant-garde publications. It may well be for similar reasons of incompatibility that Caeiro likewise had to wait to be introduced to the reading public in the pages of *Athena* in 1925.

Besides poetry, Reis and Campos were also identified as the authors of many essays, some of which remained unpublished during Pessoa's lifetime. Pessoa did publish a number of Campos's essays and shorter prose pieces; Campos also sent several letters under his name to Portuguese newspapers and staged other political interventions. At various points, Pessoa made plans to publish their works in a series of volumes, but these plans had not been fulfilled at the time of his death. In addition, starting in 1913, Pessoa published selections from a projected volume of prose fragments, entitled the *The Book of Disquiet*. He returned to this volume in 1929 after having set it aside for more than a decade, and worked on it assiduously until his death in 1935. In all, only twelve passages from *The Book of Disquiet* saw their way into print during Pessoa's lifetime, but scholars have identified more than five hundred more as belonging to this project, whose nominal author was the semiheteronym Bernardo Soares (Pessoa explained, "He is a semiheteronym because his personality, although not my own, doesn't differ from my own but is a mere mutilation of it. He's me without my logical reasoning and emotion").

In addition to Soares and the three heteronyms proper, much of whose work was published during his life time, Pessoa also created more than fifty other literary alter egos, several of whom wrote in English or French. In fact, most scholars agree that his first fully fledged alter ego was Alexander Search, the nominal author of some early poems, short stories, and essays that Pessoa wrote in English. Search first appeared to Pessoa either in Durban, South Africa, where Pessoa lived with his mother and stepfather between 1896 and 1905, or shortly after Pessoa's definitive return to Lisbon. Like many other facets of the poet's work, the existence of Search and other literary personae only came to light several decades after Pessoa's death, when scholars began to assess the vast number of unpublished papers that he left behind in a chest. Assessments of Pessoa's papers continue to the present day.

From *Orpheu* to *Presença*

While the poets and artists of *Orpheu* were products of the secular Republic, which championed values that were notably liberal for the time, many of them eventually became disillusioned with republican values and practices. In response to the social chaos of the First World War and its aftermath, they began to sympathize with conservative political causes. The initial enthusiasm of the first modernist generation for futurism and other avant-garde practices served to deflect an uneasy preoccupation with the past that had marked Portuguese intellectual and artistic production since the rise of Romanticism in the mid-nineteenth century. Many artists of the *Orpheu* generation, haunted by the glories of the Age of Discovery, and forced to inhabit a present day when Portugal's place among the modern nations of Europe was perceived as diminished, embraced an avant-garde aesthetic of rupture in the quest to renew or revive a lost cultural vibrancy. A pre-occupation with an impoverished present is evident in Sá-Carneiro's poetry, in Almada's novellas and manifestos, and in much of Álvaro de Campos's sensationist poetry; and it is most apparent in Fernando Pessoa's *Message* (1934), the only volume of poetry that the creator of the heteronyms published during his lifetime.

Message, in its evocation of figures and events from the national past and in its nod to Luís de Camões's sixteenth-century epic, *The Lusiads*, is a work that exhibits an ambitious and idiosyncratic search for a myth for modernity that is typical of high modernism. Consisting of forty-four poems divided into three parts, the work may be approached both as a single long poem and as a collection of short lyric compositions, organized around the central metaphor of the Portuguese "Fifth Empire" (which legend says will be inaugurated upon the return of the "lost" King Sebastian). While the poem is based on historical events and makes use of a messianic discourse with a long tradition in Portugal, the esoteric imagery and symbolism in *Message* is nonetheless highly personal in its vision of an apocalyptic yet redemptive future. In many respects, *Message* fulfills the desire, which Pessoa had articulated as early as 1912, to remake the national poetic tradition, bringing history to bear on his understanding of modern life and incarnating what he described as the definite indefiniteness of the national soul.

Since its publication, *Message* has been interpreted in a variety of ways. It appeared in print one year after the proclamation of António de Oliveira Salazar's authoritarian New State, and several early interpretations approached the poem as an exemplar of the regime's conservative, nationalist stance. Much of Pessoa's writing only received wide distribution beginning in the 1940s, when members of the *Presença* generation launched the publication of his *Complete Works*, in addition to the poems and novellas of Sá-Carneiro. This fact compounded the partial or equivocal interpretations of their works, and explains their reduced influence on other writers in Portugal until the 1950s.

While the *presencistas* played a crucial role in disseminating the works of Pessoa and his contemporaries, their critical and literary stance, based as it was on a premise of artistic "sincerity," was in many respects at odds with the early modernists' culture of experimentation, which posited the absolute indeterminacy of the individual subject. For this reason, some critics have labeled them modernist "counter-revolutionaries." A fairer assessment of the relationship between these two generations may lie in an understanding of late modernism's uneasy relationship to it avant-garde predecessors. The years of *Presença*'s publication coincide with the end of the First Republic and with the consolidation of the structures of Salazar's "New State." It is quite possible that many of the practices that writers of this generation championed – among them the independence of art from politics and the firm commitment to individual liberties – resulted from their initial hesitancy to ally themselves with either the Right or the Left. Although the *Presença* generation was constituted of writers whose work is less radical and transformative than that of their predecessors, they deserve credit for diffusing and elaborating the modernist canon and for continuing the early modernists' project of altering existing conventions, albeit in a careful and gradual manner.

NOTES

1. Fernando Pessoa, *Obra poética e em prosa*, vol. III, ed. António Quadros (Porto: Lello & Irmäo, 1986), p. 193.

2. From *Three Letters to Adolfo Casais Monteiro*, in *The Selected Prose of Fernando Pessoa*, ed. and trans. R. Zenith (New York: Grove Press, 2001), p. 256.

3. Excerpt of an unfinished and unpublished "preface" to what would have appeared as the first volume of his complete heteronymic works, cited in Pessoa, *Selected Prose*, ed. Zenith, p. 256.

FURTHER READING

Jackson, K. David. *Adverse Genres in Fernando Pessoa*. Oxford University Press, 2010.

Klobucka, Anna, and Mark Sabine. *Embodying Pessoa: Corporeality, Gender, Sexuality*. University of Toronto Press, 2007.

Monteiro, George, ed. *The Man Who Never Was: Essays on Fernando Pessoa*. Providence: Gávea-Brown, 1982.

Pessoa, Fernando. *A Little Larger Than the Entire Universe: Selected Poems*. Trans. Richard Zenith. London: Penguin, 2006.

The Selected Prose of Fernando Pessoa. Ed. and trans. Richard Zenith. New York: Grove Press, 2001.

Pizarro, Jerónimo, and Steffen Dix, eds. The Future of the Arcas. A special issue of *Portuguese Studies* 24.2 (2008).

Portuguese Modernisms: Multiple Perspectives on Literature and the Visual Arts. London: Legenda, 2011.

Sadlier, Darlene J. *An Introduction to Fernando Pessoa: Modernism and the Paradoxes of Authorship*. Gainesville: University Press of Florida, 1998.

Santos, Maria Irene Ramalho Sousa. *Atlantic Poets: Fernando Pessoa's Turn in Anglo-American Modernism*. Hanover, N.H.: University Press of New England, 2003.

Serra, João B., Schirn Kunsthalle Frankfurt, and Centro Cultural de Belém. *Modern Art in Portugal 1910–1940: The Artist Contemporaries of Fernando Pessoa*. Kilchberg/Zürich: Edition Stemmle, 1998.

9

C. CHRISTOPHER SOUFAS, JR.

Spain

That Spanish literature of the early twentieth century should be considered an integral part of the wider phenomenon of European modernism is a position that Spanish criticism has begun to embrace only in the last ten to fifteen years. There are many reasons for this reluctance to organize within a modernist paradigm what is generally regarded as the most important moment of Spanish literary production since the "Golden Age" of the sixteenth and seventeenth centuries – called by some a "Silver Age." Before entering into a discussion of Spain's contributions to a trans-European, indeed, global phenomenon, it will be instructive to examine briefly some of the factors within Spanish criticism that have slowed the more widespread acknowledgment of the existence of a full-fledged Spanish participation in modernism. A principal factor is the continuing tendency in continental critical circles to draw a rather sharp distinction between the notion of a progressive historical "avant-garde" and a somewhat negative and limited view of a reactionary "modernism." In this view, modernism is a rightist phenomenon whose products originate in an alienated, private, withdrawn perspective inimical to the avant-garde's more public goals and its institutional criticism of bourgeois art.[1] It is ironic that this and similar positions have emerged on the continent at precisely the moment when the concept of modernism begins to be applied to a much greater circle of literary production, one that today includes nearly all of Europe, the United States, and much of the Third World, a prominent part of which is Latin America. Just where Spanish peninsular writing fits into this larger scheme has remained a topic that Spanish criticism has been reluctant to explore.

Another significant factor for this hesitation rests within Spanish criticism itself, in the aftermath of the tragedy of the Spanish Civil War (1936–39) and the accompanying diaspora of many of its greatest modernist talents to the Americas and elsewhere. The response of Spanish criticism to the challenge of Francisco Franco's authoritarian regime, which ruled Spain from 1939 to

1975, was to retreat into a nation-centered critical paradigm that strongly reflected the extreme nationalism and isolationism of the Spanish government in the early postwar decades. There was a decidedly conservative turn in Spanish criticism during the 1940s, 1950s, and early 1960s, also largely upheld in Spanish critical circles outside of Spain, which prominently include the United States and Great Britain. The vehicle for this policy became the "literary-generation" approach to Spanish literary history. Immediately before the Spanish Civil War, there had been an attempt by Pedro Salinas to propose a generational model, patterned after the ultra-nationalistic tenets of German literary historiographer Julius Petersen.[2] Salinas strongly associated the writers identified by the press and other popular venues as the "Generation of 1898" – a group allegedly concerned with the spiritual and cultural malaise of the country after the disastrous war with the United States – with the dubious tenets that Petersen had advanced: these included difficult-to-establish notions of a generational literary language (which Salinas associated with the *modernismo* that the ex-patriot Nicaraguan poet Rubén Darío advocated, which had resonances in Spain, but was more akin to symbolism than what today is associated with modernism) and a desire for disciplined generational leadership (an "apetencia del caudillo" ["longing for the Führer"], which Salinas associates with attitudes fostered by Friedrich Nietzsche).[3] The Petersen position, which to Salinas in 1935 exemplified the most enlightened European literary criticism of the day, actually reflects many of the biases of the popular hysteria sweeping the German nation along with the ascent of Nazism during the late 1920s and early 1930s. The seminal document of postwar Spanish literary criticism, therefore, owes much to extreme positions from the outset. In the immediate aftermath of the Second World War, Salinas's approach became the basis for literary approaches to Spanish contemporary literature, as Pedro Laín-Entralgo and Dámaso Alonso strongly endorsed his position.[4] Hence by the end of the first postwar decade, the "literary generation" became, with almost no critical debate or discussion, the sole model for Spanish literary history.

According to the Petersen–Salinas model, literary generations appear at approximately fifteen-year intervals, and this largely coincides with their appearance in Spanish criticism. The first of these is the "Generation of 1898," a group of writers who started their careers in the immediate aftermath of the 1898 Spanish–American War. For the most part, these are novelists and/or essayists: Pío Baroja, Miguel de Unamuno, José Martínez Ruíz (better known by his pen name, "Azorín"), Ramón María del Valle-Inclán, and the poet Antonio Machado. A second generation, far less well-defined, is the "Generation of 1914," in which some have grouped together the philosopher and critic José Ortega y Gasset, the poet Juan Ramón Jiménez, and others. (It must be noted that these writers, although they are somewhat younger, were also often considered part of the "Generation of 1898," at least at the outset of this critical movement.) The next major generation that follows, the "Generation of 1927," is comprised primarily of poets, and includes Jorge Guillén, Pedro Salinas (these first two occasionally seen as somewhat apart from the other, younger poets), Federico García Lorca, Luis Cernuda, Rafael Alberti, Vicente Aleixandre, Gerardo Diego, Manuel Altolaguirre, and, retrospectively, the novelist Rosa Chacel. The fact that Chacel is the only woman writer of this entire period to be considered as belonging to a literary generation, and this some fifty years after the fact, points out only one of the glaring weaknesses of such a classification system. That these literary generations have proven to be little more than gentlemen's clubs is a defect that pales in comparison with the strong nationalistic bias inherent in the concept itself. In practical terms, the literary generation stops at the Spanish border. Most of these writers and poets have been associated, to one degree or another, with "Spanishness." Be it Unamuno's obsession with the character Don Quijote or Lorca's alleged sympathy for Spanish gypsies, the operating assumption underlying the Spanish literary generation is that it exists to emphasize specifically Spanish themes, and thus that such writing is fundamentally separate from developments elsewhere on the continent.

What emerges, therefore, is a rather limited choice between two fundamentally opposite tendencies within the literature of this period. Invariably, "tradition" – that is, themes and styles appropriate for expressions of specifically national concerns, such as the Spanish temperament, national or spiritual values, and even picturesqueness – is placed in opposition to peripheral, momentary forays into an avant-garde "adventure." According to this line, certain writers, mostly the poets identified with the "Generation of 1927," exhibit temporary divergences from the principal content of their (for the most part quite traditional) work, in order to try their hands at styles and techniques identified as imported.[5] Thus, for example, works such as Alberti's *Sobre los ángeles* [Concerning the Angels], and Aleixandre's *La destrucción o el amor* [Destruction or Love] reflect exceptions to the main line, rather than a full-fledged allegiance to a more continental mode of literary production. Since Spanish literary critics have not yet fully embraced the concept of a multi-faceted international literary and artistic modernist movement in which Spain is an integral part, what has often emerged in their work is a bifurcated approach to much of the writing during this period that often understands Spanish writers, and especially the poets of "1927," as "entre la tradición y la vanguardia" [between tradition and the avant-garde].

This is hardly satisfactory, given that other national literary traditions have embraced far more strongly the notion of an ideologically and stylistically diverse modernism. Literary innovation thus seems inimical to a mode of production strongly rooted in the Spanish tradition – a view that additionally makes the more experimental works of Spanish writers seem to be rather pale imitations, and thus foreign to traditional forms of national expression. Thus, the absence of a third term, like "modernism," has produced a rather skewed picture of the originality of Spanish writing of this period, one that historically has downplayed severely the European-ness of writers who for well over half a century have been made to fit within a strongly nationalistic generational framework.

The reluctance to embrace the period concept is especially puzzling in light of parallel developments in the visual arts. The great Spanish masters in painting – Diego Velázquez and Francisco de Goya – have routinely been studied as examples of the most startling modernity, to say nothing of the great modernist painters, such as Pablo Picasso, Juan Gris, and Salvador Dalí. Thus during the later decades of the twentieth century, Spanish painting was described as innovative, avant-garde, cosmopolitan, but Spanish writing as considered conservative, traditionalist, and nationalistic. It is more productive to suggest that Spanish literature, while somewhat more conservative in outlook than its literary counterparts in other parts of Europe, engages dialectically throughout the modern era with continental issues, sometimes resisting more liberal positions, yet nevertheless involving itself fully in continental discourse. This is especially evident in relation to what is arguably the fundamental theme of European modernity: the emergence of a "new man," and the accompanying political and economic order which nurtures him, beginning in the Renaissance and continuing until modernism. Indeed, it is possible to understand the various periods of European literature from 1500–1900 in terms of the evolutions and challenges this "new man" faced. Yet Spanish writers were often uncomfortable with this position, at least as it was symbolized in the Cartesian *cogito* and its historical successors. It is thus arguable to look upon Spanish attitudes at the outset of modernism in terms of a continuation of Spain's longstanding skepticism regarding autonomous subjectivity, while the rising critique of this paradigm in the rest of Europe, which ushered in modernism, began in earnest for the first time only during the late nineteenth century. The questioning, on the part of modernists, of the assumptions of European modernity and the middle-class instrumental consciousness, thus signals a *rapprochement* between the Spanish position of skepticism and much more recent European critiques. This is why such a seemingly un-modern nation such as Spain (a nation in much the same position, in this respect, as Joyce's Ireland) might be regarded as having actually led the charge that reflected a sea change in European attitudes toward subjectivity.

Charting Spanish modernism

When Virginia Woolf made her famous declaration suggesting that a new historical moment had begun, "On or about December 1910 human character changed," what she was actually acknowledging was that there now existed a critical mass of awareness that the conventional models by which the human constitution was approached and judged no longer sufficed – that modernism, as a style, is also an ideology that expresses itself prominently at the level of subjectivity. In other words, there was now a "newer" new man, requiring different approaches to account for his constitution. This was arguably the fundamental position of European modernism.

During the early contemporary period in Spain, there was likewise an intensification of competing views regarding new subject positions, more extreme models that ran counter to the constitution (which had come to seem quite shallow) of middle-class man. What Spanish modernists explored were alternate subject positions that, while corresponding more fully to emerging views of the world, also shared much with earlier models.[6] The first of these models may be called the "structural subject," influenced by Darwinian theories of evolution, and even more by the de-centered, structural model of human consciousness that Freud proposed, against which the now-superseded "autonomous thinking" model seems simplistic, to say the least. The other tendency, which also departed significantly from bourgeois norms, may be understood in relation to the "doctrines of will" that Kant had initially advanced, which intensified in the force-driven doctrines of Schopenhauer and Nietzsche. (This doctrine, which actually caricatures the conventional model of autonomous subjectivity, had in Spain long been associated with monstrosity.) One need only recall Goya's famous maxim (pronounced more than a hundred years before Woolf) in *Los caprichos*, "El sueño de la razón produce monstruos" (best translated in a double sense, "The sleep [but also the dream] of reason produces monsters"), to understand where the European disillusionment with rationalist Enlightenment values truly begins.[7]

These perceived, and postulated, changes in human character that emerge during modernism express themselves in Spanish literature as well, across the spectrum of literary genres. Astradur Eysteinsson has proposed that there is a fundamental aesthetic principle underlying most, if not all, modernist literary production: the interruption – present in larger or smaller degrees, yet identifiable in all literary genres – of the conventions of realism.[8] What this suggests is that the most typical modernist text features a rather hybrid situation that dramatizes two distinct competing perspectives: one embodying a conventional realist model grounded in the techniques of representation and dedicated to the elucidation of a parallel, autonomously functioning fictional reality; the other revealing a more unconventional dimension of what amounts to a fuller, more complex idea of what constitutes reality. In other words, modernist texts typically allude to a second reality.

The modernist strategy is to offer an alternative to "mere" representation, thus making the implied goal of such interruptions the elucidation of a more direct and, indeed, superior idea of reality. If realism's aesthetic mission centers on techniques of representation, then the modernist alternative is, in some small or large way, an overturning of such conventions in favor of an ever-elusive condition of presence. The modernist literary mode thus dramatizes writers' dissatisfaction with a realist model that has become a hindrance to what it truly means to be in the world. To one degree or another, modernist literary expression is invariably portraying a situation in which an alternate reality is aggressively seeking to supplant the conventional realist position. At its most basic level, this struggle to bring forth a different view of human subjectivity may be characterized in terms of a meta-literary style that dramatizes these competing views of reality. In other words, all modernist literature is, in some respect, meta-literary.[9]

Modernist novelistic expression certainly adopts such a posture via modifications, or outright attacks, on realism–naturalism. Even stronger positions are to be found in modernist poetic expression, often expressed in compositions of great visual expressiveness. There, poetic language becomes more difficult to understand in relation to the conventional world. In many instances, conventional symbols point to unusual referents, often seeming to function as hieroglyphs. In effect, the reader is sometimes forced to master a new mode of reading, which is not unlike formulating his own individual "Rosetta stone" in order to make sense of these texts. The themes of these types of works tend to focus directly upon modes of being that conventional representation is ill-equipped to convey. The displacement of the empirical world, of course, seeks to transcend representation altogether. That such a state is a practical impossibility does not thwart more radical practitioners from attempting it – especially practitioners of Surrealism, specifically in their early "automatic writing" techniques, in which the goal is to make unmediated contact with the surreal, the site of the fullest possibilities of being. Thus, modernists investigate the full breadth of semiotic possibility: the three positions outlined here roughly correspond to the tripartite sign system of Charles Sanders Peirce – symbol, icon, index – which describes situations that extend from the fully conventional to the fully referential.[10]

The Spanish modernist novel

The most notable Spanish contributions to the European modernist novel strongly emphasize the emergence, evolution, and consolidation of new subject positions heralded by Woolf's declaration of a changed human character, the "new European modernist man," whose attitudes toward existence and ideology turn sharply away from the rapidly deteriorating influence of middle-class models understood as stifling. Pío Baroja's *El árbol de la ciencia* [The Tree of Knowledge] (1911) marks perhaps the most expansive reflection on what this new modernist version of "human character" begins to look like, in the figure of his overly intellectualized, neurotic misfit protagonist, Andrés Hurtado. Hurtado's last name in Spanish can mean both "wounded" and "hidden" (from the past participle of the verb *hurtar*), which suggests the negative course that the life of this oversensitive young medical student (and eventually doctor) will take. Andrés Hurtado begins a search for the formula of life that is for him, although elusive, both intellectually and emotionally satisfying. Yet his highly active intellect, which analyzes everything it comes across, leaves him progressively unable to cope with the everyday world, which proves more complex and powerful than his capacity to contain it. There can be little doubt that Baroja conceives of his novel as something of a parody of French naturalism, as practiced by Emile Zola and the Goncourt brothers.[11] In effect, he portrays a situation in which the premises of the naturalist novel – objective, detached, clinical observation as the basis for the diagnosis of society's ills – succeed in achieving an effect opposite to the goal. The analytical observer struggles and drowns in a harsh, violent, grotesque social reality, unequipped to handle the real world by virtue of his obsessive effort to achieve the objective position he needs for a quite different type of understanding. Objective observation is discredited and shown to be a dangerous illusion.

Baroja's novel also becomes, in some respects, a vehicle for philosophizing, via extended dialogues between Andrés and his sometime mentor and uncle, Iturrioz, whom many commentators have taken as a stand-in for Baroja himself. At the heart of these discussions is a harsh view of the plight of the toiling classes, yet at a philosophical remove. What fascinates Iturrioz is not so much that the poor remain that way because of the oppressiveness of the conditions in which they live, but that in addition the poor rationalize their plight in a type of perverse philosophy, in which the gulf between the haves and have-nots is exacerbated by a mentality of oppression. This is forcefully conveyed in the character la Venancia's "extraña filosofía" ("strange philosophy"), which wholeheartedly maintains that the poor and the rich deserve their poverty or wealth (what Iturrioz conceptualizes as "the spirit of the poor" and "the spirit of the rich"), making the "survival of the fittest" as much an epistemological as a social phenomenon. Similarly, in parallel to the way an inhospitable reality constantly assaults the protagonist's sensibilities, Baroja's narrator continually interrupts the narrative by inserting personal commentary, and often invective, as it relates to Spanish society. The effect is to tell the reader what to think, rather than show this via a less subjective narrative style: the reader thus experiences something similar to Hurtado's progressive passivity, finding it difficult to participate in the narration actively. The effect is a narrative position that deconstructs the realist–naturalist position of omniscience as well as the reader's confidence in such a perspective. Bereft of a basis from which to act, Hurtado retreats to an ever-diminishing circle of possibilities which eventually leave him no room. His suicide at the novel's conclusion signals the victory of the outside world of nature over his capacity to resist it within his fevered consciousness. The novel's concluding sentence, that Andrés was "algo de precursor" ("something of a precursor"), offers a final, succinct commentary for the reader as to what has just taken place. Andrés is, indeed, a "new man," one whose appearance on the scene offers eloquent testimony about a significant change in "human character."

A more overt meta-fictional posture is evident in Miguel de Unamuno's *Niebla* [Mist] (1914). The protagonist, Augusto Pérez, outwardly shares little in common with Baroja's Hurtado. Yet the pampered *señorito* does share Andrés's penchant for over-intellectualization, obsessing about nearly everything, no matter how insignificant. As Augusto understands from the outset: "Los hombres no sucumbimos a las grandes penas ni a las grandes alegrías, y es porque [...] vienen embozadas en una inmensa niebla de pequeños incidentes. Y la vida es esto, la niebla" ("Men don't succumb to the great sorrows or joys; it's because [...] they come hidden in an immense mist-filled cloud of insignificant incidents. And this is what life is, mist"). Indeed, the novel itself is of the same consistency. There is no identifiable setting; description has been almost entirely eliminated; and the reader knows the characters only by what they say. To avoid monologues, a dog, Orfeo, is introduced, so that Augusto can have someone to talk to while he is alone. Another of the characters, the aspiring writer Victor Goti, who also pens a pseudo-prologue for the book, calls this new form a *nivola* and claims it as his own invention – a boast with which Unamuno, in a post-prologue, strongly begs to differ. Indeed, the presence of Unamuno is always near. When in the opening chapters Augusto falls in love (stereotypically, melodramatically, desperately) with a piano teacher who does not return the sentiment, this minimal storyline, which will constitute the novel's main plot, is first and foremost a pretext for Unamuno to present his ideas about the inefficacy of all intellectual positions. As Goti reveals in the prologue, speaking for Unamuno: "Si ha habido quien se ha burlado de Dios, ¿por qué no hemos de burlarnos de la Razón, de la Ciencia y hasta de la Verdad? Y si nos han arrebatado nuestra más cara y más íntima esperanza vital, ¿por qué no hemos de confundirlo todo para matar el tiempo y la eternidad y para vengarnos?" ("If someone has mocked God, then why not mock Reason, Science, and Truth? If they have stolen our most precious and intimate vital hope, why not confuse it all in order to kill time and eternity and take our vengeance?"). The hope that has been stolen was our belief in immortality: the hope that our consciousness, our personal *cogito*, could persist somehow. The intellectual–philosophical positions of the rationalist–empiricist tradition have undermined everything: thinking calls into question existence itself. Augusto Pérez updates Descartes: *Cogito ergo non sum*. Reason cannot affirm existence. What is left is anger and the desire to take vengeance upon the very systems which have led to an intellectual dead end. Unamuno's own desperation leads him to adopt a "confusionist" perspective, intending not merely to associate or mix concepts, but thoroughly to confuse any sense of separation among them. At least, he argues, this "mist-ifying" reflects the truer reality of the world, of the consistency of mist.

Meanwhile, Augusto takes his humiliating rejection by his beloved – she leaves him for an old flame – as proof of his non-existence. Resolving to commit suicide, he goes to speak with no less than Unamuno himself, and in the ensuing discussion, the positions get reversed. Exasperated, the author-figure Unamuno decides to kill off this character with the flick of a pen, prompting Augusto to want desperately to continue living. Hence the issue of human freedom lies at the heart of this work. Stylistically, this novel represents the maximum expression of Spanish meta-fiction, since the author is not only a character in his own novel, but is, in actual fact, the only character. Nevertheless, Augusto calls strongly into question the author's authority to decide his characters' fates. The novel thus becomes, as well, the scene of Unamuno's own impotence to act authoritatively.

A decade later, the authors Ramón María del Valle-Inclán and Ramón Gómez de la Serna advanced the Spanish modernist novel further, along a slightly more experimental course. Valle-Inclán's novel, *Tirano Banderas* [Tyrant Banderas] (1926), which deals with an uprising against the dictator of an imaginary South American country, offers a panoramic glimpse of a country whose values have been shaped by Spain and Europe as much as by its own anti-democratic traditions. In other words, Latin America is a place where the shortcomings of Spanish culture can be seen more clearly, and more grotesquely, than a direct investigation of the woes of the

Spanish peninsula would afford. Valle-Inclán's method is to focus on individual characters, standing largely in isolation from their wider milieu, in order to point out their failings. By doing so, he slows the action, such as it is, to a virtual standstill. The inclusion of vocabulary taken from every corner of the Hispanic world assists him in this strategy by showing the extent to which Hispanic culture has remained a deforming mirror of the mother country. It has the further effect of making the reader's movement through the text quite difficult. These constant verbal interruptions, as well as a complicated arrangement of the text into smaller subdivided units, combine to enhance the view of the immobility of this culture and society. The insurrection that eventually overthrows Banderas changes nothing. Revolution becomes the occasion to communicate a grotesque vision of a culture at a standstill.

Gómez de la Serna's *El novelista* [The Novelist] (1924) examines the expansive oeuvre of the artist figure Andrés Castilla, which is communicated via excerpts of novels in progress, which Castilla often writes from different locales and according to different temporal modes and schedules. These are presented patchworked together, in order to offer views about a wide variety of subjects, and also to emphasize that a novelist's work is necessarily a product in process at all times. The themes in these extended snippets range from tales of conjoined twins, to folding screens, to a street light, and even to an aborted attempt at narrating exactly what one sees in a busy city street, a seemingly endless gamut of subjects from which to construct novels. The reader is bombarded by theories of novel-writing and a myriad of other subjects, which, although seemingly unconnected, eventually weave a thematically related pattern.

In a more experimental vein is Rosa Chacel's short masterpiece, *Estación: Ida y vuelta* [Station: Round Trip] (1930). Ostensibly a narrative about two university students, called simply "él" (he) and "ella" (she), who become a couple in the springtime of their lives, the main plot proves to be a pretext around which the novelist can reflect about what is ultimately involved in bringing a new type of novel into life and form. As Chacel works out her ideas on novel writing and the most effective relationships between narrator and characters, the narrator changes from a masculine to a feminine voice. (Also in this avant-garde vein are contributions by Benjamín Jarnés and Enrique Jardiel Poncela.) It is necessary also to mention the thought-provoking and entertaining works of Ramón Pérez de Ayala, especially his short novel *Prometeo* [Prometheus], part of *Tres novelas poemáticas* [Three Poematic Novels] (1916), and his masterpiece, *Belarmino y Apolonio* (1921), in which the author's perspectival techniques achieve their most mature expression. Also noteworthy in the context of modernism is his 1926 two-volume work,

El tigre Juan [Tiger Juan] and *El curandero de su honra* [The Healer of his Honor].

Spanish modernist poetry

Although the Spanish novel certainly makes important contributions to European modernism, it is in Spanish modernist poetry that the most significant advances become evident. Yet poetry is also where the absence of a strong concept of "Spanish modernism" in the contemporary critical idiom is most keenly felt.[12] While there is recognition that much of this poetry is innovative, it continues to be cast in terms of a choice between "tradition" and a vaguely defined "avant-garde." The absence of the third term of "modernism" thus skews the critical picture; and the result is unfortunate for the study of the Spanish contributions that, to my view, represent some of the greatest achievements in European poetry of the first half of the twentieth century. Even though masterful poets such as Antonio Machado and Juan Ramón Jiménez display many of the stylistic and thematic traits that came to characterize modernist poetry in Spain, it is more correct to consider them precursors, rather than partners, in the move toward high modernism. Both Machado and Jiménez express strong interest in paralleling the physical locales of their poetry with inner existential states or longings: for Machado, the Castilian landscape in all its desolate emptiness (especially *Campos de Castilla* [Castilian Fields] (1917)); for Jiménez, often picturesque gardens and other refined settings. For Machado, the mood is often a sense of loss or existential absence in the face of the sublime yet desolate grandeur of his encounters with natural landscapes; Jiménez is more interested in the sense of existential fullness that he often intuits in his observations. Both Machado and Jiménez adopt more philosophical attitudes in their poetry as they move into their later years, setting the tone for a fuller exploration of these themes of fullness and absence in the brilliant array of poets that follow.

These poets, who wrote during the 1920s and 1930s a good deal of the poetry upon which their standing today largely rests, have been grouped together as the "Generation of 1927." (The year marks the tercentenary of the death of classical poet Luis de Góngora, whose exceedingly difficult, almost Latinate verses had won the admiration of many in this group.) More than the influence of Góngora, however, what seems to characterize this group is an intensification of the existential concerns that had characterized much of Machado's and Jiménez's verses. For the purposes of this rather brief sketch, the major poets of Spanish modernism may be grouped in two broad thematic clusters: those for whom the prospect of existential fullness or presence is a real possibility, and those for whom it is not.[13] Although there are significant stylistic disparities among these poets, the existential question remains a principal feature they share in common. Although there are a number of modernist poets who deserve prominent mention – such as Juan Larrea, Manuel Altolaguirre, Dámaso Alonso, and Gerardo Diego – I will emphasize two clusters of three poets each, characterized by their approach to the issue of existence-being. The first tendency, those for whom the fullness of being is knowable, summonable, and expressable in verse, is exemplified by Jorge Guillén, Pedro Salinas, and Vicente Aleixandre. These poets operate in a private realm in which they find themselves at the center of an aggressive struggle to achieve existential fullness or presence. The second sub-group is comprised of Luis Cernuda, Federico García Lorca, and Rafael Alberti: for them, the phenomenon of the fullness of being is never a real possibility. Unlike with their colleagues, in these poets the movement is away from private vision and toward much more public postures.

Jorge Guillén's sole work during the height of modernism is *Cántico* [Canticle] (1928), which underwent numerous re-editions as Guillén added poems over the course of more than thirty years. Of interest to students of modernism is the second, 1936 edition of only 125 poems. Despite a sustained, and often prodigious, production of poems after *Cántico*, which were brought together in a four-volume tome under the general title *Aire Nuestro* [Our Air], Guillén's standing as a poet is still largely tied to the second edition of *Cántico*, for it is here that the distinctiveness and originality of his poetry shines forth. Guillén has explicitly linked his poetry during this time with imagism, and this is certainly evident in his preference for the short poem, many of these in a modern version of the classic *décima* (one stanza of ten verses). The poet's song in *Cántico* is nearly always occasioned when the poet senses an intimate correspondence between consciousness and poetic landscape, which he is able to transform into an opportunity to celebrate the plenitude of being. Typical of many of Guillén's poems is an intellectual aggressiveness that seizes upon the poetic landscape as a pretext for a fuller elucidation of an existential state, which always seems poised to affirm its presence. (This seizure he likens in "Las alamedas" [The Poplar Grove] to "profundizando paisajes" [making the landscapes more profound].) External reality – in whatever form it comes: landscape, physical object, occasionally the human form – serves as the passive raw material that an active, aggressive consciousness can re-mold in the image (often fractured and abstract) of the inner state of being. The true protagonist of the typical Guillén poem of this period is the intellectual will, whose constant goal is to give form to the inscape of consciousness.

A similar phenomenon takes place in the poetry of Pedro Salinas, yet in terms of an extended process rather than a specific moment. In its most mature expression, this quest to affirm the fullness of being becomes an extended meditation on Salinas's somewhat unorthodox understanding of love. In *La voz a ti debida* [Voice Owed to You] (1933) and *Razón de amor* [Love's Justification] (1936), this meditation is narrated exclusively from the point of view of the poet, while the amorous other is relegated to invisibility and silence. Such a posture has not stood up as well to the passage of time, probably owing to the subject-centered nature of the amorous meditation. The goal, nevertheless, is much the same as Guillén's: the expression of the plenitude of being. As an intellectual exercise, moreover, these poems provide eloquent testimony to the meditative mode in Spanish poetic modernism.

Although Vicente Aleixandre's poetry, which was awarded the Nobel Prize for Literature in 1977, has been associated strongly with surrealism, his work is perhaps better likened to the highly intellectualized production of Salinas and Guillén, in the sense that it is also dedicated to the aggressive affirmation of the fullness of being. Expressing that struggle by often highly irrational means, Aleixandre plunges into the depths of his psyche, eventually to emerge triumphant. Like Salinas, Aleixandre addresses a shadowy female presence, who is clearly understood as a conduit, rather than as the end, to his ultimate goal. This exploration takes place over three volumes, and, although Aleixandre, like Guillén, wrote a considerable amount of poetry throughout his life, it is upon three volumes, *Pasión de la tierra* [Earth's Passion] (1929, but not published until 1935), *Espadas como labios* [Swords like Lips] (1931), and *La destrucción o el amor* [Destruction or Love] (1933), that his enduring legacy lies. These volumes chronicle the poet's experience of finding himself at a low point and his eventual recovery. Beset with the awareness that his human form has lost its consistency in *Pasión de la tierra*, a state of affairs that is also reflected in the fact that poetic verses are here expressed in prose, this and the succeeding volumes recount the re-emergence of the poet's intellectual will to refashion himself, and thus eventually, after much personal exploration and protracted struggle, to be able to proclaim the fullness of his experience of existence. These volumes are certainly among the most hermetic and challenging of the period. In fact, Aleixandre's language reflects a situation in which the poetic voice is just as confused as the bewildered reader, who must struggle to find new referents for words in an irrational context. The process toward fuller understanding progresses in much the same way as an archeologist would if confronted with a hieroglyphic inscription for which the code has not been discovered. Indeed, this highly visual poetry requires that the reader re-orient herself in order to discover the means to penetrate an alternative world in which conventional logic does not suffice. Yet as the poet exerts his intellectual will, the deciphering does proceed to the point where it becomes clear that a continuing existential narrative has unfolded, and that a full measure of understanding can be achieved. These volumes are tantamount to an extended process of self-fashioning, eventually allowing the poet to celebrate the experience of the full presence of being.

On the other side of the issue of existence is a group of poets – Lorca, Cernuda, Alberti – for whom the prospects of existential fullness are quite distant. Lorca's poetry can profitably be read as a record of progressive absence from the fullness of being, if indeed such a state is even possible.[14] Lorca's fundamentally tragic view of existence appears early on in his poetry, but it reaches perhaps its most expressive moments in two volumes that seem, on the surface, quite different: *Romancero gitano* [Gypsy Ballads] (1927) and *Poeta en Nueva York* [Poet in New York] (written during his extended visit to the United States during 1929–30 but unpublished during his lifetime). Although the publication of *Romancero gitano* won the approval of a larger portion of the general public than it had among his colleagues (this popular success occasioned the estrangement of his best friends, Salvador Dalí and Luis Buñuel, who criticized the work as a sell-out to popular taste), this volume, along with the explicitly tormented poems of *Poeta en Nueva York* that followed, traces the theme of desire misdirected beyond personal control. (This lies in sharp contrast to Guillén, Salinas, and Aleixandre, for whom the intellectual will is a principal aspect of their production.) While Lorca's gypsy characters enact scenes of frustration, violence, sexuality (real and imagined), sterility, and discord, these same forces visit their wrath on a spiritually wounded and confused poet-protagonist against the backdrop of the modern metropolis. Lorca's personal laments over a sexual orientation that runs against the expectations of conventional society becomes self-hatred in the "Oda a Walt Whitman" [Ode to Walt Whitman]. Lorca portrays Whitman as a post-sexual being, someone whose comradely ideals are compromised by the throngs of those engaging in homosexual practices, against whom the poet lashes out. As Lorca departs the metropolis, these unresolved issues accompany him and find strong resonance in his theater, discussed below.

Although he shares a similar outlook to Lorca – namely, that the poet is unequal to the task of having to confront forces that alienate him from the promise of his early youth – Luis Cernuda traces in his poetry a different kind of narrative: a hybrid autobiographical–mythical format, from his nostalgia and bitterness at being separated from his early dreams to his eventual emergence as a mature adult who discovers that his life's work is that of poet. Cernuda's poetry is organized around a multi-sectioned volume, *La realidad y el deseo* [Reality and Desire], to which he progressively added sections throughout his life. Of significant interest concerning modernism is the 1936 first edition, which recounts the trajectory from his earliest conscious thoughts to the crisis of youth to, finally, his recovery, when he acknowledges openly his homosexuality and embraces his life's vocation as a poet (that is, a modernist poet). Cernuda chronicles perhaps better than anyone the struggles of the modern artist, who is marked by impotence and bitterness yet also occupies a privileged status when all is said and done. Cernuda is one of the few poets whose later work – written in exile from Spain, to which he never returned after the civil war – compares favorably with his early poetry. His exemplary dedication to the vocation of poet has won him a growing popularity that ranks him among twentieth-century Spain's most admired poets.

Rafael Alberti's poetry is similar to Cernuda's in that his early poetry, filled with nostalgia for his early youth, cedes to estrangement and eventually full-blown crisis, from which he discovers his mature voice and a more public posture, especially political activism. Following his emergence on the scene with his first major work, *Marinero en tierra* [Sailor on Land] (1924), came volumes which document his frustrated estrangement – from *El alba del alhelí* [Dawn of Desire] (1926) to *Cal y canto* [Resistance] (1927) – culminating in his masterpiece, *Sobre los ángeles* [Concerning the Angels] (1928). Of particular note is a strong element of self-criticism, which culminates in *Sermones y moradas* [Sermons and Dwelling Places] (1930), and which provides a bridge to the politically motivated poetry collected in *Poeta en la calle* [Street Poet] (1936).

Modernist reform of the Spanish stage

Turning finally to Spanish modernist theater, two primary figures, Valle-Inclán and Lorca, stand out in the movement toward significant theater reform in the wake of the urgent awareness of crisis that followed the malaise of traditional theater during the early decades of the century. Perhaps the greatest innovation of the modernist stage was the emergence of strong stage directors, many of whom accompanied their innovative theater practices with theories of performance. Fresh ideas about acting and new schemes for staging found resonance in Spain somewhat later than in other parts of Europe. Yet with a growing wave of innovative talents, the Spanish stage made great strides during the years leading up to the Spanish Civil War. A certain dissatisfaction with the mass appeal of dramatists such as Jacinto Benavente and Eduardo Marquina led to growing concerns about the governance of theater companies (which were typically under the command of a lead actor), and also about unsatisfactory stage discipline, owing to the absence of professional stage directors. Although there were noteworthy efforts, on the part of innovative impresarios like Gregorio Martínez Sierra, a few stage professionals like Cipriano Rivas Cherif, and a scattering of the more serious acting companies, to reclaim the stage for more disciplined performances, the clumsy, outdated practice of having the theater producer stage the performance dragged on for some time, eventually bringing about a strong call for stage professionalism. This was especially important in the dramatic evolution of Lorca (see, for example, his "Charla sobre teatro" [Theater Chat]).

The most innovative modernist theater is clearly attributable to Lorca and Valle-Inclán, as well as to Rafael Alberti. Although a good bit of the Valle-Inclanesque stage belongs to an earlier moment, this dramatist's deforming, dehumanized theater of the grotesque, which he labeled the *esperpento* [grotesque], certainly participates in a modernist theater aesthetic. Along with the early *Luces de Bohemia* [Bohemian Lights], of note is the trilogy grouped together under the title *Martes de Carnaval* [Fat Tuesday], which features *Las galas del difunto* [The Dead Man's Fancy Clothes], *La hija del capitán* [The Captain's Daughter], *Los cuernos de don Friolera* [Don Friolera's Horns], a satirical spoof on classical Spanish theater (and the only play in this group to be staged during Valle's lifetime). Also of interest are Rafael Alberti's theater experiments, which feature an interesting allegorical drama patterned loosely after the Spanish *auto sacramental* [mystery play], *El hombre deshabitado* [The Vacant Man].

Without doubt, however, the most important dramatist of Spanish modernism is Federico García Lorca.[15] Lorca's mature theatrical work began in earnest during his stay in New York, where he wrote his two most experimental works, *El público* [The Public] and *Así que pasen cinco años* [As Soon as Five Years Pass]. *El público*, which has what may be a dreamscape setting, features a stage director who attempts to present Shakespeare's *Romeo and Juliet* as it was originally staged, with Juliet played by a young man. The ensuing complications allow for wide discussions about the limits of what theater can represent while still attracting the audience it needs; events reveal as well the Director's ambivalence about his homosexuality. Though *El público* itself was impossible to stage at the time, Lorca continually referred to this play in interviews during the 1930s. The issues that this work raises would strongly influence his commercial theater, notably his plays *Bodas de sangre* [Blood Wedding], *Yerma*, and *La casa de Bernarda Alba* [The House of Bernarda Alba], the last of which was finished shortly before Lorca's assassination in the early days of the Spanish Civil War.

The fateful year 1936 also witnessed the deaths of Valle-Inclán and Unamuno. The latter exited the public stage with a last spectacle: the now-legendary shouting match with a Francoist general at a public talk at the University of Salamanca, where he was rector. The general shouted his party's battle cry to the assembled audience: "Viva la muerte" [Long live death]. Unamuno replied, risking execution, "Viva la inteligencia" [Long live intelligence]. Succumbing to illness shortly after the incident, this corrosive critic of all doctrines of rationalism had made what proved to be his last stand in defense of those very ideals.

The younger modernists were forced to live at great distances from the nation in which they found their inspiration. The harsh tenor of the ensuing military dictatorship of General Franco dispersed nearly completely the brilliant flowering of literary modernism to far-flung corners of the globe. Only Aleixandre, whom Cernuda would later criticize as the "poeta en residencia" [poet in residence], remained in Spain. Whereas the great modernist painters, Picasso and Dalí, had long established themselves in Paris, their literary contemporaries fared much worse. Alberti settled in Argentina and later Rome, returning to Spain only after the death of Franco. Cernuda never returned to Spain, beginning his exile in England and eventually moving to Mexico. Guillén and Salinas resided in the United States, becoming literature professors at Wellesley and Johns Hopkins, respectively. Thus Lorca's brutal execution was but the most egregious of the terrible consequences of the fratricidal conflict that foreshadowed the coming of the Second World War. Only after Franco's death and the return of democracy to Spain did the true impact of these writers' legacies become fully evident.

By way of conclusion, it is necessary to mention the related phenomenon of modernism in the region of Catalonia and its capital, Barcelona.[16] Toward the end of the nineteenth century, a growing resurgence of interest in the Catalan language (notably Pompeu Fabra's language reforms to standardize grammar and spelling) and Catalan culture (at the vanguard of which was the group that published the journal *L'Avenç* [Forward]), invigorated a nascent Catalan nationalism. Two cultural events of great importance, the Barcelona World's Fair of 1888 (Exposició Universal) and the Modernist Festival (Festa Modernista) of 1893, in which many of Catalonia's most prominent cultural figures participated, marked the emergence of what is most frequently referred to today as Catalonian modernism, which is not so much a strictly literary movement as an interrelated phenomenon that diverges into many areas of cultural and political life. These initial forays into cultural reinvigoration mark the emergence of Barcelona as an equal to Madrid. A slightly later and more organized cultural movement, designated by the term *Noucentisme* (which might correspond to a Catalan version of "higher" modernism), emerged around 1906, with the formation of the Unified Catalan Front (Solidaritat Catalana), and remained prominent until the dictatorship of General Primo de Rivera in 1923.[17] Yet what differentiated developments in Catalonia from modernist developments in Castile was the far greater collaboration in Catalonia among artists, civic figures, and politicians. Their overriding goal was the promotion of all aspects of a renaissance for the entire region. Instrumental in the modernist effort to forge Catalan into a cosmopolitan literary language, in sharp contrast to its traditional role as a rural dialect, were the labors of Joan Maragall, perhaps best exemplified in the essay *Elogi de la paraula* [Praise for the Word] (1903), as well as the works of Eugeni D'Ors (*La ben plantada* [The Elegant Lady] 1906), Narcis Oller, Raimon Casellas (*Els sots ferèstecs* [Feral Hollows] 1901), Caterina Albert, who used the pen name Victor Català (*Solitud* [Solitude] 1905), and Josep Pous i Pagès (*La vida i la mort d'en Jordi Fraginals* [Life and Death of Jordi Fraginals] 1912).

The rivalry between Madrid and Barcelona continues in the present day, a state of affairs that is symbolized in grand fashion for the Catalonians in Antoni Gaudí's modernist masterpiece, the Temple Expiatori de la Sagrada Familia [Expiatory Temple of the Holy Family]. This work's ongoing construction, now nearing completion, stands as the greatest monument to the modern rebirth of Catalan art and culture.

NOTES

1. This is the now largely discredited view of Peter Bürger, *The Theory of the Avant-Garde*, trans. Michael Shaw (Minneapolis: University of Minnesota Press, 1984).
2. Julius Petersen, "Die literarischen Generationen," in *Philosophie der Literaturwissenschaft* (Berlin: Junker and Dünnhaupt, 1930), pp. 130–87, translated into Spanish as "Las generaciones literarias," *Filosofía de la ciencia literaria* (Mexico City: Fondo de Cultura Económica, 1946), pp. 137–93.
3. Pedro Salinas, "El concepto de 'generación literaria' aplicado a la del 98," *Literatura Española: Siglo XX* (Mexico City: Séneca, 1941), pp. 43–58.
4. Pedro Laín-Entralgo, *Las generaciones en la historia* (Madrid: Instituto de Estudios Políticos, 1945); Dámaso Alonso, "Una generación poéetica (1920–36)," *Obras completas*, vol. IV (Madrid: Gredos, 1975), pp. 755–76.
5. Andrew P. Debicki, *Spanish Poetry of the Twentieth Century: Modernity and Beyond* (Lexington: University Press of Kentucky, 1994).
6. C. Christopher Soufas, *The Subject in Question: Early Contemporary Spanish Literature and Modernism* (Washington, D.C.: The Catholic University of America Press, 2007), pp. 51–84.
7. C. Christopher Soufas, "'Esto si que es leer': Learning to Read Goya's *Los Caprichos*," *Word & Image* 2 (1986): 311–30.
8. Astradur Eysteinsson, *The Concept of Modernism* (Ithaca, N.Y.: Cornell University Press, 1990), pp. 143–78.
9. *Ibid.*, pp. 202–03.

10. Charles Sanders Peirce, "The Icon, Index, and Symbol," in *Collected Papers*, ed. Charles Hartshorne and Paul Weiss (Cambridge, Mass.: Harvard University Press, 1931–58), vol. II, pp. 274–307.
11. Soufas, *The Subject in Question*, pp. 89–91.
12. Soufas, *Conflict of Light and Wind: The Spanish "Generation of 1927" and the Ideology of Poetic Form* (Middletown, Conn.: Wesleyan University Press, 1989), pp. 25–31.
13. *Ibid.*, pp. 240–44.
14. Soufas, "Lorca y la ausencia existencial," *Estudios sobre la poesía de Federico García Lorca*, ed. Luis Fernández-Cifuentes (Madrid: Istmo, 2005), pp. 227–62.
15. For perhaps the best discussion of Lorca's' theater, see Luis Fernández-Cifuentes, *García Lorca en el teatro: la norma y la diferencia* (Zaragoza: Prensas Universitarias de Zaragoza, 1986).
16. Brad Epps, "Modernism in Catalonia," *Modernism*, 2 vols., ed. Astradur Eysteinsson and Vivian Liska (Amsterdam: John Benjamins, 2007), vol. II, pp. 781–800.
17. Joan Ramón Resisna, "Noucentismo," *The Cambridge History of Spanish Literature*, ed. David T. Gies (Cambridge University Press, 2004), p. 532.

FURTHER READING

Bretz, Mary Lee. *Encounters Across Borders: The Changing Visions of Spanish Modernism*. Lewisburg, Penn.: Bucknell University Press, 2001.
Epps, Brad. "Modernism in Catalonia." *Modernism*. Vol. II. Ed. Astradur Eysteinsson and Vivian Liska. Amsterdam: John Benjamins, 2007, pp. 781–800.
Geist, Antony L., and José B. Monleón, eds. *Modernism and its Margins: Reinscribing Cultural Modernity for Spain and Latin America*. New York: Garland, 1999.
Harris, Derek, ed. *The Spanish Avant-Garde*. Manchester: Manchester University Press, 1995.
Kirkpatrick, Susan. *Mujer, modernismo y vanguardia en España (1898–1931)*. Madrid: Cátedra, 2003.
Orringer, Nelson, ed. *Hispanic Modernisms*, special issue of *Bulletin of Spanish Studies* 79 (2002).
Robinson, William H., Jordi Falgas, and Carmen Bellon Lord. *Barcelona and Modernity: Picasso, Miró, Gaudí, Dalí*. New Haven, Conn.: Yale University Press, 2006.
Soufas, C. Christopher. "Approaching Spanish Modernism: Tradition and the 'New Man.'" *Modernism*. Vol. II. Ed. Astradur Eysteinsson and Vivian Liska. Amsterdam: John Benjamins, 2007, pp. 931–45.
Audience and Authority in the Modernist Theater of Federico García Lorca. Tuscaloosa: University of Alabama Press, 1996.
Conflict of Light and Wind: The Spanish "Generation of 1927" and the Ideology of Poetic Form. Middletown, Conn.: Wesleyan University Press, 1989.
The Subject in Question: Early Contemporary Spanish Literature and Modernism. Washington, D.C.: The Catholic University of America Press, 2007.

10

MEGAN QUIGLEY

Ireland

1922 – that great year of literary modernism with the publications of both *The Waste Land* and *Ulysses* – was also the year of the formation of the Irish Free State and the beginning of the Irish Civil War. This historical coincidence reveals the intertwined nature of Irish politics and anything we might call Irish modernism. From the political reasons behind Lady Augusta Gregory's and W. B. Yeats's founding of the Irish Literary Theater in 1899 – "We will show that Ireland is not the home of buffoonery"[1] – to the explosion of fervent unionist, nationalist, revisionist, and feminist responses in the Irish press to the 1996 *Field Day Anthology of Irish Writing*, literary events spanning twentieth-century Ireland are deeply imbricated in the political strife of a divided nation. And yet for a long time the most canonical Irish modernists – Yeats, Joyce, and Beckett – were often plucked from the Irish context, denuded (as much as possible) from purely Irish concerns, and heralded as cosmopolitan modernists free from any kind of Irish national interest or bias. As Joyce himself lamented: "condemned to express themselves in a language not their own, [the Irish] have stamped on it the mark of their own genius and compete for glory with the civilized nations. This is then called English literature."[2]

This chapter will lay out several thematic consistencies among twentieth-century Irish writers by connecting the self-evidently cosmopolitan Irish modernists – James Joyce, Elizabeth Bowen, and Samuel Beckett – to the Irish writers a generation before them, particularly Bram Stoker, Oscar Wilde, George Bernard Shaw, W. B. Yeats, and Lady Gregory. In doing so, it will also make a claim for the modernist tendencies of some of the other major figures of the Celtic Revival, including John Millington Synge and Elizabeth and Lily Yeats at the Cuala Press. Conventional accounts read Stoker, Wilde, and Shaw as barely meriting an Irish label, while the provincialism of the Irish Literary Revivalists, led by Yeats and Lady Gregory, forced the later cosmopolitan modernists to flee Ireland. In this modernist story, the Celtic Revival is expelled as the ugly stepsister, a late-Romantic creation by

Anglo-Irish Ascendency figures whose fixation on a rural past compounded the Irish modernists' need to flee a fictionalized Emerald Isle. To be modern is to leave Ireland and Irish things behind: a modernity epitomized in the multilingual *Finnegans Wake* and the Francophile Samuel Beckett. Simultaneously, nothing is more modern than the Irish condition because in their state of alienation, emigration, and internationalism, Irish writers incarnate the globalism of modernity. Yeats, however, has always disturbed this literary story, troubling the clear-cut antipathy between the Revivalists and modernists by his firm placement in – indeed, arguably leadership of – both camps.

In more recent years, post-colonial approaches to Irish literature, following the lead set by Edward Said and Seamus Deane, have worked to debunk the high modernist cosmopolitan myth. The particularities of the colonial Irish experience gave many works by Irish writers a modernist flair long before the conventional early twentieth-century demarcation of literary modernism. If modernism is characterized by a sense of exile joined with experimental technique, complete with self-conscious linguistic experimentation and a fiery anger against the status quo in sexual, political, and religious matters, many Irish writers neatly fill that bill. More specifically, key modernist obsessions – the splintering of the exiled subject, a focus on primitivism and myths, and a fascination with the idea of translation – were running themes throughout the writing that we could call Irish modernism, whether it was written in Dublin, Belfast, London, Trieste, or Paris. "Irish modernism" simultaneously adds to our concept of international modernism, confirming that many modernists were thoroughly enmeshed in national politics, and that ideological investments often underscored the apparent apolitical nature of *difficult* modernist art.

Although post-colonial approaches help to underscore the connections between twentieth-century Irish literature and the modernist movement, an important debate in contemporary Irish literary studies focuses on whether Ireland merits "post-colonial" status. Was Belfast a colonized locality akin to New Delhi or Lagos, or was it, as Joyce claimed, the "second" capital of the British Empire? Edna Longley has suggested (perhaps with tongue in cheek) that adopting the term "post-Ukanian" in reference to the Irish Free State would help to keep the specificities of the Irish colonial experience distinct from those of India or Africa.[3] Not all of Ireland, of course, is post-Ukanian; Northern Ireland rejoined Great Britain, forming the United Kingdom, two days after the declaration of the Free State in 1922. Indeed both the borders (what constitutes Ireland?) and the citizenship (who counts as "Irish"?) are violently contested. Ireland also has a long history of failed attempts of rebellion against British rule, from the "Flight of the Earls" in 1607, when the Gaelic Aristocrats fled to Catholic Europe, to the United Irish Rebellion of 1798, to the failed Easter Uprising in 1916. Under English rule, the Anglo-Irish landowners, known as the Protestant Ascendency, held political and economic power. Many of Ireland's most illustrious writers, from Swift to Yeats, stemmed from this seat of power, though the Ascendency constituted a small minority of the population. Religious and economic suppression of the rural Irish Catholic majority; the devastation of the Great Famine (1845–48) and the resulting huge waves of emigration; a violent civil war (from 1922–23); and the aftermath of partition, including the religious violence in Northern Ireland known as "the Troubles," make modern Irish history particularly divisive and violent. These historical dynamics make taking a post-colonial approach to Irish literature necessary. That said, they must always be carefully weighed against other historical factors, such as women's movements or Ireland's intimate relationship with Catholic Europe, which stretch beyond any simple Ireland / England, colonized / colonizer binary. Indeed, a simplistic post-colonial approach to Irish literature tends to reduce the complexities of Irish writing into too confining a mold. Contemporary approaches to Irish writing seek to balance post-colonial theory with a more nuanced emphasis on each Irish writer's aesthetics, influences, political commitments, and social identities.[4]

Irish history is also well suited to Marxist theories connecting literary modernism to the impact of capitalism. Joe Cleary's "Toward a Materialist-Formalist History of Twentieth-Century Irish Literature" builds on Fredric Jameson's and Perry Anderson's theories of "uneven" development to argue that Ireland's unique history made it fertile ground for breeding the canonical figures of Irish modernist literature. Modernism, according to Anderson, required in Western Europe three historical and cultural circumstances: a holdover of formal academicism and high culture from the fading aristocratic classes, new emerging technologies with the Industrial Revolution, and a sense of the imagined proximity of social revolutions. Cleary notes that in many ways Ireland's history accords perfectly with Anderson's categories. The Anglo-Irish aristocracy, in whose hands much of the production of cultural capital lay, correctly sensed the changing tides and the growing political power of the often Catholic lower classes. The aristocratic hierarchy in Ireland and its ensuing anxieties are depicted in the Irish Big House genre (portrayed in works stretching from Maria Edgeworth's *Castle Rackrent* [1800] to Bowen's *Bowen's Court* [1942]). The coexistence of old ways of life with new technologies and industries is revealed in the contrast between the largely rural and agricultural landmass of Ireland with Belfast's industrial strength. Finally, the decimation that the Great Famine caused to traditional modes of existence, leaving one million people dead and two million lost to emigration, and consequently the creation of a "global Irish populace," created exactly the sense of the "clash between old and new" that underscores much modernist aesthetics.[5]

Intriguingly, such Marxist approaches to Irish literature have often emphasized the resounding conservatism of anything called "Irish modernism."[6] Indeed, most of the canonized modernist Irish writers – Joyce and Flann O'Brien being the great exceptions – stemmed from Protestant middle- or upper-class society, and have been seen as speaking for a marginalized elite minority. For certain aspects of Yeatsian thought, for example *On the Boiler*, the conservatism is clearly true, and modernism and conservatism are not antithetical, as Marinetti, Eliot, or Pound demonstrate. However, Wilde's dandy, Joyce's Bloom, and Beckett's *Watt* undermine conservative conventions and traditions, while the modernism of the Celtic Revival collapsed the clear-cut division between "tradition" and "novel" in Irish literary history. Moreover, much of the writing deemed Irish modernism, from both sides of the political divide, formally depicts what Astradur Eysteinsson denotes a modernist "aesthetics of interruption,"[7] registering the conflicts at the heart of this divided society.

Finally, it is important to emphasize that in some ways this chapter might be working at cross-purposes with others in this volume in stressing this "Irish" modernism rather than the cosmopolitan flair of these Irish writers. To a certain extent this works to correct a historical error: Yeats, Joyce, and Beckett are too easily treated as purely international figures, with nothing in common with figures like Douglas Hyde or even Lady Gregory. Moreover, Irish literary history undermines the Irish nationalist / cosmopolitan binary – history may be a nightmare from which Stephen Dedalus is trying to awake, but Irish history, in its complex colonial past, is inevitably cosmopolitan.

Stage Irishmen: Shaw, Wilde, and Stoker

"England is the land of intellectual fogs but you have done much to clear the air: we are both Celtic, and I like to think that we are friends."

(Wilde to Shaw[8])

"The blood is the life! The blood is the life!"
(Stoker, *Dracula*)

In "On the Study of Celtic Literature" (1867), Matthew Arnold outlines the qualities of the Celtic character, in many ways affirming the caricature of the "Stage Irishman," a stereotype appearing on the stage in various guises since Shakespeare's Captain Macmorris in *Henry V*. Arnold variously defines the Celtic nature as "sentimental," "gay," and "always ready to react against the despotism of fact."[9] Though Arnold writes ostensibly to praise the Celtic temperament and to promote the creation of a Chair of Celtic Studies at Oxford University, his version of the Celt accords with the Irish buffoon all too well. Therefore Arnold vehemently warns against too much Celtic blood in the English character – "We shall perish by our Celtism!"[10] The writings and careers of George Bernard Shaw, Oscar Wilde, and Bram Stoker, all Irish men of the stage who also called themselves Celts, directly challenge Arnold's stereotype of the sentimental, feckless Celt. Arnold, the eminent Victorian man of letters, promotes a progressive vision of English civilization's hegemony for the good of all, which the later writers attack through various modern subversions; Shaw inverts the English–Irish stereotypes in *John Bull's Other Island* (1904); Wilde mocks even the moral standpoints that such an idea would foster in the dandyism of *The Importance of Being Earnest* (1895); while Stoker's gothic *Dracula* (1897) underscores the fears of miscegenation at the heart of Arnold's question of bloodlines.

Shaw, Wilde, and Stoker, all born of Protestant Anglo-Irish stock, also all left Ireland for London at a young age. In this they were hardly unique, following in the footsteps of figures such as Jonathan Swift and Edmund Burke, because as Shaw remarked:

> Every Irishman who felt that his business in life was on the higher planes of the cultural professions felt that he must have a metropolitan domicile and an international culture: that is, he felt that his first business was to get out of Ireland... For London as London, or England as England, I cared nothing... But as the English language was my weapon, there was nothing for it but London.[11]

Shaw's comment recalls Henry Craik's infamous question, "Was there ever an Irish man of genius who did not get himself turned into an Englishman as fast as he could?" – with an important difference.[12] Shaw's addition of the idea of the English language as a "weapon" highlights an adversarial rather than a submissive attitude towards the English populace, reaffirmed by his comment that "England had conquered Ireland, so there was nothing for it but to come over and conquer England."[13] All three men's chosen vehicle for "conquering" was the London stage. Shaw's theatrical career, spanning over seventy years and including over five dozen plays (as well as novels and theater criticism), earned him the accolade of being the only Nobel Prize winner also to win an Academy Award (for the screenplay of *Pygmalion*). Wilde's star burnt brightly before his fatal fall; within the three years 1892–95 he was so popular that *Lady Windermere's Fan, A Woman of No Importance*, *An Ideal Husband*, and *The Importance of Being Earnest* all had successful runs on the London stage. Stoker left Dublin to work for over thirty years as the actor Henry Irving's stage manager at the Lyceum Theater, and his most famous creation, Dracula, is in part an ambiguous embodiment of the seductive power of Irving's dynamic theatrical persona.

Shaw's career was arguably the most international of the three, as he was powerfully influenced by Henrik Ibsen (his first work was entitled *The Quintessence of Ibsenism* [1891]); he organized a theater that staged Ibsen, Hauptmann, Schnitzler, and Maeterlinck; and gained fame abroad before making his name in London. While in his lifetime he was seen as a radical, a socialist, and a consistent activist against theater censorship, contemporary critics highlight the conflicts in both his literary and political legacies. On the one hand, Shaw lambasted the idea of "the most obsolete claptrap of the stage Irishman," arguing elsewhere that "Ireland is in full reaction against both servility and the stage Irishman."[14] *John Bull's Other Island*, first staged in London, turns the feckless Irish stereotype on its head. Instead, Larry Doyle, the Irishman, is a cynical realist while the Englishman Tom Broadbent is the Romantic idealist. On the other hand, rather than appearing threatening to English audiences, *John Bull's Other Island* entertained even the British politicians superbly; the Prime Minister Arthur Balfour attended the play four times while King Edward VII allegedly broke his chair when laughing heartily at the play. In the end, after all, Broadbent does win the day, suggesting that his romantic temperament may have just been a Machiavellian act. Critics have found Shaw's play to appear to undermine Irish stereotypes while subtly affirming them and placating British audiences.[15] To a certain extent Shaw foresaw this reaction, insisting that he was really "[w]riting the play for an Irish audience" to warn and instruct them about Irish complacency, and he did not care if the English audiences "smacked their lips over it."[16]

Like Shaw, Wilde, it has often been argued, barely merits the label Irish writer, since his writing so seldom concerned itself with Irish characters or contexts. Yet in plays like *The Importance of Being Earnest*, Wilde's aestheticism, his concern with the question of heredity, and the quips of his characters assault British Victorian social niceties and morality. Indeed, very early on, Yeats tapped into Wilde's Irish viewpoint, describing Wilde's career as "an extravagant Celtic crusade against Anglo-Saxon stupidity."[17] "Never speak disrespectfully of society," Lady Bracknell warns her nephew in *The Importance of Being Earnest*, "Only people who can't get into it do that." Yet, speak disrespectfully of British aristocratic society and of nearly everything else Wilde certainly did. *Earnest* mocks marriage, religion, the foundation of the family and even the concept of "nature." By the time Jack finally learns that his name is indeed Ernest and declares, "Well it is Ernest after all. I mean it naturally is Ernest," the audience realizes that in Wilde's farcical world there is nothing "natural" about a name or identity: it all appears as haphazard as Jack / Ernest's origins in a handbag in a train station. Indeed, Wilde's play particularly parodies the British characters' obsession with family name and origin, satirizing a heredity fixation like that of Matthew Arnold.

Wilde's aestheticism is also at the forefront in *Earnest*, a world where a baby can easily be exchanged for a three-volume novel and where appearance trumps content: "In matters of grave importance," Wilde writes, "style, not sincerity is everything." Wilde's interest in promoting "art for art's sake," in *Earnest* as well as in *The Picture of Dorian Gray*, shows the influence of John Ruskin and Walter Pater, Wilde's teachers at Oxford. Dandyism, however, was always a cosmopolitan movement, embracing characters as diverse as Beau Brummell, Baudelaire, and Huysmans; and Wilde's effort to escape British confines can also be seen through his decision to write *Salomé* in French (though it was nonetheless banned on the British stage). Wilde's aestheticism furthers his attack on conventional morality and on the Victorian idea that art must teach an ethical lesson. In his Preface to *Dorian Gray* he warned: "*There is no such thing as a moral or an immoral book. Books are well written or badly written. That is all.*" Recent critics claim that for Wilde the dandy acts as a kind of terrorist and that through the Dandy Wilde worked, like Lord Henry Wotton in *Dorian Gray*, to undermine British morality and society's stability.[18] While the political efficacy of the dandy might be questionable, Wilde's social critique, in connection to his Irish upbringing, further destabilizes any nationalist or cosmopolitan label affixed to his works.

Stoker's *Dracula*, a gothic tale of vampire hunting set in Transylvania and England, might not appear to have anything to do with Ireland or with modernism on the surface. Usually considered a British Victorian novel, *Dracula* owes much to Mary Shelley's *Frankenstein* and to the vogue of gothic vampire and crime tales of the period. However, the rise of postcolonial studies has led to a flurry of interest in the "Irish Dracula." For a long time critics assumed that Stoker was of Anglo-Irish descent, though through his mother he was actually Anglo-Celtic and baptized twice in the Catholic Church as well as in the Protestant faith.[19] Is Dracula, perhaps showing Stoker's Irish sympathies, a figure of the absentee Anglo-Irish landlord, sucking the blood of the Irish peasants to stay alive? Evidence from the text to support this point includes Dracula's faded great house in Transylvania, anglophilically full of English books and maps, his obsession with blood and purity, and his need to bring Transylvanian soil in coffins to England, off of which he lives (just as the absentee landlord lives off of the Irish soil). In contrast, Dracula's ship, which crashes on the English shore, certainly resembles the coffin-ships of famine times, which brought starving Irish peasants by boat to England. In that case, showing Stoker's English sympathy, Dracula could represent the threat of nationalist or middle-class peasants bringing illness and bad Celtic blood to English shores. Dracula himself has simultaneously been compared to Henry Irving – the British actor sucking the lifeblood of the hardworking Irish Stoker – and to Parnell – the "master" of a new race.[20] *Dracula* is certainly an "overdetermined figure" demonstrating the "ideological controversies inherent in Irish studies."[21]

In fact, it is just this resistance to precise meaning that lends *Dracula* a modernist flavor, in addition to the novel's embrace of new technologies, investment in new scientific and psychological theories, and textual status as a hodge-podge of different diaries, letters, and newspaper articles. Dracula's status as a collection of rearranged "true" documents, mirrors Wilkie Collins's detective novel *The Moonstone* (1868) – another novel focused on the sinister effects of the British Empire at home in England. However, the end of *The Moonstone* expels doubt, whereas *Dracula* concludes with the suggestion that Dracula might live on yet, in the tainted blood of the young British offspring of the Dracula hunters. Through this heir, Stoker suggests that the mixing of English and Irish blood is inevitable – what the results will be, however, is a horror the novel leaves for the readers' imaginations.

What links the works of Shaw, Wilde, and Stoker together and to the high modernists who followed is the sense of being an eternal *exile*. T. S. Eliot claimed that he was always a *metoikos*, or alien, and he suggests through characters like J. Alfred Prufrock or *The Waste Land*'s Tiresias that we are all inevitably estranged from modern life. Similarly, being Irish for Shaw made him feel a "foreigner in every other country."[22] Stoker's Dracula insists he is a "stranger in a strange land" because, even when he speaks the native language, his accent always gives him away. Wilde incarnates this sense of alienation through artificiality and the idea of the "mask," an idea Yeats, too, will foster. Indeed, even in describing themselves as Celts rather than Irish, Shaw, Wilde, and Stoker highlight their sense of otherness. Laura O'Connor notes: "To declare that 'I am a Celt' is to allude to a personal identity encompassed by the pan-ethnic tag, to differentiate oneself as 'not Anglo,' and to embrace otherness in a characteristically 'je est un autre' modernist gesture."[23] Calling oneself Celtic highlights the artificiality behind the very idea of natural "Irish" character, as Wilde emphasized: nature is not the "great mother who has borne us. She is our creation."[24]

Modernist revivals: W. B. Yeats, Lady Gregory, and the Celtic Revival

> I write it out in a verse –
> MacDonagh and MacBride
> And Connolly and Pearse
> Now and in time to be,
> Wherever green is worn,
> Are changed, changed utterly:
> A terrible beauty is born.
> (Yeats, "Easter 1916")

Thematically focused on his turbulent, changing times, Yeats is considered both a modernist in content but not in form, and a modernist in form but a romantic in content. Though he initially followed the same path to England as Wilde, Shaw, and Stoker, Yeats returned to Dublin to incite a cultural renaissance. One fact seems definite: it is impossible to claim Yeats as a great modernist poet without also accepting the modernism – and cosmopolitanism – of many of the members, techniques, and literary products of the Irish Literary Revival that he spearheaded.

It is an "odd coincidence" as John Wilson Foster notes in his revisionist work on the Revival, that the dates given for the Revival and for literary modernism are often the same: 1880–1925.[25] Prominent members of the Revival include Yeats, Lady Gregory, and Edward Martyn, founders of the Irish Literary Theater in 1899; the poet, painter, and philosopher AE (George Russell); the playwrights J. M. Synge, Douglas Hyde, and Sean O'Casey; and Jack B., Elizabeth, and Susan Yeats as painters and printers. Indeed the borders of the Revivalist group are hazy, as the Revival intertwined with many other simultaneous movements occurring in Ireland. As Cleary has noted, the Revival "is best seen not as a singular phenomenon but as a matrix of cultural responses to this wider post-Famine institution-building drive to create hegemonic national institutions and a national public"; movements that include the building campaigns of the Catholic Church, the Gaelic Athletic Association (1884), The National Literary Society (1892), the Gaelic League (1893), the cooperative movement (1894), and the Irish Literary Theater (1899).[26] What was continuous throughout these movements – and which seems remarkably anti-modernist – was the nostalgic cultural nationalism driving them.

In 1892 Charles Davan Guffy gave a rough outline of the goals of the Revival, highlighting the nationalist fervor of the movement and yet somehow sounding remarkably like a young Ezra Pound:

> A group of young men, among the most generous and disinterested in our annals, were busy digging up the buried relics of our history, to enlighten the present by a knowledge of the past, setting up on their pedestals anew the overthrown statues of Irish worthies, assailing wrongs which under long impunity had become unquestioned and even venerable, and warming as with strong wine the heart of the people, by songs of valour and hope; and happily not standing isolated in their pious work, but encouraged and sustained by just such an army of students and sympathizers as I see here to-day.[27]

The Revivalists, through works like Lady Gregory's collections of Irish Folklore, Douglas Hyde's staging of *The Twisting of the Rope* (*Casadh an tSugain*), the first modern production of an Irish language play, and Yeats's fervent resurrection of ancient Gaelic mythology, worked to bring the Celtic past to the Irish present. The modernist mantra to *Make it New* and the Revivalist's goal to *revive* a lost past seem patently at odds. Indeed, the Revival is usually characterized as an anti-modern movement, at best a demonstration of Celtic patriotism, at worst the product of a declining Anglo-Irish elite desperate to appropriate the Gaelic past.

And yet, without meaning to minimize either the nationalist aspirations or the political ramifications of the Literary Revival, it is important to remember that the movement shared many philosophical underpinnings with international modernism – particularly in its perception of history and the use of myth. Where the modernists turned to primitivism (African masks, poetry's origins as a "savage beating a drum in the jungle"), the Revivalists turned, using similar new anthropological ideas, to the "local primitive" in the Gaeltacht (Irish-speaking areas).[28] Where modernists turned to classical myth, Revivalists turned to Celtic mythology. The most famous articulation of the modernists' avowed Classicism (Hulme, Pound, Eliot, H. D.), their desire to skip over the recent past to tap into the strengths of a "stricter" era, was a gloss on the methods of an Irish author, Eliot's "*Ulysses*, Order and Myth" (1923).

The Revivalists, as Guffy noted, similarly "dug up relics," collecting folklore and the myths of famed Gaelic heroes to recapture a lost glorious past in order to give meaning to the present. From his early *The Wandering of Oisin*, and "Cuchulain's Fight with the Sea" to his final collection's "Cuchulain Comforted," Yeats consistently used Irish myth to underscore his own mystical symbolism, and his early reputation was based on his three collections of folklore. (In fact, Eliot pointed out that Joyce had borrowed the "mythical method" from Yeats.) Standish O'Grady's translations of the Cuchulain and Finn MacCool sagas, Lord Dunsany's (Edward Plunkett's) *The Gods of Pegana* and *King Argimenes and the Unknown Warrior*, and Lady Gregory's *Cuchulain of Muirthemne*, similarly used Irish myths and traditions. Perhaps most memorably, Yeats and Lady Gregory embodied the simultaneity of past and present Ireland through the figure of *Cathleen Ni Houlihan* (1902). In that play, Cathleen symbolizes Ireland's past and comes to make the young Michael abandon marriage plans to fight for Ireland. The play forces the past into the present, so that Michael goes to join the pantheon of Irish heroes, and Cathleen, though initially seeming old and frail, finally reveals herself to be a young girl walking like a queen. When Maud Gonne played this role to packed audiences and great acclaim in Dublin in 1902, her intoxicating patriotism made Shaw ask whether it was a play which "might lead a man to do something foolish."[29] Similarly, Yeats later wondered about the way the play used the past to encourage nationalism and particularly its influence on the Easter 1916 uprising: "Did that play of mine send out / Certain men the English shot?"[30]

The methods of the Revivalists, including its coterie qualities, manifestos, small presses, and little magazines solidify its modernity. In collecting folklore, collaborating, and "translating" existing Gaelic oral traditions or written texts into English modern versions, the status of the texts as a constructed document also shares much with the aesthetic of modernism, such as Pound's "translations" from Cathay or the collaboration of Eliot and Pound on *The Waste Land*. Terence Brown succinctly notes about the Revival: "a literature so dependent on versions, redactions, editions, translation could scarcely have avoided making literature itself seem a matter of construction rather than creation, of objective, impersonal work, rather than an opportunity for personal expression."[31] Coole Park, Lady Gregory's estate, where Yeats stayed for twenty summers and where other figures such as George Moore, Synge, Hyde, Shaw, and O'Casey frequently visited, and the powerful Abbey Theatre, established 1904, created a "coterie" aspect to the Revival, mirroring other modernist groups such as London's Bloomsbury or Gertrude Stein's Paris soirées. Lady Gregory's urgent letter setting forth the necessity of the Irish Literary Theater resounds with manifesto-like language mirroring that of the futurist manifesto or the imagist manifesto. Arguing for "that freedom to experiment which is not found in theatres of England," Lady Gregory urges her essential "new movement in art." Small presses, like the Cuala Press, formerly the Dun Emer Press, where the Yeats sisters published beautiful editions of works by authors including W. B. Yeats, Bowen, Oliver St. John Gogarty, and Louis MacNiece, paralleled small presses like the Woolfs' Hogarth Press. Finally, 1892–1922 has been called "the second golden age of Irish literary magazines": small periodicals like *Irish Homestead*, *Beltaine*, and *Dana* flourished, publishing not only short stories by writers like George Moore and Joyce, but also modernist Irish artwork by painters like Jack B. Yeats.[32]

Though Terry Eagleton has declared that there was no avant-garde equivalent in Irish modernism, the reactions by audiences to many Abbey Theatre productions were as outraged as the Parisians were to the Paris art salon of 1905. From Yeats's first play at the Irish Literary Theatre, *The Countess Kathleen*, where a Protestant noblewoman trades her soul to help her tenants who have traded their souls for food, the Abbey productions were sure to lead to complaints of being anti-Irish, anti-Catholic, or conversely of being too nationalistic and anti-English. Synge's *Playboy of the Western World* (1907) led to nightly riots at the Abbey due to its portrayal of the rural peasantry who support a father-murderer. Sean O'Casey's *The Plough and the Stars* (1925) similarly led to riots amongst nationalists, leading Yeats to need to defend O'Casey's genius. On the flip side, the staging of Shaw's *Shewing-Up of Blanco Posnet* (1909), which was censored on the British stage because of alleged blasphemy, led to a show-down between Lady Gregory and the British authorities, who accused the Abbey of defying the King's authority. "GLORIOUS RECEPTION SPLENDID VICTORY WHERE IS THE CENSOR NOW," gloated the telegram from Lady Gregory and Yeats to Shaw as his opening night was greeted with cheers inside the theater and from crowds in the street outside.[33]

In *A Portrait of the Artist as a Young Man*, Joyce shows Stephen hearing the angered cries of his fellow students against *The Countess Kathleen*, "A libel on Ireland! Made in Germany! Blasphemy!" And, indeed, the parallels between the Irish Literary Revival and international modernism were often due to cross currents between Ireland and mainland Europe, England, and the United States. Lady Gregory's nationalism was encouraged by her youthful affair with Wilfrid Scawan Blunt, the British poet and anti-imperialist whose opinions about British affairs in Egypt caused her, slowly, to rethink her attitude toward Home Rule. Synge lived in Paris for much of his short life, reading Nietzsche, Schopenhauer, Darwin, Marx, and Ibsen. John Quinn, the New York lawyer and patron of modernism, often assisted Lady Gregory and Yeats as well as Joyce, Eliot, and Pound. Paige Reynolds points out that George Moore, Maud Gonne, James and Margaret Cousins, and Mary and Padraic Colum, who are often considered isolated Revivalists, were actually involved with international modernist movements.[34] Yeats himself spent nearly as much of his life in cosmopolitan London as in Dublin or Thoor

Ballylee (his Norman Tower constructed in Galway), and he traced his own symbolism to the international flow of ideas: "That mood which Edgar Poe found in a wine-cup ... passed into France and took possession of Baudelaire, and from Baudelaire passed to England and the Pre-Raphaelites, and then again returned to France, and still wanders the world ..."[35] Yeats's own late "modernization" is – contestedly – often ascribed to his relationship with Ezra Pound and the winters they spent at Stone cottage. As Yeats wrote to Lady Gregory, he "helps me to get back to the definite and the concrete away from modern abstractions. To talk over a poem w/ him is like getting you to put a sentence into dialect ... all become clear and natural."[36]

Elizabeth Bowen's *The Last September*, a novel set in County Cork in 1920 in the last days of British rule, depicts the violent conflict between nationalism and a cosmopolitanism fostered by British imperialism. The novel simultaneously resounds with Revivalist nostalgia and presents a modernist exploration of time and identity. *The Last September* acts as the *Bildungsroman* of the young Lois Farquar, whose attempts to find love and friendship prove fruitless in the face of the bloody struggle for Irish independence that surrounds her. As the Big House she lives in and its aristocratic traditions go up in flames, Lois sets out for a European tour with hopes of art school. Lois acts as another figure of the Irish "artist" in exile, though a female Irish artist, conflicted about her artistic, gendered, and national identities.

Ireland in translation: Joyce, Beckett, O'Brien

About 1900 anyone who foresaw International Modernism might have expected its language to be French; what would have been absent from his calculations was the birth in a Dublin suburb, 1882, of James Joyce.

(Hugh Kenner, *A Colder Eye*)

In "The Necessity for De-Anglicizing Ireland" (1892), Douglas Hyde, the first President of Ireland and founder of the Gaelic League, called upon Ireland "to keep alive our once great national tongue."[37] Indeed, for any Irish writer after Hyde's Gaelic Revival, the choice to write in Gaelic, English, both or neither, constituted a politicized decision even before pen touched paper. Yeats's ambivalence crystallizes the bind of the English-speaking Irish writer: "Everything I love has come to me through English; my hatred tortures me with love, my love with hate."[38] And, in one of the most cited passages on Joyce's relationship to language, Stephen Dedalus in *A Portrait of the Artist as a Young Man* thinks to himself when speaking to the English dean of studies:

> The language in which we are speaking is his before it is mine. How different are the words *home*, *Christ*, *ale*, *master*, on his lips and on mine! I cannot speak or write these words without unrest of spirit. His language, so familiar and so foreign, will always be for me an acquired speech. I have not made or accepted its words. My voice holds them at bay. My soul frets in the shadow of his language.

For Joyce, this sense of an "acquired speech" – enforced by the English Crown and the Roman Catholic Church – leads to the stylistic and linguistic revolutions of *Ulysses* and *Finnegans Wake*. For Samuel Beckett and Flann O'Brien, writing in Joyce's wake, questions about language and translation remain key to their withering satires on nationhood and subjectivity. Indeed, reading Beckett's defense of *Works in Progress* in the light of Ireland's bilingual history underscores the links among high modernism, politics, and translation studies: "Here form *is* content. Content *is* form. You complain that this stuff is not written in English. It is not written at all."

Though the writers' paths diverge in most other ways, Joyce, Beckett, and O'Brien shared a mocking attitude toward the Irish Literary Revival and nationalist rhetoric. Joyce opted for exile over the "paralysis" of his childhood Dublin, choosing instead to write, mostly in English – and in a multi-lingual, idiosyncratic language in *Finnegans Wake* – in Europe: in Trieste, Zurich, and Paris. Beckett, in contrast, after 1946 wrote mostly in Paris in French, self-translating famed works like *En attendant Godot* (*Waiting for Godot*) and *Fin de Partie* (*Endgame*) into English later. O'Brien decided to stay in Dublin where he (or Myles na gCopaleen, Brother Barnabas, John James Doe, Peter the Painter, Winnie Wedge, George Knowall, etc., which – like Flann O'Brien – were all pseudonyms for Brian O'Nolan) wrote his comic masterpiece, *At Swim-Two-Birds* (1939) in English, though many of his other works, including his column "Cruiskeen Lawn" [a full jug], were written in both Irish and English.

While critics have amply documented the animosity of Joyce, Beckett, and O'Brien toward the nationalist rhetorical strategies of the Revival, this antagonism has led to the myth of Irish modernist apolitical art, an error that occurs particularly often in the case of Joyce. Joyce's own comments about politics, "Don't talk to me of politics, all I am interested in is style"; his dismissive portrayal of Ireland as "an old sow who eats her farrow" and the Irish as having GPI (General Paralysis of the Insane); and his exile status, lend support to reading his works as providing a purely cosmopolitan world view. Beckett, too, with his existentialist themes set in minimalist waste lands has earned a reputation of universality.

However, both post-structuralism and post-colonial studies have fostered an upsurge in politicized readings of all three figures.[39] Joyce's verbal and stylistic experimentation, from Stephen's loss of faith in the logos in *Portrait* through to the Tower of Babel that is *Finnegans Wake*, is fueled by his anti-imperialist ideology, particularly connected to language. In his critical writings this ideology is clear, although he also rebukes Ireland for its own participation in its subjugation. As early as 1899, as part of a university essay, Joyce laments the impact of an "overcoming power" which can lead to "the complete disuse of the original tongue, save in solitary, dear phrases, spontaneous in grief or sadness."[40] In "Ireland: Island of Saints and Sages" (1907), Joyce writes "I do not see what good it does to fulminate against English tyranny while the tyranny of Rome still holds the dwelling place of the soul," insisting, as does Stephen throughout *Portrait* and *Ulysses*, that the Catholic Church as well as the British Empire are guilty in Ireland's oppression.[41] Joyce wraps up the essay by imagining a new dream Ireland: "a rival, bilingual, republican, self-centred and enterprising island next to England . . . "[42]

Joyce's imagined multilingual Ireland recurs in Bloom's dream of the "new Bloomusalem":

> New worlds for old. Union of all, jew, moslem, and gentile . . . General amnesty, weekly carnival with masked license, bonuses for all, Esperanto the universal language with universal brotherhood . . . Mixed races and mixed marriage.

Of course, a nationalist like the Citizen in "Cyclops" would prefer a more Irish Ireland than Bloom's utopia; and, if the Citizen embodies the figure of the nationalist (Joyce arguably modeled the character after Michael Cusack, the founder of the Gaelic Athletic Association), then in *Ulysses* nationalism leads to prejudice, exclusion, and bloodshed, encapsulated in the Citizen's anger and violence toward Bloom. In contrast, Bloom embodies the new cosmopolitan citizen, defining a nation as "the same people living in the same place [. . .] Or also living in different places." The endeavor in *Ulysses* to write Ireland's new epic – since the genre of the epic is connected to the program of creating a national history and myth – may very well be Joyce's own answer to the question of how to form a community, not based on blood or a national tongue, in a multi-cultural, inclusive Dublin. And *Finnegans Wake*, a linguistic epic of sorts, takes this conception of the Irish epic one step further, using as its dialect Bloom's "universal language." Indeed, if Joyce begins in *Portrait* to divorce the word from the word of

God, as Stephen realizes that language is not God-given but "acquired," *Finnegans Wake* represents the fulfillment of this new deconstructed speech, which throws off the yokes of both the logos and imperial English.

Beckett, who began his career as a writer in the shadow of Joyce's *Wake*, chose bilingualism and made a consistent theme of the need to speak even when the failure to communicate is inevitable. In "Dante . . . Bruno. Vico.. Joyce" (1929), Beckett defends Joyce's *Finnegans Wake*: "His writing is not *about* something; *it is that something itself*." Beckett proclaimed this "desophisticated language" to be the ultimate union of form and content. Ironically, however, while Beckett's "Dante" piece can be seen as the ultimate artistic credo of high modernist autotelic art, apparently making the task of the translator impossible, Beckett himself was soon engaged in translating the ALP section of the *Wake* into French.[43] Beckett's early demonstration that autotelic art must inevitably fail, a breakdown of the modernist dream, contributes to his reputation as the first postmodernist.

Indeed, if Joyce in *Finnegans Wake* wished to create an omnivorous language that could overtake an imperial tongue, Beckett instead chose to pare language down to its barest bones, revealing the "impoverishment" of all communication. "Joyce had gone as far as one could in the direction of knowing more," Beckett wrote, "I realized my own way was in impoverishment, in lack of knowledge and in taking away, in subtracting rather than adding."[44] In works such as *Waiting for Godot* and *The Unnameable*, Beckett emphasizes his characters' ignorance and their lack of power, and yet their need to communicate regardless: "I can't go on, I'll go on!" (*The Unnameable*). Critics have tied Beckett's nihilism to many factors including his readings in philosophy (particularly Hegel, Husserl, and Heidegger) and his wartime experiences serving in the Resistance (he was awarded both the Croix de Guerre and the Médaille de la Reconnaissance Française). In addition, recent studies read Beckett in the Irish tradition, suggesting connections between the style of Irish oral storytelling and the narrative repetitions in his trilogy, *Molloy*, *Malone Dies*, and *The Unnameable* as well as understanding the negativity of *Watt* as potentially a savage satire on Ireland's neutrality during the war. Indeed, most of Beckett's settings are implicitly or explicitly Irish, suggesting that his nihilistic human comedy was tied to that landscape. Finally, critics have suggested that Beckett's anger against Irish censorship contributed to his decision to move abroad and to write in French.[45]

"Flann O'Brien" wrote in the new de Valera Ireland, and takes as one of his targets the new Irish citizenry (The "Plain People of Ireland") who support censorship in their new free Irish state. His other major target is high modernism. Although O'Brien wrote that *At Swim-Two-Birds* has "nothing in the world to do with James Joyce," he was proud that the novel was allegedly the last book that Joyce read (and liked). It is clear why critics consistently trace a connection between O'Brien's style and Joyce's experimentalism: with multiple beginnings and endings, a narrative web deeply layered, characters borrowed from other novels, and extravagant punning, *At Swim-Two-Birds* delights in meta-fictional play. In his twenty-six years as a columnist for the *Irish Times*, writing under the name Myles na gCopaleen (or Myles of the little ponies), O'Nolan entertained his readership by forcing them to examine through parody the new bureaucratic society in which they lived.

Flann O'Brien found his place amongst a significant group of Irish-language modernists that arose as Irish writing flourished after the formation of the Gaelic League (1893) and *Irisleabhar na Gaedhilge* (*The Gaelic Journal*, 1882). The Great Blasket Island autobiographies that O'Brien satirizes in *An Béal Bocht* include *An tOileánach* (*The Islandman*) by Tomás Ó Criomhthain and *Fiche Bliain ag Fás* (*Twenty Years a-Growing*) by Muiris Ó Súilleabháin (Maurice O'Sullivan); but sentimental autobiographies were certainly not the only writing in Irish of the period. Patrick Pearse's poetry and short stories revitalized Irish writing in these years with Pádraic Ó Conaire and Liam Ó Flaithearta further developing his lead. Máirtín Ó Cadhain (1905–70) provides the preeminent example of Irish language modernist fiction with his novel *Churchyard Clay* (1949) (*Cré na Cille*). *Churchyard Clay* is as much "about" the multiplicity of Irish dialects in which it is written as it is about life in an Irish small town recalled by the inhabitants of its local churchyard. Seán Ó Ríordáin, whose experimental poetics in collections such as *Eireaball Spideoige* [A Robin's Tail] (1952) led him to be called the chief modernist in Irish poetry, noted the importance of "wordplay" to Irish writing:

> I'm reading Joyce's *Ulysses*. Corkery once said that eighteenth-century [Irish] poets wrung a music out of the [Irish] language that had never been wrung out of it before. They played tricks with the music and the language and a shower of music fell down on them. As for us [modern poets in Irish], we ought to play with the meaning of words and a shower of meaning will fall on us. So let's play with the meaning of words. Wordplay.[46]

Such self-conscious "wordplay," perhaps stemming from the nation's bilingual condition, is manifestly characteristic of Irish modernism, whether written in Irish or English.

The critical focus on the "universal" aspects of Irish modernists such as Joyce, Beckett, and O'Brien, has made the gap between Irish modernism and Irish nationalism (embodied in the Revival) seem at times unbridgeable. If, as this chapter has traced, the "modernism" in much modern Irish writing stems from the social fragmentation incurred by a colonial history, the link between modernism and nationalism needs to be re-established. Nonetheless it remains true that texts like *Finnegans Wake* and *Waiting for Godot*, as well as predecessors like *The Importance of Being Earnest* and *Dracula*, might ultimately prove impotent as tools for political rebuilding, eviscerating national difference and lacking an Irish audience.[47] Yeats remains once again the great exception: politically suspect as a conservative loathing the majority of the Irish populace, yet capable of writing emphatically Irish lyrics like "Easter 1916," which became synonymous with a rebellion, or "The Lake Isle of Innisfree," whose lyrics greet you as you land at Dublin airport. The trend to realism in Irish fiction after the 1930s exhibits a turning away from the cosmopolitan experimentalism of the Irish modernists and towards more Yeatsian, self-consciously Irish, themes and settings. The popularity of "Irish" themes in contemporary culture – embodied in the poetry of the Nobel Laureate Seamus Heaney or in the fortune amassed by the band U2 – demonstrates the continued universal appeal of Irish experience in the twenty-first century. Joyce's own advice to the Irish writer Arthur Power at once supports those who criticize the modernist drive to universality and highlights the importance of the Irish tradition to Joyce's craft:

> You are Irishmen and you must write in your own tradition. Borrowed styles are no good. You must write what is in your blood and not what is in your brain . . . For myself, I always write about Dublin because if I can get to the heart of Dublin I can get to the heart of all the cities of the world. In the particular is contained the universal.[48]

NOTES

1. Lady Gregory, *Our Irish Theatre* (Oxford University Press, 1972), p. 20.
2. Richard Ellmann, *James Joyce* (Oxford University Press, 1965), p. 217.
3. Longley adopts the term from Tom Nairn; Longley, "Multi-Culturalism and Northern Ireland: Making Differences Fruitful," *Multiculturalism: The View from the Two Irelands* (Cork University Press, 2001), p. 4.
4. See for example, Emer Nolan, "Postcolonial Literary Studies, Nationalism and Feminist Critique in Contemporary Ireland," *Éire-Ireland* 42 (2007): 336–61; John McCourt, "Joyce's Well of the Saints," *Joyce Studies Annual* (2007): 109–33; Glenn Hooper and Colin Graham, eds., *Irish and Postcolonial Writing* (New York: Palgrave Macmillan, 2002); Clare Carroll and Patricia King, eds., *Ireland and Postcolonial Theory* (Cork University Press, 2003).
5. Joe Cleary, "Toward a Materialist–Formalist History of Twentieth-Century Irish Literature," *Boundary 2* 31 (2004): 207–41. See also Perry Anderson, "Modernity and Revolution," *New Left Review* 144 (1984): 96–113; Jameson,

"Modernism and Imperialism," *Nationalism, Colonialism and Literature*, pp. 43–95.

6. See Terry Eagleton, *Heathcliff and the Great Hunger* (London: Verso, 1995), p. 299.

7. Astradur Eysteinsson, *The Concept of Modernism* (Ithaca, N.Y.: Cornell University Press, 1990).

8. Wilde to Shaw (February 23, 1893), *The Letters of Oscar Wilde*, ed. Rupert Hart-Davis (New York: Harcourt, Brace & World, 1962), p. 332.

9. Arnold, "On the Study of Celtic Literature," *The Complete Prose Works of Matthew Arnold*, vol. III, ed. R. H. Stuper (Ann Arbor: University of Michigan Press, 1980), pp. 343–44.

10. *Ibid.*, p. 382.

11. Shaw, *The Matter with Ireland*, ed. Dan. H. Laurence and David H. Greene (New York: Hill and Wang, 1962), p. 10.

12. Kiberd, *Inventing Ireland* (London: Jonathan Cape, 1995), p. 33.

13. Shaw, quoted in Lillah McCarthy, *Myself and My Friends* (London: Thornton Butterworth, Ltd., 1933), p. 14.

14. Shaw, *The Matter with Ireland*, pp. 100, 99.

15. Kiberd, *Inventing Ireland*, p. 61.

16. Shaw, Preface to *John Bull's Other Island, Complete Plays with Prefaces*, vol. II, pp. 443–44.

17. Karl Beckson, ed., *Oscar Wilde: The Critical Heritage* (London: Routledge & Kegan Paul, 1970), p. 111.

18. Jerusha McCormack, "The Wilde Irishman: Oscar as Aesthete and Anarchist," *Wilde the Irishman*, ed. McCormack (New Haven, Conn.: Yale University Press, 1998), p. 85. See also Stephen Calloway, "Wilde and the Dandyism of the Senses," *The Cambridge Companion to Oscar Wilde*, ed. Peter Raby (Cambridge University Press, 1997), p. 45.

19. Joseph Valente, *Dracula's Crypt* (Urbana: University of Illinois Press, 2002), pp. 15–16.

20. See Christopher Frayling, "Preface," *Dracula*, pp. ix–x and Michael Valdez Moses, "Dracula, Parnell, and the Troubled Dreams of Nationhood," *Journal X: A Journal in Culture and Criticism* 2 (1997): 67–111. For a largely nationalist approach to *Dracula*, see Terry Eagleton, *Heathcliff and the Great Hunger* and Seamus Deane, *Strange Country* (Oxford: Clarendon Press, 1997). Bruce Stewart takes the opposite angle in "Bram Stoker's *Dracula*: Possessed by the Spirit of the Nation?" *Irish University Review* 29 (1999): 238–55. Finally, for fantastic reproductions of 1880s newspaper cartoons, showing both the Irish peasant and the British Empire as bats feeding off the other, see Luke Gibbons, *Gaelic Gothic: Race, Colonialization and Irish Culture* (Galway: Arlen House, 2004), pp. 82–3.

21. Moses, "Dracula, Parnell, and the Troubled Dreams of Nationhood," 69, and Raphael Ingelbien, "Gothic Genealogies: *Dracula, Bowen's Court*, and Anglo-Irish Psychology," *ELH* 70 (2003): 1089.

22. Shaw, *The Matter with Ireland*, p. ix.

23. O'Connor, *Haunted English* (Baltimore, Md.: The Johns Hopkins University Press, 2006), p. xiii.

24. Wilde, *De Profundis* (London: Penguin Books, 1973), p. 79.

25. John Wilson Foster, *Colonial Consequences: Essays in Irish Literature and Culture* (Dublin: The Lilliput Press, 1991), p. 44.
26. Cleary, "Toward a Materialist–Formalist History of Twentieth-Century Irish Literature," p. 220.
27. Gregory Castle, *Modernism and the Celtic Revival* (Cambridge University Press, 2001), p. 239.
28. Eliot, *The Use of Poetry and the Use of Criticism* (London: Faber, 1933), p. 155.
29. Lady Gregory, *Seventy Years* (Gerrards Cross: Smythe, 1972), p. 444.
30. Yeats, *The Variorum Edition of the Poems of W. B. Yeats*, ed. Peter Allt and Russell K. Alspach (New York: Macmillan, 1957), p. 632.
31. Terence Brown, "Ireland, Modernism, and the 1930s," in *Modernism and Ireland: The Poetry of the 1930s*, ed. Patricia Coughlan and Alex Davis (Cork University Press, 1995), p. 34.
32. See Gifford Lewis, *The Yeats Sisters and the Cuala Press* (Dublin: Irish Academic Press, 1994); Frank Shovlin, *The Irish Literary Periodical: 1923–1958* (Oxford: Clarendon Press, 2003).
33. See, for discussion, Lucy McDiarmid, "Augusta Gregory, Bernard Shaw, and the Shewing-Up of Dublin Castle," *PMLA* 109 (1994): 26–44.
34. Paige Reynolds, *Modernism, Drama, and the Audience for Irish Spectacle* (Cambridge University Press, 2007), p. 7.
35. Yeats, *The Secret Rose* (Ithaca, N.Y.: Cornell University Press, 1981), pp. 143–44.
36. James Longenbach, *Stone Cottage: Pound, Yeats and Modernism* (Oxford University Press, 1988), p. 19.
37. Hyde, in *1,000 Years of Irish Prose*, ed. Vivian Mercier and David H. Greene (New York: Devin-Adair, 1952), p. 87.
38. Yeats, *Essays and Introductions* (New York: Collier Books, 1968), p. 519.
39. See Vincent Cheng, *Joyce, Race and Empire* (Cambridge University Press, 1995); John McCourt, ed., *James Joyce in Context* (Cambridge University Press, 2009); Pascale Casanova, *Samuel Beckett: Anatomy of a Literary Revolution*, trans. Gregory Elliott (London: Verso, 2006); Kim McMullen, "Flann O'Brien's Postmodern Dialogue with Irish Tradition," *Novel* 27 (1993): 62–84 and Gregory Dobbins, "Constitutional Laziness and the Novel: Idleness, Irish Modernism, and Flann O'Brien's *At Swim Two Birds*," *Novel* 42 (2009): 86–108.
40. Joyce, *Occasional, Critical, and Political Writings*, ed. Kevin Barry (Oxford University Press, 2000), p. 15.
41. *Ibid.*, p. 125.
42. *Ibid.*, p. 125.
43. For discussion see Megan Quigley, "Justice for the 'Illstarred Punster': Samuel Beckett's & Alfred Peron's Revisions of 'Anna Lyvia Pluratself'," *James Joyce Quarterly* 41 (2004): 469–87.
44. James Knowlson, *Damned to Fame* (New York: Simon & Schuster, 1996), p. 319.
45. See Brown, "Ireland, Modernism, and the 1930s," p. 36; Ann Beer, "Beckett's Bilingualism," *The Cambridge Companion to Samuel Beckett*, ed. John Piling (Cambridge University Press, 1994), p. 216; and Brown, "Beckett and Irish

Society," *Samuel Beckett: 100 Years*, ed. Christopher Murray (Dublin: New Island, 2006), p. 19.

46. Quoted in Frank Sewell, "James Joyce's Influence on Writers in Irish," *The Reception of James Joyce in Europe*, vol. II, ed. Geert Lernout and Wim Van Mierlo (London: Thoemmes Continuum, 2004), p. 478.

47. See Seamus Deane, "Heroic Styles: The Tradition of an Idea," *Ireland's Field Day: Field Day Theatre Company* (Notre Dame: University of Notre Dame Press, 1986), pp. 45–58, and Emer Nolan, *James Joyce and Nationalism* (London: Routledge, 1994).

48. Arthur Power, *From the Old Waterford House* (London: Mellifont Press, n.d.), pp. 63–64.

FURTHER READING

Banville, John. *The Sea*. New York: Vintage, 2006.

Beckett, Samuel. *The Letters of Samuel Beckett*. Vol. I. Ed. Martha Dow Fehsenfeld, Lois More Overbeck, in association with Dan Gunn and George Craig. Cambridge University Press, 2009.

Ó Cadhain, Máirtín. *The Road to Brightcity*. Trans. Eoghan Ó Tuairisc. Dublin: Poolbeg Press, 1981.

Cronin, Michael. *Translating Ireland*. Cork University Press, 1996.

Deane, Seamus. *Celtic Revivals: Essays in Modern Irish Literature*. London: Faber, 1985.

Deane, Seamus, and Angela Borke, eds. *The Field Day Anthology of Irish Writing*. 5 vols. Derry: Field Day, 1991–2002.

Foster, R. F. *W. B. Yeats: A Life*. 2 vols. Oxford University Press, 1998, 2003.

Kiberd, Declan. *Irish Classics*. Cambridge, Mass.: Harvard University Press, 2002.

Lloyd, David. *Anomalous States: Irish Writing and the Postcolonial Moment*. Durham, N.C.: Duke University Press, 1993.

New Voices in Irish Literary Criticism. Vols. I–V. Dublin: Four Courts Press. Vol. I, ed. P. J. Mathews (2000); vol. II, ed. Alan A. Gillis and Aaron Kelly (2001); vol. III, ed. Karen Vandevelde (2002); vol. IV, ed. Fionnuala Dillane and Ronan Kelly (2003); vol. V, ed. Ruth Connolly and Ann Coughlan (2005).

Toibin, Colm. *Lady Gregory's Toothbrush*. New York: Picador. 2003.

11

LEONARDO LISI

Scandinavia

If one judges solely from contemporary accounts, the central role of Scandinavian authors in European modernism can be in little doubt. To name but a few examples, in 1897 Henry James proclaimed Henrik Ibsen the greatest living author, while three years later the young James Joyce wrote his first publication on the Norwegian dramatist's final play. Joyce, moreover, learned Norwegian so that he could read the master in the original, just as Rainer Maria Rilke taught himself Danish in order to study his beloved novelist and poet J. P. Jacobsen. Jacobsen was also an object of adulation for Robert Musil, Sigmund Freud, and Stefan George, among others; and his compatriot, Herman Bang (who was in turn highly esteemed by Thomas Mann) was central to the development of Lugné-Poë's experimental theatre in France. Ibsen's *The Master Builder* provided the foundation for the Belgian symbolist Maurice Maeterlinck's theory of modern tragedy, even as Bernard Shaw and William Archer in England vigorously championed the revolutionary realism of that same play. In 1924, the American Eugene O'Neill named "among the most modern of moderns" the Swede August Strindberg, whom Joyce had imitated in his celebrated *Circe* episode, and whose influence can be felt with equal force in expressionist drama and epic theater, Antonin Artaud and Samuel Beckett's *Waiting for Godot*. Walter Benjamin, for his part, wrote of the Norwegian novelist Knut Hamsun that "his language bridges a gap of incomprehension more vast than any other," while Kafka in his diary noted that the Danish philosopher Søren Kierkegaard "confirms me as does a friend." Theodor Adorno, Martin Heidegger, and Karl Jaspers likewise drew heavily on Kierkegaard, who in the 1920s, as Georg Lukács would recall forty years later, "was present everywhere." In Spain, Miguel de Unamuno developed a similar infatuation after reading of Kierkegaard in an article by the Danish critic Georg Brandes, who also gave Nietzsche his first fame, and whose influence on the literature of the time was such that the modernist journal *The Dial*, on his arrival to the United States in 1914, could "doubt if this country has ever entertained a more distinguished representative of European letters." In short, during the years of the modernist breakthrough, Europe was enjoying a Scandinavian craze.[1]

Although it is now completely overlooked by the secondary literature, this tremendous fertility and influence of Scandinavian letters is arguably not difficult to explain. Like most of Europe, Scandinavia underwent significant social, political, and cultural transformations during the nineteenth and early twentieth centuries, yet with its position at the linguistic, cultural, and political periphery of Europe as their defining characteristic. Far from being the obstacle that it has frequently been assumed to constitute, the acute awareness of this peripheral position by leading figures in Scandinavian culture in fact meant that the calls for newness, innovation, and rupture that pervade modernist aesthetics were heard earlier here than many other places.

The height of productivity in Scandinavian modernism spans two crucial historical events: Denmark's loss of Schleswig-Holstein to Prussia in 1864 and Norway's independence from Sweden in 1905. Together, these events spelled the unequivocal end of the popular dream of a pan-Scandinavianism that might return the region to political greatness. Coupled with the absence of any large urban centers, this situation led many of the figures in Scandinavian modernism, including Brandes, Ibsen, Strindberg, Hamsun, and Bang, into extended periods of voluntary exile, where they served as crucial mediators between the European cultural core and its peripheries. Thus the cosmopolitan spirit that in large part came to define modernism in the early twentieth century was already a necessity for Scandinavians a generation earlier, giving rise to a particularly fertile combination of global and local perspectives on the trials of modernity.

That this fact has yet to be properly appreciated among critics is due, not least, to the absence in Scandinavia of the kind of self-consciously modernist movements that express themselves in the various "-isms" of other European countries. As a consequence, the secondary literature has so far almost completely neglected this field, and a consensus has instead emerged that modernism only reached Scandinavia after the Second World War.[2] It is possible to identify, however, in a variety of works produced in Scandinavia during the late nineteenth century, a set of shared presuppositions that provide the conditions for their possibility, analogous to the function of a literary movement, and on the basis of which such works can be classified as modernist. As I shall argue here, these grounding presuppositions are exemplified in the writings of Georg Brandes and Søren Kierkegaard: in Brandes, a commitment to the objective, social conditions of the modern world, and in Kierkegaard, the examination of modes of experience and representation that transgress the laws of language and objective reason. The particular vibrancy of Scandinavian modernism from the late nineteenth century onward can be said to derive precisely from the early prominence and uneasy coexistence of the principles that these two thinkers represented.

Kierkegaard and Brandes

Among the first figures in Scandinavia to formulate a view resonant with modernist tenets was the Danish philosopher Søren Kierkegaard, who, in his attacks on the Danish Hegelians during the 1840s, rejected the epistemological monism that dominated post-Kantian thought. In what he calls in *The Concept of Anxiety* his project for a *"secunda philosophia,"* Kierkegaard insists on the absolute gap between ideal and real, reason and experience, as the necessary starting-point for any understanding of existence. This dualism leads Kierkegaard to insist, among other things, that the individual is fundamentally irreducible to the structures of reason and language. Accordingly, the possibility of mediating such gaps exceeds philosophy itself, and must instead be found in a religious relation to a transcendent Other.

Much of Kierkegaard's philosophy presages central modernist themes. Yet the explicit concern in Scandinavian culture with modernity and its challenges is traditionally taken to begin some two decades after his death, in what has come to be known as "the modern breakthrough." Although this latter term was not in fact coined until an 1883 collection of essays by Georg Brandes,[3] it is traditionally associated with Brandes's incendiary attack on contemporary Danish literature during a series of lectures delivered in 1871. In the introduction to his talks, Brandes claimed that the Danish literature of the day was determined by the fact that the country had remained unaffected by the progressive aims of the 1789 revolution, while nevertheless fully absorbing the reaction against them. Accordingly, whereas the rest of Europe had by the mid-nineteenth century moved away from the reactionary politics and values that had culminated with the Bourbon Restoration, Denmark continued to be stuck in an escapist idealism that failed to engage with the actual world. Where Danish writers, in Brandes's view, concern themselves "not with our life, but with our dreams," truly modern authors frankly discuss contemporary issues, such as the institution of marriage, religion, property, and the relations between the sexes. As Brandes put it in a phrase that resonated throughout Scandinavia: "What keeps a literature alive in our days is that it submits problems to debate."[4] By the 1870s, a literary program that insisted both on a radical break with past aesthetic practices and an active engagement with the conditions of modernity had left its unmistakable mark on Scandinavian literature.

It is important to note, however, that in spite of Brandes's extraordinary attention to, and influence on, the literary trends of his times (as late as 1922, Stephen Dedalus still borrowed his interpretation of *Hamlet* from him), he remained in an important sense fundamentally at odds with some of the central impulses of modernism. He dismisses Mallarmé's *Un coup de dés*, for example, as "so impenetrable, so insane, that certainly nothing to that degree incomprehensible is produced in a mental institution,"[5] and characterizes the Italian futurists as "charlatans" reciting "nonsense."[6] Such objections arguably stem from the fact that Brandes, for all his radicalism, ultimately derived his philosophical presuppositions from the Enlightenment tradition, retaining a faith in reason as the standard of reality and art that remained fundamentally unaffected by the epistemological crisis of the nineteenth century. As such, he rejected the dualisms, the fascination with ambiguity and the irrational, and the explorations of an irreducible subjectivity that underlie many of modernism's most important innovations.[7] If Brandes added to Kierkegaard's influence an attention to contemporary social structures that the earlier thinker arguably neglected, he nevertheless lacked Kierkegaard's modern philosophical foundation, which rejects the primacy of reason and complicates the very possibility of representation. Yet the combination of these two concerns, one predominantly thematic and the other formal, provided the conditions necessary for the emergence of modernist art.

Ibsen and Strindberg

Among the many authors who followed Brandes's call for a modern breakthrough, including Bjørnstjerne Bjørnson, Holger Drachmann, Anne Charlotte Lefler, Alfhild Agrell, and Olivia Levison, it is Henrik Ibsen, with his plays written during the late 1870s and 1880s, who has been most widely associated with this program. During these years, Ibsen revolutionized the theater, not only by turning to prose rather than verse as the medium for high drama, and doing away with such conventions as character asides and unmotivated monologues, but also by openly discussing issues like women's rights, venereal disease, incest, and the corruption and hypocrisy of good society.[8] However, Ibsen had in fact already proclaimed aims similar to Brandes's several years earlier, in an early draft of his dramatic poem, *Brand* (1866):

> See, therefore have I turned my sight and mind
> Away from soulless sagas of our past
> Away from lying dreams of future days
> And instead walk into the fog-world of today.[9]

The turn "Away from soulless sagas of our past" constituted a significant break with Ibsen's own works prior to 1866, which had consisted predominantly of romantic history plays. The few exceptions to this rule, such as *St. John's Night* and *Love's Comedy*, were in turn written largely under the influence of the idealist aesthetics championed by J. L. Heiberg. If *Brand* signals a new departure in the Scandinavian representations of the contemporary world, this is accordingly due primarily to its radical rejection of the kind of formal reconciliation between ideal and real that Heiberg favored.

The title character of *Brand* is a priest on Norway's western coast, whose commitment to his religious calling is guided by the uncompromising maxim, "all or nothing." Sacrificing his mother, his son, his wife, and finally himself in the service of God, Brand's example reveals through stark contrast the hypocrisy and pusillanimity of state officials and common people alike, who live by the principle of compromise governing the modern world. Yet what is particularly interesting about this critique of contemporary society is that, even while it appears to give Brand's position moral and exegetical priority over the remaining characters, every juncture in the plot (Brand's decision to stay in the parish in acts II and III; his decision to build a new church, and then to force his wife to give up the clothes of their deceased son, in act IV; his repudiation of the very church he built in act V) is in fact dictated to him by other people's discourses, or only comes into existence through their mediation. Thus, although Brand continually interprets the utterances of the surrounding characters as the manifestation of God's will, his actions nevertheless appear arbitrary, because they are based on parts of discourse that either constitute reinterpretations of the meaning and value of previous statements, or that have been delivered as a matter of pure chance. His uncompromising maxim of "all or nothing" in this way depends for its content and actualization on the presence in language of the very contingency and nuance that he seeks to shame. The suffering caused by the pursuit of his ideal cannot escape the sense of the gratuitous.

Interestingly, such vacillation, as equally active determinants of plot, between the necessity embodied in the principle of "all or nothing" and the contingency of its actualization in the world, is in agreement with what Kierkegaard, in *Either/Or*, had prophesied some twenty years earlier would be the form of modern tragedy. From the perspective Kierkegaard proposed, tragedy in the modern world no longer arises from the fact *that* a necessary order opposes our individuality (on the basis of which criterion George Steiner has influentially argued there can be no such thing as modern tragedy[10]), but rather from the inability to know for certain *whether* such an order is operative, and thus what determination the events we witness carry.

The deployment of two opposed representational principles to generate this conflict in his plays is central to Ibsen's mature poetics and places the crisis of representation that haunts modernism at the forefront of his works. This is true no less of the prose plays of his middle period, of which *A Doll's House* arguably constitutes his greatest success. Again heeding Brandes's call to engage with contemporary problems, Ibsen in *A Doll's House* focuses on the heroine Nora, who in the play's famous final scene suddenly breaks with her preceding character, and rejects the traditional obligations of family, religion, and morality in order to abandon her home and educate herself. The ending of *A Doll's House* has remained among the most famous and powerful in modern drama not only for the critique of the social position of women that it contains, but also for the way it breaks with theatrical convention. Until the moment of Nora's final departure, the events of the play are organized, on the one hand, according to the rigid rules of the nineteenth-century "well-made play," which structure Nora's attempt to escape the legal and economic consequences of her forgery eight years ago. Yet, on the other hand, Ibsen also continually defers the origin of those events beyond this neat causal framework. Rather than simply being the effect of Nora's original forgery, it turns out that the play's crisis might be due as well to the fact that her father, too, was guilty of a crime; or that her husband let her father off the hook in exchange for Nora's hand in marriage; or that the loan-shark, Krogstad, was abandoned by his lover for a richer man; or that Krogstad knew Nora's husband in his youth and therefore now addresses him with the informal "du," rather than formal "De"; and so on. The play thus denies the possibility of a happy alternative to its particular plot, as every action is shown to derive its meaning from an all-pervasive network of guilt and tragic errors that exceeds all control. By breaking with both of these structures, the causal logic of the well-made play and the infinite deferral of a universal guilt, Nora's departure reveals the inability of the moral taxonomy of nineteenth-century melodrama to grasp the instability of inter-subjective relations, and imposes a new response to that crisis.[11]

The exploration, in both *Brand* and *A Doll's House*, of the relation of the structures of the modern world to a sphere of contingent or anarchic determinations, became more dominant still in Ibsen's final four plays, which have frequently been identified with a "symbolist" phase in his authorship. Particularly in *The Master Builder* and *When We Dead Awaken*, Ibsen reduces plot to a minimum and increases the deliberate challenge to realist conventions, thereby forcing his audience to discover alternative modes of motivation among textual units. These plays resonated not only with symbolists abroad, but also those within Scandinavia, where authors such as Oscar Levertin, Sigbjørn Obstfelder, and the young Verner von Heidenstam turned to related poetic principles. The most radical exploration of non-realist techniques was pursued in the late plays of August Strindberg.

Strindberg achieved his first major breakthrough as a dramatist with works such as *The Father*, *Miss Julie*, and *Creditors*, which, in agreement with the author's own term, have traditionally been designated "naturalist." Yet this label is somewhat misplaced; for already in these plays Strindberg, following the path set out by Kierkegaard and Ibsen, shows a far greater interest in the irrational, particular, and unconscious determinations of subjectivity than what the social and objective perspectives advocated by a narrower naturalist program would allow for.[12] This interest is, in fact, one of the sources for Strindberg's formal innovations in these works, such as the deployment of erratic dialogue and the rapid shifts in characters' behavior and interrelations.

Strindberg broke free entirely of nineteenth-century conventions in his subsequent plays, such as *To Damascus*, *A Dream Play*, and *The Ghost Sonata*. Unlike in traditional drama, here Strindberg does not make his primary material objective events in the external world, but rather seeks to represent subjective experience directly. The revolutionary thrust of this shift is captured in the note attached to the opening of *A Dream Play*:

> In this dream play the author has, as in his former dream play, *To Damascus*, attempted to imitate the disjointed yet seemingly logical form of a dream. Everything can happen, everything is possible and probable. Time and place do not exist; on an insignificant basis of reality, the imagination spins and weaves new patterns; a blend of memories, experiences, spontaneous ideas, absurdities, and improvisations.[13]

Strindberg's rejection of the Aristotelian unities of time, place, and action – to which Ibsen still adheres for the construction of his plots – is clear. In *A Dream Play*, Strindberg instead provides a minimum of overt motivation (the descent to earth of Indra's Daughter to experience the human condition) in order to allow for the largest amount of material to be gathered under the most general purpose. The play's different scenes appear to be only contingently related, as a character from one reappears in a new function in the next, or the function of an earlier character is echoed in a different figure later on. Moreover, the stage settings through which these characters move are subject to a similar instability of value and meaning, as the props in one scene transform into those of the next in full view of the audience, with little justification as to why one rather than another setting should follow.

In spite of this dominant centrifugal tendency, however, *A Dream Play* also operates with a number of opposing, centripetal principles. For example, the apparent chaos of the changing characters, scenes, and unconnected discourse is centered on the variation of a limited set of themes: the claim that one person's happiness necessarily implies another's misery; the adage that love conquers all; and the pursuit of the secret of life. As in a musical composition, these themes are repeated throughout the play's polyphonic register, and in the final moments they are gathered into a whole, when the Daughter reveals to the Poet that the secret of life simply is that love and suffering are eternally at odds. Furthermore, *A Dream Play*, like *To Damascus*, displays a strict cyclic movement at its base, as the play proceeds from the growing castle, to the theater corridor, to Fingal's Cave, through Fairstrand and Foulhaven, back to Fingal's Cave, and to the theater corridor and finally the growing castle once more.

The dynamic interaction of these two organizational principles – one anarchic and deferring; the other static and organizing – suggests that for all their apparent differences, Strindberg's late dramas work on a structural binary that is in fact similar to Ibsen's, particularly as we find it in Ibsen's *Peer Gynt*. This shared reliance on opposed representational principles to capture the dynamics of the modern world lends further credence to Fredric Jameson's claim that modernism must be understood as the product of an incomplete process of modernization, in which the temporality of the new, urban modernity dialectically confronts that of the old, feudal countryside.[14] Scandinavia's position at the periphery of the modern economic world-system seems to have accentuated the awareness of this conflict.

Jacobsen and Hamsun

While Strindberg's radical experimentation found few immediate heirs in Scandinavian drama (although one might point to the early plays of Pär Lagerkvist), his impact on European symbolism, expressionism, and the theater of the absurd was immense. Moreover, Strindberg's erratic genius proved seminal in other genres too, as in poetry, where he was among the first Scandinavians to experiment with free verse, laying the foundations for modern Nordic poetry alongside figures such as Ola Hansson, Johannes V. Jensen, and Vilhelm Ekelund. No less importantly, Strindberg's *The Red Room* has traditionally been considered the first modern Swedish novel, with its rapid narrative pace, urban setting, and critique of antiquated social institutions.

As Georg Brandes was quick to note, however, it is the Dane, J. P. Jacobsen, who counts as the first stylistic modernizer in Scandinavian prose. Turning away from the large social canvases typical of the nineteenth-century novel, Jacobsen focused instead on the detailed depiction of subjective experience. In a representative instance from his short-story "Mogens," for example, Jacobsen deploys the kind of "delayed decoding" that became a hallmark of Joseph Conrad's art a generation later. The title character is looking at a mole heap:

> Suddenly a little, round, dark dot appeared on the light-grey soil; one more, three, four, many, still more, the entire heap was completely dark-grey. The air was full of long, dark lines, the leaves nodded and swayed, and a whistling came, which moved toward the south: it poured down water.[15]

The passage first presents the reader with the sensuous attributes of an experience (colors, shapes, sounds) before providing the concept that determines it (rain), thereby making us partake of the character's impressionistic process of cognition. Techniques such as these combine with Jacobsen's use of free indirect discourse and the reduction of authorial commentary to provide a more direct representation of subjectivity. Further, his prose fiction frequently restricts the appearances of minor characters to a single or a few consecutive episodes before those characters suddenly disappear for good – a strategy that enacts what might be described as a radical secularization of the novelistic world, in which the contingencies of an individual's linear temporality replace an overarching teleology as the organizing principle of character-spaces.

Jacobsen's attention to the subjective dimensions of experience is taken up most effectively in the works of Knut Hamsun. In his seminal novel, *Hunger*, written in the first person and recounting the experience of a starving writer in the Norwegian capital, Hamsun not only filters the description of events through the eyes of his narrator, but even transfers the principles of subjectivity onto the unfolding of occurrences themselves. The problem that governs the plot, the necessity of acquiring the means to survive, changes shape according to the contingencies of memory, passion, and impulse, as the narrator struggles to swallow his pride sufficiently to accept someone's generosity, or suddenly remembers another acquaintance from whom he can beg for money, or pursues a random idea for no apparent reason. Not only the unpredictability of the narrator's own subjectivity interferes with the course of events, however, but also that of others: whether a particular pawnbroker will be interested in his goods, if a shopkeeper makes a mistake when giving back change, whether the police take him to be a tramp, or if a friend should suddenly appear and offer food and drink of his own accord, and so on. The combination of these two forces, the continual decline imposed on the narrator against his will and the incalculable movements of subjectivity that persist in generating it, gives the narrative a nightmarish feeling that easily explains the fascination Hamsun held for Kafka.[16]

In his subsequent novel, *Mysteries*, Hamsun provides some of the earliest and most sustained uses of the stream-of-consciousness technique. The novel's central character, Johan Nagel, spends the morning in his bed, letting his mind roam free:

> What was it Hauge, the butcher, said to me once, Hauge, the butcher, who had a strong laughter and would impose himself so much with it? He said that no one who had all his five senses...
>
> And what a delightful child he had! The day I met her on the street, it was raining. [...] At that moment the band marched by; the pretty girl who works at the parish turned and smiled at me [...] But a man with a long beard in a soft felt hat suddenly grabbed me by the arm, or else I would have been run over. Yes by God I would have been...
>
> Quiet! One...two...three; how slowly it strikes! Four...five...six... seven...eight...is it already eight o'clock? Nine...ten. Ten o'clock? I must get up. Where did that clock strike? It couldn't have been in that café, could it? [...] But that was really an amusing scene in the café last night, wasn't it?[17]

Nagel's thoughts move freely from prior events in the narrative, to moments even earlier in his past, to contemporary political affairs, to the maid's enticing figure, to external stimuli and meditations on the human condition at large. In light of Franco Moretti's brilliant discussion of the evolution of the stream-of-consciousness technique, it is remarkable that Hamsun's use of it is not made subservient to the plot as the representation of a mind in distress (as in Tolstoi's *Anna Karenina* or Schnitzler's *Leutnant Gustl*), nor a state that the individual is somehow involuntarily forced into and which he rapidly leaves again when given the chance (as in Dujardin's *Les lauriers sont coupés*), nor a means to capture the poetic essence of life (as in Virginia Woolf's *Mrs. Dalloway*). Rather, the movement of Nagel's thought is concerned with the utterly mundane, is superfluous to the course of events, and is presumably operative at all times. The immediate predecessor to James Joyce's *Ulysses* is thus arguably to be found not in St. Petersburg, Vienna, Paris or London, but in a small coastal town in Norway.[18]

In the first decades of the twentieth century, many of the innovations first found in Jacobsen and Hamsun reappear and are expanded by others. Authors such as Karen Blixen, Tom Kristensen, and Eyvind Johnson, to name but a very few, continue exploring the ambiguity of language and experience in its opposition to realist conventions. The expressionist revolution in Fenno-Swedish poetry at this time would likewise need to be considered in a more detailed discussion of Scandinavian modernism. As mentioned above, however, it is not these writers that literary history has come to consider representative of modernism proper, but those of the generation that followed: writers such as Villy Sørensen, Erik Lindegren, or Paal Brekke, whose predilection for fragmentation and non-referential writing can be seen to assimilate some of the more radical elements of European modernism. The scholarly privileging of these authors is possibly based on the fact that modernism was only fully institutionalized in Scandinavia during this later period;[19] as such, it is arguably in large part an effect of the belated recognition of modernist writers by the Swedish Academy, which awards the Nobel Prize for literature. This latter institution, another crucial aspect of Scandinavia's influence on the development of modernism, was notoriously resistant during its initial years to experimental literature, but eventually it came to bestow the international recognition that has helped establish the more restricted canon of modernist studies: Thomas Mann in 1929, Luigi Pirandello in 1934, T. S. Eliot in 1948, William Faulkner in 1950, Ernest Hemingway in 1954, and Samuel Beckett in 1969, among others.[20] Modernism in Scandinavia after the Second World War is defined primarily in terms of its resemblance to such models; however, this overlooks the fact that these models depend in turn on their now largely ignored Scandinavian predecessors. Reincorporating the latter into the dynamic and comparative context of the modernist years is a project much to be desired.

NOTES

1. For some of these sources, see Henry James, *Literary Criticism: Essays on Literature, American Writers, English Writers*, ed. Leon Edel (New York: Library of America, 1984), p. 1388; James Joyce, *Occasional, Critical, and Political Writings*, ed. Kevin Barry (Oxford University Press, 2000), pp. 30–49; Rainer Maria Rilke and Lou Andreas-Salomé, *Briefwechsel*, ed. Ernst Pfeiffer (Frankfurt am Main: Insel, 1979), p. 139; Maurice Maeterlinck, "A propos de *Solness le Constructeur*," in *Le Figaro*, April 2, 1894; George Bernard Shaw, *Major Critical Essays* (London: Penguin, 1986), pp. 115–19; William Archer, *The Theatrical Year for 1893* (London: Walter Scott, 1893), pp. 63–70; Eugene O'Neill, *The Unknown O'Neill*, ed. Travis Bogard (New Haven, Conn.: Yale University Press, 1988), p. 387; Walter Benjamin, *Gesammelte Schriften*, ed. Rolf Tiedemann and Hermann Schweppenhäuser (Franfurt am Main: Suhrkamp, 1985), vol. VI, p. 142; Franz Kafka, *Tagebücher 1910–1923*, ed. Max Brod (Frankfurt am Main: Fischer, 1998), pp. 232–33; Miguel de Unamuno, *Obras Completas* (Madrid: Escelicer, 1968), vol. III, pp. 289–93; Georg Lukács, *The Theory of the Novel*, trans. Anna Bostock (Cambridge, Mass.: The MIT Press, 1971), p. 19; Friedrich Nietzsche, *Ecce Homo, Werke*, vol. II (Darmstadt: Wissenschaftliche Buchgesellschaft, 1997), p. 1151; *The Dial* 56 (June 1, 1914): pp. 447–40. Unless otherwise noted, all translations in this chapter are my own.

2. Recent instances of this view can be found in the contributions to "Modernism in the Nordic World," in *Modernisms*, vol. II, ed. Astradur Eysteinsson and Vivian Liska (Amsterdam: John Benjamins, 2007), pp. 833–77. Two current exceptions to this consensus are Toril Moi, *Henrik Ibsen and the Birth of Modernism* (Oxford University Press, 2006); and Arnold Weinstein, *Northern Arts* (Princeton University Press, 2008).

3. Georg Brandes, *Det moderne Gennembruds Mænd* (Copenhagen: Gyldendal, 1883).

4. Georg Brandes, "Inaugural Lecture, 1871," trans. Everet Sprinchorn, in Eric Bentley, ed., *The Theory of the Modern Stage* (Harmondsworth: Penguin Books, 1968), p. 388.

5. Georg Brandes, *Samlede Værker* (Copenhagen: Gyldendal, 1901), vol. VII, p. 277.

6. Georg Brandes, *Fugleperspektiv* (Copenhagen: Gyldendal, 1913), pp. 348; 350.

7. See e.g. Brandes, *Samlede Værker*, vol. XIII, pp. 43–84; and *Levned* (Copenhagen: Gyldendal, 1905–08), vol. I, p. 63 and vol. II, p. 145.

8. Ibsen's social polemics were especially influential in England, where they led to the heated "Ibsen Controversy" of the 1890s. See Michael Egan, ed., *Ibsen: The Critical Heritage* (London: Routledge and Kegan Paul, 1972). The relation of Ibsen's representation of women to his modernism has been explored by Joan Templeton in *Ibsen's Women* (Cambridge University Press, 1997), pp. 323–35.

9. Henrik Ibsen, *Samlede Værker*, vol. V, ed. Francis Bull, *et al.* (Oslo: Gyldendal, 1928), p. 367.

10. George Steiner, *The Death of Tragedy* (New Haven, Conn.: Yale University Press, 1996).

11. I have explored this issue at greater length in Chapter 4 of my book *Marginal Modernity: The Aesthetics of Dependency from Kierkegaard to Joyce* (Fordham University Press, forthcoming).

12. Significantly, Zola complained that Strindberg's characters lacked the "état civil complet" necessary to make them real. See August Strindberg, *Père: Tragédie en trois actes, Précédée d'une lettre de m. Émile Zola* (Helsingborg: H. Österling & Comp., 1888), p. 3.

13. August Strindberg, *Miss Julie and Other Plays*, trans. Michael Robinson (Oxford University Press, 1998), p. 176; translation modified.

14. Fredric Jameson, *A Singular Modernity* (London: Verso, 2002), p. 142.

15. J. P. Jacobsen, *Samlede Skrifter* (Copenhagen: Gyldendal, 1893), vol. II, p. 274. On Conrad's use of "delayed decoding," see Ian Watt, *Conrad in the Nineteenth Century* (Berkeley: University of California Press, 1979).

16. See Franz Kafka, *Briefe 1902–1924*, ed. Max Brod (Frankfurt am Main: Fischer, 1998), p. 519.

17. Knut Hamsun, *Mysteries*, trans. Gerry Bothmer (New York: Farrar, Straus and Giroux, 1971), pp. 37–38; translation modified.

18. Franco Moretti, *Modern Epic* (London: Verso, 1996), pp. 168–81. Unfortunately Moretti does not take Hamsun's works into consideration, and his argument that the stream-of-consciousness in *Ulysses* stands apart from all predecessors thus suffers from a significant oversight. Further still, Hamsun's position in the evolution of this technique problematizes the usual claim that it is grounded in metropolitan experience.

19. See Susan Brantley, "Into the Twentieth Century: 1890–1950," in *A History of Swedish Literature*, ed. Lars G. Warme (Lincoln: University of Nebraska Press, 1996), p. 364.
20. On the history and criteria of the Nobel, see Kjell Espmark, *The Nobel Prize in Literature* (Boston: G. K. Hall & Co., 1986).

FURTHER READING

Eysteinsson, Astradur and Vivian Liska, eds. *Modernisms.* vol. II. Amsterdam: John Benjamins, 2007, pp. 833–77.

Jansson, Mats, *et al.*, eds. *European and Nordic Modernisms.* Norwich: Norvik, 2004.

McFarlane, James. "Intimate Theatre: Maeterlinck to Strindberg," in *Modernism*, ed. Malcolm Bradbury and James McFarlane. London: Penguin, 1991, pp. 514–26.

McFarlane, James, ed. *The Cambridge Companion to Ibsen.* Cambridge University Press, 1994.

Moi, Toril. *Henrik Ibsen and the Birth of Modernism: Art, Theatre, Philosophy.* Oxford University Press, 2006.

Moretti, Franco. "The Moment of Truth," in *Signs Taken for Wonders.* Rev. edn. London: Verso, 1997, pp. 249–61.

Robinson, Michael, ed. *The Cambridge Companion to August Strindberg.* Cambridge University Press, 2009.

Rossel, Sven H. *A History of Scandinavian Literatures.* 5 vols. Lincoln: University of Nebraska Press, 1992–2006.

Stewart, Jon, ed. *Kierkegaard's Influence on Literature and Criticism.* Vols. I–IV. Surrey: Ashgate, 2011.

Tysdahl, Bjørn, *et al.*, eds. *English and Nordic Modernism.* Norwich: Norvik, 2002.

Weinstein, Arnold. *Northern Arts: The Breakthrough of Scandinavian Literature and Art, from Ibsen to Bergman.* Princeton University Press, 2008.

12

RUDOLF KUENZLI

Switzerland

Heidi and her grandfather in the Swiss Alps, the provincialism of Swiss cities, and the obsession with order and common sense have hardly been conducive to the development of modernism in Switzerland. In European modernist literature, Switzerland tends to serve as the model for a pre-modern, idyllic vision of life that European writers often invoked as a refuge from the chaos of the modern metropolis. Yet Zurich, the largest Swiss city, was the center of European modernism during the two world wars. After these two invasions of modernist writers, artists, composers, dancers, and theater people, the Swiss launched their own modernism after 1945.

First World War

During the First World War, neutral Switzerland became the chosen refuge for European pacifists, revolutionaries, anarchists, and anti-war protesters. James Joyce, Romain Rolland, V. I. Lenin, and the German Expressionists and socialists Ludwig Rubiner, Ernst Bloch, Otto Flake, René Schickele, Klabund, and Annette Kolb were among the thousands of refugees living in Switzerland during these years (and keeping the Swiss police very busy). They primarily settled in Zurich, which thereby became *the* center of modernism in Europe during the First World War.

In June 1915, Joyce brought his family to Zurich from Trieste. Sentimentally, he first stayed at the same inn where he and Nora had lived in 1904 after their elopement from Dublin, the Gasthaus Hoffnung. During the four years he spent in Zurich, Joyce wrote the major part of *Ulysses*, which he sent in sections to Ezra Pound for serial publication in *The Little Review*.[1] His other chief occupation in Zurich was his involvement with the English Players. In his attempt to get his play, *Exiles*, staged, Joyce made the acquaintance of an English actor, Claud Sykes, who suggested they form a theater company to stage plays in English and to counter the many German theater companies that were in Zurich. Joyce agreed to be the business manager of the firm, Sykes the producer and director. They chose as their first play Oscar Wilde's *The Importance of Being Earnest*. Although many professional British actors lived in Zurich during the war, Joyce proposed Henry Carr, an official at the British Consulate, for the role of Algernon. The performance was a success, but Carr became a major problem for Joyce. He wanted to be paid for the pair of trousers, hat, and gloves that he had bought for the role. Carr's repeated threats and slanders prompted Joyce to take him to court. Richard Ellmann comments that this "affair colored the rest of his [Joyce's] stay in Zurich."[2] Joyce's English Players, minus Carr, went on to perform in Zurich an ambitious program of modern plays, among them John Synge's *Riders to the Sea* and Bernard Shaw's *The Dark Ladies of the Sonnets* and *Mrs. Warren's Profession* (the latter play was still banned in England). Yet the company never performed Joyce's *Exiles*. At war's end, when the refugees' departure changed Zurich back from a cosmopolitan city to a provincial one, Joyce returned with his family to Trieste. He moved to Paris a year later.

Tom Stoppard later used Joyce's antagonist, Henry Carr, as the figure of the narrator in his play, *Travesties* (1975). In that play Carr recalls the fierce debates between Joyce, Tristan Tzara, and Lenin concerning the function of modernist literature. Yet although these three writers surely knew of each other and frequented the same cafés, they did not meet in the way Stoppard suggests. Nevertheless, the play provides a vivid glimpse of the dynamic atmosphere in Zurich during the war. "Great days," Carr reminisces at the end of the play, "Zurich during the war. Refugees, spies, exiles, painters, poets, writers, radicals of all kinds. I knew them all. Used to argue far into the night."

The historical Lenin arrived in Zurich in September 1914, where he wrote *Imperialism, the Highest Stage of Capitalism* (1916). He spoke at two international anti-war conferences that were held in Swiss towns, Zimmerwald (1915) and Kienthal (1916). At both meetings, he unsuccessfully urged that the imperialist war should be transformed into a class war. In 1917, after the abdication of Tsar Nicholas II, Lenin received permission to travel in a sealed railway carriage through Germany in order to reach Russia.

Lenin was certainly aware of Tristan Tzara and the Dadas, who opened their Cabaret Voltaire only 200 yards from his apartment. The founding of Dada in Zurich was in retrospect the most important event in the annals of modernism in Switzerland. The founder, Hugo Ball, left Germany in 1915 and arrived in Zurich with his girlfriend, Emmy Hennings, a professional cabaret singer and poet. Prior to his arrival in Switzerland, Ball had worked as a playwright in Munich, where he knew Wassily Kandinsky and the members of the Blaue Reiter group. On February 5, 1916, in the back room of a bar, Ball and Hennings founded their own cabaret, out of which the Dada movement emerged. Ball explained in his diary the name of the cabaret and its purpose:

> The ideals of culture and of art as a program for a variety show – that is our kind of Candide against the times. People act as if nothing had happened. The slaughter increases, and they cling to the prestige of European glory. They are trying to make the impossible possible and pass off the betrayal of human beings, the exploitation of body and soul, and all this civilized carnage as a triumph.[3]

In a rather quixotic way, Ball and Hennings intended to oppose, reject, and destroy the war mentality through a satirical, anarchic variety show. The Romanian refugees Tristan Tzara and Marcel Janco, as well as the Alsatian poet and painter Hans Arp and his Swiss girlfriend, Sophie Taeuber, a teacher of applied arts and dancer trained by Rudolf Laban, joined the cabaret. A week later, Ball's close friend, Richard Huelsenbeck, a poet and medical student, arrived from Berlin. Against the backdrop of fierce nationalism raging in Europe, this nucleus of artists and writers formed an international group that aimed to change people's mentality through a radical critique and transformation of contemporary art and poetry. Their common experience of the War prompted them to question their former hopes and beliefs; the ecstasy of expressionism, the pathos of futurism, and the rigor of cubism came to be replaced by irony, nihilism, and cynicism.

From the opening of the cabaret to its closing four months later, nightly performances were the focus of the Dada group in Zurich. On the small stage in the bar and restaurant, Holländische Meierei, everything seemed possible. The programs ranged from simultaneous recitations of poems in three different languages to songs, cubist dances, performances of short plays, such as Ball's bruitist *Nativity Play*, and skits with audience participation. Hans Arp's description gives an idea of the chaotic atmosphere in the cabaret:

> Total Pandemonium. The people around us are shouting, laughing and gesticulating. Our replies are sighs of love, volleys of hiccups, poems, moos, and meowing of medieval Bruitists. Tzara is wiggling his behind like the belly of an Oriental dancer. Janco is playing an invisible violin and bowing and scraping. Madame Hennings, with a Madonna face, is doing the splits. Huelsenbeck is banging away nonstop on the great drum, with Ball accompanying him on the piano, pale as a chalky ghost.[4]

According to Ball, Huelsenbeck injected a more aggressive tone: "He pleads for a stronger rhythm (Negro rhythm). He would prefer to drum literature into the ground."[5] Huelsenbeck's drum beats and recitations of pseudo-African poems, Janco's masks for the performance of improvised dances, Tzara's appropriations of African songs, which he found in the periodicals of anthropologists and missionaries – all of these point to the group's search for "primitive" art, an art that predated the derailment of European culture. In his sound poems, such as "Karawane," Ball wanted to find a language that emerges from the "primeval strata untouched and not reached by logic and by social apparatuses."[6] He drew parallels between what he was doing in sound and what Kandinsky did in abstract paintings: rejecting the representational as "impure," going "back to the true form, the sound of a thing, its essence, its essential curve."[7]

The word "Dada," multivalent as it is, can refer to the first sounds a baby makes, but it can also mean nothing. In his "Dada Manifesto," which he read on July 14, 1916, Ball states that Dada is "the heart of words."[8] Yet he distinguishes two different uses of "Dada": as a primal word for a new beginning which he advocated, and as a strategic trade mark, an empty, mystifying label that reduces everything to nonsense, which he realized Huelsenbeck and Tzara were eager to promote. The rift between himself and Tzara and Huelsenbeck was in Ball's assessment so deep that he and Hennings left the Zurich group after four months and went to Ascona.

In early 1917, Ball and Hennings returned to Zurich to participate in the group's performances, which now took place in a much more sedate space, the Gallery Dada. These evening performances included Ball reciting his sound poems while Taeuber wore one of Janco's masks and performed abstract dances; the group's performance of Oskar Kokoschka's play, *Sphinx and Straw Man*; Hans Heusser, a Swiss composer, performing his new music; and the Dadas creating connections between African poems, Western mystical texts, and Arabic dance rhythms. After three months, again due to financial difficulties, the gallery closed in May 1917. Ball and Hennings again returned to the Ticino. Their departure signaled the increasing influence of the twenty-year-old Tzara, who promoted Dada strategically and tirelessly – by launching the Collection Dada, a series of collaborative publications between artists and poets; by founding the journal *Dada*, copies of which he sent everywhere, from Paris to New York to Moscow, and by organizing large Dada manifestations in Zurich. In the third issue of *Dada*, he published his "Dada Manifesto 1918," which André Breton in Paris immediately recognized as "a violent explosion. It proclaims art's rupture with logic, the need of accomplishing a great negative work."[9] Indeed, in this manifesto Tzara rejects any guidelines for creating art, when he writes, "We don't accept any theories. We've had enough of the cubist and futurist academies:

laboratories of formal ideas."[10] The text of the manifesto consists of a series of contradictions, thus deconstructing logic and common sense. In a later manifesto, Tzara recommends writing only illogical poems by literally cutting up the sentences of a newspaper article, shaking the snippets in a paper bag, and then arranging them via the principle of chance.

Hans Arp also tore apart his own earlier paintings and arbitrarily arranged the resulting fragments. He saw in this deconstruction his attempt to undermine "the trumpets, the flags and money, through which repeatedly killings of millions were organized on the field of honor."[11] He singled out human reliance on logic and reason as the major cause of the War: "Modern times, with their science and technology, turned man towards megalomania. The confusion of our epoch results from this overestimation of reason."[12] The destruction of the cultural construct of reason was the principal function of his and the other Dadas' performances and works. Yet while Tzara saw in randomness and chance a strategy to transform sense into nonsense, Arp's "law of chance" took on mystical connotations. His automatic drawings and *Cloud Pump* poems point to a deeper, non-rational order, not unlike the one Ball suggested in his sound poems.

The end of the War brought about the end of Dada in Zurich. The refugees were again free to travel. Tzara joined the group around André Breton in Paris and launched Paris Dada; Arp went to Max Ernst in Cologne, where they formed Cologne Dada; and Huelsenbeck, who was able to leave earlier to go to Berlin, founded Berlin Dada. In joining other avant-garde groups in these European cities, they brought with them from Zurich the magic word "Dada" as well as their experimental performances and works, which transformed the activities and manifestations of other writers and artists.

When Ball and Hennings left Zurich, they joined friends in another important Swiss center of modernism, Ascona. From 1900 to 1920, this small town in the Italian-speaking region, located near Locarno on the shores of Lago Maggiore, became a major center of European counter-culture. In part a sanatorium for wealthy people who wanted to recover from mental and physical ills, in part an artists' colony and commune, it promoted vegetarianism, nature cure, matriarchy, anarchism, pacifism, eroticism, and withdrawal from the modernity of big cities. Some stayed for years, others visited for a few weeks. The spirit of Ascona (and Monte Verità, the hill behind Ascona) was well known throughout Europe. H. G. Wells presented some of these ideas in his novels, *A Modern Utopia* (1905) and *The World Set Free* (1913). Franz Kafka's friend Max Brod wrote a more critical assessment of Monte Verità in his novel, *Das grosse Wagnis* (*The Great*

Risk), in which the psychoanalyst Otto Gross, a key figure of this movement, figures as Doctor Askonas. Robert Landmann, Harald Szeemann, and Martin Green have established lists and information on hundreds of writers, artists, dancers, mystics, and prophets, who lived in this countercultural community, the underbelly of civilization.[13] Peter Kropotkin, one of Russia's foremost anarchists, was in Ascona every summer from 1908 to 1913. Hermann Hesse was also a frequent visitor. In his early novel, *Peter Camenzind* (1904), set in Switzerland, he introduced his well-known dualisms between city and countryside, art and life, civilization and nature. The real-life embodiment of many of Hesse's heroes, particularly in his stories from 1907 to 1914, was Gusto Gräser, the footloose pilgrim in tunic and sandals from Ascona. The most influential person on Monte Verità was the psychoanalyst Gross, the prophet of eroticism, matriarchy, and suppression of the ego. He attacked patriarchy, Christianity, property, progress, and the work ethic. After his arrival in Ascona in 1905, he went back and forth between Ascona and Munich, where he worked in a psychiatric clinic. In 1912, Gross even conceived of establishing a free university in Ascona that would teach anarchy and his anti-Freudian psychoanalysis. His wife's friends, Else and Frieda von Richthofen, came to Ascona and were inspired by Gross. In his biography *The Von Richthofen Sisters*, Martin Green traces the impact of Gross's ideas on the writings of D. H. Lawrence (who married Frieda von Richthofen). Gross's critique of patriarchy and Freudian notions of repression also received wide dissemination in Berlin Dada, particularly through the writings of the prominent figures Franz Jung and Raoul Hausmann.

Significant connections existed between these two centers of modernism in Switzerland, particularly between the Dada camps in Zurich and Ascona during the war years. Ball and Hennings settled in the Italian-speaking part of Switzerland, near Ascona and near Hermann Hesse, who became their friend and supporter. Ball wrote the first biography of Hesse, and Hesse in turn wrote a Preface to Ball's diary, *Flight Out of Time*. Yet the major connection between Zurich and Ascona was Rudolf Laban's School of Dance, which emphasized free and spontaneous movement that was liberated from the constraints of music and theater. When the war broke out, Laban moved his dance school from Munich to Zurich, and in summers he taught on Monte Verità. His major students, Sophie Taeuber, Suzanne Perrottet, Mary Wigman, and Katja Wulff, all participated in the Dada performances at the Gallery Dada. Perrottet, who was an excellent pianist, played music by Erik Satie and Arnold Schoenberg, and Arp collaborated with Taeuber on many works that were exhibited in the gallery.

Participants in these two centers of modernism, Zurich and Ascona, were, as we have noted, primarily foreigners who sought refuge in neutral Switzerland during the First World War.[14] The Swiss themselves were generally suspicious of these foreigners – to the extent that much of the activities of these émigrés can be learned from police files. Swiss writers showed little interest in Dada. When the Zurich Dadas exploited the gullibility of newspaper editors and sent them a fictitious report about a gun duel between Tzara and Arp, with the prominent Swiss writer J.C. Heer as witness, Heer was deeply insulted, since the story wrongly associated him with "these kinds of people." Swiss newspaper reports of Dada evenings at best parodied their presentations, but generally the papers simply dismissed these events as worthless. At least in literature, Dada had little impact on Swiss writing at the time of the First World War.

Second World War

Extreme patriotism and conservative thinking marks the period in Swiss literature from 1933 to 1945. In light of the political threat of Nazi Germany from the north and fascist Italy from the south, the Swiss government instituted an elaborate program to promote and defend Swiss traditions and values, which implied a rejection of everything foreign. Some Swiss writers even began to write in Swiss-German, since they believed that this spoken language was able to convey more directly true Swiss feelings and emotions. The organization Pro Helvetia was founded to support financially those Swiss writers who were producing patriotic works that glorified Swiss traditions and promoted the myth of Switzerland as the most democratic and beautiful of countries. Performances of Friedrich Schiller's play, *William Tell*, which depicts the founding of the Swiss nation in the Middle Ages, took place everywhere. The climax of Swiss pride and Swiss myths occurred at the Swiss National Exhibition of 1939, which served as a mirror to reflect Swiss greatness and tradition back to the thousands of visitors. This massive propagation of Swiss tradition and values had dire consequences for the hundreds of foreign writers who sought refuge in Switzerland during the Second World War. While foreign pacifists came to Switzerland during the First World War to write and publish their attacks against the war, foreigners were forbidden between 1933 and 1945 to be politically active or to publish in Switzerland, for fear of provoking Nazi Germany. Bertolt Brecht, who in 1933 conceived the notion of forming an anti-fascistic artist colony in Switzerland, came to understand that "Switzerland is a country which is famous for allowing refugees to be free. But they have to remain tourists."[15] Yet even this assessment depicts the situation more favorably than it really was. The Association of Swiss Writers, with full support of the government and the police, limited the number of foreign writers permitted to enter the country, and they also severely limited the duration of their stay. The Swiss politics of appeasement also led to the rejection of many Jewish writers. Joyce, who desperately sought a visa to come to Switzerland from occupied France in 1941, had to wait for months, because Swiss officials mistakenly thought that he was a Jew.

Nevertheless, even in this difficult political situation, Zurich became once again the center of European modernism. Thomas Mann, who had lived in Switzerland since 1933, received special treatment in his adoptive country. He founded the journal *Measure and Value* in 1937, which courageously published contributions by émigrés, including Walter Benjamin, Ernst Bloch, Alfred Döblin, Robert Musil, and Heinrich and Klaus Mann. The Swiss socialist Emil Oprecht, who published this journal, also distributed books that criticized fascism, such as Bloch's *Inheritance of This Time* (1935) and Heinrich Mann's *The Day Will Come: A German Reader* (1936).

Yet the cabaret was again the chosen form of critique and attack in Zurich. From 1933 to 1937, Erika Mann, married to W. H. Auden, and daughter of Thomas Mann, directed the Cabaret Die Pfeffermühle, which was located in the same area as the Cabaret Voltaire. She wrote most of the scripts and performed on stage, but the star of the cabaret was the German-Jewish actress, Therese Giehse, who in her performances could transform the most harmless texts into biting satires of Hitler and the Nazis. Klaus Mann, Erika's brother, who also wrote for the cabaret, called Die Pfeffermühle "the most successful and most effective theatrical undertaking of the German emigration."[16] The cabaret gave more than 1,000 performances in Zurich, before it was closed in 1937 on account of its pointed critiques of Nazi Germany. In 1934, the Swiss Walter Lesch founded in Zurich the Cabaret Cornichon, which stayed open until 1951. It primarily attacked the Swiss petit bourgeois and their smug, selfish attitudes towards refugees and world events. Major Swiss actors participated, and their use of Swiss-German increased the effectiveness of their critique for Swiss audiences.

The major center of modernism in Zurich during the Second World War, however, was the Schauspielhaus, the main theater in the city. From 1933 to 1945, this stage was the center of modern German-language theater. It attracted the best actors and directors from Germany and served as a major institution against fascism. The owner of the Schauspielhaus was the Swiss Ferdinand Rieser, a Jewish wine merchant married to Franz Werfel's sister. In 1933, Rieser chose for performance, with the help of his newly acquired German directors and actors, Ferdinand Bruckner's play *Rassen*, which critiques the Nazi politics of race; he followed this with Hermann Broch's

They Do Not Know What They Do, as well as plays by Else Lasker-Schüler and Karel Capek. Between 1933 and 1938, Rieser's theater staged nineteen plays by playwrights living in exile. Yet massive attacks in the Swiss press and protests by Swiss Nazi-sympathizers at performances forced Rieser, in 1938, to put the theater up for sale. A group of investors (organized by Emil Oprecht) bought the theater and chose the Swiss Oskar Wälterlin as the new director, but they kept the group of excellent actors and stage designers. This new director achieved a balance between the critique of fascism and the demand for Swiss patriotism by selecting plays that portrayed human freedom and dignity. Naturally, he had to stage Schiller's *William Tell* (the Swiss audiences spontaneously burst out singing the Swiss national anthem in the middle of the performances), but he also chose plays that emphasized themes of humanism and tolerance, such as Gotthold Ephraim Lessing's *Nathan the Wise* or certain works from German classical theater, as an indirect critique of Nazi brutality. The contemporary works he staged included plays by Paul Claudel, Jean Giraudoux, Jean-Paul Sartre, Eugene O'Neill, and Thornton Wilder. Remarkably, several of Bertolt Brecht's plays received their world premiere in the Schauspielhaus in Zurich: *Mother Courage* in 1941, with Therese Giehse playing the mother, *The Good Woman of Setzuan* (1943), and *The Life of Galileo* (1943).

Swiss modernism

Freed after 1945 from the political and social pressures to produce patriotic literature, many Swiss writers came to reject Swiss provincialism, and instead eagerly embraced the inventions, themes, and techniques of European modernism. In adopting uncertainty, unreliability, irresolution, and self-reflexivity, these writers directly criticized the certainties and "truths" about Switzerland that the previous generation had established. Swiss modernism, the period in Swiss literature after the Second World War, can be characterized as an intense critique of these myths.

The plays performed at the Schauspielhaus in Zurich from 1933 to 1945 constituted optimal training for the young Swiss dramatists Max Frisch and Friedrich Dürrenmatt who, unlike their colleagues in Germany, became acquainted during the War with international theater, and particularly with Brecht's and Wilder's use of parables. Frisch and Dürrenmatt attended rehearsals of plays by Brecht, Claudel, Sartre, and Giraudoux, and they both met with Brecht, who came to Zurich from America in 1947. In using Brecht's technique of the parable as distancing effect, Dürrenmatt and Frisch could write about the Nazi past right after the war. Yet, instead of implying Brecht's socialism as an answer, their parables aimed to open different, often clashing possibilities. Their plays and prose writings also question the myth of Switzerland that Swiss writers so fervently promoted from 1933 to 1945. Frisch's play *Andorra* (1957), which has as its subject anti-Semitism, can easily be read as an indictment of the Swiss myth of the hedgehog that, sufficient to itself and to its own greatness, attempted to keep out everything foreign. His prose text, *Wilhelm Tell for the School* (1971), questions the central Swiss legend of Tell as the great revolutionary defender of freedom. Frisch depicts him as a reactionary, even selfish, traditionalist who protects the financial interests of his people. In his *Dienstbüchlein* (*Army Service Booklet*) of 1973, he attacks the sacrosanct myth of the Swiss army as a defender of democracy by showing that it primarily defends the Swiss banks and the possessions of the rich. The famous opening statement of his novel, *Stiller* (1954), "I am not Stiller," questions the identity of the first-person narrator, who does not want to be "Swiss" any longer. Dürrenmatt's play, *The Visit* (1955), which takes place in Güllen – the Swiss-German word for manure – can easily be read as an attack on what he saw as the all-too-practical selfishness of the Swiss; the citizens are willing to give up their high ideals, even to kill a fellow citizen, for money.

And then there is Robert Walser, who was born in Switzerland in 1876, but lived in Berlin from 1905 to 1913, where he published his novels, *The Assistant* (1908) and *Jacob von Gunten* (1909), as well as many stories and poems. Franz Kafka read Walser's stories aloud to friends, and German writers celebrated him as one of the important figures of literary modernism. When Walser returned to Switzerland in 1913, he continued to write, but the Swiss literary establishment, which wanted to keep the myth of idyllic Switzerland alive, found his stories too playful, critical, and sarcastic. When Walser died in 1956, he was almost totally forgotten. Only in the 1970s did Swiss writers rediscover Walser's witty, burlesque, and often absurd stories. In the past twenty years, Swiss and foreign writers have celebrated him as *the* modernist Swiss writer. J. M. Coetzee wrote of Walser's novel, *The Robber*, written in 1925, but only published after his death in 1972: "Fundamentally *The Robber* is 'about' nothing more than the adventure of its own writing." He continues: "*The Robber* is more or less contemporary in composition with Joyce's *Ulysses* and with the later volumes of Proust's *Recherche*. Had it been published in 1926 it might have affected the course of modern German literature, opening up and even legitimating as a subject the adventures of the writing (or dreaming) self and of the meandering line of ink (or pencil) that emerges under the writing hand."[17]

Robert Walser's fate might serve as an emblem for the relationship between literary modernism and Switzerland prior to 1945. In 1933, Swiss authorities declared Walser insane. Although he lived until 1956, he claimed that he stopped writing after that official declaration. When someone asked why he did not write anymore, he answered: "How can I write when I am declared insane and put into an asylum?"

NOTES

1. Frank Budgen, Joyce's closest friend in Zurich, provides insight into the writing of *Ulysses* in his *James Joyce and the Making of Ulysses* (1934; Bloomington: Indiana University Press, 1960). *The Little Review* published *Ulysses* from March 1918 to December 1920.
2. Richard Ellmann, *James Joyce*, rev. edn. (New York: Oxford University Press, 1982), p. 428.
3. Hugo Ball, *Flight Out of Time: A Dada Diary* (New York: Viking, 1974), p. 67.
4. Hans Arp, "Dadaland," 1938, in *Arp on Arp*, ed. Marcel Jean (New York: Viking, 1972), p. 234.
5. Ball, *Flight Out of Time*, p. 51.
6. *Ibid.*, p. 75.
7. Hugo Ball, "Lecture on Kandinsky," 1917, in *Flight Out of Time*, p. 226.
8. Hugo Ball, "Dada Manifesto 1916," in *Flight Out of Time*, p. 221.
9. André Breton, *Entretiens* (Paris: Gallimard, 1969), p. 33.
10. Tristan Tzara, "Dada Manifesto 1918," in *Dada Painters and Poets*, ed. Robert Motherwell (Cambridge, Mass.: Harvard University Press, 1989), p. 77.
11. Hans Arp, *Unsern täglichen Traum* (Zurich: Arche, 1955), p. 41.
12. Arp, "Dadaland," 232.
13. See Robert Landmann, *Ascona Monte Verità* (Zurich: Benziger, 1973); Harald Szeemann, *Monte Verità – Ascona* [exhibition catalogue] (Milan: Electa Editrice, 1978); Martin Green, *Mountain of Truth* (Hanover, N.H.: University Press of New England, 1986).
14. Exceptions are the Swiss writer Friedrich Glauser, who performed on the Dada stage, Perrottet, and Taeuber. Yet because Taeuber taught applied arts in Zurich, her name could never be mentioned in the Dada programs. Some Swiss artists did exhibit with the Dadas, and they formed together the group New Life in 1919.
15. Bertolt Brecht, *Prosa* (Berlin and Weimar, 1973), vol. III, p. 256; quoted in Werner Mittenzwei, *Exil in der Schweiz* (Frankfurt: Röderberg-Verlag, 1981), p. 21.
16. Quoted in Mittenzwei, *Exil in der Schweiz*, p. 226.
17. J. M. Coetzee, "The Genius of Robert Walser," *The New York Review of Books*, November, 2, 2000, pp. 14, 16.

FURTHER READING

Amrein, Ursula. *Phantasma Moderne: Die literarische Schweiz 1880 bis 1950*. Zurich: Chronos, 2007.
Ball, Hugo. *Flight Out of Time: A Dada Diary*. New York: Viking, 1974.
Butler, Michael, and Malcolm Pender, eds. *Rejection and Emancipation: Writing in German-Speaking Switzerland 1945–1991*. New York: Berg, 1991.

Flood, John L., ed. *Modern Swiss Literature*. London: Oswald Wolff, 1985.

Green, Martin. *Mountain of Truth*. Hanover, N.H.: University Press of New England, 1986.

Kuenzli, Rudolf. *Dada 1916–23*. London: Phaidon, 2006.

The Review of Contemporary Fiction. Special issue on Robert Walser 12.1 (Spring 1992).

Rusterholz, Peter, and Andreas Solbach, eds. *Schweizer Literaturgeschichte*. Stuttgart: Metzler, 2007.

13

MARCI SHORE

Eastern Europe

In August 1913, the Czech poet S. K. Neumann published the essay "Open Windows":

> Our villagers dislike ventilation... Their windows are closed in winter and in summer. Mine are open... Let air come in!... Until we caught up to Europe, we'd let things in indiscriminately. Today we've caught up to Europe, that is, there's no reason why what happens in 1913 in Paris, in London, in Rome, in Berlin, could not happen in 1913 in Prague. How it happens, though, this is a different question.

"To live with contemporaneity!" Neumann exclaimed.[1]

In 1913, Neumann was a modernist in an age of imperialism, residing still in an empire of polyglots. Austria–Hungary was a vast domain, extending from Kraków to Sarajevo, from Vienna to Lemberg. Its cultural centers – like those of its imperial neighbor to the east – were marked by a cosmopolitanism inseparable from empire. In Warsaw and Kraków, Prague and Lemberg, Kiev and Budapest, art and literature from Paris and Berlin encountered philosophy and aesthetics from Moscow and Petersburg, making Eastern Europe the most cosmopolitan of European spaces.[2]

A wrinkle in time

Neumann wrote "Open Windows" only a year before the Habsburg monarchy declared war on Serbia, thus beginning the end of the old Europe. It was only then that the twentieth century truly revealed itself – and for this no one was quite ready. The First World War brought previously unimagined violence. It also brought four land empires to their knees: Russian, German, Habsburg and Ottoman. In these lands, the Great War was even more of a caesura than it was in Europe's West: in the eastern half of the continent, the map was radically redrawn. Great imperia dissolved in smoke;

modern nation-states were conjured up in drawing rooms. Vienna lost its uncontested position as literary and artistic capital.

Something else happened as well. In Eastern Europe, the twenty-five years or so before the First World War had seen the birth of *moderna*, a term that encompassed symbolists, decadents, neo-Romantics, and an assortment of other modernists. *Moderna* was about aestheticism and lyricism, about nature, about religious longings, about the soul. In a world where spiritual values seemed lost, a world that utilitarian positivism had drained of color, these fin-de-siècle writers sought redemption in art. Almost all of the poets were translators as well, and the works of Rimbaud, Mallarmé, Baudelaire, Keats, Shelley, Nietzsche, Balzac, Stendhal, Poe, Verlaine, and many others were lovingly rendered in Slavic languages. The *moderna* writers suffered, too, from metaphysical despondence and what the Russians call *bogoiska-tel'stvo* – a weakness for God-seeking. Subjectivism was at the center of their literary experimentation. For Stanisław Przybyszewski, editor of the Polish journal *Życie* (*Life*), most important was the "naked soul," full of irrational instincts and elemental passion. "Art has no aim, it is aim in itself," Przybyszewski wrote in 1899.[3] Then the war came and broke the reign of this passionate aestheticism. The battle against positivism continued, yet in a new key: *l'art pour l'art* gave way to life as a work of art. *Moderna* belonged to empire. The avant-garde was modernism in a post-imperial age.

One Sunday, not long after, in November 1918, an independent Poland had risen from the ashes of three different empires, the young poet Anatol Stern pushed his friend Aleksander Wat in a wheelbarrow for some two miles from Łazienki Park to Castle Square. Later Stern recited their poetry wearing only a fig leaf. The two took seriously Charles Baudelaire's imperative: *épater les bourgeois*. These were the Polish futurists, who sometimes called themselves neo-futurists, and in time declared that they were really Dadaists. Soon they were joined by a young man from Kraków named Bruno Jasieński, who had completed secondary school in Moscow, who had seen the October Revolution, who had seen it all. Jasieński's charm was that of a dandy: a monocle on one eye, a wide tie harkening back to nineteenth-century Romanticism. Girls fell for him.

It was a time of animated sociability. In the evenings these young men met at a Warsaw café called Ziemiańska, where all the futurist and non-futurist poets gathered. "One entered from the street into darkness," the Polish novelist Witold Gombrowicz recalled,

> a fearful haze of smoke and stale air, from which abyss there loomed astonishing faces striving to communicate by shouts and gestures in the ever-present din. The aquiline features of various *schöngeists*, in other words intellectual aesthetes, fraternized with honest, round, peasant mugs from the

country . . . The second floor was above all the "poets of the proletariat." This name included not just working class bards but also those who, originating in the lower social spheres, had become worshippers of all sorts of surrealism, Dadaism, and other such ultramodernism, with which they compensated for the more glaring problems arising from their primitivism and backwardness.[4]

The end of empires brought a special kind of freedom: with the achievement of the nation-state, a nationalist mandate had been lifted. That he was a Czech, S. K. Neumann now wrote, was "only a matter of course, / neither a merit, nor a virtue." He went further: "in my blood, in my nerves is something that dares / to feel international."[5] "Amongst us," Gombrowicz explained, "there arose a great embarrassment on the subject of our homeland."[6] "And in the spring," wrote the young poet Jan Lechoń more simply, "let me see spring, not Poland."[7]

The First World War marked not only the beginning of a new freedom, but also the end of an age of innocence: no longer could one travel without a passport – and thus did a natural polyglotism, an imperial cosmopolitanism, give way to the self-conscious internationalism of the avant-garde. Now borders were something to be overcome – an overcoming that betrayed first a recognition.

The First World War marked the end of an age of innocence in another way as well. In 1921 Aleksander Wat wrote an absurdist vignette, which included the following scene:

To the great terror of the peaceful bystanders, when the walls were torn down, 500 corpses presented themselves to the eyes of the curious, corpses in the second month of decomposition, in which strange roiled worms joined together in chains. The oxygen left the air at once and the predacious worms multiplied themselves everywhere. In connection with this, the bodies of those present swelled, reddened, and burst into quivering, as it were pulverized pieces.[8]

"No one," the avant-garde poet Adam Ważyk explained, "could have written that before 1914. That was postwar black humor."[9]

The sense of temporal rupture brought with it an acute self-consciousness of linear time. There could be no cyclical return to what was past. "Our age has been split in two," declared the 1920 founding statement of the Czech avant-garde collective Devětsil; "Behind us are left the old times, condemned to being turned into dust in libraries; before us sparkles a new day."[10] Wat and Stern's *GGA*, the "first Polish almanac of futurist poetry," began:

PRIMITIVES TO THE NATIONS OF THE WORLD AND TO POLAND
the great rainbow monkey named Dionysus took his last breath long ago.
we are throwing away his rotten legacy.[11]

As Filippo Tommaso Marinetti told the Polish poets in 1923, "*le passé tremble.*"[12]

The First World War was more than a European war marking the end of empires. In 1917 came the Bolshevik Revolution, a wild fire more than an historical event. What it meant, no one yet knew. 1917 was a wrinkle in time, a cosmic leap from the old world to the new. "An idea flared up in the Russian darkness," the Polish avant-garde poet Tadeusz Peiper wrote, "which, though blind and crazy, reached beyond the borders of its fatherland with the shadow of its vibrating wings."[13]

From that Russian darkness came the Yiddish poet Peretz Markish. In Warsaw he found other Yiddish poets: Melekh Ravitch from Vienna and Uri Zvi Grinberg, from what had been Austrian Lemberg and what was by then Polish Lwów. In 1921 the three joined together to form "Khalyastre," that is, "gang."

> Khalyastre is coming!
>
> *Year – 1922. Late spring.*
> *Country – Poland.*
> *Time period – between two planetary spasms, universal explosions of bloody*
> *madness.*[14]

Khalyastre was only one of many such "gangs." As elsewhere, in Eastern Europe the avant-garde was a coterie phenomenon. Cliquishness reigned. There was a fetish for "programs" and manifestos, and the avant-garde produced nearly as many declarations as it did works of literature. Avant-garde journals were filled with programmatic theory – often opposing both programs and theory. "Dada can be applied to everything, and yet is nothing," Dada's Romanian creator Tristan Tzara wrote to the Polish poets.[15] "Without a Program," Konrad Winkler titled his own introduction to a Polish avant-garde journal devoted to the ambiguously defined "*Formizm.*"[16] The journals were internationalist, interdisciplinary, and multilingual – as well as ephemeral. Time sped – "*Vitesse! Vitesse!*" Marinetti wrote to the Polish poets – and all avant-garde endeavors suffered from short half-lives.[17] In Poland economic hyperinflation was accompanied by literary "inflation," a kind of relentless intensification in an effort to sustain liminality. "The right of identity," Wat explained, "ceased to obtain. A thing ceased to be itself. The day after tomorrow it would no longer be what it had been the day before."[18]

Falling in love with Maiakovskii

Marinetti's futurism exalted not only violence and will, but also speed and technology. It was a modernism inspired by modernization. In

Eastern Europe, modernization proceeded more slowly than it did in Rome, Paris, or Berlin. And liberalism, modernization's erstwhile political counterpart, was a latecomer – it was over almost as soon as it had arrived. So, too, did time suddenly expedite in the aesthetic realm: imperial to post-imperial modernism sped from symbolism, decadence, and neo-Romanticism to modernism's "second wave": the avant-garde. Everything arrived, seemingly at once: expressionism, futurism, dadaism, constructivism, variations on variations. The East European avant-gardists read – and loved – Apollinaire and Maiakovskii, Marinetti and Khlebnikov, Tzara and Goll, Gropius and Breton, Aragon and Rimbaud and Blok.

In July 1921, Wat, Stern, and Jasieński, "in the name of the Polish futurists" – that is, themselves – sent a letter to Vladimir Maiakovskii. "Polish futurists, establishing contact with futurists from all countries, send the Russian futurists fraternal greetings," the letter began. "Beginning in September of the present year," it continued, "we will publish in Warsaw the first large international journal-newspaper devoted to universal futurist poetry in all languages. In addition to Polish futurists, taking part are Italian, French, German and Spanish futurists."[19] The "first large international-journal newspaper devoted to universal futurist poetry in all languages" lasted for just two issues. Their love for Maiakovskii lasted for the rest of their lives.

Maiakovskii and the Russian futurists had a personal emissary in central Europe. In 1920, a young Muscovite, a futurist–linguist named Roman Jakobson, arrived in Prague on a Soviet Red Cross mission. A diminutive man with a larger-than-life personality, Jakobson possessed a certain magnetism. People were drawn to him; things happened around him. In Prague, Jakobson joined Devĕtsil, whose members included Konstantin Biebl, František Halas, Vitĕslav Nezval, Jaroslav Seifert, and Karel Teige. Jakobson was an exceptional *animateur*: interwar Prague would not have been what it was had he not appeared there. Not long after his own arrival, Jakobson wrote to his friend Maiakovskii to join him. S. K. Neumann had already translated his poem "150 Million." "Come, my dear," Jakobson urged.[20]

Maiakovskii came to Prague only in the spring of 1927. Jakobson was waiting at the train station. "He's the same as before. He's put on a bit of weight," Maiakovskii noted. Jakobson introduced him to his friends from Devĕtsil. At the Národní Dům in Vinohrady all 700 tickets for Maiakovskii's reading were sold. In the end, nearly twice as many people crowded into the hall, and Maiakovskii spent the intermission signing copies of his books. He found this boring. "Signatures – a Czechoslovak passion," he wrote afterwards.[21]

On the same trip, Maiakovskii visited Warsaw, where the Polish poets were awed by his voice. Rooms trembled when he read his poetry. "I assume," Wat wrote of an evening that spring with Maiakovskii, "that chills went up the spines of quite a few of the people there, for that truly was imperious power. That wasn't a man, that wasn't a poet; that was an empire, the coming world empire."[22] Of the Polish poets Maiakovskii wrote in turn, "They chase the youth to the Louvre."[23] In Maiakovskii's opinion, if Warsaw was Paris, then it was "a very small Paris." As for the Polish writers who claimed that Warsaw was another Moscow, this was, Maiakovskii believed, "simply a mistake."[24]

"Laying Bare": freedom, nothingness, and the seduction of form

The revolt of the avant-garde was a revolt against both positivism and Romanticism, but also against *passéisme*, against boredom, against the bourgeoisie – who were themselves harbingers of modernity. For the avant-garde, modernity was both ecstasy and trauma, joy and despair, with little in between. Modernity was also emptiness – that is, a space for play. It was a nihilism that resembled less catastrophism than it did nothingness, in the sense that Jean-Paul Sartre would later articulate it: nothingness as absolute freedom. Thrown into empty space, man was compelled to act. In an introduction to the Polish journal *Formiśći* (*The Formists*), Winkler explained, "For contemporary man realizes ever more vividly that he has entered a new historical era – he stands on the border of two opposing worlds." It was a precarious position. Modern man could be saved only by "some kind of Promethean gesture, a mad leap into a void, an act born of creative lunacy."[25]

Cliquishness aside, this was a leap that in some way each had to make on his own, and the first-person singular became a preoccupation. Peretz Markish titled one poem "I." "I don't know, whether I am at home / Or abroad – " he wrote. "I am no one's, my own master, / Without beginning and without end . . . "[26] In this enticingly empty time-space of no beginning and no end, the three poets of Khalastrye came together in 1921. There in Warsaw "they went crazy for some five years, then they scattered and parted company."[27] Yet the solipsistic "I" was at once part of an infinite crowd. The Devětsil poet Jaroslav Seifert began his "A speech to the crowd" with the lines, "Loving myself, / I am a crowd." Some ten lines later, the poem concluded: "I am miracle beyond miracle, / multitudes made joyous / from nothing we will create nothing / the world."[28] The self was everything – and yet it remained but a breath away from nothingness.

In this void, the new world was being created. "The panegyric of *passéisme* we will betroth to the flaming torch of futurism," S. K. Neumann wrote. He included a long list of things that must be allowed to perish, among them: mysticism, snobbism, Czech culture, *Malleus maleficarum*, folklore, boredom, bourgeois beneficence, and socialist sentimentality. Other things should live long: expressionism, cubism, dynamism, flowing life, *moderna*, the liberated word.[29] The liberated word perhaps mattered most. In a time of play, words were toys. Later Aleksander Wat explained: "You see, that slogan, the idea of words being liberated, that words were things and you could do whatever you liked with them, that was an enormous revolution in literature; that was a revolution like, let's say, Nietzsche's 'God is dead.'"[30]

In May 1913, Marinetti had announced the slogan, "*parole in libertà*": words were to be liberated from syntax. The following month Apollinaire published "*L'Antitradition Futuriste*," calling for *paroxysme, suppression de l'ennui, pas de regrets, polyglottisme, invention de mots*, and *mots en liberté*.[31] That same summer, Neumann tried to convey to his Czech readers the magnitude of what Apollinaire had done: "One would need to inhabit the skin of such a strident, ruthless mongrel as is Apollinaire, in order to be able to reproduce faithfully the ingeniously provocative and logical pastiche of humor, solemnity, defiance, theory, and consequentiality of *words in freedom*."[32]

The Polish poets lacked Marinetti's infatuation with technology, war, and violence. What meant much more was the freeing of words – and this proceeded at a breathtaking pace. The same year, in 1913, the Russian futurists Aleksei Kruchenykh and Velimir Khlebnikov went a step further: they announced that the future belonged to *slovo kak takovoe*, "the word as such." Now words were to be liberated not only from syntax, but also from their referents. No one did more to effect this coupling of literature and linguistics than Roman Jakobson. This was just at the moment when the Swiss linguist Ferdinand de Saussure had declared that language was a form, not a substance, and the relationship between signifier (*signifiant*) and signified (*signifié*) was an arbitrary one. For Roman Jakobson and the Prague Linguistic Circle, whose origins lay in Russian formalism, poetic language was language conscious of itself: it was words that drew attention to themselves as signifiers.

Polish formism was related but not identical to Russian formalism: it was less literary analysis and more artistic practice. One of its leading practitioners, Leon Chwistek, was best known for his theory of "the multiplicity of reality in art."[33] "There is no defined way," he insisted, "of presenting what is real – on the contrary: the same object can be presented in many different ways."[34] In the journal *Formiści*, Chwistek explained: "Those who desire poetry in truth know that it's possible to find in it only one great value and only one feeling worthy of satisfaction, namely: perfect form and drunkenness on that form."[35] This aspiration was formism.

Chwistek's sometime friend, the marvelous painter and poet and philosopher who called himself Witkacy, had his own idea of "Pure Form." Witkacy's conception involved treating "pictures as certain constructions of shapes imbued with life of their own, possessing a formal unity independent of the objects being depicted" – that is, treating pictures as Pure Form, "rather than as some kind of reflection or individual interpretation of the visible world."[36] Both Chwistek and Witkacy, like Jakobson and Wat and Neumann, were preoccupied with the decoupling of form and content. "Form as the construction of the complete work is everything," Witkacy wrote, "and so called 'content' is an inessential addition."[37]

Release from the imperative of mimesis was especially tempting for those whose relationship with reality was so angst-laden. The East European avant-gardists were polyglots who reveled in the liberation from syntax, in the rupture of referentiality, in the newly discovered materiality of language. They experimented with unconventional typesettings and deliberate misspellings. They played with atonal meters, with rhyme and assonance and alliteration, disregarding what would traditionally be considered the meaning of words. Marinetti's emancipation of words from syntax, Apollinaire's poetry in graphic form, Khlebnikov's notion of the self-valuing word, all inspired the East European avant-garde poets. Wat's *namopaniki*, like the Russian *zaum* poetry, were in essence sound experiments. Disciplinary distinctions among the arts fell away. The Devětsil theorist Teige declared that a poem was to be read like a modern picture, and a modern picture like a poem, for poetry was expanding its boundaries.[38] Chwistek played with mathematics, the Czech journal *Disk* played with alphabet and numbering as poetic structure. The Polish poets worked with graphic artists like Mieczysław Szczuka and Teresa Żarnerówna; the Czech poets with architects like Teige and Jaromír Krejcar; the Yiddish poets with designers like El Lissitzky and Henryk Berlewi. In 1923 Berlewi returned to Warsaw from Berlin and soon founded, together with Wat and another futurist friend, Stanisław Brucz, a graphic design advertising agency. Among "Reklama Mechano's" projects was a brochure for the Warsaw chocolate manufacturer "Plutos."

The break not only from mimesis, but also from referentiality more broadly, meant attention paid to the signifier – that is, the form – *as such*. In this way was language – and the artistic-poetic device – "laid bare." Berlewi wrote, "We have been bereaved of tradition, we are naked like Adam and . . . stand before a great task: to create a new world, a world of our own forms."[39] Now "nakedness" – laying bare – became a motif. The "laying bare" of the word – of the aesthetic device – had sensual overtones, and "nakedness" slid into a new openness about sexuality. "A woman's nakedness is not a fetish, but life itself," read a line of Neumann's poem "In Praise of Nakedness."[40] Ważyk wrote of "A body, naked, vast," which "withdraws and grasps: / clings with its mouth, hugs with its hands. // Lavish and tender velvet of caresses / nakedness set in flutter and swing."[41] And Peiper titled one poem simply "Naked." There he expressed the joy and sensuality of laying bare – as well as the thrill of transgression. Amidst tenderness a hint of violence revealed itself: "you, a leaf of paper on which I will write, / or perhaps instead will throw, burn, on the grate / naked, affixed to the silence, be silent and be sublime."[42] The Krakowian dandy Jasieński was less gentle: "And I want to stroke your breasts without the blouse, / I want to be wildly insolent and powerful, like an untamed ox."[43]

Hunger for wholeness

Most rhapsodic – and most painful – was the "laying bare" of the "I." In Poland, futurism and expressionism arrived as contemporaries; at moments they blended and merged. Aleksander Wat's debut literary work, "I from One Side and I from the Other Side of My Cast Iron Stove," was written in a fever that approached delirium. Wat swam into the depths of his soul; it was *l'écriture automatique* of the French surrealists *avant la lettre*.

"Having gained the joyful knowledge of the mask," an eighteen-year-old Wat wrote, "I burned with a miraculous lust: to turn myself into space! But once I was terrified by a bottomless crack, which I perceived just *beyond* the surface of the nose, when I looked at it with my right eye. The accursed crack, the accursed *principium individuationis*, horrifies me, plagues me, whips me, twists me, paralyzes me like a golden caftan."[44] Selfhood was too heavy. "Away with consciousness," Wat declared, "I go to 'Liberate my own phantoms.'"[45] But the escape was unsuccessful. The long prose poem concluded with the end of the implied author:

THE END OF ALEKSANDER WAT. Gothic dreams 'modern' souls and orgies satanic faiths come under mandrake-mildewed impotencies of doric columns.
It brings desperation it calls forth the spirit of the abyss, which *breaks you away from yourself*. Aha! the used key to the abyss!
Idiot beast moron fuck.
It is I who am burning in the inquisitorial insides of my cast-iron stove . . .[46]

The "I" was an unbearable burden. Absolute subjectivity brought absolute suffering. The affirmation of multiplicity, the license to indulge in the many faces of the "I," made for a certain narcissistic fulfillment; yet pathological narcissism was less something one reveled in than something one suffered from. The liberated word, now luxuriating in its autonomy, made for wonderful play. Nothingness and nakedness made for exhilarating freedom. Dadaism was all individuality and fragmentation, a willful refusal to order, to conform, to tone down. Yet the absence of any firm grounding grew impossible to endure, and in time the avant-gardists longed for wholeness.

To Czech modernists – avant-garde and otherwise – the French philosopher Henri Bergson was an inspiration. "A woman's nakedness is...but life itself," Neumann wrote, and it was to this "life itself" that they aspired. Bergson described an *élan vital*, an all-pervasive impulse to life. This was a revolt against positivism – and against what Bergson called "mechanism" and "finalism," in essence teleology. He insisted on vitalism, pluridimensionality, division, contingency. He insisted, too, on the limited ability of the intellect to grasp life in all its richness. Instinct, in contrast, was "molded on the very form of life."[47]

The *élan vital* was a "virtual multiplicity," yet not a hopelessly fragmentary one: there could be unity in plurality.[48] Like Chwistek, Bergson insisted on heterogeneity. Yet this was a heterogeneity that did not suggest nihilistic discontinuity without end. In his 1913 essay "Long Live Life!", Neumann wrote of Bergson's appeal – the appeal of wholeness:

> Yet Bergson with his sense for the *continuousness of life*, for the interrelation of events in the flow of time, is leading us only now on the right path...Following Bergson's words we can say that, if we are to express our intuition of the symphonic unity of all things, our ever-present feeling of life's internal rhythm, then it's necessary that we do so by diverse images, taken from varied sources...because in truth, life is relatedness.[49]

In Czechoslovakia this "hunger for wholeness" found expression in Devětsil, whose members were a generation younger than Neumann.[50] Devětsil was explicitly collectivist; it insisted on the unity of art and life. In his 1924 Poetism manifesto Teige wrote, "Poetism knows that one of the greatest values embraced by mankind is human individuality harnessed to the discipline of the collective fellowship of man." He called for "poetry for all senses." Here Teige embraced socialism, constructivism, hedonism, sensualism, and relativism. The time of the decadents had passed. Poetism was a rebellion against aestheticism and "art for art's sake," in favor of dissolving the boundary between life and art. "Poetism," he declared, "is, above all, a way of life."[51]

The same year Teige's Devětsil colleague František Halas sent a letter to the Polish journal *Blok*. "**Art=life**," Halas wrote.[52] The same issue of *Blok* included a long manifesto from Serbia, presenting the philosophy of "Zenitism" and its "words in space." The Zenitists called upon the cultural nihilism and madness of the Balkans, "a cradle of pure barbarism," to reinvigorate art and the world with elementalism, vitality, and "barbarogenius." Zenitism was "an elixir of eternal youth and a realization that one must tirelessly and eternally strive upward." In this striving "all individual forces should be concentrated in the great circle of the whole."[53] Zenitism's founding manifesto was clear about this: "**ZENITISM=∞=TOTALITY**."[54]

Zenitism saw itself as "a crazed phantom dancer on the burning Balkan sky of brilliant beyond-sense."[55] Chwistek's formism aspired to "pure beauty and the feelings of joy and enthusiasm connected to beauty."[56] Seifert wrote of how "I am a poet, / of the joy of life I am a poet singing."[57] At a Khalastrye poetry matinee, Markish insisted that Mojsze Broderzon, his fellow Yiddish poet from Łódź, read his poem with the refrain: "We, the young ones, a joyous gang [*khalyastre*], full of song."[58] "Joy" was among the East European avant-garde's favorite words; others included dreaming, dancing, going, I, youth, hermaphrodite, abyss. "I" was yoked to both "joy" and "abyss." Joy was headiness, only a moment's distance from despair. Radical contingency and radical nihilism meant the infinite freedom, and infinite subjectivity, of nothingness, and this absence of stable meaning proved unbearable. Ultimately the avant-garde fled. From nothingness they reached for totality.

Endgame

The East European avant-gardists hated the bourgeoisie from the very beginning – despite the fact that the East European bourgeoisie was but a nascent one, small and weak. This hatred was in large part a self-hatred, even prior to Marxist inspiration – and Marxist guilt. For the futurists understood "bourgeois" above all as Rousseau had: superficiality and conformity, pretentiousness devoid of content, inauthenticity. *Passéisme*. Their impulse to "shock the bourgeoisie" followed Baudelaire's: the joy of transgression preceded solidarity with the proletariat.

When the avant-garde poets found their way to the Russian Revolution, their new hatred of the bourgeoisie was a derivative one: a revolt against exploitation grew from a revolt against inauthenticity. A Slovak journalist could not believe that the internationalist avant-garde writers of the Slovak group DAV ("crowd") had truly rid themselves of "national feeling." One day the journalist encountered one of the DAVists on "entirely neutral territory." Both believed they had things to discuss. Yet "first," the DAVist told the journalist, "we have to break your bourgeois spirit."[59] By then, the mid-1920s, the DAVists had already given their hearts to the Revolution.

In 1923, Jasieński and Stern together published a collection of poetry titled *Ziemia na lewo* [The Earth to the Left]. "We hate the bourgeoisie," they wrote in their introduction, " – not only that which today obstructs our world with a shabby banknote – but the bourgeoisie as an abstraction, its view of the world and everything that belongs to it."[60] There was a proletarian modernism that preceded socialist realism, and Bruno Jasieński was at the center of it.

While Marinetti and the Italian futurists joined forces with Mussolini, the Polish futurists, the Czech Devětsil artists and poets, the Slovak DAVists, the Ukrainian Panfuturists, and many of the avant-garde Yiddish poets leaped into the fire of communist revolution. "Revolution is a painful tragedy," the Polish poet Witold Wandurski told a friend, "a glorious fire, in which you must burn yourself, descend into savagery, into barbarism – in order to discover in yourself the simple joy of life."[61] "Revolution," wrote the Devětsil theater director Jindřich Honzl, "this is life's catharsis, this is the passion and drama of the times . . . evil and goodness are mixed in a carnal collective with no less ferocity and instinctual savagery than in Macbeth."[62] Revolution was conflagration.

The East European avant-garde's feeling of being on the threshold was prescient: something *was* coming. Maiakovskii was the first to go. In April of 1930, the beautiful Russian futurist committed suicide. Four years later, Wandurski became the first of the Polish communist poets to fall victim to the Great Terror in the Soviet Union. He was shot in Soviet Ukraine in June 1934. In January 1938, in a Soviet prison cell awaiting execution, Bruno Jasieński wrote of his favorite poet Maiakovskii, who had brought him to the October Revolution.[63]

Stalinism provoked, too, a falling-out among the Czech avant-gardists, who by now had taken to Freudian-influenced Surrealism and had grown close to André Breton and Paul Eluard. Teige, Biebl, and others broke with Nezval. It was the time of Stalin's show trials of the Old Bolsheviks, and the issue was one of loyalty to Moscow. Breton was horrified. It was absolutely impermissible, he insisted, that in a time when at any moment the fate of civilization could be decided, his Czech friends could lose their sense of what united them.[64]

The Second World War was a bloodbath. In Eastern Europe, the avant-garde poets, many of them of Jewish origin, often lost their families, if not their own lives. Then the war ended, and Stalinism came. The Soviet Terror of the 1930s was replayed in Eastern Europe. In 1950, the Czech surrealist literary critic Záviš Kalandra was tortured, show tried, and hanged. His friend Eluard declined to join those of Kalandra's colleagues who protested the execution – he would not betray the Communist Party. Breton was disgusted. "How can you tolerate, deep down," he wrote to Eluard, "such degradation to be inflicted on a man who was a friend to you?"[65]

Peretz Markish, who had long since given his loyalty to Stalin, was arrested in 1948. Like so many other Soviet Yiddish writers, in 1952 Markish died with a bullet to the base of his skull. The founders of Slovak DAV, Laco Novomeský and Vladimir Clementis, were both purged after the war. Novomeský was sent to prison; Clementis was hanged. Teige, terrorized by the purges of his friends, died of a heart attack in 1951. He was fifty years old. His friend Biebl, following a peculiar Czech tradition of death by defenestration, committed suicide the same year. In 1967, Wat, a veteran of Stalinist prison and one of very few Polish modernists still among the living, took his own life.

In Eastern Europe as elsewhere, the aesthetic "crisis of representation" was a crisis of modernity, a crisis intensified by Eastern Europe's leapfrogging. The principle of the *Gleichzeitigkeit des Ungleichzeitigen* (simultaneity of the unsimultaneous) very much applied. Everything arrived nearly at once: Freud and Husserl, expressionism and futurism, Dadaism and proletarian poetry. The East European avant-gardes were afflicted from the outset with internal tensions: national identity versus cosmopolitanism, subjectivity versus collectivism, glorification of civilization versus calls for a primitivist paradise.

The movement from the transparency of language to the materiality of language was breathtakingly quick. So, too, was the movement from art as representation to art as transformation. The East European avant-gardists read Dostoevskii and Nietzsche; they believed that terrifying hatred was only a hair's breadth away from the maddest, most desperate love, and that what was falling should still be pushed. If the avant-garde followed this maxim of Nietzsche, suggested the literary critic Boris Groys of its Russian artists, "it was only because it was deeply convinced that the fall could not be broken."[66]

In Eastern Europe, the avant-garde was post-imperial modernism. And for Eastern Europe, there was no post-imperial moment uninflected by the Bolshevik Revolution. Was the avant-gardists' leap into the fire of revolution overdetermined? The nihilism of the pure empty space of the 1920s gave way to the catastrophism of a no-longer empty space of the 1930s. The Revolution devoured its children, adults who had aspired to eternal youth. No one managed to escape with clean hands. Heinrich Heine is said to have remarked, "Jews are like those among whom they live – only more so." So was the avant-garde in Eastern Europe just like the avant-garde elsewhere in Europe – obsessed with subjectivity, the rejection of mimesis, formal experimentation. To this was added an anxiety about backwardness, which made it only more so.

Epilogue

In Eastern Europe, the avant-garde's engagement with communism has cast a shadow over all literary accomplishment. Largely condemned during the socialist realist years, the avant-garde was rehabilitated in the 1950s, its members reinscribed in the communist pantheon. Much of the secondary literature published during the communist years was accordingly hagiographic. With communism's fall, the avant-garde once again fell largely out of favor: after all, if not Party members, these were at the very least fellow travelers who had lent their talents to a murderous revolution. In recent years, the question posed about the East European avant-gardists has been much like that posed about Martin Heidegger: should – can – their aesthetic and ideological legacies be decoupled?

In June 2008, a Polish–Jewish monthly devoted a special issue to Bruno Jasieński.[67] The following spring of 2009, the president of Poland's Institute for National Remembrance sent a letter to the governing council of Jasieński's hometown. It had come to the Institute's attention that in the small town there remained a certain street named after Jasieński – a street that was in effect "a glorification... of the criminal ideology of communism." A Polish literary critic stepped forward with a letter of protest:

> Was Jasieński a communist? He was an antifascist, a romantic of proletarian revolution, a victim of Soviet pathology, a deeply tragic figure. Painfully sensitive to injury and intolerance, he believed – naively? – in a utopia of humanity liberated from national and social conflicts, just as, in the early twentieth century, believed so many of the great thinkers and artists. Anyone unable to distinguish human dreams from brutal totalitarian politics does not understand the twentieth century.[68]

NOTES

1. S. K. Neumann, "Otevřená okna," in *Osma a skupina výtvarných umělců: teorie, kritika, polemika, 1907–1917*, ed. Jiří Padrta and Miroslav Lamač (Prague: Odeon, 1988), pp. 138–40.

2. For comments on an earlier draft of this essay, I would like to thank Amelia Glaser and Timothy Snyder, who was also my collaborator in translating certain passages by Wat. While this essay will focus on northern Eastern Europe, there

were lively modernist movements in Hungary, Romania, and the Balkans as well.

3. Quoted in Czeslaw Milosz, *The History of Polish Literature* (London: Macmillan, 1969), p. 330.

4. Witold Gombrowicz, *Polish Memories*, trans. Bill Johnston (New Haven: Yale University Press, 2004), pp. 109–10.

5. Stanislav K. Neumann, "Moje vlastenectví," in *Básně* (Prague: Nakladatel Fr. Borový, 1920), p. 145.

6. Gombrowicz, *Polish Memories*, p. 91.

7. Jan Lechoń, "Herostrates," quoted in Milosz, *The History of Polish Literature*, p. 385.

8. Aleksander Wat, "Powieść," in *Ucieczka Lotha: Proza*, ed. Krzysztof Rutkowski (London: Polonia, 1988), p. 13.

9. Adam Ważyk, *Dziwna Historia Awangardy* (Warsaw: Czytelnik, 1976), p. 52.

10. The Devětsil Association of Artists, "Statement," in *Between Worlds: A Sourcebook of Central European Avant-Gardes, 1910–1930*, ed. Timothy O. Beson and Éva Forgács (Cambridge, Mass.: MIT Press, 2002), pp. 240–41.

11. Stern and Wat, "GGA," in *Antologia Polskiego Futuryzmu i Nowej Sztuki*, ed. Helena Zaworska (Wrocław: Zakład Narodowy im. Ossolińskich, 1978), p. 3.

12. F. T. Marinetti, "List," Milan 1923, *Zwrotnica* 6 (October 1923): 161.

13. Tadeusz Peiper, "Point of Departure," in *Between Worlds*, pp. 265–66.

14. Melekh Ravitsh, "A kurtse geshikhte fun a dinamisher grupe fun dray yidishe poetn in varshe 1921–1925," in *Warszawska awangarda jidysz*, ed. Karolina Szymaniak and Monika Polit (Gdańsk: słowo/obraz terytoria, 2005), pp. 266–301.

15. Tristan Tzara, "Trzeci list z Paryża: DADA," *Zwrotnica* 3 (November 1922): 76–78.

16. Konrad Winkler, "Bez programu," *Formiści* 2.4 (April 1921): 1–2.

17. F. T. Marinetti, "List," Milan 1923, *Zwrotnica* 6 (October 1923): 161.

18. Aleksander Wat, "Wspomnienia o Futuryzmie," *Miesięcznik Literacki* 2 (January 1930): 68–77.

19. Bruno Iasenskii, Aleksander Vat, and Anatol' Stern to Vladimir Maiakovskii, Warsaw, July 1, 1921, 2852/1/599, Rossiiskii Gosudarstvennyi Arkhiv Literatury i lskusstva (RGALI), Moscow.

20. Roman Jakobson to Vladimir Maiakovskii, Prague, February 8, 1921, fond 336/5/119, RGALI, Moscow.

21. Vladimir Maiakovskii, "Ezdil ia tak," in *Polnoe sobranie sochinenii*, vol. VIII (Moscow: Khudozhestvennoi Literatury, 1958), pp. 331–38.

22. Aleksander Wat, *My Century*, trans. Richard Lourie (New York and London: W.W. Norton and Company, 1988), p. 44. On Maiakovskii in Prague: Jiří Weil, "Vladimir Majakovskij a Praha," in fond Jiří Weil, Literární archiv Památníku národního písemnictví, Prague.

23. Maiakovskii, "Poverkh Varshavy," in *Polnoe sobranie sochinenii*, vol. VIII, pp. 347–57.

24. Maiakovskii, "Naruzhnost' Varshavy," in *Polnoe sobranie sochinenii*, vol. VIII, pp. 344–46.

25. Konrad Winkler, "Bez programu," *Formiści* 2.4 (April 1921): 1–2.

26. Peretz Markish, "Ikh," in *Warszawska awangarda jidysz*, pp. 44–45.

27. Melekh Ravitsh, "A kurtse geshikhte fun a dinamisher grupe fun dray yidishe poetn in varshe 1921–1925," in *Warszawska awangarda jidysz*, pp. 266–301.

28. Jaroslav Seifert, "Řeč davu," in *Dílo Jaroslava Seiferta*, vol. I, ed. Jiří Brabec and Marie Jirásková (Prague: Akropolis, 2001), pp. 27–28.

29. Neumann, "Otevřená okna," in *Osma a skupina výtvarných umělců*, pp. 138–40.

30. Wat, *My Century*, p. 5.

31. Guillaume Apollinaire, "L'Antitradition Futuriste," in Mary Ann Caws, *Manifesto: A Century of isms* (Lincoln: University of Nebraska Press, 2001).

32. Neumann, "Otevřená okna," in *Osma a skupina výtvarných umělců*, pp. 138–40.

33. Leon Chwistek, "About Multiplicity of Reality in Art," in *Between Worlds*, pp. 253–60.

34. Leon Chwistek, "Formizm," *Katalog Formiści: wystawa III* (20 August 1919): 2–8.

35. Leon Chwistek, "Formizm," *Formiści* 2 (April 1920): 2–3.

36. Stanisław Ignacy Witkiewicz, "On 'Deformation' in Pictures," in *Between Worlds*, 251–53.

37. Witkiewicz, "Aesthetic Sketches," in *Between Worlds*, pp. 261–64.

38. Karel Teige, "Malířství a poesie," *Disk* 1 (1923): 19–20.

39. Henryk Berlewi, "In kamf far der nayer forem," in *Warszawska awangarda jidysz*, pp. 122–25.

40. Stanislav K. Neumann, "Chvála nahoty," in *Básně* (Prague: Nakladatel Fr. Borový, 1920), pp. 38–40.

41. Adam Ważyk, "Niedziela," in *Poezja polska okresu międywojennego*, vol. II, ed. Michał Głowiński, Janusz Sławiński, and Janusz Stradecki (Wrocław: Zakład Narodowy imienia Ossolińskich), pp. 301–2.

42. Tadeusz Peiper, "Naga," in *Poezja polska okresu międywojennego*, vol. II, p. 317. English translation by Timothy Snyder.

43. Bruno Jasieński, "Trupy z Kawiorem," in *Poezja polska okresu międywojennego*, vol. II, pp. 280–83.

44. Aleksander Wat, "JA z jednej strony a JA z drugiej strony mego mopsożelaznego piecyka," in *Poezje*, ed. Anna Micińska and Jan Zieliński (Warsaw: Czytelnik, 1997), pp. 307–35.

45. *Ibid.*, p. 312.

46. *Ibid.*, p. 335.

47. Henri Bergson, *Creative Evolution*, trans. Arthur Mitchell (Mineola: Dover Publications, 1998), p. 165.

48. On the influence of Bergson on the Czech writers, see Thomas Ort, "Men without Qualities: Karel Čapek and his Generation, 1911–1938," Ph.D dissertation, New York University, September 2005.

49. S. K. Neumann, "Ať žije život!", *Osma a skupina výtvarných umělců*, pp. 140–142.

50. This phrase is used both by Mary Gluck in *Georg Lukács and His Generation 1900–1918* (Cambridge, Mass.: Harvard University Press, 1985) and by Peter Gay in *Weimar Culture: The Outsider as Insider* (New York: Norton, 2001).

51. Karel Teige, "Poetism," *Between Worlds*, pp. 579–82.

52. Fr. Halas, "List z Czechosłowacji," *Blok* no. 6–7 (September 1924).
53. Lioubomir Mitzich, "No Made in Serbia: Zenitozofja czyli energetyka twórczego zenityzmu," trans. E. Miller, *Blok* no. 6–7 (September 1924). English translation taken from: Ljubomir Micić, "Zenithosophy: or the Energetics of Creative Zenithism," in *Between Worlds*, pp. 514–18.
54. Ljubomir Micić, "Zenitist Manifesto," in *Impossible Histories: Historical Avant-gardes, Neo-avant-gardes, and Post-avant-gardes in Yugoslavia, 1918–1991*, ed. Dubravka Djurić and Miško Šuvakovič (Cambridge, Mass.: MIT Press, 1993), pp. 525–31.
55. Micić, "Zenithosophy," in *Between Worlds*, pp. 514–18.
56. Leon Chwistek, "Formizm," *Katalog Formiśći: wystawa III* (August 20, 1919): 2–8.
57. Jaroslav Seifert, "Ballada o krásné myślence," in *Dílo Jaroslava Seiferta*, vol. I, ed. Jiří Brabec and Marie Jirásková (Prague: Akropolis, 2001), p. 144.
58. Melekh Ravitsh, "A kurtse geshikhte fun a dinamisher grupe fun dray yidishe poetn in varshe 1921–1925," in *Warszawska awangarda jidysz*, pp. 266–301.
59. Ladislav Novomeský, "Slovensko – DAV – Komunizmus (Fragment zo spomienok)," in *DAV: Spomienky a štúdie*, ed. Štefan Drug (Bratislava: Vydatel'stvo Slovenskej akadémie vied, 1965), p. 279.
60. Jasieński and Stern, *Ziemia na lewo*; reprinted in *Antologia Polskiego Futuryzmu i Nowej Sztuki*, ed. Helena Zaworska (Wróclaw: Zakład Narodowy im. Ossolińskich, 1978), p. 74.
61. Feliksa Lichodziejewska, ed., *Od bliskich i dalekich: Korespondencja do Władysława Broniewskiego*, vol. I (Warsaw: Państwowy Instytut Wydawniczy, 1981), pp. 118–20.
62. Jindřich Honzl, "O proletářském divadle," in *Revoluční sborník Devětsil* (Prague: Večernice V. Vortel, 1922), p. 89.
63. Quoted in Piotr Mitzner, "Śmierć futurysty," *Karta* 11 (1993): 58–76; quotation p. 76.
64. See André Breton to Vitěslav Nezval, Paris, March 18, 1938 in Nezval *et al.*, *Korespondence Vítěslava Nezvala*, pp. 96–99; Karel Teige, *Surrealismus proti proudu* (Prague: Surrealistická skupina, 1938).
65. André Breton, "Open Letter to Paul Eluard," in *Free Rein (La Clé des champs)*, trans. Michel Parmentier and Jacqueline d'Amboise (Lincoln: University of Nebraska Press, 1996), pp. 229–31.
66. Boris Groys, *The Total Art of Stalinism*, trans. Charles Rougle (Princeton University Press, 1992), pp. 14–15.
67. See *Midrasz* 6: 134 (June 2008).
68. Edward Balcerzan to Rada gminy Klimontów, Poznań, 23 April 2009, *Gazeta Wyborcza* (25–26 April 2009): 4.

FURTHER READING

Benson, Timothy O., ed. *Central European Avant-gardes: Exchange and Transformation, 1910–1930*. Cambridge, Mass.: MIT Press, 2002.
Benson, Timothy O., and Éva Forgács, eds. *Between Worlds: A Sourcebook of Central European Avant-Gardes, 1910–1930*. Cambridge, Mass.: MIT Press, 2002.

Bojtár, Endre. *East European Avant-Garde Literature*. Budapest: Akademiai Kiado, 1992.

Carpenter, Bogdana. *The Poetic Avant-Garde in Poland, 1918–1939*. Seattle: University of Washington Press, 1983.

Cornis-Pope, Marcel, and John Neubauer, eds. *History of the Literary Cultures of East-Central Europe: Junctures and Disjunctures in the 19th and 20th centuries*. Vol. I. Amsterdam: John Benjamins Publishing Company, 2004.

Djurić, Dubravka, and Miško Šuvaković, eds. *Impossible Histories: Historical Avant-gardes, Neo-avant-gardes, and Post-avant-gardes in Yugoslavia, 1918–1991*. Cambridge, Mass.: MIT Press, 1993.

French, Alfred. *The Poets of Prague: Czech Poetry between the Wars*. Oxford University Press, 1969.

Janacek, G., ed. *Crisis and the Arts: The History of Dada*. Vol. IV: *The Eastern Dada Orbit*. New York: Hall, 1997.

Lodge, Kirsten, trans. and ed. *Solitude, Vanity, Night: An Anthology of Czech Decadent Poetry*. Prague: Charles University, 2008.

Milosz, Czeslaw. *The History of Polish Literature*. London: Macmillan, 1969.

Moss, Kenneth B. *Jewish Renaissance in the Russian Revolution*. Cambridge, Mass.: Harvard University Press, 2009.

Novák, Arne. *Czech Literature*. Trans. Peter Kussi, ed. William E. Harkins. Ann Arbor: Michigan Slavic Publications, 1976.

Sandqvist, Tom. *Dada East: The Romanians of Cabaret Voltaire*. Cambridge, Mass.: MIT Press, 2006.

Shore, Marci. *Caviar and Ashes: A Warsaw Generation's Life and Death in Marxism, 1918–1968*. New Haven, Conn.: Yale University Press, 2006.

Venclova, Tomas. *Aleksander Wat: Life and Art of an Iconoclast*. New Haven, Conn.: Yale University Press, 1996.

14

RODERICK BEATON

Greece

On the tenth day of April, 1910, it was raining hard in Athens. A handsome man, aged forty, dressed in a white flannel suit and matching gloves, hired a two-horse carriage for the short drive to Skaramanga, a port on the coast facing the island of Salamis. Today, the shipyards of Skaramanga and the rusting tankers lying offshore are among the ugliest sights in Greece; a hundred years ago, there was not even a fashionable beach. There was, at least, an inn, where the visitor ordered lunch and a beer. Then, rising from the table, he called for the driver to unhitch one of the horses. Mounting without stirrups, he kicked the horse to a gallop and rode bareback straight into the sea. Far out from the shore, he raised a pistol, held it to his temple, and pulled the trigger. The rider disappeared; the horse swam back to shore. It would be another two weeks before the body washed up.

Pericles Yannopoulos had made a name for himself with a series of newspaper articles and two very thin cultural manifestos published in 1906 and 1907. In one of them, he had written, perhaps prefiguring his suicide:

> A boy who was nothing, running in the light of the sweet mountains of Attica that is like Adonis, saw pass across the pure azure heavens of brilliant noontime the pure-white steed of rebirth with its enormous pure-white wings, and dared, threw himself after it, put out his hand to the base of its wings, and held them upright, burning white. Man and horse descended, trod the earth.
>
> [. . .]
>
> With the first powerful clap of its wings, the male child will be struck by its wing and will fall dead voluptuously, his lips drenched in the honey of voluptuousness.[1]

The style of the extract, no less than that of the clearly deliberated act, will not seem out of place in a collection of essays on European modernism. *Décadentisme* may have begun and been christened in France, but, as this book shows, in the early years of the last century it had a wide reach. The story of Yannopoulos's end is as ironic as it is tragic. The self-appointed apostle of "Greekness," a version of extreme nationalism that was meant to transform his own people and then the universe, Yannopoulos wrote and died in ways that no Greek had ever quite done before him. To a present-day audience, at least with the benefit of a century of hindsight, the whole story seems to come straight from the heart of literary Paris.

In extreme form, the example of Yannopoulos typifies the two poles of Greek modernism as it would develop over the next half century. On the one hand, there was the imperative to define and defend, in the new world of the twentieth century, a modern national identity predicated on the ancient Greek past. On the other hand, there was a strong urge to engage with European modernity, so as not to be left behind as "backward" or "provincial." In short, the dilemma of Greek modernism was the dilemma of how to be both modern *and* Greek at the same time.

This, too, is a matter of hindsight. In Greece, the term "modernism" has only recently begun to find acceptance. Traditionally, histories of Greek literature have been more comfortable speaking of "generations" and "schools." Most of the writers that we think of today as modernists have historically been grouped into either the Athens-based "Generation of the 1930s" or the regionally defined "School of Thessaloniki." The most convincing account of modernism in Greece to date proposes a chronological span defined by two influential essays that were published, respectively, in 1929 and 1961.[2] But in the context of the present volume, even these dates, which are confessedly schematic, are too restrictive. As the example of Yannopoulos shows, from the very beginning of the century, Greek writers were engaging fully with trends that today would be classified as modernist.

Before 1930

No Greek writer active before 1930 has yet been hailed as an out-and-out modernist, although this could change as hindsight continues to be applied. Nevertheless, at least some aspects of modernism have been identified in some of the most important figures of the period.

Newly arrived in Athens from Crete at the start of the century, the young writer Nikos Kazantzakis made his literary debut in 1906 with a bizarre novella in the high *décadentiste* manner: *Serpent and Lily*, where a young couple commits suicide together amidst the voluptuous fragrance of flowers.[3] Kazantzakis followed this fable with several dramas that clearly show the influence of Ibsen and Nietzsche. He would repudiate these early experiments later in his career, when he went on to become Greece's only modern novelist of international renown and a candidate for the Nobel Prize. But that is to get ahead of ourselves.

In 1907, Kostis Palamas, the most prolific poet of the age, published *The Twelve Lays of the Gypsy*. In this poem of epic length and ambition, the narrative coherence is fragmented, and metrical experiments often come close to free verse.[4] The poem views Greek history and culture through the eyes of an "outsider," the unnamed gypsy, and in the process it questions many of the most cherished pillars of Greek society and culture.

For these two writers, and for most of their generation, the natural center of the Greek world was the national capital, Athens. An exception to this general rule was C. P. Cavafy. Much has been made of Cavafy's background in Alexandria, that cosmopolitan city on Egyptian soil, and of his aloofness from the politics and personalities of the Greek state. E. M. Forster, who made Cavafy's acquaintance in 1917, described him unforgettably as "a Greek gentleman in a straw hat, standing absolutely motionless at a slight angle to the universe."[5] Today Cavafy is the only Greek writer of modern times whose name, and even some of whose poems, are widely known and cited in translation around the world. But for all his de-centered position in relation to Greece, Cavafy was not indifferent to the issue of redefining Greek identity for the twentieth century. Almost half the poems he published in his lifetime evoke the historical world that Alexander the Great built up with his conquests, including Cavafy's own Alexandria. These poems celebrate a hybrid world of fluid boundaries, rejecting neat categorizations. But for all the cosmopolitanism that appeals to readers today, there is hierarchy as well as hybridity in lines like the following, spoken by a young man in Alexandria under Ptolemaic or Roman rule in the poem "In the Town of Osroene" (1917):

> We are a mixture here: Syrians, expatriate Greeks, Armenians, Medes.
> Remon is one of us. But last night when
> the moon lit up his sensual features,
> we saw in our minds' eye Plato's Charmides.

A mixture of races, yes. But in the minds of all in that mixture, it is the *Greek* aesthetic ideal of male beauty that stands supreme – as does the Greek language, that same language that once gave expression to the male ideal in Plato's dialogue on the subject, and does again today in the poem we are reading.

This attempt to reconstruct a lost or overlaid collective past is only one aspect of Cavafy's engagement with modernism. When his poems are not set in the historical past, they often explore the ways in which we experience time. In this, Cavafy has been compared with Proust.[6] Finally, throughout his poems there can be found a quasi-religious faith in the permanent aesthetic value of the work of art, something that places Cavafy among other modernists of his time.

Greekness and the national center: the "Generation of the 1930s"

For Greeks, the most shattering impact of modernity on their lives in the early twentieth century came in the form of military defeat by Turkey in September 1922. Greece had been relatively untouched by the horrors of the First World War: it fully engaged as a combatant nation only during the final sixteen months of the War. Yet the Paris Peace Conference of 1919 unintentionally set off a new conflict, which saw Greek troops land at Smyrna (modern Izmir) and advance far into the interior of Anatolia, before they were repulsed by the emerging Turkish nationalist forces that, in 1923, would establish the present-day Republic of Turkey. The defeat was for the Greeks not only a military humiliation: it also became a humanitarian emergency, when more than a million Orthodox Christians, most of them Greek-speaking, were forcibly displaced from their homelands in the former Ottoman Empire, in exchange for the smaller number of Muslims living in Greece.[7] To this day, these events are known in Greece as the "Asia Minor Catastrophe," or simply "the Catastrophe."

It was against this background that the most far-reaching developments towards a distinctively Greek expression of European modernism came about. In 1929, a short polemical book with the title *Free Spirit* appeared in Athens. The book begins with the author imagining himself looking down at the European continent from an airplane far above: from such a height, the distinctions between one country and another begin to fade. *Free Spirit* argues that Europe, for all its tribal differences, is a single entity, and that Greeks ought to go out and embrace their destiny within it: "A litera-ture acquires international significance when it begins to exert an influence, without of course ever ceasing to be influenced itself."[8] The author was the twenty-four-year-old George Theotokas, whose first novel, *Argo*, would take the myth of Jason's legendary voyage and apply it as a metaphor for the youth of Greece growing up in the 1920s, somewhat as Joyce had done with the Ulysses legend in Ireland. The experience of Theotokas's gener-ation is summed up in the novel: "There is no Golden Fleece. But there *is* the voyage of the Argo."[9] If myth could be mobilized as a balancing counterweight against modernity, as T. S. Eliot had proposed in 1923, then lying here at hand was a resource that Greek writers had in abundance, one that at the same time could have compelling power for writers determined to redefine their own national identity in the new geopolitical world of the 1930s.[10]

All of these ideas came together in Athens under the guiding hand of the literary impresario George Katsimbalis, whom Henry Miller would immortalize as the "Colossus of Maroussi." In 1935, Katsimbalis established the literary journal *Ta Nea Grammata (New Letters)*. While avoiding anything so programmatic as a manifesto, this journal would for the next five years provide a platform for poetry, fiction, essays, criticism, and translations, in which new aesthetic ideas from lands abroad (primarily France, Britain, and the United States) came together with a politically cautious attempt to redefine the Hellenic tradition. At the same time as it published some of the earliest poetry of the writers who would become Greece's only two Nobel laureates, George Seferis and Odysseus Elytis, *Ta Nea Grammata* also looked back to the early years of the century, running special issues, for instance, on Palamas and on Pericles Yannopoulos, that doomed high priest of Greekness with whom we began. Theotokas became a contributor to the journal, as did other novelists whose work would for many years define mainstream literary fiction, such as Angelos Terzakis and Kosmas Politis. An editorial in 1936 coined the term "Generation of the 1930s," which has remained in use ever since, and is still largely synonymous with what today might be termed "high modernism" in Greece. Even the Marxist Yannis Ritsos, who would later be retrospectively assimilated to the Generation of the 1930s, published some of his earliest poems in the journal pseudonymously, thus launching one of the most prolific careers in Greek poetry.

The fusion of Greek myth and Greek landscape with a new, modernist aesthetic was brought about in a variety of ways. The curriculum vitae of George Seferis is that of the exemplary modernist: brought up bilingually in Greek and French in the cosmopolitan city of Smyrna, Seferis spent six years at university in Paris, where he imbibed everything that had been happening in French poetry from Moréas (his compatriot) to Fargue and Claudel. On returning to Greece, he entered his country's diplomatic service (as did Claudel and Saint-John Perse). Then in 1931, while on his first diplomatic posting in London, Seferis discovered the poetry of T. S. Eliot – and with it, his own role as a new kind of Greek poet. Beginning with the sequence of twenty-four short poems to which he gave the daring title *Mythistorema*, or *Novel* (1935), which he wrote while he was translating *The Waste Land*, Seferis introduced into Greek poetry a fragmentary, allusive style in which, as in Eliot, what coherence can be said to exist is to be found in the lost resources of ancient myth. But in Seferis's poetry of the 1930s, myth is not so much a *counter*weight to modernity (as it was was for Eliot) as a *weight* from which the modern poet struggles to escape. One of the poems of *Mythistorema* begins:

> I awoke with this head of marble in my arms,
> it exhausts my elbows and I have nowhere to put it down.

In this nightmare encounter with the ancient past, it is the living who come off the worse:

> my arms disappear and come towards me
> truncated.[11]

Odysseus Elytis, like Seferis, spent time in Paris during the 1920s. Born eleven years after Seferis, he had been young enough to learn from the Surrealism of André Breton and Paul Eluard, although he would always distance himself afterwards from Surrealism as a movement. In 1936, Seferis had written the much-quoted line, "Wherever I travel Greece wounds me." Six years later, Elytis would turn this idea on its head – while yet using very similar images of Hellenic continuity:

> I spoke of love of the health of the rose the sun's ray
> which all by itself finds its way to the heart
> of Greece that treads with assurance on the sea
> of Greece that takes me travelling always
> to naked mountains crowned with snow.[12]

In an essay he wrote shortly after *Mythistorema*, Seferis declared the need for Greek artists to *take back* from Europe the cultural inheritance of ancient Greece (which had spread far and wide since the Renaissance) and graft it onto their own indigenous traditions and lived experience.[13] This is still an entirely modernist agenda – and, characteristically, the essay was part of a debate, conducted in the columns of *Ta Nea Grammata*, about the nature of "Greekness."

By 1938, however, the Generation of the 1930s had moved away from the outward-looking optimism of *Free Spirit*. The future no longer lay, they argued, in reaching out to *export* to Europe the best that Greek artists can do, but in *bringing back* what is "ours," to work on at home. What has happened here? Once again, the answer is to be found in the geopolitics of the period. Greece had weathered the economic crisis of the early 1930s relatively well, but (as elsewhere in continental Europe) at terrible political cost.[14] On August 4, 1936, a bloodless *coup d'état* marked the beginning of a military dictatorship that would last five years. The official rhetoric of the Metaxas regime, echoing Mussolini and Hitler, proclaimed the "Third Greek Civilization" (after the classical and the Byzantine). But the regime's simplistic ideology had (of course) nothing to do with those earlier Greek civilizations. This was raw nationalism of a distinctively twentieth-century cast. In the name of this "civilization," censorship was imposed. What we now call modernism was not directly threatened, as it was in Nazi Germany. Still, writers found it necessary and prudent to draw their material, at least ostensibly, from their imaginations or from the past. There was no longer a potentially harmonious modern Europe to reach out to. The modernity that Theotokas had celebrated less than a decade earlier had turned by 1938 into the harbinger of a new world war to come.

Cosmopolitan peripheries

The quest that Theotokas and Seferis had initiated to redefine Greek national identity in a new relationship with Europe did not, as a rule, engage very far with the most radical manifestations of modernism abroad. With few exceptions, novelists in Athens avoided the kind of formal experiments that we associate with, say, the later work of Joyce or Woolf. In poetry, the most obvious formal indication of the arrival of modernism was the rise of free verse during the 1930s. Yet liberation from the constraints of form, at least among the Athens-based "Generation of the 1930s," never became a complete break from intelligibility. More radical experiments took place outside the mainstream. In Athens, the self-proclaimed Surrealists, Andreas Embirikos and Nikos Engonopoulos, were ridiculed when they first began publishing their work. Embirikos's first book of prose poems, published in 1935, was allegedly the product of automatic writing. A psychoanalyst trained in France, Embirikos would become an outspoken advocate of complete sexual liberation. It was not until 1980, five years after his death, that all of his poetry would be published in unexpurgated editions, where it would win belated critical acclaim. Engonopoulos, today, is better known for his paintings, which follow a style in the school of De Chirico, than for his poetry, which blends deliberate pomposity with self-deprecating humor.

Despite their avowed admiration for Breton, the Greek Surrealists never produced a manifesto of their own. For this, they have come in for some negative criticism in recent years; they have also been accused of political conservatism, in contrast with the progressive commitment of Breton's second manifesto. In one respect, however, they *were* radical for their Greek context, and this is in their cosmopolitanism. Embirikos, who was born in Romania and had spent part of his childhood in the Crimea, exults in landscapes and people remote from Greece; Engonopoulos, descended from a minor hero of the Greek War of Independence of the 1820s, nudges his readers to remember that the famed Hellenic patriots of his ancestral island, Hydra, had been ethnic Albanians. Engonopoulos's most famous poem has the paradoxical title *Bolivár: A Greek Poem* (1944): it juxtaposes characters and situations from modern Greek history with exotic characters and locations from South America.[15]

In fiction, the most experimental innovations came out of Greece's second city, or "co-capital," Thessaloniki (also known as Salonica).[16] It was here that a group of writers, loosely grouped around the early 1930s periodical *Makedonikes Imeres* [Macedonian Days], became the first to translate Joyce, Woolf, Rilke, and Zweig (among others) into Greek. In time, this group, among whom the best known was the novelist Nikos Gabriel Pentzikis, would become known as the "School of Thessaloniki."[17] These novelists turn their backs ostentatiously on the traditional business of storytelling, preferring instead to bring the reader inside the artist's workshop to witness the tribulations of trying to convey the experience of life on paper. Like such experimenters elsewhere in Europe, these writers are fearless in treading the uncharted territory of the subjective consciousness, and in trampling on the conventions of realism.

It is tempting to wonder whether the avoidance of conventional realism, and the evident cosmopolitanism, of the "School of Thessaloniki" have their origins in the very different character of their home city from the national capital. Until its incorporation into the Greek state in November 1912, Thessaloniki had been for many centuries a truly multicultural city: the largest community within its population in 1912 was Jewish, mainly Sephardim whose first language was Judeo-Spanish. After a devastating fire in 1917, much of the city's central area came to be rebuilt by the French architect and archaeologist Ernest Hébrard – along uncompromisingly modernist architectural lines. When the armies of the Third Reich arrived on April 9, 1941, Thessaloniki was still only halfway to finding its modern identity. The city's substantial Bulgarian- and Turkish-speaking communities were by then long gone. In the spring of 1943, almost 50,000 Jews were rounded up and deported to Auschwitz; very few survived, and even fewer returned to their home city. From 1943 until the early 1990s, when economic migrants began to arrive from a newly opening Albania, Thessaloniki was, for the only time in its modern history, a homogeneous Greek city. And it was only in the midst of that period, beginning in the 1960s, that writers like Yorgos Ioannou and Nikos Bakolas would begin to record the historical fabric and feel, the memories and the inhabitants, of what had by that time become, as the subtitle of a recent book has it, a "city of ghosts."[18]

War, civil war, and their aftermath

Between April 1941 and September 1943, Greece was occupied and partitioned among three Axis powers: Germany, Italy, and Bulgaria. After the

Italian capitulation, the Germans and Bulgarians remained until October 1944. Then, in the aftermath of the war, the political tensions that had been created all over Europe by Nazi occupation broke into open civil war, which lasted until 1949. Under the occupation and in the years that followed, poets who had begun publishing during the previous decade turned to the longer poem as a medium. Perhaps drawing on the epic tradition and its modernist revival (in works such as Pound's *Cantos*, *In Parenthesis* by David Jones, and the *Anabasis* of Saint-John Perse), these writers found common ground, in the face of appalling conditions of defeat and privation, in a more or less visionary affirmation.

By contrast, the younger poets who began publishing at the end of the war or a little later adopted a much bleaker perspective, one that had more in common with the contemporary writings of Sartre and Camus. What is the point of writing at all, Manolis Anagnostakis demanded, when everybody knows that "poems don't bring down regimes"?[19] As an eighteen-year-old medical student, Anagnostakis had dodged bullets in Thessaloniki while the Germans were still there. Later, in the civil war, he had been condemned to death for being a communist, only winning reprieve at the last minute. The poems of Anagnostakis and his like-minded contemporaries Aris Alexandrou and Titos Patrikios have precious little to say about "Greekness"; for them, the "imagined community" is that of the political left. And what these Marxist idealists shared from 1949 onwards was the knowledge of defeat.

Out of that same experience would come, in the early 1960s, Greece's most fully realized modernist novel: the trilogy known collectively as *Drifting Cities*, by Stratis Tsirkas.[20] Like Cavafy before him, Tsirkas was born into the Greek community of Egypt, moving to Greece in the 1950s. A lifelong Marxist, he witnessed the events he describes in his trilogy, which is set in Jerusalem, Cairo, and Alexandria during the Second World War. *Drifting Cities* has a huge cast of characters – British, Austrian, German, Jewish, and Egyptian, as well as Greek – making the trilogy one of the most cosmopolitan Greek works of the century. At the same time, the novels draw on the ideas of Eliot and Seferis about myth, and they perhaps also represent the fullest working-out, after Joyce's *Ulysses*, of what Eliot called the "mythical method." The trilogy has an acknowledged political agenda: to vindicate the position of the defeated Greek left, and to understand the causes of that defeat. To this end, Tsirkas avails himself fully of modernist techniques such as stream-of-consciousness, alternating viewpoints, and elliptical narration, as well as the controlling use of myth.

I end this brief survey of modernism in Greece with a return to a figure mentioned near the beginning. Nikos Kazantzakis, after almost twenty years of travelling abroad, returned to Greece in the late 1930s to publish his verse epic, a monster-sequel to Homer's *Odyssey*, in 1938.[21] Kazantzakis was still in Greece, living on the nearby island of Aegina, when war broke out and the occupying troops arrived. Confined to his small island alongside the woman who would soon become his second wife, the tethered wanderer submitted to her pestering: "why don't you write the story of that devilish Zorba?" So he did, and the result, first published in 1946, was the novel known in most languages, though not in Greek, as *Zorba the Greek*. When he began writing *Zorba* in 1941, Kazantzakis was fifty-eight years old. This book launched the elderly Kazantzakis on a new career as a writer, one that would bring him international fame, with three of his books made into films in French and English – the only Greek novelist ever to be so rewarded.[22]

Until recently, the novels of Kazantzakis's final years were thought of as a throwback to the Romanticism of the previous century. Their plots are linear; with one (albeit notable) exception, they eschew formal experiment; and their epic-style clash of personalities and ideologies can be compared with justice to the novels of Dostoevskii and Thomas Mann. But Kazantzakis had lived through the heyday of modernism and could not be untouched by it: his own earliest work, as we saw, bore the hallmarks of *décadentisme*, Ibsen, and Nietzsche. Beneath the surface realism of his later novels, Kazantzakis makes much subtler, but telling, use of modernist aesthetics. *Zorba* is not only the story of the lovable, footloose rogue whose zest for life and home-spun philosophy are enough to sweep away all intellectual cobwebs and overcome any disaster. The book also establishes itself, through allusion and the kind of "continuous parallel" that Eliot advocated, as a modern equivalent of the Socratic dialogue and the medieval saint's life. In Kazantzakis's *Christ Recrucified* (written 1948, and published in the United States as *The Greek Passion*), Eliot's "mythical method" is still more evident. The whole story is built upon a sustained parallel between events in a Greek village in Anatolia at the beginning of the 1920s and the Biblical story of Christ's Passion. Similarly, *Freedom and Death* (1950), Kazantzakis's take on inter-communal warfare in his native Crete at the time of his childhood, has justly been described as a "modern *Iliad*": once again, a "continuous parallel" is maintained, through allusive details, between the events of the story and the ancient myth. And in *The Last Temptation of Christ* (1951), Kazantzakis goes further still. The last four chapters of the novel extend Jesus' life for more than thirty years, describing events that might have been, and which seem really to unfold in the narrative, before returning the hero to complete his mission and die on the Cross. This startling departure from realist conventions, the inheritance certainly of Bergson, and possibly also of Borges, who used a similar distortion of time in one of his stories, brings Kazantzakis beyond modernism to the threshold of the later postmodernism.[23]

NOTES

1. P. Yannopoulos, Ἄπαντα [*Complete Works*], vol. I, ed. D. Lazogiorgos-Ellinikos (Athens: n.p. 1963), p. 222. For the story of his suicide see pp. xl–xliii and 283–4 of the same book.
2. D. Tziovas, "Introduction," in *Greek Modernism and Beyond* (Lanham, MD: Lexington 1997), pp. 1–23.
3. Trans. Theodora Vasils (Berkeley: University of California Press, 1980).
4. Trans. and ed. G. Thomson (London: Lawrence and Wishart, 1969).
5. "The Poetry of C. P. Cavafy," in E. M. Forster, *Pharos and Pharillon* (Richmond: Hogarth Press, 1923), reprinted in *The Mind and Art of C.P. Cavafy: Essays on His Life and Work* (Athens: Denise Harvey 1983), p. 13.
6. R. Beaton, "Cavafy and Proust," *Grand Street* (New York) 6 (1987): 127–41.
7. For a moving account of the population exchange and its consequences, down to the present day, see B. Clark, *Twice a Stranger: The Mass Expulsions that Forged Modern Greece and Turkey* (London: Granta; Cambridge, Mass.: Harvard University Press, 2006).
8. G. Theotokas, Ελεύθερο πνεύμα, ed. K.Th. Dimaras (Athens, 1973), p. 37; for translation see *Modern Greek Studies Yearbook*, 2 (1986): 153–200.
9. Αργώ, vol. 1 (Athens, n.d.): 310.
10. T. S. Eliot, "Ulysses, Order and Myth," in *James Joyce: The Critical Heritage*, ed. R. Deming, vol. I (New York: Routledge & Kegan Paul, 1970), pp. 268–71.
11. *Mythistorema*, 3 (the poem is untitled).
12. Ήλιος ο πρώτος [Sun the First], section 3 (1942; Athens: Ikaros 1971), p. 14, probably written in 1940.
13. Δοκιμές [Essays], ed. G. P. Savvidis, 3rd edn, vol. I (Athens, 1981). For translation, see G. Seferis, *On the Greek Style*, trans. R. Warner and Th.D. Frangopoulos (London: Bodley Head, 1966), pp. 73–97.
14. M. Mazower, *Greece and the Inter-War Economic Crisis* (Oxford University Press, 1991).
15. For a good bilingual selection, see Nikos Engonopoulos, *The Beauty of a Greek: Poems*, ed. and trans. David Connolly (Athens: Ypsilon, 2007).
16. See, most fully in English, P. Mackridge and E. Yannakaki, *Ourselves and Others: The Development of a Greek Macedonian Cultural Identity since 1912* (Oxford: Berg, 1997).
17. Of Pentzikis's fiction, only *Mother Thessaloniki* has been translated, by L. Marshall (Athens: Kedros, 1998); see also G. Thaniel, *Homage to Byzantium: The Life and Work of Nikos Gabriel Pentzikis* (St. Paul, Minn.: North Central Publishing, 1983).
18. M. Mazower, *Salonica: City of Ghosts* (London: HarperCollins, 2004).
19. Book-length translations of Anagnostakis's poems are by K. Friar (*The Target: Selected Poems*, New York: Pella, 1980) and P. Ramp (*Poems*, Nottingham: Shoestring 1998), both out of print.
20. Trans. K. Cicellis (New York: Simon and Schuster, 1974; rpt. Athens: Kedros, 1995).
21. *The Odyssey: A Modern Sequel*, trans. K. Friar (London: Secker and Warburg, 1958).

22. *He Who Must Die* (Dassin, 1956), *Zorba the Greek* (Cacoyannis, 1966), *The Last Temptation of Christ* (Scorsese, 1988).
23. R. Beaton, "The Temptation that Never Was: Kazantzakis and Borges," in D. Middleton, ed., *Scandalizing Jesus? "The Last Temptation of Christ" Fifty Years On* (New York: Continuum, 2005), pp. 85–95.

FURTHER READING

There are two good comprehensive anthologies: David Ricks, ed., *Modern Greek Writing* (London: Peter Owen, 2003) and the bilingual *A Century of Greek Poetry 1900–2000*, edited by Peter Bien, Karen Van Dyck, and others (available from http://www.greeceinprint.com). The fullest treatment of the subject of this chapter is to be found in Dimitris Tziovas, ed., *Greek Modernism and Beyond* (Lanham, Md.: Lexington, 1997). For more information on the writers discussed here and their context see Roderick Beaton, *An Introduction to Modern Greek Literature*, 2nd edn. (Oxford University Press, 1999).

Of the writers mentioned in this chapter, only those listed below have generated a significant bibliography of translations and commentary in English. For all others, see the information given in notes to the chapter.

Cavafy

There have been no fewer than eight complete translations of Cavafy's 154 "canonical" poems published in English, half of them in the twenty-first century. Recommended are *The Collected Poems*, trans. Evangelos Sachperoglou (Oxford University Press, 2007) for its facing Greek text (ed. Anthony Hirst) and introduction by Peter Mackridge and, as a taster, the *Selected Poems*, trans. Avi Sharon (London: Penguin Classics, 2008).

Elytis

The Collected Poems of Odysseus Elytis, trans. Jeffrey Carson and Nikos Sarris, expanded edn. (Baltimore, Md.: Johns Hopkins University Press, 2004).

Kazantzakis

All seven of the major novels, originally published by Cassirer (Oxford) and Simon and Schuster (New York) in the 1950s and early 1960s are currently in print (London: Faber). For an authoritative study of the author and his work, see Peter Bien, *Kazantzakis: Politics of the Spirit*, 2 vols. (Princeton University Press, 1989–2007).

Ritsos

Repetitions, Testimonies, Parentheses, trans. Edmund Keeley (Princeton University Press, 1990).
The Fourth Dimension, trans. Peter Green and Beverly Bardsley (Princeton University Press and London: Anvil, 1993).

Seferis

The standard translation is the *Complete Poems*, translated, edited and introduced by Edmund Keeley and Philip Sherrard (Princeton University Press and London: Anvil, 1995). See also Roderick Beaton, *George Seferis: Waiting for the Angel: A Biography* (London and New Haven: Yale University Press, 2003).

All quotations from Greek in this chapter are in my own translation.

15

NERGIS ERTÜRK

Turkey

In an essay entitled "Some Europes in Their History," J. G. A. Pocock describes a sixteenth-century map of Europe composed in the figure of "a crowned woman, whose head was the Iberian Peninsula and whose heart was situated at Prague."[1] What is striking about this map, Pocock observes, is how its authors push "the Baltic as far East and the Black Sea as far North as they dare, hoping to bring them close enough to each other to justify the description of Europe as a continent."[2] Though it is no more than a peninsula or extension of Asia, the European subcontinent continues to this day to map itself as an autonomous territory demarcated by what Étienne Balibar has called a "great Wall of Europe."[3]

As a geographic *and* cultural copula linking the subcontinent of Europe to Asia, Turkey has always been a volatile element of this fantasy, in the figure of the "terrible Turk" produced by Europeans consolidating for them-selves a European identity. With the nineteenth-century integration of the Ottoman Empire into the geopolitical network of capitalist modernity, a reciprocal dynamic of identity formation began to take shape on the other side of Europe's "great Wall," with a fantasy of "Europe" taking center stage in the consolidation of a new Turkish identity. As an object of often intense desire, Europe continues to function in the Turkish social imaginary, today, as an idealized figure of modernity with which one must "catch up" – or else as a threat to Turkish culture to be avoided. In analyz-ing the performative repertoire through which the Turkish subject projects the fantasy of Europe, the sociologist Meltem Ahıska has described the "temporal/spatial imagining of modern Turkish national identity" in what she calls "Occidentalism."[4] Neither an "internalized Orientalism," nor a simple "defensive reaction against the West,"[5] Occidentalism, as Ahıska uses the term, points to the *structure* of fantasy that mediates both positive and negative Turkish desire for Europe. My argument in what follows is that in Turkey, the emergence of literary modernism, in all its plural, discontinu-ous, and at times contradictory forms, cannot be understood independently of this Occidentalist social imaginary.[6]

In many ways, Turkish literary modernism begins with the symbolist poetry of Yahya Kemal [Beyatlı] (1884–1958)[7] and his formative exile in Paris between 1903 and 1912. Modernism in the visual and plastic arts in Turkey can be dated to the same period, appearing with the emergence of the impressionist painting of the "1914 Generation" (1914 Kuşağı).[8] These artists were educated at the Ottoman School of Fine Arts (Sanayi-i Nefise Mekteb-i Âlisi) and sent to Paris on government fellowships for study at the atelier of Fernand Cormon. Such sponsorship is as good an example as any, we might say, of complicity between the creative appetite in Turkey for aesthetic modernism, and the political vanguardism of both the Ottoman imperial state and the Turkish Republic, which emerged with a state program of modernization.

In the writings of Kemal and his contemporaries, Ahmet Hamdi [Tanpınar] (1901–62) and Peyami [Safa] (1899–1961), the desire for modernism was more ambivalent. Kemal, Tanpınar, and Safa turned to the writings of Mallarmé, Bergson, Rimbaud, and Baudelaire in search of a *traditionalist* modernism consonant with the critique of extreme rationalization they saw emerging in Europe itself. In this sense, it was not to Europe as an uncomplicated modernity of progress, but to a Europe of internal contradiction and dissent that Kemal, Tanpınar, and Safa looked, seeking a model for their own discontent with extreme modernization in Turkey. Favoring new forms of poetic and prosaic expression, but looking simultaneously to the past, these authors produced their own culturally modernist discourses of melancholy and loss.

The heterogeneous history of Turkish modernism, which left to the second half of the twentieth century a unique legacy, would take a remarkable turn in the poetry of the İkinci Yeni (Second New) poets and the novels of Oğuz Atay and Orhan Pamuk. To be sure, the oscillations of these writers themselves, within the Occidentalist binary, demonstrate that the canonical texts of Western European modernism continue to serve as a rich source of new critical openings in and onto Turkish literature. But this observation should not obscure the fact that the Turkish encounter with European modernism, in a dynamic one ought not to celebrate too hastily, is in many ways determined by an uneven transnational history positing Europe as the object of desire, at the expense of any other.

Conservative modernism

The *Tanzimat* (Reorganization) period of the nineteenth century is a crucial turning point in the history of the Ottoman Empire, since it marks the advent of a wide range of modernizing measures. These include the abolition of the Janissary forces and their replacement with a modern army, the reorganization of imperial bureaucracy on a European model, the adoption of new penal and commercial codes, and the establishment of new naval and engineering schools.[9] To observe that many of these measures were undertaken for the defense of the state apparatus itself, against the encroachment of the European Great Powers, is not to diminish their novelty to the culture they were meant to guard. Indeed, Auguste Comte, the founding philosopher of positivism, was impressed enough with the imperial reform project to invite the Turks, in an enthusiastic letter delivered to the reformist Grand Vizier Mustafa Reşit Paşa in 1853, to join his new "positive religion" of humanity.[10]

Thus it was that the most important promoters of modernism in Turkey, during the first half of the twentieth century, were the bureaucratic agents of the Ottoman imperial and Turkish Republican states, themselves. The first encounter of Ottoman Turkish painters with European modernism took place in this context, as the artists of the "1914 Generation," educated in new imperial schools as well as abroad in Europe, rejected the pictorial realism of their instructors at the Ottoman School of Fine Arts, introducing new impressionist techniques to the Turkish scene.[11] These impressionist painters were among the founders, in 1908, of the Ottoman Painters Society (Osmanlı Ressamlar Cemiyeti), which staged exhibitions of work by new painters at the Galatasaray Lycée in Istanbul, starting in 1916.

Educated in both the traditional and the reformed imperial schools, Yahya Kemal had long since left Turkey to study at the École des Sciences Politiques in Paris. A journey that began at the age of eighteen, as a Young Turk sympathizer, would take a turn in Paris, as Kemal, unable to complete his studies, embraced the bohemian life of the Latin Quarter. In his posthumously published memoir, *Çocukluğum, Gençliğim, Siyâsî ve Edebî Hatıralarım* [My Childhood, My Youth, My Political and Literary Memories] (1973), Kemal describes the detour he made through the writings of Hugo, Gautier, Baudelaire, and Mallarmé, emphasizing the special influence of José-Maria de Heredia. "In the Quartier-Latin of 1907," Kemal explained, "a young follower of Heredia appeared behind the times . . . [but] I realized I finally discovered through Heredia the new Turkish that I had been searching for. Our spoken Turkish was like the white language [*beyaz lisan*] of ancient Greek and Latin."[12]

Although Kemal's identification with Heredia's neo-Classicism may seem incompatible with his commitment to Baudelairean and Mallarméan symbolism, this contradiction can be understood in the context of the Ottoman Turkish poetics and language politics of the day. The traditions of Ottoman classical poetry had been transformed when the Western-influenced Young

Ottomans of the second half of the nineteenth century introduced new poetic themes. With the advent of mass print culture, the high written Ottoman Turkish of the literati and the state was simplified for public use, and the intensification of translation and printing activities narrowed the gap between the spoken and written registers of Ottoman Turkish. During this time of linguistic and literary transformation, Heredia's neo-Classicism pointed Kemal to the possibility of using older poetic forms within the new, simplified Turkish language. Mallarmé's "pure poetics," meanwhile, shaped Kemal's conception of "derûnî âhenk," or "inner harmony," a term that describes the poetic unity of word order, meter, and rhythm.[13] Kemal's adapted neo-Classicism *is* modernist to the extent that his melancholic thematization of ruin and decadence, despite and against his own cultural agenda, registers something essential in the tensions and ambiguities of traditionalism in the vanishing Turkish present (a quality that in many ways places his work in the company of Baudelaire and Benjamin).

After the War, Kemal founded the bi-monthly literary journal *Dergâh* [Convent] in Istanbul, publishing it between April 1921 and January 1923, while the Turkish War of Independence (1919–22) against the occupying forces of Great Britain, France, Italy, and Greece was fought to a close. The *Dergâh* editorial collective planned to publish a series of volumes of poetry, but this project evidently got no further than the appearance of Ahmet Haşim's symbolist *Göl Saatleri* [The Hours of the Lake] (1921). In many ways, the centrality of *Dergâh* to Turkish literary modernism lay in its support for the work of a group of Bergsonist intellectuals that included the pedagogue, academic, and practitioner of traditional arts Ismayil Hakkı [Baltacıoğlu] (1886–1978), and the novelist, poet, and critic Ahmet Hamdi [Tanpınar]. These Bergsonist intellectuals opposed the rationalist and positivist conceptual underpinnings of the Ottoman modernization project, supporting the Turkish national struggle for liberation as a spontaneous and "creative leap," or *élan vital* (*hayat hamlesi*), set against the technological determinism of imperial Europe.[14]

Although the *Dergâh* intellectuals had been marginalized, in political terms, by the foundation of the Turkish Republic in 1923, they constituted one of the most important counter-cultures of the Republican period of 1923–50. During this period, Mustafa Kemal [Atatürk] (1881–1938) and the ruling Republican People's Party (CHP) intensified the state-led social engineering projects of the defunct empire, implementing a new series of radical civic, judicial, and cultural reforms. Edicts that Atatürk issued abolished the sultanate (1922) and the caliphate (1924); banned traditional attire and mandated Western attire (1925); replaced the Perso-Arabic script of Ottoman Turkish with the Latin phonetic alphabet (1928); and mandated that the call to prayer (*ezan*) be performed in Turkish (1932).[15] Against the nationalism and secularism of this Republican state agenda, which sought to break every tie with Ottoman–Islamic institutions, many former members of the *Dergâh* collective took a position of "conservative modernism" committed to linking the Republican present to the Ottoman past. For many of these intellectuals, the concept of *gelenek*, or tradition, described not a set of dead customs, but still-living practices to be located in the flux of *durée* of the Republican present.

In a 1938 article entitled "Yeni Türk San'atkârı yahut Frenkten Türke Dönüş" [The New Turkish Artist, or the Return from the Frank to the Turk], the scholar and translator Sabahattin [Eyüboğlu] (1908–73), who worked with Leo Spitzer and Erich Auerbach during their exile in Turkey, described the trajectory of the new Turkish artist as one of homecoming through the "Frank." He pointed to Yahya Kemal as the exemplary figure of such homecoming. "To return from Europe," Eyüboğlu observed, "does not mean to leave it behind, but rather to mix it with ourselves. (Failing to return from Europe means to mix into it, to be digested instead of digesting it.)"[16] While it might be said that in Eyüboğlu's hands, both "Europe" and "Turkey" are improbably monolithic and homogeneous categories, his narrative illuminates the extent to which no account of the Turkish desire for modernism, even those more nuanced than his own, can extricate itself entirely from the Occidentalist historical imaginary.

"Occidentalism" thus accounts for the process by which the projection of fantasies of "Europe" becomes an integral component of socially elite Turkish identity formation. The term is critically useful precisely in its emphasis on the *uneven* process and historical field in which the fantasy of Europe operates – whether it is constructed, as in that portion of Kemal's memoirs written before his departure, as a passion "for the radiant [*nurlu*] world of Europe,"[17] or, as in those written after his return, as a "homecoming through the Frank." Meanwhile, Eyüboğlu's own account of modernist homecoming via Paris stands as a useful complication of currently fashionable celebrations of diasporic modernism, insofar as Eyüboğlu, unmoved by the liberatory potential of transnational migration, settled, in this essay, into the nationalist modernism that such liberation *also* enabled.

As prominent conservative modernists, Tanpınar and Safa are also worth mentioning in this context. Considered by many to be the most important writer of the Turkish Republican period, Tanpınar openly identified Kemal, Mallarmé, and Valéry as his most important literary influences,[18] and his writings circle continuously the question of what he saw as the "schism" of Turkish identity. Tanpınar's majestic work of encyclopedic literary historiography, *XIX. Asır Türk Edebiyatı Tarihi* [History of Nineteenth-Century

Turkish Literature] (1942; rev. 1956), revisits this most contested period of Turkish literary history, in an effort to overcome the division between "East" and "West" that Tanpınar saw as blemishing Turkish cultural identity.

Tanpınar's use of the monolithic Occidentalist categories "East" and "West" can be as uncritical as Eyüboğlu's. Yet Tanpınar's novels, *Huzur* [A Mind at Peace] (1949) and *Saatleri Ayarlama Enstitüsü* [The Time Regulation Institute] (1954),[19] work in many ways against his worst impulses as a critic, dramatizing the limitations of Occidentalist discourse by showing the futility of any quest for national cultural authenticity. The melancholic tale of a failed love affair, *A Mind at Peace* ends by acknowledging the impossibility of restoring the past. (It is in this sense that, as the critic Nurdan Gürbilek has said of Tanpınar, "[p]recisely because he was obsessed with unity, he was able to narrate loss so well."[20]) In the novel, the classical Ottoman music that the protagonist's lover sings transports him to "the age of Sultan Selim III, to Shaykh Galip, to the era of Sultan Mahmud II, to Mümtaz's own aestival reminiscences, to Kanlıca twilights, to the Kandilli hill, and to the astounding Play of Light on Bosphorus daybreaks"; yet it also "conjure[s] the phantom of a hindrance between her voice and himself."[21] And the satire of Turkish modernization that drives *The Time Regulation Institute*, a hyperbolic account of an agency charged with synchronizing all the clocks in Turkey (and later the world), stages the hollowness of the quest for genealogical narratives, with architectural metaphors of rootless dwelling.

The literary and journalistic career of Safa, one of the most important ideologues of Turkish nationalist conservatism (*milliyetçi muhafazakârlık*), was marked by the tumultuous political climate of the Republican and postwar periods. An influential member of bohemian literary and artistic circles in the late 1920s, Safa was close to Nâzım Hikmet, the futurist communist poet, from 1928 through the early 1930s. Safa endorsed Nâzım's radical poetics, dedicating to Nâzım his most successful psychological novel, *Dokuzuncu Hariciye Koğuşu* [The Ninth Surgical Ward] (1930), in an expression of friendship. By the mid-1930s the two had parted ways, however, publishing columns attacking each other in the left-leaning newspaper *Tan* (Safa eventually left for the weekly *Hafta*), in one of the best-known episodes of "fight literature" (*kavga yazıları*) in Turkish cultural history.[22]

Safa's modernism survived his embrace of the political right entirely intact. His most important (if neglected) novel, *Matmazel Noraliya'nın Koltuğu* [Mademoiselle Noralia's Armchair] (1949), is a document of what we might call Safa's corporatist nationalism, composed in broken Turkish and larded with Arabic and French terminology and extracts from Rimbaud's "L'Éternité" and Aldous Huxley's *The Perennial Philosophy*. Written during a period of engagement with parapsychology, *Matmazel Noraliya'nın Koltuğu* might be said to register the crisis of a disenchanted modernity in linguistic fragmentation, attempting to supplement the extreme rationalization of the Republican state with a new form of spiritualism.[23] Without a doubt, Safa's novel risks reproducing the most vulgar instantiations of the Occidentalist social imaginary, in its attribution of the leading role in resolving global moral crisis to the Turkish nation as a synthesis of the East and the West. But we cannot ignore that in many ways, Safa's dialogues with Rimbaud and Huxley, in *Matmazel Noraliya'nın Koltuğu*, work against his own political and cultural agenda as its author, and that the very untenability of the Occidentalist binarism itself (East/West; spirit/body; ideal/material) tends to force our attention to "Europe" and "Turkey" as radically heterogeneous sites of a *crisis* of the modern, rather than of its settled progress.

The avant-garde in Turkey

At the other end of the political spectrum, by this time, we can find Nâzım Hikmet [Ran] (1901–1963), who is without doubt the most influential figure of Turkish modernism known outside Turkey (his writings have been translated into more than fifty languages). Arriving in the Soviet Union in 1921, Nâzım studied between 1922 and 1924 at the Communist University for the Workers of the East in Moscow. At a time when Russian futurist and constructivist experimentation was in many ways reaching its peak, Nâzım found inspiration in the drama of Meyerhold and the free verse poetry of Maiakovskii, joining both authors for literary events and performances during 1923.[24]

In Turkey, the publication of Nâzım's poetry collection *835 Satır* (*835 Lines*, 1929) in the Latin alphabet announced the birth of a new Turkish poetics, introducing to Turkish poetry free verse, typographic innovation, and revolutionary political themes. Nâzım's poem "San'at Telâkkisi" [Regarding Art] (1929) outlined the principles of this new aesthetics, as opposed to those of traditionalist modernism: "Sometimes I, too, tell the ah's / of my heart one by one / like the blood-red beads / of a ruby rosary strung / on strands of golden hair! / But my / poetry's muse / takes to the air / on wings made of steel / like the I-beams / of my suspension bridges!"[25] Meanwhile, Nâzım's 1929 essays, published in the monthly *Resimli Ay* [Monthly Illustrated] under the title "Putları Yıkıyoruz" [Demolishing the Idols], produced public outrage at Nâzım's redefinition of literary "genius" and the "national poet" through Marxist aesthetics. While the machine aesthetic of Nâzım's early work is consonant in many ways with the Eurocentrist futurist vanguardism of the Turkish Republican state itself, in his narrative poems, "Jokond ile Si-Ya-U" [La Gioconda and Si-Ya-U] (1929), "Benerci Kendini Niçin Öldürdü?" [Why Did Banerjee Kill Himself?] (1932), and "Taranta-Babu'ya Mektuplar" [Letters to Taranta-Babu] (1935), Nâzım looked beyond Occidentalist discourse and toward the possibility of new para-national collectives that would include Indian, Chinese, and Ethiopian revolutionaries.

Although the political pressure on Nâzım and other Turkish socialists increased throughout the 1930s – Nâzım was sentenced to twenty-eight years' imprisonment in 1938 – the Republican regime left many other avant-garde artists and poets more or less unmolested. The critic Duygu Köksal has noted that Republican governing elites "never displayed a harsh and uncompromising rejection of Modernism in art or literature"; instead, they generally welcomed it "as the most recent and contemporary movements in Europe, and not as movements challenging bourgeois modernity."[26] In the art world, the early 1930s witnessed the emergence of two new oppositional groups: the Müstakil Ressamlar ve Heykeltraşlar Birliği [Association of Independent Painters and Sculptors], modeling itself on the French Société des Artistes Indépendants; and the d Grubu [d Group], which became the most controversial promoter of constructivist and cubist art in Turkey.[27] The members of the "d Group," educated in the ateliers of André Lhôte and Fernand Léger, embraced the shock value of radical novelty, testing the limits of the ruling elite's tolerance with aggressively abstract styles. By the 1940s, however, the d Group had become fully absorbed into the national cultural establishment, mixing their cubist forms with folkloric themes, and participating in the painting tours (*yurt sergileri*) of the ruling Republican People's Party (CHP), which visited many Anatolian provinces.[28]

Meanwhile, the trio of Orhan Veli [Kanık] (1914–50), Oktay Rifat [Horozcu] (1914–88), and Melih Cevdet [Anday] (1915–2002), who would become known as the Garip [Strange] or Birinci Yeni [First New] poets, brought a new neo-Surrealist poetics to the cultural space that Nâzım had vacated. In his 1941 preface to the collection *Garip*, Orhan Veli, the group's most vocal member, outlined a new poetics freed of any formal, rhythmic, and syllabic conventions, designed to eliminate the gap separating aesthetic experience from ordinary life.[29] Although Veli regarded poets as cultural figures of unique sensibility, he argued that the poet should serve the tastes of ordinary people and focus on the beauty of the everyday. Rejecting ornate metaphor and other forms of poetic artifice, Veli described a direct poetics of simple, colloquial Turkish. His poem "Kitabe-i Seng-i Mezar" [Epitaph], composed for an ordinary citizen named Süleyman and published in three parts in 1938, 1940, and 1941, created an uproar in literary circles,

redirecting the elegiac form traditionally reserved for sultans and other emi-
nences: "He suffered from nothing in the world / The way he suffered from
his corns; / He didn't even feel so badly / About having been created ugly. /
Though he wouldn't utter the Lord's name / Unless his shoe pinched, / He
couldn't be considered a sinner either. / It's a pity Süleyman Efendi had to
die."[30]

Although Veli's preface describes Surrealist automatic writing as one possible model for the direct poetics he proposes, he disassociates Garip poetry
from any categorical affiliation with European Surrealism. At the same time,
he goes out of his way to emphasize differences between French Surrealist
and Turkish Garip poetic practice. While the Garip poets did share with
the Surrealists an interest in poetic play and the absurdity of the everyday,
Veli's insistence on separateness is borne out by the fact that, his own sugges-
tions notwithstanding, the Garip group never actually engaged in automatic
writing in Breton's sense (and practice).[31]

Postwar trajectories

In many ways, the work of the Garip had lost its novelty by the time of Veli's
death in 1950. The two other members of the group joined a new wave of
neo-Surrealism that critics have called the İkinci Yeni [Second New]. The
continuity of the First and Second New movements is more chronological
than structural, since the Second New was committed to countering what
they saw as the "simple" Surrealism of the First, and to pushing experimental
techniques to the brink of incomprehensibility. Along with the novelist Oğuz
Atay (1934–77), Second New poets, who include Ece Ayhan Çağlar (1931–
2002), Cemal Süreya (1931–90), and Sezai Karakoç (b. 1933), have emerged
as the most important Turkish modernist writers of the second half of the
twentieth century.

Arguably, the most important difference between these postwar writers and their Republican predecessors is the political distance they placed
between themselves and the state.[32] During the tumultuous quarter century
that included the military coups of 1960, 1971, and 1980, Ayhan's "civil
poetry" (sivil şiir) and Atay's novel Tutunamayanlar [The Disconnected]
(1970) sought to give voice to the outsiders within the Turkish nation –
intellectuals, gay men and women, prostitutes, street children – and also
to expose both the costs and limits of the state's violent exercise of its
sovereignty. If, as Ahıska has observed, the Occidentalist social imaginary is
a device "through which those in power consume and reproduce the projection of the 'West' to negotiate and consolidate their hegemony in line with

their pragmatic interests,"[33] then the broken languages of postwar Turkish modernism have registered the violence through which that hegemony was consolidated.

The 1980s are considered a crucial turning point in Turkish literary history and its historiography, as the transformation of Turkish society by the brutal suppression of the left, along with the opening of the economy to world markets, spurred the formation of new literary currents that some have characterized as "postmodern."[34] Although the work of Orhan Pamuk is often classified as postmodernist, one might read Pamuk's first two novels, *Cevdet Bey ve Oğulları* [Cevdet and Sons] (1982) and *Sessiz Ev* [The Silent House] (1983), as well as the recent memoir *Istanbul* (2003), as noteworthy examples of contemporary modernism in Turkish letters. *Cevdet Bey ve Oğulları*, which critics often compare with Thomas Mann's *Buddenbrooks*, is an ironic–epic account of Turkish modernity, as lived by three successive generations of a bourgeois Istanbul family between 1905 and 1970. By contrast, the narrative time frame of *Sessiz Ev* is confined to one week, during which three grandchildren visit their grandmother's home in a fictional coastal town near Istanbul, with embedded historical time recounted from multiple viewpoints in flashback. More than a by-now formulaic modernist literary technique, however, *Sessiz Ev*'s paratactic juxtaposition of five individual voices is a device for undoing the otherwise continuous patriarchal narrative of fathers and sons, exposing, in the interpolation of women's voices among those of men, the heterogeneous multiplicity of a gendered modernity.

In awarding the 2006 Nobel Prize in Literature to Pamuk, the Permanent Secretary of the Swedish Academy praised *Istanbul* for rendering the city as "an indispensable literary territory, equal to Dostoevsky's St. Petersburg, Joyce's Dublin or Proust's Paris."[35] Arguably, however, *Istanbul* is an important work of contemporary Turkish modernism *not* in its reproduction of a kind of Turkish *Ulysses*, so much as in the profound metacommentary that it affords on the way such modernist mimicry is produced within the uneven transnational histories of Occidentalism itself.

NOTES

1. Pocock, "Some Europes in Their History," *The Idea of Europe*, ed. Anthony Pagden (New York: Woodrow Wilson Center Press and Cambridge University Press, 2002), pp. 57–58.
2. Pocock, "Some Europes," p. 58.
3. Balibar, "Strangers as Enemies," *Globalization and Autonomy Online Compendium*, www.globalautonomy.ca/global1/article.jsp?index=RA_Balibar_Strangers.xml (1 March 2009), 3.

4. Ahıska, "Occidentalism," *South Atlantic Quarterly* 102 (2003): 353. Throughout this chapter, I have cited Ahıska's article "Occidentalism." For a more comprehensive discussion of Occidentalism, see Ahıska's *Radyonun Sihirli Kapısı* (Istanbul: Metis, 2005), pp. 51–100. Given the scope and space limitations of this chapter, I am able to engage, here, with only one portion of Ahıska's both wide-ranging and nuanced argument.

5. Ahıska, "Occidentalism," p. 365.

6. What is designated as "Turkish modernism" is doubtless an historical abstraction, far from capacious enough to represent the dynamics of modern Turkish literature as a whole. By "modernism," I understand the European literary movements enduring from the second half of the nineteenth century through the Second World War. With the phrase "Turkish modernism," I am marking a set of varied and heterogeneous engagements with European modernist currents in Turkey during the twentieth century. While "modernism" is not used as a period term in Turkish national-literary historiography, the concept of "Turkish modernism" can be useful at the national level, in tracing important continuities and discontinuities with European modernist literature. (The critic Hasan Bülent Kahraman's writings are important contributions, in this regard.) At the comparative level, meanwhile, attention to the ambiguities, tensions, and negations of a "Turkish modernism" can be useful in exposing the uncritical limits of any transnational modernist studies that goes seeking primarily a reflection of itself, in what it "finds" outside Europe.

7. The Surname Law of 1934 required each Turkish citizen to adopt a family name. Throughout this chapter, I have marked adopted family names with brackets.

8. The "1914 Generation" included, among others, İbrahim [Çallı] (1882–1960), Hikmet [Onat] (1882–1977), and Namık İsmail [Yeğenoğlu] (1890–1935).

9. For an historical overview, see Erik J. Zürcher, *Turkey* (New York: I. B. Tauris, 2004), pp. 9–90. Historians of the Ottoman Empire use the term *Tanzimat* to denote the period between 1839–76. The reformist spirit certainly persists through the reign of Sultan Abdülhamid II (1876–1909), despite his repressions.

10. Comte, "Reşit Paşa'ya Mektup," *İslâmiyet ve Positivism*, ed. Christian Cherfils, trans. Özkan Gözel (Istanbul: Dergâh, 2008), p. 26.

11. For an historical overview (in English), see Turan Erol, "Painting in Turkey in Nineteenth and Early Twentieth Century," *A History of Turkish Painting*, ed. Gürsel Renda *et al.* (Geneva: PALASAR, 1988), pp. 87–234.

12. Beyatlı, *Çocukluğum, Gençliğim, Siyâsî ve Edebî Hatıralarım* (Istanbul: İstanbul Fetih Cemiyeti, 1999), p. 108. Unless noted otherwise, all translations from Turkish into English, here, are my own.

13. See Beyatlı, "Derûnî Âhenk ve Öz Şiir," *Edebiyata Dair* (Istanbul: İstanbul Fetih Cemiyeti, 1997), pp. 20–21.

14. For a more comprehensive history of the activities of the Bergsonist intellectuals, see Nazım İrem, "Undercurrents of European Modernity and the Foundations of Modern Turkish Conservatism: Bergsonism in Retrospect," *Middle Eastern Studies* 40.4 (July 2004): 79–112. I have drawn on İrem's work in the present chapter. For more on Baltacıoğlu, see Nergis Ertürk, "Surrealism and Turkish Script Arts," *Modernism/modernity* 17 (2010): 47–60.

15. On the history of the Kemalist reforms, see Zürcher, *Turkey*, pp. 166–205.

16. Eyüboğlu, "Yeni Türk San'atkârı," *İnsan* (April 15, 1938), p. 31. For an influential contemporary intellectual biography of Kemal that deploys this narrative of homecoming, see Beşir Ayvazoğlu, *Yahya Kemal* (Ankara: Birlik Yayınları, 1985).

17. Beyatlı, *Çocukluğum*, p. 74.

18. Tanpınar, "Antalyalı Genç Kıza Mektup," *Seçmeler*, ed. Enis Batur (Istanbul: Yapı Kredi Yayınları [YKY], 1992), pp. 20–24.

19. The English translations appeared in 2008 and 2001 respectively. *Saatleri Ayarlama Enstitüsü* was serialized in 1954 and published in book form in 1961.

20. Gürbilek, "Kurumuş Pınar, Kör Ayna, Kayıp Şark," *Kör Ayna, Kayıp Şark* (Istanbul: Metis, 2004), p. 137.

21. Tanpınar, *A Mind at Peace*, trans. Erdağ Göknar (New York: Archipelago Books, 2008), pp. 316, 317.

22. Safa's polemical articles have been collected and republished by Ali Ergenekon under the title *Kavga Yazıları* (Istanbul: Boğaziçi Yayınları, 1989).

23. I devote a chapter to a reading of this novel in my forthcoming book *Grammatology and Literary Modernity in Turkey*.

24. For a biography of Nâzım in English, see Saime Göksu and Edward Timms, *Romantic Communist: The Life and Work of Nazım Hikmet* (New York: St. Martin's Press, 1999).

25. Nâzım Hikmet, "Regarding Art," *Poems of Nazım Hikmet*, trans. Randy Blasing and Mutlu Konuk (New York: Persea Books, 2002), p. 4.

26. Köksal, "Art and Power in Turkey: Culture, Aesthetics and Nationalism during the Single Party Era," *New Perspectives on Turkey* 31 (Fall 2004): 100.

27. For an account in English of the activities of these groups, see Erol, "Painting," pp. 174–234. On the exhibitions of the d group, see Nihal Elvan, ed., *d Grubu = d Group, 1933–1951* (Istanbul: YKY, 2002).

28. Köksal, "Art," pp. 102–04.

29. Kanık, "Garip," *Şairin İşi* (Istanbul: YKY, 2001), pp. 11–22.

30. Kanık, "Epitaph 1," *Just For the Hell of It*, trans. Talât Sait Halman (Istanbul: Multilingual Yabancı Dil Yayınları, 1997).

31. On this point, see Hasan Bülent Kahraman, *Türk Şiiri, Modernizm, Şiir* (Istanbul: Agora Kitaplığı, 2004), pp. 118–19.

32. Nâzım is an important exception. The conservative modernists were critical of official nationalism, but not of the institution of the state.

33. Ahıska, "Occidentalism," p. 366.

34. For more on this development, see Parla, "The Wounded Tongue," *PMLA* 123 (2008): 34–38.

35. Horace Engdahl, "Presentation Speech for the 2006 Nobel Prize in Literature" (Nobel Prize Award Ceremony, Stockholm, Sweden, December 10, 2006).

FURTHER READING

Bozdoğan, Sibel. *Modernism and Nation Building: Turkish Architectural Culture in the Early Republic*. Seattle: University of Washington Press, 2001.

Kanık, Orhan Veli. *Just For the Hell of It: 111 Poems*. Trans. Talât Sait Halman. Istanbul: Multilingual Yabancı Dil Yayınları, 1997.

Nemet-Nejat, Murat, ed. *Eda: An Anthology of Contemporary Turkish Poetry.* Jersey City, N.J.: Talisman House Publishers, 2004.

Ran, Nâzım Hikmet. *Beyond the Walls: Selected Poems.* Trans. Ruth Christie, Richard McKane, and Talât Sait Halman. London: Anvil Press Poetry, 2002.

Human Landscapes from My Country: An Epic Novel in Verse. Trans. Randy Blasing and Mutlu Konuk. New York: Persea Books, 2002.

Tanpınar, Ahmet Hamdi. *A Mind at Peace.* Trans. Erdağ Göknar. Brooklyn, N.Y.: Archipelago Books, 2008.

The Time Regulation Institute. Trans. Ender Gürol. Madison, Wisc.: Turko-Tatar Press, 2001.

INDEX

Cambridge Companions to . . .

AUTHORS

TOPICS